Hawthorne's Histories,
Hawthorne's World

Hawthorne's Histories, Hawthorne's World

From Salem to Somewhere Else

Michael J. Colacurcio

ANTHEM PRESS

Anthem Press
An imprint of Wimbledon Publishing Company
www.anthempress.com

This edition first published in UK and USA 2024
by ANTHEM PRESS
75–76 Blackfriars Road, London SE1 8HA, UK
or PO Box 9779, London SW19 7ZG, UK
and
244 Madison Ave #116, New York, NY 10016, USA

First published in the UK and USA by Anthem Press in 2022

Copyright © Michael J. Colacurcio 2024

The author asserts the moral right to be identified as the author of this work.

All rights reserved. Without limiting the rights under copyright reserved above,
no part of this publication may be reproduced, stored or introduced into
a retrieval system, or transmitted, in any form or by any means
(electronic, mechanical, photocopying, recording or otherwise),
without the prior written permission of both the copyright
owner and the above publisher of this book.

British Library Cataloguing-in-Publication Data
A catalogue record for this book is available from the British Library.

Library of Congress Cataloging-in-Publication Data
Names: Colacurcio, Michael J., author.
Title: Hawthorne's histories, Hawthorne's world : from Salem to somewhere else /
Michael J. Colacurcio.
Description: London; New York, NY : Anthem Press, 2024. |
Includes bibliographical references and index. |
Identifiers: LCCN 2024942537 | ISBN 9781839993497 (paperback) |
ISBN 9781839983245 (epub) | ISBN 9781839983238 (pdf)
Subjects: LCSH: Hawthorne, Nathaniel, 1804-1864–Homes and haunts–Massachusetts–Salem.
| Hawthorne, Nathaniel, 1804-1864–Homes and haunts. | Hawthorne, Nathaniel,
1804-1864–Knowledge and learning. | Historical fiction, American–History and criticism. |
Puritan movements in literature. | LCGFT: Essays. | Literary criticism.
Classification: LCC PS1884.C65 2022 | DDC 813/.3–dc23/eng/20220209
LC record available at https://lccn.loc.gov/2024942537

ISBN-13: 978-1-83999-349-7 (Pbk)
ISBN-10: 1-83999-349-9 (Pbk)

Cover image: Clockwise from left, the artists are Charles Osgood,
Cephas Thompson, J. J. E. Mayall, and J. A. Whipple. From
"Images from Hawthorne's Adult Life," hawthorneinsalem.org.

This title is also available as an e-book.

CONTENTS

Introduction: Here and Elsewhere		1
Chapter One	Summons of the Past: Hawthorne and the Theme(s) of Puritanism	11
Chapter Two	Cosmopolitan and Provincial: Hawthorne and the Reference of American Studies	21
Chapter Three	Moments' Monuments: Hawthorne and the Scene of History	37
Chapter Four	"Certain Circumstances": Hawthorne and the Interest of History	57
Chapter Five	"Life within the Life": Sin and Self in Hawthorne's New England	77
Chapter Six	The Teller and the Tale: A Note on Hawthorne's Narrators	99
Chapter Seven	A Better Mode of Evidence: The Transcendental Problem of Faith and Spirit	123
Chapter Eight	"Artificial Fire": Reading Melville (Re-)reading Hawthorne	137
Chapter Nine	"Red Man's Grave": Art and Destiny in Hawthorne's "Main-Street"	153
Chapter Ten	"Such Ancestors": The Spirit of History in *The Scarlet Letter*	167
Chapter Eleven	Inheritance, Repetition, Complicity, Redemption: Sin and Salvation in *The House of the Seven Gables*	193
Chapter Twelve	"Inextricable Knot of Polygamy": Transcendental Husbandry in Hawthorne's *Blithedale*	215
Chapter Thirteen	Innocence Abroad: Here and There in Hawthorne's "Last Phase"	245
Index		293

INTRODUCTION: HERE AND ELSEWHERE

Probably no classic American author is more closely associated with a single place than Hawthorne is with Salem, Massachusetts.[1] Born there (in 1804), raised there, except for summers in Maine, he returned there after college (at Bowdoin) in Maine and lived a quiet, some would say a reclusive life there from 1825 to 1837. Salem was his ancestral home, infamous for the witch trials of 1692, about which he wrote more than once, and for his great-great grandfather's involvement in which he seemed now and then to be doing penance. In "Young Goodman Brown," most famously, but also in the curious story called "Alice Doane's Appeal" in which the tangled question of Satan's power to appear in the guise of human beings is explored for the morose delectation of some innocent (and ignorant) latter-day inhabitants of that fateful little village.

Later on, *The House of the Seven Gables* (1851)—more popular in his century than in ours—was set there, self-consciously, and as knowledgeably as *The Scarlet Letter* (1850) is set in John Winthrop's Boston;[2] and many readers find the Salem "Custom House" preface to that historical masterpiece quite as memorable as any of its studied references to the site of Puritanism's capital city. Indeed, undergraduates often tell you that Hester Prynne is ostracized from Salem. Less well known, perhaps, a dramatic sketch called "Main-street" (1849) offers us a selective and, as it turns out, a truncated history of that very town, displeasing an internally represented audience, and offering a well-considered and carefully crafted revision of the more patriotic account then in print. The audience is not amused. Given all this, it may strike us as significant when a Narrator, pretty close to Hawthorne "himself," in his bio-satiric sketch on what it was like to work at and be fired from the customs house of that city, declares himself henceforth "a citizen of somewhere else." Literally, at the moment any contemporary could read that querulous valedictory, Hawthorne was living in Lenox in the Berkshire Mountains of Western Massachusetts, where he wrote both *The House of the Seven Gables* and *The Blithedale Romance*—and where,

---

1. Suitably emphasized in most biographies—but oddly passed over in Robert Milder's *Hawthorne's Habitations* (Oxford: Oxford University Press, 2013)—the issue is made central in Margaret B. Moore, *The Salem World of Nathaniel Hawthorne* (Columbia: University of Missouri Press, 1998); and Edwin Haviland Miller—noticing the absence of the word "home" from a famous Hawthorne quote—entitles his comprehensive study *Salem Is My Dwelling Place* (Iowa City: University of Iowa Press, 1991).
2. The quasi-scholarly background of *The House of the Seven Gables* is ably demonstrated by Allan M. Emery, "Salem History and *The House of the Seven Gables*," in Bernard Rosenthal, ed., *Critical Essays on Hawthorne's "House of the Seven Gables"* (Boston, MA: G. K. Hall, 1995), pp. 129–49.

as it turns out, he would meet and become, for a time at least, good friends with Herman Melville. And, having shaken the dust off his feet, he would never again take up residence in his ancestral Salem.

After a dispute with his landlord in Lenox, Hawthorne moved to Concord, briefly, in 1852. Moved *back*, one is tempted to say, for, after a stint in the customs house of Boston, and the better (or worse) part of 1841 spent at an idealistic social experiment called Brook Farm—where two could live as cheap as one, but the one could get no writing done—a newly married Hawthorne and his bride had lived there, happily enough, as it seems, from 1842 to 1845. One severely selective version of his life there is offered to the public in the sketch called "The Old Manse," written to introduce a volume of tales and sketches published in 1846, *Mosses from an Old Manse*. The marriage would develop serious strains, as a modern study would labor to demonstrate,[3] but by his own account Hawthorne seemed on the verge of discovering there something approaching a stable and satisfactory sense of self, a condition that appeared to elude him in all the years he spent reading and writing "moral history" in the garret of his mother's house in Salem.

Not much like the Transcendentalists, who made Concord their literary capital, Hawthorne nevertheless got on rather well with a number of persons who carried that card. At a minimum, they would visit the newly married couple, take a rest from their agitated, overintellectual lives, and in the best case take a restorative nap. But there was more: canoe trips with the poet Ellery Channing, forest excursions with Thoreau, long walks with Emerson; even some not entirely metaphorical ice-skating on the sluggish and quick-to-freeze Concord River, with that notable theorist of "surfaces." And of course a whole new set of tales and sketches, composed, as we are told, at the desk where Emerson wrote *Nature*. Not a full, rich and interesting social life, perhaps, but better than retiring to an attic to brood over the sinful past.

But the second stay in Concord was relatively brief. Asked to produce a campaign biography for his college friend, Franklin Pierce, Hawthorne responded with a book which, though its doctrine of compromise and conciliation angered the Abolitionists, was good enough to aid in Pierce's election and to secure for its author his third political job: not a customs house this time, but a consulship to the important British seaport of Liverpool. Not quite a sinecure, it was sufficiently remunerative to solve the nagging financial problems of this now famous but never very well paid author of highly original tales and romances. It ended when Congress changed the terms of the salary paid to foreign consuls, from a percentage of the value of goods passing through a port to a fixed stipend.

More so than those written in America, the author's *English Notebooks* reveals a vital curiosity about contemporary political and social affairs—as well as a genuine satisfaction with the part a relatively important person might enjoy in a genuinely cosmopolitan situation. On the other hand, however, this third job of work proved no more conducive

---

3. To the patient analyses of T. Walter Herbert, we owe our chastened sense that the wedded union Sophia Peabody and Nathaniel Hawthorne did not create and exhaust the perfection of middle-class marriage in the nineteenth century; see *Dearest Beloved* (Berkeley: University of California, 1995).

to the production of imaginative literature than had the two previous experiments. The period from 1850 to 1852 has been called, with a nod to the career of Henry James, "Hawthorne's Major Phase,"[4] producing as it did three important novels in as many years. And also, into the bargain, another significant contribution to his high-level writings for children, *A Wonder-Book for Boys and Girls* (1851) and *Tanglewood Tales* (1853). Of course, it would be hard for any human writer to keep up that pace very long, however much he needed the money. Which now, finally, he did not. Then too, life itself was so interesting.

In any event, the signal public production of the Liverpool years was *Our Old Home* (1863), a highly personal, reflective, and on the whole favorable account, for a still rather homogeneous collection of Americans, on what it meant to have the British for ancestors. Puritanism, it appeared, was only part of the story. Overall, it is one of the two best books on England written by an American in the nineteenth century; and compared with Emerson's more philosophical *English Traits* (1856), it reveals a warmer sort of emotional acceptance; so that one is not too surprised to learn that after several years traveling in France and Italy—and in near despair over a native land on the verge of civil war—Hawthorne seriously considered moving his family there. Yet he would have been there as an expat and not at all a citizen. And, evidently, he felt some deep loyalty, not to Salem, to be sure, but to the United States; and especially to New England, which he, unlike Lincoln, seemed perfectly happy to imagine in separation from the Slave Power.

Hawthorne's "Last Phase," critically so called,[5] lies beyond the scope of the essays offered in this volume. An extended Coda will indicate what a scholar with a longer life—as imagined in one of several uncompleted romances that litter and dignify the years after his 1860 return to America—might make of this period of final power and precipitous decline. Treated here, after a reminder of what Hawthorne accomplished in his Salem years, is an account of what happened after that and before the final turn. The Concord phase a little sketchily, perhaps, but the career after that—if I may say so—big time: "Ethan Brand," if only through the lens of Melville's condescension and the inspired reprise; "Main-street," a way back into earlier materials and a reminder that those Puritan materials were occupying a space that was far from uninhabited; and then the three "American Romances," proof positive, is any such were still required, that the once isolated Nathaniel Hawthorne had become a fully enfranchised citizen of the post-Jacksonian and mid-Victorian literary world.

But even the first of these essays conveys the sense that the writer who immersed himself in the morale of America's colonial past was never, properly speaking, a full-fledged citizen of his most provincial Salem. Not a "citizen of the world," quite yet, though his deep interest in the literary traditions of England and France clearly suggest a bias in that direction. A champion, since college, of the cause of an authentic and original American literature, and bound and determined from the first to tell his contemporaries some home truths about the conscience of New England, he seems a man whose deepest loyalty is

---

4. See Nina Baym, *The Shape of Hawthorne's Career* (Ithaca, NY: Cornell, 1976).
5. The phrase—and the attendant problematic—appears to originate with Edward H. Davidson, *Hawthorne's Last Phase* (New Haven, CT: Yale University Press, 1949).

not to a place as to a cause, namely, the power—and the right, even the duty—of the imagination to create a meaningful sense of the past. Puritanical Salem was indeed his "dwelling place,"[6] but it was less a home than a point of departure. Everybody is born somewhere, and it is merely fantastic to suppose that one can completely resist or entirely shed all that one hears said before the birth of original thought. But from the moment he began to publish imaginative literature, Hawthorne displayed interests and gifts that had the astonishing marks of having been conceived somewhere else. On another planet, almost.

In literal fact it took quite a long time for Hawthorne to find another dwelling place, let alone a home. But the Declaration of Independence from Salem Citizenship may well be said to have begun much earlier, unconsciously with the commitment to the life of the imagination, consciously, formally, when, standing on the blighted ground where arbitrarily accused and oddly convicted "witches" once met their paralegal doom, one of his consciously crafted narrators distinguishes himself from those representative Salemites who "could not tell, within half a century, as much as the date of the witchcraft delusion." Hawthorne's more famous response, "Young Goodman Brown," offers us a version of that delusion, but from the vantage of one who, having read Spenser's account of the Redcrosse Knight's delusions at the hands of Archimago, found himself writing a twice-told tale. A tale like "The May-Pole of Merry Mount" makes the town of Pessonagesset—later Mount Wollaston, Merry Mount, Mount Dagon, and Quincy—as foundational as Salem, and the long shadow of Milton reveals an authorial identity well formed in a world elsewhere. And political tales like "Roger Malvin's Burial" and "My Kinsman, Major Molineux" reveal a sophisticated detachment as far from local as one can imagine. What was the birthplace of Oliver Stone?

All this I covered in a book written long since, *The Province of Piety* (1984). Published here are many of the essays on Hawthorne I have written since—a couple on the early stories, as a reminder, but mostly on what came after. As I suggested in *Province*, there could easily be three more volumes on that same scale: the Old Manse Period, the so-called Major Phase, and the years after that. No one has quite taken up the suggestion. Including me. Other things came along: Edwards, the earliest American Puritans, their place in the larger scope of early American religion, Melville, and then (now) Emerson. We do what we can.

Reprinted (and re-titled) from a collection called *Nathaniel Hawthorne in Context*,[7] "Summons of the Past" reminds the reader that, early on, American Puritanism appeared to be Hawthorne's flood subject, but that there are important distinctions to be made. "Young Goodman Brown" and "Alice Doane's Appeal" refer us to the matter of 1692 but "The Hollow of Three Hills" does not. Some of the tales are frankly political, as "The Gray Champion" and "Endicott and the Red Cross" and even the apparently moralistic "May-Pole of Merry Mount," but the politics is complex and ironic. And even

---

6. Again, see Miller, *Dwelling Place*, esp. pp. 11–19.
7. See Monika M. Elbert, *Nathaniel Hawthorne in Context* (Cambridge: Cambridge University Press, 2018), pp. 21–34.

the old-time questions of bigotry and "gloom" are delicate and touchy subjects, looking one way in "The Man of Adamant" but several others in "The Minister's Black Veil." So that by the time Hawthorne returns to this material in *The Scarlet Letter*, informed critics will have to check their clichés at the door.

"Certain Circumstances" rereads "Young Goodman Brown" in the context of a larger argument about the play and the place of historical criticism. The reader always reads "now," in a moment when the overdeterminations of history make plausible a wide range of meanings; but the work itself was written "then": what if it was all different? Was Brown's nightmarish experience in the forest a dream or was it real? Or, was it the kind of waking experience the seventeenth century soberly believed the Devil could easily supply? It happened in Spenser, well before the famous witch trials; and here it is again, look out! How might the knowledge of "specter evidence" alter our range of interpretation?

But if Hawthorne's fictions consciously occupy a space that is significantly historical, they are also, more often than not, delivered in a way that is more hypothetical than categorical. That is to say, they have Narrators. "Hawthorne"—whoever he turns out to be this time—sometimes thinks something like what to tell us to conclude, but not always and seldom without either internal dialogue or contextual discount. Sadly, the narratological tour de force called "The Story-Teller" got all broken up, leaving without any sense of when and where to place the tales of Goodman Brown and Parson Hooper: does the speaker know, in the one case, about specter evidence or, in the other, what Hooper's darkened sermons exactly said? And, more troubling still, do we really think "The Birthmark" is about Aylmer's unhappy loss of Warland's ideal of the "Beautiful"? And, in the context of Giovanni Guasconti's trial of faith and evidence, are we really instructed to learn that "there is something truer and more real, than we can [...] touch with the finger"? Plato lives!—but so does D. H. Lawrence: "Trust the tale, not the teller." Or else, don't read *The Blithedale Romance* at all. (Or even *The Scarlet Letter*, for that matter.)

Narratorwise (or foolish), no instance could be more instructive than the pair of tales Hawthorne linked together as "Allegories of the Heart." First, a sympathetic but somewhat literal-minded sculptor tries to tell the story of a guilt-ridden and self-obsessed man who keeps insisting he has a snake in his bosom; the narrator concedes that this may be a metaphor, but he is rather tolerant of the learned physicians who keep trying to flush the thing out, one end or the other. And he allows to stand, unchallenged, the concluding claim of the crazy man's wife that to be well he has but to lose himself in "the idea of another." Not the arms, not the love, not the life; no, the *idea*. Emerson as a cure for what ails New England? Well, let's see. Recovered or not, the Puritanic Crazy—associated with Jones Very, but also figuring as a version of the Hawthorne called down from his "dismal and squalid" attic by one or another of the Peabody sisters, so they could all go to Emerson's lectures or Margaret Fuller's conversations—tells the story of a selfhood disorder that might not be so easy to cure. A certain otherwise successful man can no way make life real to himself: it's all like "shadows, flickering on the wall." Plato, of course, but enough like Emerson's not-yet published "Experience" to make one wonder what those two talked about in their long walks in Concord. And whether a cure can be worse than a disease.

Transcendentalist epistemology also hides out in the omni-referential tale of Giovanni Guasconti's ill-starred affair with Rappaccini's lovely but apparently deadly daughter. Well before my students taught me that the preface implicates George Ripley, and that Padua matters at least as much as Concord, I managed to recognize a perverse version of the logic that liberal Divinity Students mounted against their massively conservative Professor of Biblical Theology; faith is about spiritual recognition not miraculous evidences. Fine: tell that to the hapless medical student lately come up from Naples: he hears her voice and loves the soul therein revealed, but what about those dead insects. So, ask those Divinity Students, what if the message and the miracles pointed in opposite directions? What if I heard His voice, touched the hem of His garment, then died of the virus?

A similar logic lurks in the multiform ambiguities of Melville's *Pierre*, but already, in *Moby-Dick*, the hectic ephebe is beginning to rewrite the lucid precursor. Flatly (and naively) critical of the moral tendency of Hawthorne's abortive study of the Unpardonable Sin, Melville gets it right, proffers in fact an authoritative reading of "Ethan Brand," in his study of another man, one Ishmael, who also lost his way—almost—by looking too long into the fire. Quite like Ahab, Ethan Brand is a Prometheus figure, indeed more literally so: tending the civilizing fire a once-upon-a-time almost-Christ figure stole from the gods, this fire-gazing lime burner envisions hell and tries to imagine what "unpardonable" sin could possibly be its eternal reward. Ah yes, the one Big Secret the heavens still hide from the mortal man. If only one could find it out: would not men then avoid it like the plague? Or, if it were, on Calvinist premise, somehow predestined, at least one could *know*. Generous motive, but evidently hubristic, as with Ahab, whose monstrous egotism may well have begun in sympathy and with a mind to vindicate a suffering humanity.

Less mythic, more locally historical, "Red Man's Grave" tells the story of a storyteller telling, with the assistance of a show box, the history of the Main Street in Salem, Massachusetts, USA, from its seventeenth-century invention to his own moment in the nineteenth century. The show box breaks down before the showman can bring the story up to his and his audience's present moment, but not before we witness a moccasin-shoed (and silent) native to notice, then wonder at, then learn to suspect and fear an invading populace whose heavy boots leave a pretty deep mark on the earth they have invaded. And then the natives disappear, leaving us to suspect that the famous blizzard of 1717 stands for something like a "white-out." And leaving it to the showman, whose main interest appears to be the morale of Puritanism, to point out that, wherever it may be thought to be headed in Remarkable Providence or in Manifest Destiny, the town's Main Street began as a path lightly trodden by the soft moccasins of the native inhabitants. A thought we may need to keep in mind when, later, we visit Salem's *House of the Seven Gables*.

Before that, though, in a formal introduction to *The Scarlet Letter*, a look at John Winthrop's Boston of the 1640s, where Hester Prynne is mocked and scorned and where her partner in something or other suffers in guilty silence. Footsteps of Anne Hutchinson indeed, as Hester's career seems predicted in the sexual rhetoric the Puritan patriarchy had applied to that dangerous "seductress." Where Arthur Dimmesdale's tortured logic of doomed endurance owes something to John Cotton's theory of "the usefulness of hypocrites." And where, in widest view, an entire novel—Puritan Romance, if you will—seems predicated on Winthrop's (and others') sexualization of the theory of covenant. What might human love be like in a world where the only *real* bridegroom is Christ? Hester eventually gets over it; Dimmesdale never does: "Is this not better?" (I.e., I *do* love God more.) And poor ugly Chillingworth: all that monster had wanted was a little warm relief from bad science.

Attempting to bridge the gap between the witch-haunted and otherwise superstitious seventeenth century and the author's own more quotidian present, *The House of the Seven Gables* turns from control of language to ownership of land—beginning with a guilty usurpation and ending just short of the conclusion that property is theft. At the very least, the Pyncheons recommit the original sin by passively accepting the stolen house and land. "Pyncheon"—familiar name—wasn't he the biggest landlord in the Connecticut River Valley? And didn't he also write a forbidden book about original sin? The plot must be thicker than we had thought. Leftover Maule marries off-brand Pyncheon; but do we all live innocently ever after in the guilt-ridden world we fall into?

If the invention of the cent shop that sells gingerbread men is one "novelistic" mark of the go-ahead nineteenth century, the formation of communes, Fourierist and otherwise, is another, more enduring sign. Hawthorne went to one of the more conservative of these, but the fictional outgrowth of the experience reflects the wider and more radical interest being expressed: families nowhere very welcome, and at least one free-love experiment. And so, with an important essay by James Baldwin clearly in mind,[8] "Nobody's Protest Novel" attempts to read the not anti- yet not quite pro-feminist politics that get both obscured and expressed in the aging and perhaps guilty memory of Hawthorne's full-blown Untrustworthy Narrator. Coverdale may be impercipient, an inept storyteller; or he may be a brilliant sociopath; or, just possibly both, if only his unconscious knows why after many years he has returned in fiction to the scene of *somebody's* crime. Yet none of this narrative ambiguity can conceal the fact that, in the name of gender equity and social justice, people are doing some very bad things. In a world well predicted by Hester Prynne turned proto-feminist, where anyone can fall in love with anyone else, regardless, the rule appears to be sexual jealousy pretty much as usual. Maybe the time of Hester's radical prediction was not yet.

Without world enough and time, a final essay tries to provide a firm outline of what did and did not get done in the period after all this prolific production: three major fictions in three years, then England, then Italy. From the very last years, several uncomplete romances count for something, especially the one which protests the fact that evidently "God wants short lives." Noteworthy too is the magazine essay in which the writer who had defended the temporizing policies of Franklin Pierce expresses his "Peaceable Man's" conservative refusal to revel in patriotic gore. More significant, however, is the book-long work he called *Our Old Home*. Published in 1863—and problematizing the

---

8. Obviously enough, my title alludes to the definitive deconstruction of the otherwise iconic Uncle Tom's Cabin: see "Everybody's Protest Novel," in *Notes of a Native Son* (Boston, MA: Beacon, 1955), pp. 113–23.

matter of "home"—it consists of twelve essays growing out of the years (1853–56) Hawthorne spent as American Consul to Liverpool. Based largely on side trips taken around the countryside, and conceived in the style of the Romantic-Victorian "excursion," the essays are far more personal—and on the whole a little more friendly to the hereditary English culture—than Emerson's quasi-scientific and in literary fact deconstructive *English Traits* (1856). But the two together suggest that in the nineteenth century, Americans do England better than vice versa.

But the master work of Hawthorne's later years—flawed though it is judged to be on many accounts—is the romance which grew out of the months the Hawthorne family spent in Italy. Embarrassingly famous for its guide-book-like attention to the contents of Roman museums, and with a narrator who often seems unsure of what he is supposed to know about the off-stage lives of his major characters, the work is nevertheless a major effort in the "international" mode of testing the limits of American character by immersing it in the culture of a world more bound to the past, more superstitious, perhaps, but also more sensuous and more accepting of merely human norms than the puritanic one even Henry James would recognize as the American morale. An archetypal American pair find something like affection under the outstretched arms of some pope or other; but finding themselves unable to deal with a tangled question of love and death, in a world far older than the "old home" called England, they flee to the thin idealism of a Fatherland where the incorrigibly innocent woman will help her less dogmatic but still confused partner to see "sunlight on the mountain-tops." Not since "The May-Pole of Merry Mount" had Hawthorne thought so hard about the American difference.

In the end, one thing should be clear about the essays in this volume: written for different occasions, with different moments of local inspiration, they share a commitment to the more or less conservative principles of historical scholarship. All readers read *now*, with the mentality of their own historical present; and as there is, outside of an odd graduate seminar here and there, no such thing as a Criticism Police, everybody is pretty much free to respond to a literary work as in fact they do and to say so out loud. But the literary work *itself*—ah yes, that antique but still lively premise—was written *then*, when very many things were probably very different. So that, one thing professional criticism can try to do is to compensate for the epistemic difference. Hawthorne lived in New England; not everyone does. Hawthorne worried a lot about America's Puritan inheritance; we are more concerned with systemic racism and the legacy of slavery. Additionally, Hawthorne had read more than anybody I know, and he appeared almost always to reference his readings; our life is too short. But we can try.

We can try to ask not just what we happen to notice, but what some determined writer appeared to wish somebody or other to *get*. Problem is, of course, we can never know if we are right. But the attempt continues to seem worth it.[9] We read in context and share our conclusions. Others do the same. We compare and contrast. And who knows? Another world, recognizable but different, might well arise. No law requires. But none forbids.

---

9. For the lucid (and all-but-needless) defense of this minimalist theory, see "Everybody's Protest Novel," in *Notes of a Native Son* (Boston, MA: Beacon, 1955), pp. 113–23.

But if the method here is all pretty much the same, the inspiration, occasion, audience are all a little various. As I have said at the outset, this is not the overgrown monograph another life and career trajectory might well have produced. Essays by different hands, they well might seem, except all of them are mine. I think they all "add up" pretty well, offering intimations of a literary person who had deep roots in a strong but problematic religious culture, which he studied hard to understand and then to outgrow. That is to say, Hawthorne nearly always writes as something of an historian. His Transcendentalist contemporaries lay great stress on what they called "consciousness"; for Hawthorne, the literary faculty was something more like "reflection."

Written in relative seclusion, the best early stories want to recall the power and the problems of a Puritan religious and political culture that insisted on itself and did not give ground easily: what must the moral life have been like among "such ancestors"? Then, moving from his ancestral Salem to Boston, to Brook Farm in Roxbury, to that Emersonville they called Concord, his fiction engages with the liberated morale of his own generation. Critically, from the perspective of some atavistic (and largely unconscious) bias, but always with the sympathetic sense that new ideas are not created *ex nihilo*, and that the first job of criticism is archeological: not "how could they possibly think that?" but "where in God's name did that come from?" And to what F. O. Matthiessen identified long since an age of Swedenborg and Fourier, there can hardly be a better introduction than the tales and sketches in *Mosses from an Old Manse*. *The Scarlet Letter* self-consciously revisits the Puritan past, but it ends with Hester Prynne's prediction of the dangerously free-loving world of *The Blithedale Romance*. In between, *The House of the Seven Gables* dares to draw a line from a decaying Puritan Sanctocracy to some self-presuming Aristoi of his present; the "Claimant" manuscripts push the search for the authority of ancestry back to the old country; and, without hint of jingoism, *Our Old Home* tries hard to separate the longing for a traditional identity from the fact of a horrific failure of social policy.

Not the only story of course. Easier to say, Hawthorne was not much of a feminist. Or poor guy: looked at a world of particulars and kept seeing an Allegory; should have read Emerson's "Nominalist and Realist" more carefully. Or again, could never quite make his moral standard explicit enough to try conclusions with Emerson or even, at any great length, with Melville. For other views, see other critics. Meanwhile, having done what I could, I trust my audience will tolerate the absence of some Totalitarian Thesis, even as Hawthorne's narrator keeps asking his "Gentle Reader" to forgive the absence of an encompassing moral. History is plural. So is Hawthorne.

Chapter One

SUMMONS OF THE PAST: HAWTHORNE AND THE THEME(S) OF PURITANISM

Once it all seemed so simple: "Puritanism" was "the haunting fear that somewhere, someone may be happy." Then, more professionally, a Harvard Scholar named Perry Miller began to convince us that Puritan theology was a rather sophisticated affair, and that the Puritan affect would not be that easy to represent. Still, the sensation persists: Hawthorne's Puritans are nowhere very cheerful; and, in Hawthorne's own century, a liberal minister charged, in what he called a "moral argument" against their Calvinism, that "gloom" was one almost certain outcome of that religious creed. Did Hawthorne perhaps think he was right?

In something like his master allegory of Puritans and Others, his Revelers overflow with Jollity and Mirth, their more aggressive competitors bespeak and predict only Gloom. It turns out that in "The May-Pole of Merry Mount" Hawthorne is reproducing rather than inventing the allegory of this more-than-twice-told tale; but even when traced to its historical sources, it does little or nothing to undo the claim that, at or near the outset, "Gloom and Jollity" were contending for something or other. And gloom is of course the last word in what may be Hawthorne's signature story: poor Goodman Brown gets more than he was asking for, but who ever said playing with the devil was not an extreme sport? In any event he goes through life, even to his grave, a very unhappy man. In "The Minister's Black Veil," a certain Parson Hooper seems to have got his gloom a little more innocently: unlike Goodman Brown, his awakened sense of sin begins with himself; and whether he was right or wrong to express his private insight in the obliqueness of a symbol, the fact is that he can no longer chat comfortably with his parishioners after divine service, he misses out on his Sunday lunches with the local squire, and he doesn't even get the girl. If sentiment is the only standard, he might just as well be that "Man of Adamant," whose hysterical fear of praying with the unregenerate keeps him locked up inside himself. And then, famously, but somewhat later in Hawthorne's career, there is the sad case of the Reverend Mr. Dimmesdale: convinced that he needs to stay in his appointed place of worshipful suffering, he preaches his sermon of sin at all occasions, but never is quite able to "show forth" even a token "by which the worst may be inferred." Perhaps Hawthorne's Puritanism is better defined as the conscientious determination that no one shall ever be in fact happy.

Hawthorne's most explicit verdict on the Puritan past is given at a stroke in the meta-historical sketch called "Main-street": "Such a life was sinister to the intellect and sinister to the heart." Period, we are tempted to say. Yet not quite—for why then the lingering fascination? Not exactly a "flood subject," the legacy of Puritanism remains for Hawthorne a concern of lifelong meditation. Somewhat overshadowed by the "Transcendental" themes of the early 1840s, the problem of puritanic inheritance lies just beneath the surface of several important tales and sketches; one tale, "Egotism: Or, the Bosom Serpent," even appears to be a re-writing of "The Minister's Black Veil." And after the masterful recapitulation of *The Scarlet Letter*, the concern with Puritan inheritance and repetition refuses to relent. Evidently a topic survives: not so much the psychological question of what about Puritanism so arrested Hawthorne and bent his otherwise worldly literary intentions; not even the more historical one of why in the words of "Main-street" should "we" be in *any* sense "happy to have had such ancestors." But simply this: from whom exactly are we descended? Utopians or inspired visionaries? De facto bigots or would-be libertarians? Doctrinaire killjoys or sober moral realists? Maybe "gloom" is not so simple a fact as it first appears.

2

Appropriately, perhaps, what we likely encounter first from the still-green pen of Nathaniel Hawthorne is a story about witchcraft—the ugly blot on the record of exemplary New England. Part of an early "projected" but never published collection titled "Seven Tales of My Native Land," "The Hollow of the Three Hills" survives to offer us the scene of a young woman who has deserted her family, but now, in a fit of remorse, visits a very-very old crone, who tells her what she most fears to learn about those she has deserted: desolate parents, husband driven insane from grief, and (of course) a dead baby. At all this, the witchy woman smiles in pleasure, while the fecklessly repentant young woman dies, of shame as much as of guilt, perhaps, as she is shocked to learn that the privileged source of all this information is not at all a clear medium: What? Did she hear the voices "too"?

Not a bad story for a college kid to have written. And gloomy enough. Yet not about the witchcraft we learn of in the Salem in 1692 nor, famously, in "Young Goodman Brown." There, as we have taken some time to learn, the issue concerns the unhappy surrender of weak faith in the face of suspicious evidence. Here it is the wish for privileged information: if she was *so* concerned, why did she leave? And also, perhaps, about the nature and possibility of diabolical evil. Guilty to the domestic limit, the young woman still cares, and this counts to us in her favor. But that witch—if that's what she is—is a bad one indeed, taking rare delight in the agony of others. Of course, she may be only a moderately competent fortune teller, practicing her shameless art on a woman who seems to have escaped from a seduced-and-abandoned novel of the 1780s—guessing what her client fears yet wishes to hear—but her perverse sense of pleasure seems not human. Capital-letter Evil, no doubt; but not "What Happened in Salem."

A glimpse of which we see in a revised version of another early story. Framed by the experience of a storyteller who recalls the time he read one of his early stories to a couple of fair maidens from Salem—who, like their oblivious neighbors, cannot come close to dating the witch trials. Standing on the graves of the supposed witches, he reads a tale in which a young man, separated by time and education from his twin brother, develops an unwholesome attachment to their sister. Brother returns and presents Other Brother with "indubitable proofs" that he and the sister are guilty lovers. Enacting what a Freud critic has called the killing of a "personified incest wish, he angrily murders his guilty double. We do not witness the murder, but learn of it only as confessed to a Wizard, who had in fact arranged the whole affair—caused, somehow, the "evidences" against poor Alice to *appear* "indubitable." Full of suspicion, he killed a person no more guilty than himself. What was he thinking?

Indeed. What were they thinking in Salem when, instructed that, as "the Devil has often appeared as an Angel of Light," so he may in fact have the power to create "spectral" impersonations of saints, implicating them in darkly evil deeds and testing thereby the credence of the otherwise faithful, the court went right on listening to testimony about "specters." A lot to ask of an unsuspecting audience, perhaps, but a final gothic scene confirms the learned reading. A scene in a graveyard: all the devils have come to celebrate the foul crime, "all the incidents [of which] were results of the machinations of the Wizard." And then the "spectral" fantasy comes literal: just as at the forest-scene climax of "Young Goodman Brown," absolutely everybody seems to be there—husbands, wives, young mothers, defenders of the colony, pastors, illustrious early settlers—

> All, in short, were there; the dead of other generations, whose moss-grown names could scarce be read upon their tombstones, and their successors, whose graves were not yet green; all whom black funerals had followed slowly thither, now re-appeared where the mourners had left them. Yet none but souls accursed were there, and fiends counterfeiting the likeness of departed saints.

One accomplished critic found this passage self-contradictory: were they all in league with the devil or not? Another, however, spotted the abstruse point at once: "specters" all, some representing persons actually given over to the Devil and some illicitly simulated by that gifted but evil magician. All a spectral deceit—whatever this superstitious belief might be made to signify.

Significantly, the point transfers perfectly to "Young Goodman Brown": the question is not, how evil does Hawthorne think we all are, but what sort of evidence leads Goodman Brown to decide that everyone (except, in the end, himself) is given over to the Devil? Isn't the thing just a little too easy? Brown goes to meet the devil, on a purpose fixed enough to be called a "covenant." He suspects his wife suspects his motives for not "tarrying" with her this one peculiar night; but no, he convinces himself, the thought would kill her. Besides, it's just one night; after that, he'll "cling to her skirts and follow her to heaven." And this is all we know for sure. Was Goody Cloyse really there? Or only her specter? And if that, was it surrendered to the Devil in her personal covenant or merely usurped by the Father of Lies for his own malicious purposes? And so with the others: The Deacon, the Pastor, all the Church-people, promiscuously intermixed in with all the Tavern-People. "All, in short," including Faith herself. Was *she* really there? OK, let's say she really was, in person and not in spectral simulation: what then? Let's see: she lost her pink ribbons; but did she "look up to heaven and resist the evil one" when Goodman Brown cried out in torment for her soul? Well, did she? How could he know? Any more than Othello can know about Desdemona. How, that is to say, can anyone ever know what exactly goes on in that privacy of soul which Hawthorne's generation was learning to call the "subject"? Perhaps it all depends on faith. As indeed it had in Spenser's *Faerie Queene*; Archimago first tempts Redcrosse with an erotic dream of sex with Una, and then produces specters of Una disporting herself with that knight's own squire. As if to say: specter evidence is guilty suspicion.

As Faith is Brown's faith as well as his wife, his cry appears to signal his own last-minute refusal. And not a moment too soon: it seems hard to come back from the blasphemous declaration that "There is no good on earth; and sin is but a name"; but maybe it's just possible. Maybe it ain't over till it's over. Be that as it may, Brown's suspicions are evidently stronger than his faith: unable to believe that a wife may resist the Devil as soon as would a husband, he lives out a most unhappy life—hearing the blasphemous forest songs when his snug little congregation intones its familiar hymns and never again quite trusting the wife he meant to deceive for one night only. Ah, yes guilt is like that: "Maybe you're accusin' me of what you're doin' yourself."

One general name for the region in which Hawthorne re-interprets the superstitious belief in specters might be "The Haunted Mind." Indeed, he has a sketch (1835) with that very title: it's not very interesting and it ends, implausibly, with the suggestion that sharing a bed with some gentle lover will keep all the spooks away; but the name suggests his belief that night-thoughts inhabit pretty much the same mental space as love and virtue. And it suggests that ghosts and goblins are not the only thing that may trouble our consciousness. Sin too might haunt an otherwise sane and sober man—not *theirs* but, as in the grave case of Parson Hooper, his very own sin; possibly some literal act or omission, but just as likely something not "actual" but "original," like being born with a nature selfishly unable to love the good for its own sake. There he was, going along just fine, in the less stressful latter days of some New England parish when it hit him: "I'm not ok, and neither are you." Sinfulness is inherent and, buried in the individual subject, its exact sense is essentially incommunicable. Except perhaps by symbol: don't we all wear the black veil?

Ink has been spilt trying to determine whether this veiled but oddly smiling minister is to be admired for his moral consciousness or shunned as obsessive and egotistical, but the more important point, surely, is to notice that his new, more searching manner of preaching divides his own congregation into factions: to one side, he is either a lunatic or a moral monster; to the other, a necessary if painful introduction to the idea that the good news of salvation can come only after the bad news of sin. When we learn that this fictional composite once gave an election sermon before Governor Belcher, and that it brought back "all the gloom and piety of our earliest ancestral sway." we begin to see that, with an obliqueness that may depend on the limitation of our storytelling Narrator, we are dealing with a version of New England's revival; and when we notice that the Reverend Mr. Hooper—called a "Parson" by those who have forgot the historical meaning of that term of Anglican art—has had to stop having Sunday dinner with a local squire who rejoices in the most famous pen-name of Benjamin Franklin, we realize that the moment in question is the one in which Awakening and Enlightenment stopped talking to one another. Famously, Franklin learns to call his sins, errata, misprints, so to speak. And so goodbye to one famous source of gloom; but farewell also to that level of consciousness one original Puritan had called the true sight of sin.

3

One most able critic has identified "sin" as the essential feature of the Puritan sense of identity and, though it has more than one sight, it is, obviously enough, one way into Hawthorne's dungeon of puritanic gloom. Not love in itself, exactly, or love truly discovered and honestly enjoyed, but the fear that some human loves might compete with and even come to replace the all-important love of God. Following St. Augustine in this regard, the majority of Puritans believed there was really only one sin, idolatry, loving anything more than God. Neither monks nor hermits, they well knew that they lived in and were expected to work effectively in the world; but they were not *of* the world, and they learned to call their cautious engagement with mortal things—and persons!—loving the world with "weaned affections."

The original American poet Anne Bradstreet has to ask herself repeatedly about the worldly temptation: had she loved the house that burned down a little too much? Or, elsewhere, the natural world itself, which seemed to work so much more happily that the social. Or, in the most tense case, the grandchildren who were born only to die almost at once: had she loved them too much? Tempted to blame God, she feared she had been in danger of loving them *more*. More revealing still is the case of Thomas Shepard, whose *Autobiography* expresses the painful sense that, in the death of wives and children, God is constantly warning him to keep his loves in order. In check, we might almost say—especially if we were looking for a source of sober self-discipline where one ought to expect only joy. In fact, the Puritans had about the same conservative sexual ethic as most Christians in the seventeenth century, but they may yet be remarkable for their fear of the way love itself might be related to sin.

As their most common figure of idolatry was adultery, no doubt some of this fear affects the secret but hysterical guilt of Arthur Dimmesdale: does he repent his adultery? And if not, does this not prove he loves Hester more than God? But an early tale presents the problem in a somewhat more subtle form: in "The Gentle Boy," more than one character has to face the painful choice of simple human love and the sense of some higher religious calling. A simple reading may see the story as somewhat sentimental, but it may also take us to the heart of something quite as essentially Puritan as the sight and suspicion of sin.

After a lengthy head-note, the tale opens with a scene in which a less-than-single-minded Puritan named Tobias Pearson encounters a grieving and helpless child: his natural sympathies want to help, but they are opposed by his discovery that the child is the offspring of an "accursed sect." The reader may think of the parable of the outcast Samaritan who yet proves himself singularly a "neighbor" to the man lying helpless in the ditch; or to the New Testament suggestion that "true religion" is caring for widows and orphans. Orphan this gentle child effectively proves to be, his father having been executed by the latter-day rulers of Winthrop's Holy City, and his mother having been called by the Spirit to testify against sectarian violations of conscience. A decisive moment.

Surely, if slowly, the warm heart wins out over the well-chilled head: Tobias takes the outlandishly named Ilbrahim home where he is more than welcomed by a wife who, having lost all her own beloved children, has never managed to wean herself from the need to love and nurture. The child's mother appears, asking Dorothy Pearson whether she can raise the child in the spiritual way of the Quakers. Her answer is both ironic and cogent: "we must do towards him according to the dictates of our consciences, and not of yours." The scene is meant to be quite telling: "rational piety" versus "unbridled fanaticism," and both in the figure of a woman. But as the "rational" is also significantly the "domestic," we begin to suspect that, deeper than the discrimination of sects, the issue concerns the place of what Jonathan Edwards would have called "natural virtue" in the orderly working of the world. Or even whether, in somebody's theology, "adoption" might precede and not follow "justification."

In any event, adoption occurs and problems ensue: the Pearsons are scorned by their neighbors for harboring a heretic; and their children vent their righteousness on the foundling. One seeming friend betrays him with a blow which all but breaks his gentle spirit. But then, just as we begin to feel that Hawthorne's will-to-sentiment is pushing some anti-Calvinist argument from nature a little too far, the emphasis shifts from stricture to enthusiasm. Drifting toward the newness, Tobias becomes acquainted with an elderly Quaker who, in a discussion about the difficulty of true piety, tells the chilling tale of how, in a triumphant epitome of virtue over life, he left a dying daughter to follow a call of the Spirit. Joined by Quaker Catherine, he tells her the good news that the King has demanded that New England give up its bloody crusade against Quakers but also, less happily, the news that her son is dying. Too much, finally. "Will He try me beyond my strength?" Will He, that is to say, insist on a virtue so painfully at odds with ordinary nature?

Of course, a politics is also involved, as the reader cannot fail to notice that "toleration," when it comes, comes from England. And one may well wonder why Hawthorne has associated the theme of "weaned affections" with those left-leaning Puritans known as Quakers. Certain it is, however, that this early tale has identified an ethic which threatened to set religion *against* caring. And that he has associated both the exaggeration of and the opposition to this sad premise with the instincts of womanhood. Very much as in *The Scarlet Letter*, where only Pearl prevents Hester—for a time at least—from turning into a prophet like Anne Hutchinson.

By comparison, Hawthorne's tales of the Revolution—a topic for separate treatment in this volume—do not strike us as communicating the same affect. They may be ironic, subtly taking away with narrative irony the patriotism they seem heavily to pronounce, but in general Hawthorne's Puritan revolutionaries seem, if a trifle paranoid, more strong and determined than gloomy. Their pronounced "Champion" may be gray, but more significantly he is steadfast. In one tale only do the topics of gloom and resistance seem on purpose to coexist—namely "The May-Pole of Merry Mount," which is not always taken as a political statement. Yet it involves the same John Endicott who elsewhere mars the banner used by the American trainbands; and an historical reading is able to identify the maypole as a symbol every bit as definitively British as that definitive Red Cross.

Morally, so to speak, the earliest Puritans battle it out with a group of straying Revelers, and the learned have defended both sides. Or perhaps Hawthorne was simply "ambivalent." More revealing, surely, is a reading which sets this future-determining contest of Gloom and Jollity in the context of a project Hawthorne called "The Story-Teller": running away from the strict control of a step-parent who insists on some warrantable calling, a scapegrace aspiring to a career in storytelling meets up at once with an orthodox evangelist; journeying together, the two itinerant wordsmiths epitomize two opposed yet hardly comprehensive "literary" careers. Unhappily, the richly composite work never appeared as designed, but what if, running away from the latter-day Thumpcushion, the Story-Teller introduces us to the aboriginal Endicott?—whom "no fantastic foolery could look [...] in the face." Evidently Endicott's destruction of "the only may-pole in New England" amounts to a revolution that is esthetic as well as moral: in merry old England they love to play merry old games. But not here. If Endicott has his revolutionary way, New England never will figure as a culture of play. Any more than of love. What then if "literature" as we know it is some composite of exactly these?

A small but tensely ironic headnote refers the reader to a certain "Book of Sports," compiled by a dauntingly learned antiquarian of the eighteenth century. But has no one heard of King James' own so-called "Book of Sports"—that public list of games Englishmen are allowed, indeed encouraged to play on their Sabbath? Probably Plymouth's Governor Bradford—who first told a version of the story in which the sober Puritans overcome the shameless Revelers with their "idol or idle may-pole" had not; but the newly arrived John Endicott most certainly had; so he made haste to cut down the pine tree a promiscuous Thomas Morton had used in the celebration of England's May Day—long after that pettifogger had been deported for trading guns and rum for beaver? Evidently something very essential is at issue. James saith, in my Merry Kingdom, my subjects may have merry maypoles; Endicott replieth, as in the "Red Cross," "What have we to do with England?" Evidently something somehow like Gloom is not an exclusively moral issue. Perhaps a certain cultural sobriety, involving the exclusion of play, can be considered the meta-politics of American Puritanism. At any rate, the famous preface to *The Scarlet Letter* will still present us with a Hawthorne still worrying about what his ancestors would think of his more or less idle literariness.

4

Gloom or not, the issue of Puritan affect continues. Favorably reprised, for once, in the reverent parody we know as "The Celestial Rail-road"; with curious ambivalence in "Egotism," where a self-styled analyst of secret sin gets himself put in a mental hospital for posing a Parson Hooper-like challenge; and with fear and trembling in "The Birthmark," where a puritanic scientist tries to transform his otherwise idolized lover into an entirely new creature; and in "Rappaccini's Daughter," which looks suspiciously like a troubled response to the idea that original sin is seminally transmitted. It floats in the air above sketches like "The Hall of Fantasy" and especially "Earth's Holocaust"—where the familiar wish for purity seems to require the extirpation of all created being. And then the novels after *The Scarlet Letter*: beginning with an episode of witchcraft, clearly some quasi-original sin lingers within *The House of the Seven Gables*; some will to reform by separated example informs the morale of *The Blithedale Romance*; and some atavistic moral fear reveals itself when, in *The Marble Faun*, a pair of New England innocents find themselves, respectively, trying to confess away some oddly imputed guilt, and trying to survive the moral shock of a fertility festival.

Too complex for adequate discussion here, the gloom of *The Scarlet Letter* might almost speak for itself. Suffice it to say that, in this sober tale of love and sin—this "Puritan Love Story" once stigmatized as an account of "the nauseous amour of a puritan pastor"—the characters are historically conceived and are made to endure and to live out a set of premises we might wish to correct, if only history would permit. Trying for seven long years to persuade himself that he may be a Saint even though a serious sinner, and that he does indeed love God more, Dimmesdale eventually decides to "seize the day" and then, reversing himself, makes a confession only a little less oblique than the ones his remorseful hypocrisy has all along attempted. Pearl kisses him on the scaffold, but he himself refuses to predict a divine reconciliation. Hester appears to fare a little better, yet both her heroism and her "liberation" are easy to overstate. Associated with the figure of Anne Hutchinson from the outset, she is said (but not shown) to reason her way out of her early wish to be near Dimmesdale, even in hell, and into something like an "antinomian" position, the world's law being "no law to her mind." And she well survives Dimmesdale's death, as Chillingworth does not. But then, back she comes, to take up her letter and to predict—but not at all to work for—a more equitable understanding of love and marriage. That task being left for the women obliquely represented in *The Blithedale Romance*.

Beneath it all there appears to lurk some extraordinary sense that the Puritans, who feared the sin of excessive affection, but who made their Covenant of Grace look a lot like a loving marriage, were connoisseurs of guilty conscience but inspired failures in the theory of human love. Unequivocally serious about faith and morals, monumentally determined to pursue their understanding of God's plan, and potently influential in determining the psychological complexion of New England, they were also, in some fundamental sense, wrong. And what on earth could make us gloomier than that?

Works Cited

Coxe, Arthur C. "The Writings of Hawthorne." *Church Review.* January 1851: 489–511.
Crews, Frederick C. *The Sins of the Fathers: Hawthorne's Psychological Themes*. Oxford: Oxford University Press, 1966.
Gura, Philip F. *A Glimpse of Sion's Glory: Puritan Radicalism in New England, 1620–1660*. Middletown, CT: Wesleyan University Press, 1984.
Knight, Janice. *Orthodoxies in New England*. Cambridge, MA: Harvard University Press, 1994.
Levin, David. "Shadows of Doubt: Specter Evidence in Hawthorne's 'Young Goodman Brown.'" *American Literature* 34 (1962): 344–52.

———, ed. *What Happened in Salem: Documents Pertaining to the Seventeenth Century Witchcraft Trials.* Boston, MA: Harcourt, 1960.

Miller, Perry. "From the Covenant to the Revival." In *Nature's Nation.* Cambridge, MA: Harvard University Press, Belknap Press, 1976: 90–120.

Sanders, Ernest. "*The Scarlet Letter* as a Love Story." *PMLA* 1977 (1962): 425–35.

Waggoner, Hyatt. *Hawthorne.* Cambridge, MA: Harvard University Press, 1955.

Warden, G. B. *Boston, 1689–1776.* Boston, MA: Little, Brown, 1970.

Chapter Two

COSMOPOLITAN AND PROVINCIAL: HAWTHORNE AND THE REFERENCE OF AMERICAN STUDIES

It might almost go without saying: a certain provincialism has been the besetting fault of the American Studies Movement. And surely it is this intense local bias of explanatory "style"—and not some more abstract failure of interdisciplinary "method," or yet some ingrained resistance to "theory"—which explains why literary "Americanists" seem a little distrusted by many of their departmental colleagues. In an age committed to the transcendence, or else the self-reference, of literary speech, they have been somewhat more "historicist" in their persuasion. Worse, perhaps, they have meant to give a distinctly "American" explanation to phenomena which other trained observers cannot imagine as nationally distinct and would not consider privileged if they did. Americanists have been concerned with divergences from tradition; in their relentless pursuit of some American "difference," they have elaborated the local and the peculiar at the expense of the universal, the traditional, or the generic. And this has seemed indeed provincial.[1]

Observing this much (and suspecting much more), the critic would be rash to insist on the cardinal significance of every local reference in the learned but never pedantic tales and sketches of Hawthorne. The utter worldliness of Hawthorne's tone must count for something, surely. So too must the fact that his range of reference is almost as cosmopolitan as his reading was omnivorous. Yet there are strategies of reference to consider: hierarchies and directions and dependencies. And these are, in Hawthorne, often pointed toward the local, suggesting the mentality, if not always the methods, of American Studies.

Indeed, Hawthorne is the writer, I mean to suggest, who throws us back on ourselves, in spite of ourselves; in spite of himself even. He aspired to the condition of the world-class authors whose meanings his allusions went out to touch; and we should like to admit him to that world. Yet the assimilation can never be complete, for he is the sort of writer who can scarcely be grasped at all without constant attention to his own local allusions—in a series of tales he himself entitled "Provincial"—to a sequence of writers one never

---

1. For a recent response to the provincial bias of "American Studies," see Jonathan Arac, "F. O. Matthiessen: Authorizing an American Renaissance," in Walter Benn Michaels and Donald E. Pease, eds, *The American Renaissance Reconsidered* (Baltimore, MD: Johns Hopkins University Press, 1985), pp. 90–112; and cp. Gerald Graff, *Professing Literature* (Chicago: University of Chicago Press, 1987), pp. 209–25.

expects to see on the syllabus of a course in "English" or in "Theory." And, though his mood is more nearly one of political Irony than patriotic Hurrah, he seems to have felt that making sense of "The American Experience" was the only way he could become a writer of significance at all.

1

Only a limited case for Hawthorne's cosmopolitanism could be based on his use of John Bunyan, perhaps; particularly in these latter days when Bunyan's masterpiece—once the very lingua franca of Western Christianity—survives chiefly as a marker of popular English Puritanism or else as an early misstep in the otherwise steady course of the rising novel. Still, we may as well begin with the most obvious instance: "The Celestial Railroad" rewrites *The Pilgrim's Progress* as flagrantly as possible; but this prime literary fact tells us much less about the workings of Hawthorne's whimsical performance than we might suppose.[2]

It is scarcely a question of "parody," in the usual sense: nineteenth-century religious institutions and attitudes make their own mockery of Bunyan's antique tropes; but in this satire, his old-time standard of religious seriousness is the source of authority rather than the object of ridicule. Taking Bunyan absolutely for granted, Hawthorne revivifies him in order to try conclusions with various forms of an emergent American liberalism. Quite unlike the more famous example of Joyce and Homer, the relation to the pre-text is altogether obvious and insistent, even a bit mechanical. The fun lies not in detecting the repetition of episodes from the pilgrimage of Christian—for these are in fact announced—but in identifying and measuring the local objects of satire.

Students usually fasten first on the timely replacement of those "two cruel giants, Pope and Pagan": in their stead, Emerson—or some "Giant Transcendentalist"—is said to prophesy "in so strange a phraseology" that the would-be Christian knows "not what he meant, nor whether to be encouraged or affrighted" (X, 197).[3] The point, clearly enough, is that a text like the Divinity School "Address" redefines Christianity so radically that one can scarcely tell whether it is an act of pious reform or of daring apostasy; and the question will indeed bear looking into. Still, it is the Unitarians who draw the more direct and consistent attention. Avoiding all roads that lead near a "sight of the cross" (192), the Liberal Christians might be trying to have the good news of salvation

---

2. In the patient formulation of Lea Bertani Vozar Newman, "the story's internal evidence is sufficient to establish Bunyan's allegory as Hawthorne's model without additional documentation," but the reader will "better understand 'The Celestial Rail-road' if he knows the history of the [religious] changes in New England"; see *Reader's Guide to the Short Stories of Nathaniel Hawthorne* (Boston, MA: G. K. Hall, 1979), p. 46. For the received moral of Hawthorne's use of Bunyan, see W. Stacey Johnson, "Hawthorne and 'The Pilgrim's Progress,'" *Journal of English and Germanic Philology*, 50 (1951), pp. 156–66; and Hyatt H. Waggoner, *Hawthorne: A Critical Study* (Cambridge: Belknap Press, 1963), pp. 17–19.
3. All citations of Hawthorne are from the Centenary Edition of his *Works* (Columbus: Ohio State University Press, 1962 ff.); volume and page are given in the text.

without the bad news of sin and the need of redemption. In their creed, and in their liberal world more generally, Franklin's extra-sectarian wish to invent a creed which would "satisfy the professors of all religions and shock none" has reached its liberal-Christian perfection: "Even an infidel would have heard little or nothing to shock his sensibility" (189). And a whole preaching, lecturing, conversing, and conventioneering age is ironically praised for making it possible to "acquire an omnigenous erudition, without the trouble of even learning to read" (198). All these socio-religious questions are just the sort Americanists love to worry about; but they are also, just as clearly, the ones this sketch forces on our attention.

Bunyan furnishes us the moral a priori we need to judge the phenomena of present interest; but he is not, so far as Hawthorne's enterprise is concerned, himself one of those phenomena. He comes to us as a given, almost a "structure"—as if his transformation of Everyman into Christian had altogether succeeded in transferring solitude, sobriety, and substitutionary atonement from the stock of religious culture to the store of original nature. This makes him, of course, a prime candidate for deconstruction. In fact Edward Taylor's account of "God's Determinations" had seen and seized the opportunity at once: one rides to salvation, singing and in concert; sober, single walking may seem "natural," but it is surely not the Bible's Way.[4] But unlike Taylor's wonderful "Coach," Hawthorne's "Rail-road" parodies only itself, leaving the Bunyan standard entirely in place. Not itself subject to further investigation, the worldly given merely convicts the local deviance of latter-day reduction.

It further appears, however, that Bunyan is not the only standard we need—and are given—to estimate "the liberality of the age" (190) that followed the end of Calvinist hegemony. Behind the example of his mechanic preaching, on the one hand, lurks someone else's more early archetypal "tolle, lege." And, on the other hand, the harder we press the orthodoxy of *The Pilgrim's Progress*, the more anxious we grow about the quality of Hawthorne's own (ambiguous) belief.[5] We are helped along considerably, however, as soon as we discover that "The Celestial Rail-road" has at least one other major pre-text—thoroughly provincial, and mediating, so to speak, the otherwise too simple influence of Bunyan.

Aside from the narrator, the principal character in Hawthorne's sketch is a quintessential Liberal named "Mr. Smooth-it-Away," whose function it is to assure everyone that there is nothing difficult or paradoxical about the Christian plan of salvation. And it turns out that Smooth-it-Away has a clear and direct precursor in an intensely doctrinaire poem by a Connecticut Wit, who was also a staunch Edwardsian Calvinist. In a poem entitled "The Triumph of Infidelity," Timothy Dwight offers us, along with an extended reflection by Satan on the ups and downs of his earthly reign, the following evocation

---

4. Cf. Edward Taylor, "The Joy of Church Fellowship Rightly Attended," in Donald E. Stanford, ed., *The Poems of Edward Taylor* (New Haven, CT: Yale University Press, 1960), pp. 458–59.
5. Of recent commentators, only Agnes McNeill Donohue holds out for "H's consistently Calvinist habit of mind"; see *Hawthorne: Calvin's Ironic Stepchild* (Kent, OH: Kent State University Press, 1985), p. 1. Donohue offers no reading of "The Celestial Rail-road."

of a liberal "character" named "Smooth Divine"—a favorite of Satan, clearly—as his theological project involves eliminating all harsh and discordant elements from the public preaching of Christianity.

> There smil'd the "smooth" Divine, unus'd to wound
> The sinners' heart, with hell's alarming sound.
> No terrors on his gentle tongue attend:
> No grating truths the nicest ear offend.
> That strange new-birth, that methodistic grace,
> Nor in his heart, nor sermons, found a place.
> Plato's fine tales he clumsily retold,
> Trite, fireside, moral seesaws, dull as old;
> His Christ, and bible, plac'd at good remove,
> Guilt hell-deserving, and forgiving love.
> 'Twas best, he said, mankind should cease to sin;
> Good fame requir'd it; so did peace within.[6]

A plausible doctrine without question: what one of my students called "Christianity Light"; just the sort of distraction from guilt we count on humanistic culture to arrange.

And if it does not cover Hawthorne's entire case, the lack is immediately supplied when, two or three satiric "characters" later, somebody—whose initials suggest Charles Chauncy—ransacks the Bible to disprove the doctrine of Hell. In Dwight's original account, the deed requires considerable torture of linguistic interpretation, as "kai's and epi's build the glorious scheme! And gar's and pro's unfold their proof supreme!"[7] But in Hawthorne's still later redaction, Smooth-it-Away merely takes the occasion of a passage through a "smoky and lurid cavern" to propose some offhand proof "that Tophet has not even a metaphorical existence" (194).

Of course some plot is thickened by the discovery that Timothy Dwight is rewriting Alexander Pope—that his heroic couplets and literary characters are turning the *Dunciad*'s mock-heroic theme of dullness back into the sober theology of sin; producing, thereby, some quaintly pseudo-Miltonic Infideliad. But our own problem, here, is a little simpler: the quality of Dwight's doctrinal involvement with his subject lets us know at once what an embattled Calvinism will sound like, suggesting thereby the Hawthornean "difference." Dwight's hysterical attack on the actual propositions of liberal Christianity assures us at once that Hawthorne's protest is largely, perhaps mainly tonal and, in a special sense, structural: certain ways of talking are just not Christian; and the element of offense to the natural man is of the essence. Leaving someone else's text to live (and quickly die) in pursuit of doctrinal purity, Hawthorne suggests only that it is safer to sound earnest, like Bunyan, than plausible, like the Liberal Christians of the American

---

6. Timothy Dwight, *The Major Poems of Timothy Dwight: (1752–1817)* (Gainesville, FL: Scholars' Facsimiles and Reprints, 1969), p. 356.
7. Dwight, *Major Poems*, p. 362.

nineteenth century, whose tone we are being taught to recognize and to disdain. "No Featherbed to Heaven," as they used to say; and no railroad either.

By itself, perhaps, "The Celestial Rail-road" would seem an insignificant example: a formally peculiar tale, which we seldom emphasize, turns out to be determined by even more provincial coordinates than we had feared. Yet the pattern of allusion operating in the more famous (and more dramatic) tales will scarcely alter the figure. Hawthorne's taste and indeed his moral sense are nourished by the literature of the great world, but his public eye and his own creative attention are fixed on his "native land." In case after case.

Though it has come to seem compacted of more or less subtle allusions to almost everything, "Rappaccini's Daughter" nevertheless begins with a perfectly explicit—and most assuring—reference to Dante: Giovanni Guasconti is "not unstudied in the great poem of his country"; indeed one of his own ancestors "had been pictured by Dante as a partaker of the immortal agonies of the Inferno" (X, 93). We may doubt, from the outset, that this most suggestive literary placement will aid the allegorical protagonist, imperceptient by generic demand, but surely it will guide the worldly reader.

Yet not so much, unhappily, as we should like to hope. It makes some sense to imagine that Giovanni's (symbolic) ancestor may be Averroes, whose philosophical researches forced him to discover the unhappy notion of the "Two Truths"—the undeniable ones of faith and, in conflict, the necessary ones of experience. The narrator himself, flawed as he is, seems trembling on the verge of some such discovery: "Blessed are all simple emotions" (105), he ponderously prays, as he writes but cannot sufficiently interpret Giovanni's conflict of love and horror. Beyond this telling definition of Giovanni's mental division, however, the world-class example of Dante offers only a little help, all of it "ironic." Criticism is all but unnerved by the suggestion of a "poisoned" Beatrice. And no "guide" appears to tell us whether we are in heaven, purgatory, or hell.[8]

Worse, perhaps—for the critic who would wish to make a "Modernist" virtue of this medieval conundrum—we swiftly learn that such interpretative help as we do get is coming to us in the language of a nineteenth-century American controversy about faith and miracles; and that our narrative preceptor has been made to sound distressingly like George Ripley, whose idealist theory of some "better mode of evidence" can convict but scarcely assist Giovanni in solving an allegory that works only when you already know. "Faith is a fine invention," that is to say, when Gentlemen are Narrators. True, we can defer, perhaps evade, this faithful "Americanist" reading by sticking to the tale's fascinating "Road to Padua"—and to the medical interventions of a certain Benvenuto Cellini—but this will hardly solve the problem of provincial reference as such; for the

---

8. For the radical argument—that the allusions in "Rappaccini's Daughter" all unsay themselves—see Robert J. Daly, "Fideism and the Allusive Mode in 'Rappaccini's Daughter,'" *Nineteenth-Century Fiction*, 28 (1973), pp. 25–37. For recent "returns" to Dante, in the mode of irony, see David L. Cowles, "A Profane Tragedy: Dante in Hawthorne's "Rappaccini's Daughter,'" *American Transcendental Quarterly*, 60 (1986), pp. 5–24; and Lois A. Cuddy, "The Purgatorial Gardens of Hawthorne and Dante," *Modern Language Studies*, 17 (1987), pp. 39–53.

"black-letter tracts" which indicate the emergence of modern medical practice from the crisis of medieval epistemology do not at present count as part of the Great Tradition.[9]

Similar problems embarrass the worldly reference of "Ethan Brand." Here, surely, is the single concentrated center of the theme called "Hawthorne's Faust." Yet our interest in the allusions to Goethe—and to a whole tradition of blasted, dark-romantic wanderers—is overbalanced by the intensity of the tale's insistence on the local details of some more drastic case of conscience. A more "Puritan" case, somehow, despite the latter-day setting. Brand's relentless and inspired attempt to discover and embrace the unpardonable sin reads as if it were designed to balk the entire history of Puritan casuistry, the proudest boast of which was its power to restore spiritual health to the sober person who, fearing reprobation, trembled on the brink of a covenant with Satan. As if this sinner meant to defy Cotton Mather (and Thomas Hooker before him) as well as to defy God. Aspiring to some sort of negative transcendence, he would constitute himself the one "Brand" that never could be "Pluck'd out the Burning."[10] But it cannot be done with Goethe alone: his Faust gets a second chance, as a humane social engineer, a happy ending parodied in the fact that Brand's remains go into the civil elements of fertilizer and cement; but the terror comes from the local tradition.

And just so, elsewhere, do the provinces assert their awkward interest. The imagery—and even the suppressed plot—of "Egotism; or, The Bosom Serpent" conceals and reveals its debt to Spenser; but its application, indeed its motive, is scarcely intelligible without the example of Jones Very who, in the wake of Emerson's call for some new Bards of the Holy Ghost, went about identifying the "Bosom Idols" of his fellow Salemites. To his ministrations, Hawthorne alone proved immune: negative capability, it appears, had deprived him of any proper ego. "The Christmas Banquet" shows traces of a fateful reading of Voltaire, but it begins to make emotional sense only in relation to that unique complex of grief, idealism, and the failure of noumenal selfhood we know as Emerson's "Experience"—even if we are forced to conclude that Hawthorne learned the case from Emerson's Journals.[11] "The Birthmark" rewrites the "Platonic" career of a

---

9. See my own essay, "A Better Mode of Evidence," *Emerson Society Quarterly*, 54 (1959), pp. 12–22; and cp. Carol Marie Bensick, *La Nouvelle Beatrice* (New Brunswick, NJ: Rutgers University Press, 1985), esp. pp. 29–43, 113–30.
10. For the presence of Goethe in "Ethan Brand," see William Bysshe Stein, *Hawthorne's Faust* (Gainesville: University of Florida Press, 1953); and cp. Joan E. Klingel, "'Ethan Brand' as Hawthorne's Faust," *Studies in Short Fiction*, 19 (1982), pp. 74–76. For the surrounding tradition, see Newman, *Guide*, pp. 101–3. And for a brief hint of the "Puritan connection," see John McElroy, "The Brand Metaphor in 'Ethan Brand,'" *American Literature*, 43 (1972), pp. 633–37.
11. The classic study of Spenser in "Egotism; or The Bosom-Serpent" is John W. Shroeder, "Hawthorne's 'Egotism' and Its Sources," *American Literature*, 31 (1959), pp. 150–62; but see also David Van Leer, "Roderick's Other Serpent," *ESQ*, 27 (1981), pp. 73–84. Alfred H. Marks infers the presence of Poe; see "Two Rodericks and Two Worms," *PMLA*, 74 (1959), pp. 607–12. But the more cogent example is that of Jones Very: see Robert D. Arner, "Hawthorne and Jones Very," *New England Quarterly*, 42 (1969), pp. 267–75; and cp. Edwin Gittleman, *Jones Very: The Effective Years, 1833–1840* (New York: Columbia University Press, 1967). For the presence of Voltaire in "The Christmas Banquet," see Frank Davidson, "Voltaire and Hawthorne's 'The Christmas Banquet,'" *Boston Public Library Quarterly*, 3 (1951), pp. 244–46. The most

seventeenth-century virtuoso, and "The Artist of the Beautiful" invokes a familiar array of high Romantic ideas about art, but both are most urgently read in their local relations—to the Swedenborgian spiritualism of Emerson and the Transcendental esthetics of Poe.[12]

So far, of course, all of our instances are taken from tales written in the 1840s, when Hawthorne has emerged, finally, from his self-imposed and studious isolation at Salem, to open his "intercourse with the world." What isolation of literary reference may we not expect from the earlier stories, which come to us from the closet of Hawthorne's colonialism?

But first, a brief mention of *The Scarlet Letter*: surely here, in a work recognized as a worthy addition to the world-class canon can be made to escape the charge of intense localism. And to be sure, what a hostile critic then seemed to recognize as an invasion of the "French era," has been recognized as well as a significant and unashamed addition to an emergent multinational tradition of the "Novel of Adultery." And yet, there she is, Anne Hutchinson, right there on the first page—and again, very emphatically, in a chapter explaining why the private but un-repentant Hester Prynne has not come down to us as a prophet of gender equality. We seem always to have known that this masterwork was written with the pages of Caleb Snow's *History of Boston* open before him; and elsewhere I have made a strong enough case for the pages of Winthrop's *Journal* as well. So that, even if we reject the notion that Hawthorne has offered us but the "nauseous amour of a Puritan pastor," we have to confess that he has given the problem of "Women's Rights and Women's Wrongs" a local habitation and a name.

2

Back at the historical beginnings, "Young Goodman Brown" may well deserve to be regarded as "Hawthorne's Spenser." Brown's unhappy loss of Faith clearly reprises the outsetting episode of *The Faerie Queene*: the false forms by which Archimago manages to "abuse [the] fantasy" of Redcrosse, and so to separate him from his Una, are Spenser's way of predicting a career of guilty projection: Brown slips into the forest on a guilty errand and then "sees" his wife (and everyone else) as up to the same evil. But even as this tale validates the famous argument about the deceitful—spectral—powers of the guilty

---

revealing treatment of "Egotism; or, The Bosom-Serpent" and "The Christmas Banquet"—separately and together—remains unpublished: see Bruce W. Jorgensen, "The True Madmen of This Nineteenth Century," Doctoral Dissertation (Cornell University, 1978), pp. 229–307. Jorgensen is especially suggestive on Hawthorne's timely exchange of journals with Emerson.

12. For the cosmopolitan contexts in question, see Alfred S. Reid, "Hawthorne's Humanism: "'The Birthmark' and Sir Kenelm Digby," *American Literature*, 38 (1966), pp. 337–51; and Millicent Bell, *Hawthorne's View of the Artist* (New York: New York State University Press, 1962), pp. 94–113. The relation of "The Artist of the Beautiful" to Emerson's ideal of "The Poet," for whom "the ideal shall be made real" has been often remarked. More telling is the possibility that both "The Birthmark" and "The Artist of the Beautiful" may implicate Poe, whose women are more beautiful dead, and whose esthetic everywhere values spiritual aspiration over material artifact.

imagination, it plainly applies the Spenserian argument to the vexing Americanist question of "What Happened in Salem?" And the tendency of its most open references—to Martha Carrier, for example—is to insist on a sort of catholicity of pretext: Cotton Mather also belongs on our table of cultural contents. Perhaps we should found a society for those who have read all of the *Magnalia*.[13]

Just behind this most famous tale, and serving as a sort of workshop for it, "Alice Doane's Appeal" goes over much the same ground; and it also comes to rest squarely in the midst of the provinces. Opening with an image of unburied guilt that can come from nowhere but the skeptical critique of Robert Calef, it works out the psychology of "specter evidence" with an astonishing literalness. It even extends the concept to cover the ambiguities discovered by the Wieland circle, in Brockden Brown's latter-day test of unsupported faith.[14]

And the pattern appears invariable, without regard to the century or decade of setting in American time. "The Minister's Black Veil" evokes the paradigm of "The Romantic Solitary," but it imitates a moment of provincial Awakening; and it absolutely turns on the significance of certain election sermons delivered before an eighteenth-century governor of provincial Massachusetts. "My Kinsman, Major Molineux" creates its world out of the atmospheric fragments of some "Mid-Summer Night's Dream," but it makes its point by comparing the American Revolution to the workings of a rum-riot in the 1730s. Focusing on a protagonist named Ilbrahim, "The Gentle Boy" appears to reflect an Orientalism quite modish in the nineteenth century, but not powerfully enough to efface a moral texture supplied by the painful researches of the Quaker prophet and historian Willem Sewel.[15] And "The May-Pole of Merry Mount"—which insists on itself as "Hawthorne's Milton," almost as clearly as "The Celestial Rail-road" is his "Bunyan"—nevertheless forces our attentions directly back into the matter of some entirely obscure annalists of earliest New England.

This last example we may well regard as an epitome of our problem, the most perfect provincialism of our most perfect provincialist; and I am willing to offer it as the centerpiece of the argument for an "American Studies Hawthorne." Or else, more soberly, for Hawthorne's perfection as "Artist of the Provincial."

---

13. For the detection of Spenser in "Young Goodman Brown," see Randall Stewart, ed., *The American Notebooks of Nathaniel Hawthorne* (New Haven, CT: Yale University Press, 1932), p. 11; and Herbert A. Leibowitz, "Hawthorne and Spenser," *American Literature*, 30 (1959), pp. 459–66. The classic account of Hawthorne's American application of the doctrine of "specter evidence" is, of course, David Levin, "Shadows of Doubt," *American Literature*, 34 (1962), pp. 344–52. And on both issues, see my own "Visible Sanctity and Specter Evidence," in *The Province of Piety* (Cambridge, MA: Harvard University Press, 1984), pp. 283–313.
14. See *Province*, pp. 78–93.
15. The provincial side of these questions is fully argued in *Province*, pp. 314–85, 130–53, 160–202. For the discovery of *A Midsummer Night's Dream* in "My Kinsman, Major Molineux," see Newman, *Guide*, p. 220. And for the orientalism of "The Gentle Boy," see Luther Luedke, "Turkish Hospitality and Natural Religion," in *Nathaniel Hawthorne and the Romance of the Orient* (Bloomington: Indiana University Press, 1989), pp. 93–103.

3

"The May-Pole" has seemed to insist we read it, even though its nominal protagonists are utterly without distinguishing psychological marks. Unlike the more complex and psychically troubled figures of Goodman Brown and Robin Molineux, the Edith and Edgar of this curiously mythic tale are merely young. Yet their mere growing up is said to recapitulate moral experience and also to prefigure the problem of "America": a cliché struggling to become an archetype. Of course it required the "system" of a Frederick Crews to notice the ugly strain of sadism in their all too severe antagonist, who wants to turn their pagan maypole into a Puritan whipping post; and this after he has already performed a painful enough, if only symbolic, castration.[16] As if the chief distinction of Puritanism were that it ruined our sex life.

But as soon as we notice that the Narrator can absorb even this class of insight into his own metatheme of the triumph of Gloom over Jollity, we may well find ourselves looking elsewhere for the main point. Doggerel is doggerel, even out of Civilization and Its Discontents. And besides, Hawthorne here calls deliberate attention to the quintessentially "Americanist" project—the origin and progress of the puritanic mind. Already trusting the (biological) images more than the (moralistic) narrator, we must learn to explore the allusions as well.

Yet even in these terms some critics have felt entirely free to decline the "Americanist" invitation. For above and behind this local spectacle of Puritanism's Quarrel With Nature looms the cosmic example of Milton which, if it does not quite proclaim "Christ's Victory and Triumph," at least announces an historic end to the fantasy of innocence. Perhaps we should be gracious enough to profess Comparatism after all, in the language of one of its own high priests: "The May-Pole of Merry Mount" is essentially "a Paradise Lost in provincial miniature," with the difference that Hawthorne "went much further into the subliminal," daring to "center his graceful parable upon the most primitive archetype of sexuality."[17] Thus join hands the cosmopolitan and the elemental—preventing, at the outset, an indefinite future of nationalistic analysis. In Adam's phallus we sinned all: abandon R. W. B. Lewis, all you who enter here.

But if Milton lurks, like his own crew of Comus, and nowhere more potently than in the tale's final moral summation, still a flagrant colonialism positively flaunts itself in the very first line of an irreducibly historical headnote: the "foundation" of his "philosophic romance" lies in the "curious history" of Merry Mount, and in the "allegory" that seems "spontaneously" there. Reader: think the altogether obscure problem of American origins; avoid, thereby, the problem of getting, once more, too far too fast. It is a tense moment, critically speaking. Two roads diverge, testing our loyalties and perhaps our epistemologies as well. Perhaps there is a middle way.

One scarcely needs to be a professional Deconstructionist to notice that Hawthorne himself has clearly marked, at just the center of his tale, its own very "navel." But

---

16. See Frederick C. Crews, *The Sins of the Fathers* (New York: Oxford University Press, 1966), pp. 17–25.
17. See Harry Levin, *The Power of Blackness* (New York: Vintage Books, 1960), pp. 53–54.

evidently it requires somewhat more elan than provincial source-hunters usually display to unscrew it. Who knows what we might discover if we pressed to explain the full force of the absolutely outrageous footnote which Hawthorne himself has caused to depend from his story's own most tensely charged moment of ideological opposition? The moment, that is, when Endicott boldly identifies the man marrying Edith and Edgar as the eccentric Anglican minister Blackstone; and blasts him, once and for all, as a "priest of Baal" (IX, 63). And to the footnote which says, essentially, "What?"

Nothing in the Narrator's own modestly historical value system quite prepares us for this moment. He knows Endicott is coming, of course, even as he knows more Milton than anyone in 1628 could possibly know; and he has thoroughly prepared us to expect that Endicott will be, all allegorically, the very strictest and sternest of an entirely puritanical band of settlers, who will utterly execrate the pointless Jollity of Merry Mount. Furthermore, the mature sobriety of his tone suggests that he expects us also to realize, though more temperately, that in these chilly, northern, latter-days of the real world the whole Merry Mount Way must go down to Reality. But he himself—or perhaps some other, more dutifully antiquarian "editor," overseeing his text—is genuinely surprised when Endicott comes on in quite so blatant and prophetical a manner. Worst of all, he is positively shocked by the historical slander expressed in the hot haste of Endicott's enthusiasm. And so a footnote, one of only a few such in Hawthorne's highly researched but utterly unpedantic canon: "Did Governor Endicott speak less positively, we should suspect a mistake here. The Rev. Mr. Blackstone, though an eccentric, is not known to have been an immoral man. We rather doubt his identity with the priest of Merry Mount" (63).

By now of course we are indeed committed—to the colonialist, the provincial road. For if this really bizarre literary tactic does not arouse our obscure historical suspicions, the reason can only be some a priori commitment to the possibility of cosmopolitan explanation for its own sake: cultural politeness as critical bad faith. Trapped, we may find ourselves fuming at the author: "it's your story, Hawthorne; why tell us one thing in your tightly over-wrought fiction and then deny it in your own fey footnote?"

Why indeed? Unless to suggest that there really is something more we need to know before we can justly construe an allegory that seems to impose itself on us inevitably, as if it were our very own meaning. Unless to emphasize what has already been suggested in the story's otherwise innocent headnote—that the "allegory" here has wrought itself so "spontaneously" as not to be the present writer's own at all, but rather that of those nameless "New England annalists," whose pages often seem "grave" to the point of some quotidian insignificance. Obviously they have suggested this tale; clearly what happens here is "literally" insignificant without some reference to events recorded by them and no one else. Perhaps we are being encouraged to discover just a bit more about the exact nature of their own literary project; or, at very least, about the account they gave of the Merry Mount affair. Perhaps we are required to ask if there is indeed, from their point of view, some sober if outrageous point in having Endicott "misidentify" Blackstone. Perhaps this is the key to their own "allegory," of which "The May-Pole of Merry Mount" is merely a critical imitation—a twice-told tale with a certain purposive historical vengeance.

Forced to ask, we readily discover that something like this is indeed the case; and forced to discover, we readily conclude that some most provincialist criticism is precisely what the tale itself has absolutely required of us. That Puritanism overcame we scarcely need to be told. And that this fact more or less agrees with our prevailing suspicion that human life is everywhere sadder and less satisfactory in historic reality than in originary myth we will hardly regard as a surprising illumination. But what really happened in 1628? Who is Endicott, that all our annalists commend him? And what, dear God, may Blackstone signify?

Of course Blackstone cannot be identified as an "immoral" practitioner of phallic paganism—unless, of course, we are prepared to identify Anglicanism as such as precisely that. And how can we associate him with the historical goings on at Merry Mount, when he is known to have contributed money to support the military expedition organized to shut down those revels, and to arrest and deport their infamous (but here unmentioned) master, Thomas Morton?—unless, of course, we accept the entirely tendentious proposition of Puritan typology, that things equal to the same paganism all belong together in the same history.[18] Certain New England annalists might seem to believe that a pagan maypole at Merry Mount and an Anglican surplice on Beacon Hill mean exactly the same un-American thing, but evidently the worldly reader is supposed to protest; even if this means reducing a world-class allegory to its most utterly provincial components. Even if it means reducing America to mere history.

The full story of Hawthorne's wickedly twice-told tale is a little too long to rehearse in its entirety, but its main outlines may be quickly set forth.[19] Without benefit of William Bradford's original account of the complex meta-political problem of Merry Mount, Hawthorne was nevertheless fully aware that much more—or much less, depending on one's point of view—was at issue than the "pagan" symbolism of the maypole. If he knew from Strutt's *Book of Sports* (to which he alludes in his headnote) that maypoles and maygames had been officially endorsed by King James I as an authentic way for English people to recreate themselves on Sundays, in explicit insult to puritanic sabbatarianism, he also knew, from Bradford's very own "Letter-Book," that the official charge against Merry Mount and Morton involved selling guns and rum to the Indians, and abusing their women. We cannot know whether he believed these charges, on which Morton was never convicted, and about which regular historians are still fussing.[20] But he

---

18. For attempts to explain Endicott's misidentification of Blackstone, see G. Harrison Orians, "Hawthorne and 'The May-Pole of Merry Mount,'" *Modern Language Notes*, 53 (1938), pp. 159–67; Terence Martin, *Nathaniel Hawthorne* (New York: Twayne, 1965), p. 87; and J. Gary Williams, "History in Hawthorne's 'The May-Pole of Merry Mount,'" *Essex Institute Historical Collections*, 108 (1972), pp. 173–89. And for a learned account of what Endicott might mean by calling anybody a "priest of Baal," see Thomas Pribeck, "The Conquest of Canaan," *Nineteenth-Century Fiction*, 40 (1985), pp. 345–54.
19. For a fully documented version of Hawthorne's retelling of the tale of Merry Mount, see *Province*, pp. 251–77, 602–10.
20. See John P. McWilliams, "Fictions of Merry Mount," *American Quarterly*, 29 (1977), pp. 3–30; and cp. Minor W. Major, "William Bradford versus Thomas Morton," *Early American Literature*, 5 (1970), pp. 1–13.

clearly knew that this was not the problem his various annalists had chosen to emphasize. He could not have observed how the matter of paganism tended to warp Bradford's account in the Plymouth Plantation; but he plainly observed how a surprising number of later writers all emphasized the symbolic theology at the expense of the real politics, to the point where the full story could hardly be reconstructed at all. Indeed the very chronology of events became disarranged, by men who called themselves mere "annalists"—until a nineteenth-century antiquarian editor of the Massachusetts Historical Collections was forced to correct it all, in a respectful but puzzled footnote, which Hawthorne's own outrageous footnote wickedly mocks: there seems to be some mistake.

Of course Blackstone was no pagan. Nor was he anywhere near Merry Mount the day Endicott cut down the maypole. For in fact nobody of any significance was there that day. By the time Endicott came on the scene at all—as late in the political reality as he appears in the fictional account—Captain Miles Standish, about whom we hear nothing, had already arrested Morton, about whom we also hear nothing, in an encounter that can only be called mock-heroic, and sent him back to England, on charges of political misconduct as grave as they are dubious. It was all over but the allegory. But as that thing seemed needful, Endicott appears to have provided it: "What? You deported Morton and left his maypole standing, the only one such in New England? We'll fix that." And off he marched, utterly unopposed, except by the symbol of paganism generated in his own mind, to cut down that symbol. Some sober colleague may well have been baffled: "Begging the Governor's pardon, the thing is now only a common pine tree, such as grow erect everywhere in these parts. No dancing and frisking now, good Sir; no streamers, no flowers, no lascivious poetry; only naked nature. A tree is a tree is a tree." The little lower layer, then: "Fool. Things mean what they mean. The symbolism is evident to me. As soon tolerate a surplice-bearing eccentric to tend garden on Beacon Hill. They both must fall."

Such are not the literal words, of course. None such survive. Indeed nothing at all survives except a closely connected series of annalistic accounts which emphasize the symbols while they distort or ignore some other reality, and which universally place Endicott at Merry Mount well before he had ever heard of the place. And yet some such words must be imagined if we are to understand what actually occurred, as that blasted footnote insists we must—namely, that first Bradford and then a whole string of too faithful followers too plainly saw that their "real" story was in fact a sort of allegory: not guns, Standish, and the para-constitutional deportation of a clear and present political danger; but Anglocatholic-Paganism, Endicott, and the castration, at the very outset, of the idea of America as Nature's Nation; or the King's; or the Pope's. Without some such speculation we can scarcely understand "The May-Pole of Merry Mount" as anything but a curiosity, a pale moral allegory which yet calls awkward attention to the utter falsity of its own historical terms; and which inspires, perhaps, two cheers for the sort of imagination which uses historical sources "selectively" and for its "own special purposes" of myth, romance, or allegory.[21]

---

21. See Gayle L. Smith, "Transcending the Myth of the Fall in Hawthorne's 'The May-Pole of Merry Mount,'" *ESQ*, 29 (1983), p. 74; Smith's formula merely repeats the commonplace of

With some such effort, I think, the tale appears as one of Hawthorne's subtlest and most devastatingly crafted: eschewing psychological questions almost entirely, it nevertheless solves certain crucial problems of American intellectual history—and even historiography—at their very outset, even as it forces the honest reader to recover certain obscure and otherwise uncanonical texts in which those problems are first posed. The effect cannot quite be intuited. The text begs for historical interpretation, but then balks the one it seems to provide. It literally forces us back into its own provincial pretexts, or else into critical bad faith. We tend to know about Thomas Morton, who appears (ever so briefly) in our anthologies as William Bradford's classic antagonist. But this tale forces us to read Nathaniel Morton as well, for it is his altogether obscure *New-England's Memoriall* which set the seal on Bradford's allegory. Bungling chronology so as to make Endicott appear original and not hysterically after the fact, and apologizing for including any mention of guns and Indians at all, Nathaniel Morton it was who composed the urtext of "Endicott and the Merry May-Pole," which this most incisive of Hawthorne's twice-told tales exists to deconstruct.[22]

4

Yet where will all this leave Milton? Evidently the story insists that we remember his truths as somehow prior, perhaps as universal, even as we poke about to discover certain provincial errors which seem to antedate his own historical existence. Must we relegate him to the tale's moralistic level, as providing merely some "authoritative" way to know that fallen men who play at phallic myth can well discover a way to behave like animals? Certainly we may hope otherwise. For that, once again, were to redeem the provincial with the banal.[23]

Probably it is merely "humorous" to recognize that Endicott (elsewhere conceived as some parodically separatist Redcrosse Knight) is here presented as a sort of omnipotent mock-Samson—demolishing some pillar of paganism even as he gives the Philistines themselves a puritanic haircut. And possibly not all readers will require a full "explication" of the (apparently) explicit Comus allusion: conservative moralists will be heartened to learn that the narrator's moral disapproval of the Revellers enjoys full Miltonic sanction; yet it would be hard to show, against the grain of William Carlos Williams, that Hawthorne himself utterly disavows "the Dionysian connection" of Merry Mount.[24]

---

many previous critics who cannot quite believe Hawthorne seriously engages his historical sources.

22. For a recent attempt to evade this logic—by stressing the status of "The May-Pole of Merry Mount" as "story"—see Alan O. Weltzien, "The Picture of History in 'The May-Pole of Merry Mount,'" *Arizona Quarterly*, 45 (1989), pp. 29–48.
23. The case for a somewhat more "playful" reading of MM is well made by John N. Miller, "'The May-Pole of Merry Mount': Hawthorne's Festive Irony," *Studies in Short Fiction*, 26 (1989), pp. 111–23.
24. See Sacvan Bercovitch, "Diabolus in Salem," English Language Notes, 6 (1969), pp. 280–85; and Sheldon W. Liebman, "Hawthorne's Comus: A Miltonic Source for 'The May-Pole of Merry Mount,'" *Nineteenth-Century Fiction*, 27 (1972), pp. 345–51.

Somewhat closer to the story's deconstructive point would be the recognition that the narrator's entire, pregnant morphology of "Jollity" and "Gloom" finds its full naturalistic anticipation in "L'Allegro" and "Il Penseroso": tempted (by the narrator's sobriety) to erect an historic ontology on some "poetic" translation of Endicott's own unforgiving dichotomies, the reader may yet be rescued by recalling that somewhere these insatiable opposites signify no more than "the pleasures of the imagination," as these rhyme with nothing more ultimate than the alternating moods of any man.

Absolutely indispensable, however—and every bit as central to the historic theme of "The May-Pole" as the matter of the annalists—is the gentle reminder, in the very last paragraph, of the momentous conclusion of *Paradise Lost*.[25] Endicott himself is, to be sure, only a very parodic archangel, turning this newly fallen (yet strangely loving) couple out of their provincial Eden. But the newly conscious pair—Lord and Lady no more—are designed to be every bit as sympathetic as that truly original couple whose archetypal example alone rescues them from psychological nullity. And yet their own situation is significantly, painfully different: where Milton's Adam and Eve had ("fortunately," we all agree) a whole "world" before them, "where to choose," Edith and Edgar have literally, no choice—only Salem and the enforced definitions of Puritan Sainthood. The worst of their luck, apparently, is to be forever trapped in the triumph of Endicott's new-world allegory, in terms of which everything that is merely natural must perforce be regarded as pagan. Historical process, we take the occasion to observe, is actually quite miscellaneous, relative, and slow: years elapse as Pessonagessit turns to Mount Wollaston, Wollaston to Merry Mount, Merry Mount to the Mount of Dagon, and finally—as the provinces assert their own ridiculous authority—the Boston suburb of Quincy, Mass. But Puritan dialectic knows no such moral evolution. Two sites alone exist: the bestial assemblages of ordinary history and the disciplined congregations of a nation truly in Covenant. So off are dragged our end-time Adam and Eve, to Endicott's proleptic New Jerusalem.

Of course we can easily soften our sense of their unhappy fate. On the one hand, they clearly win their own sort of victory over Endicott, softening that "iron man" till he almost sighs "for the inevitable blight of early hopes" (p. 66). Just so, we could argue, humanity and the comparative sense will eventually humanize and make relative even the most doctrinaire Puritanism: Nature is not an allegory; the slippery Proteus is not so easily caught. And, on the other, it seems only accurate to notice that Hawthorne's couple draws its best strength not so much from the institutions of Endicott's typic "Israel" as from "each other"—which is, after all, the reason they manage to remind us of Adam and Eve in the first place. Perhaps it may yet appear that some covenants really are more fundamental than others. And yet, in the near term, some sense of historic misfortune remains: Adam and Eve could work it out for themselves; nobody knowing better was standing right there, just waiting to place their brand-new consciences under puritanic arrest, to explain all that is implied when "the Lord hath sanctified [a] wilderness for [a] peculiar people" (p. 63). Something or other seems unhappily short-circuited.

---

25. See Smith, "Transcending the Myth," pp. 76–79; and cp. Newman, *Guide*, pp. 191–92.

Or, again, we can even defend the present outcome—if we wish, ourselves, to invoke an orthodoxy rather than a humanism. After all, Milton's Adam and Eve are quintessentially "pre-Christian." Altogether "historical" they may now finally be, so that no romantic myth of pristine simplicity and unrestriction need apply. And bearers of the promise of eventual redemption they now most assuredly are, so that no Melvillean myth of the "upright barbarian" will quite cover their case. Still, lacking the advantages of Abraham, of Moses, of the historic Christ (not to mention the Reformation), what more can in honesty be expected or in justice exacted of them? Of course they will have to make it up as they go along. We may think of them as long-range candidates for the unique advantages of some "Israel" sanctified for a "peculiar people." But all this is not yet. They must wander. They must both choose and endure all the ravages that mere history will hold in store. Wise they were, beyond their mere hours of knowledge, to pray for Salem, even as an end of their natural liberty.

Unless, of course, this plot should come to seem a bit too orthodox. Unless Hawthorne—with Milton behind him—should conclude that, though Christianity might alter and redirect history—not even America could end it.

What Milton's Adam and Eve enter, even as they leave the altogether mythic realm of Eden, is precisely history; at the very beginning of whatever stages or phases it is to have. What follows—Providence superintending, and even perhaps a Redeemer interrupting—is exactly what they shall choose. Inelegant, no doubt, as the argumentative messiness of "Book Three" exists to confess. But there really is no other way. If you want a real world at all, you have to take what you can get. The whole thing may yet be saved. But it cannot be abrogated. Thus history will be in large measure, a plot that shall write itself. In America as elsewhere.

This same history, we somehow sense, is what Edith and Edgar ought to be entering as well. Or indeed what they are entering, beneath the ideological overspecifications of Endicott—and despite the latter-day weariness of the narrator. Softened, but not converted, Endicott insists that they are being spared to join an enclave of Covenant, an Israel which sanctifies policy as easily as it turns the ragged realities of current events into some divinely guaranteed Allegory of the Kingdom of God. If the narrator understands the nature of Endicott's "mistake" here, the editor yet provides no footnote. But the Miltonic paradigm survives to give the lie to Endicott's puritanic metahistory: all history is the same history; the City of God is exactly where Augustine had said it was—elsewhere, always, regardless of the progress of piety from East to West.

Thus the reader is left to discover for himself the outlines of the authentic "Americanist" criticism implied everywhere in the text: the historical discovery of the provincial roots of the fateful notion of some American difference—the project is indeed "genitive." Others might learn to be more explicit about the American shortcut to glory, to criticize it as an abridgment of history and a truly chauvinist species of false transcendence. But Hawthorne seems to have got there first. He saw it in our earliest annalists, to whom his own texts do indeed force us awkwardly back. And he seems to have possessed the truly rare literary grace to found his Americanist criticism on the memory of an author who was, merely, English.

Still, before we take too much cosmopolitan comfort in the revelation that Hawthorne discovered in Milton a significant denial of the separate moral existence of America, we should yet recall that this discovery is itself a prime achievement of American Studies—then, in Hawthorne, or now, again, in Bercovitch. The example of Milton is, here, next to meaningless except in precise, if critical, relation to that of Endicott and Nathaniel Morton. Their story is not his, and it is this difference which constitutes the effective meaning of Hawthorne's most cunning tale. Clearly, that is, "The May-Pole of Merry Mount" presumes and ironically applies but does not simply rewrite the matter of Milton.[26] And without our knowledge of the case in point, the story collapses into repetition and cliché.

Thus teachers of English, whatever the basis of their cosmopolitan prejudice; and theorists, whatever their loyalty to the laws of writing as such; and even Americanists, whatever their growing awareness of nativist provincialism, may find reason to tolerate that old-time historicism which insists on referring American texts to American reality. The point is not at all "separatist"—to privilege America, in the manner of the Puritans' own political typology. Rather it is simply to admit that writers have the duty to consider, even if only to problematize, what they find distinctive in their own national culture. Certainly this task lies close to the source of Hawthorne's enduring achievement, even as some generalized form of his inquiry offers the best rationale for our own efforts at a distinctive American Studies.

A pretty good book once confidently satirized the close interest in local sources as producing an "American Studies Hawthorne"—preferring, for a time at least, the high road of Freudianism. Nothing more cosmopolitan than that: the deep soul of all human beings there before us. Fine. Henry James too thought Hawthorne's interest lay in this direction. But not this only. Very nearly born to write—as Emerson was to preach—Hawthorne read just about everything he could lay his hands on. Spenser, Shakespeare, Milton, Bunyan, French literature of the eighteenth century, British Romanticism, novels from all over, gothic and otherwise: evidently some writers learn to write by reading; and there is little doubt that, unlike Melville stumbling into the travel narrative, Hawthorne from the first meant to write for the canon. But he had another reading list as well, records and documents and literary text form America's colonial period; and at college, unlike classmate Longfellow, he joined the club favoring a distinctive American literature. Witness, almost at once, "Seven Tales of My Native Land." Canonic literature may have taught him how to write. But not what. Required for that was a home-made Americanist education. The amazing result: stories that begin in the provinces and take their place in the world.

---

26. See Smith, "Transcending the Myth," p. 76; and cp. Q. D. Leavis, "Hawthorne as Poet," in A. N. Kaul, ed., *Hawthorne* (Englewood Cliffs, NJ: Prentice-Hall, 1966), pp. 34–35.

Chapter Three

MOMENTS' MONUMENTS: HAWTHORNE AND THE SCENE OF HISTORY

Like the man said, Poetry is more philosophical than History. Not that we still care that much about philosophy: most people would agree with my post-Jesuit brother who defines it as that one thing with or without which everything else remains the same. Or poetry either, for that matter, as the enrollments in our English classes will testify: long lines for the American novel; for any period of American verse, not so much. But still we appear to take the point: literature—though Aristotle hardly had that concept—can scarcely afford to care about the over-determining details of one singular event; give us, if not the generalization, then at least the present application. Especially in a classroom situation: Hawthorne's once-famous "ambivalence" about his Puritans and his Revelers is more likely to generate enthusiasm than a cautious account of how his self-proclaimed "allegory" appeared in fact to assemble itself out of a series of footnotes to William Bradford.

But somewhat more is at issue than the limitations of our ever-more-distracted undergraduates. We too expect literature to offer us more than a contrived version of something that just happened to happen. Once. In a more or less endless list of events that mattered no doubt, but which probably could have been otherwise, and which in any event seem controlled by forces no longer in visible operation. Humanity may or not progress, but things change. History *itself*, we think, must do more than state the facts: find the connection or reveal the law; otherwise, life is just too short, the press of the present too insistent. And if history, then literature a fortiori. Hawthorne himself warns the too-literal reader not to go looking for *The* House of the Seven Gables, and assures us that the writer of romance binds himself less to the facts of the local case than to the "laws of the human heart." So what exactly does this moral essentialist mean by also insisting, as it has come to seem he most certainly does, that we attend to the historical references in so many of his best wrought tales? Where does he get off in loading his tales and sketches, and even his long-form fictions, with historical allusions that beg to be identified and that, often enough, lead us to some necessary historical pretext of the fiction in question? Can Hawthorne presume history without actually doing it? How is the general law supposed to arise from facts not yet for all of us in evidence?

Or put it this way: Who is supposed to get the subtle irony of "Roger Malvin's Burial" when many of the details of the "well remembered" instance of protective retaliation called "Lovell's Fight" have been so long forgot? Nor does the less obscure case of the American Revolution change the case very much: everybody sees that "My Kinsman, Major Molineux" has *something* to do with the events of the 1760s or 70s; but then why is it set in the 1730s when, except for the beginning of the Great Awakening, perhaps, few people now alive can name a single event? And why is the nominal protagonist named Molineux, when no such name appears in the ranks of the arch-Tories, and whose case sounds more like that of the notorious Tommy Hutchinson? All explainable enough, it turns out, but only a fair way into the archive. Where a person can easily get lost—trying, for example, to explain how the four "Legends of the Province House" are supposed to work. To be sure, "Malvin" and "Molineux" are very early works, tempting us to hope that Hawthorne might get over his pedantry; but those "Legends" are written late in the 1830s, by somebody whose first published collection had to suffer silent subvention. By age thirty-five you're supposed to know better. Not to mention the past-mid-life *Scarlet Letter*, whose Puritan pretext only begins with the "footsteps" of Anne Hutchinson. And if the truth were told, the donnee of the *Seven Gables* is further back than any witchcraft episode; and, though Hawthorne's letters appear to protest otherwise, the choice of the name Pynchon, infamous in the history of New England real estate, is far from accidental. Evidently historical fact and general law are not a simple either/or.

So how *is* it supposed to work? Taking Hawthorne's ancestral and culturally definitive Puritans as a test case, what can we say about the figure of history in some of Hawthorne's most enduringly intriguing fictions? Pretty clearly he does not mean to imitate, in any close or continuous way, the social surface of the everyday life of other generations, something even the avowed novelist of manners would dare undertake at serious epistemological risk: when did the self-consciously uxorious Thomas Shepard stop having sex with the pregnant second wife, who told him they "should love exceedingly together because [they] should not live long together"? Or, less intimately, what in fact did the Bradstreets and their expatriated friends talk about in the long reminiscent evenings before the untimely burning of their house? Or more generally, what did the "civil-honest" half-way members of all those awesomely provisioned Congregational Churches really think about their chances for salvation? If only we could know—as Hawthorne knows we cannot. The specific past-as-it-really-was is simply lost. And yet Hawthorne's Puritan characters ask to be seen as much more than The Human Heart dressed up sable garments and tall gray hats. What exactly is his interest in these self-confessed "ancestors"? And what is his approximate mode of literary address? If not the approximate affect of their quotidian life, then what does he seek to imitate? And why? Which is to ask: can we in the end understand Hawthorne's historical fiction as something other than an excuse for our own will to pedantry or a self-erected bar to avid student participation?

2

The first thing to be noticed about Hawthorne as a writer of historical fiction is how long it took him to get around to attempting a novel in that form. The eponymous hero of *Fanshawe* (1828) may have some latter-day Mather in mind, but no one has ever thought of this mock-academic exercise as an attempt to reverse the ever-steady declension or to lift the burden of the "Hathorne" family guilt. And *The Scarlet Letter* (1850)—itself first conceived as a (long) tale among others—comes along way too late to correct any of the historical sins of efforts like Child's *Hobomok* or, somewhat less egregiously, Sedgwick's

Hope Leslie. These and other less famous writers may still be "scribbling" in the 1850s, but they will have long since ceased to blame their theory of women's rights and women's wrongs on John Winthrop. And, starting out in the late 1820s and 30s, Hawthorne has only a few highly stylized magazine tales and sketches to prefigure his most insistent subject. Evidently a studious apprentice—armed with his aunt's library card—already knew enough to know he knew way too little to treat a morally subtle and epistemologically risky subject at length.

Accordingly, therefore—and predictively, perhaps—the historical sketches (of Mrs. Hutchinson, Governor Phips, and Dr. Bullivant) take care to get in and out pretty fast. Context is amply provided, and enough is told of Hutchinson's career as a serious heretic to let us know that Puritanism is not *all* about gender; but no one, certainly not any of Hawthorne's female competitors, could not fail to notice that, beginning with a competitive prefatorial reference to "cisatlantic" female writers, its emphasis comes to rest, "at the center of all eyes," upon a vivid image of "The Woman." That's right: the Godmother of American feminism had dared to speak theology to an audience who found her not-so-nomian emphasis quite cogent; and worse, had thought it proper to suggest that not all the licensed male preachers in New England had quite taken the point of Protestantism. Perhaps it was *almost* all about gender.

Well then, let's just see: what sort of a "man" was the first king-appointed governor of godly Massachusetts? Trailing clouds of filiopietistic glory conferred by a well-intentioned but essentially meretricious biography in Mather's *Magnalia*, "Sir William Phips" is evoked as the long un-churched rowdy from the wilds of Maine turned magically into the first new-charter governor of Winthrop's Holy City—the best a petitioning Increase Mather could secure—who got where he got by finding some Spanish treasure and turning it over to the King of England. His story is prefaced by a long-enough, fairly serious meditation on how we do and do not remember the past; but the new-world career of this quondam adventurer is represented by a day-long set of fictionally invented and chronologically arranged scenes: "a day in the life." For purposes of formal introduction, the Mathers have dressed up their man in the robes of a Godly Magistrate, but they are learning, to their chagrin, that you can't take him anywhere. Or not, at least, to lunch with the rest of New England's dignified dignitaries: he gets quite drunk and betrays the life and manners of a rough-and-ready seaman. A truly embarrassing moment—worse, in its way, than Silas Lapham at the tensely comic dinner party of the Bromfield Coreys.

Learnedly introduced, then understated and euphemistic in its drama, this little sketch can seem rather gratuitous; but with the rags-of-works-to-riches-of grace pretext of the *Magnalia*, its ironic point is sharp and precise: Phips may have ended the witch trials—and gone on to win glory at the battle of Louisburg—but in 1692 he was a redneck still and, by all *other* accounts, a piss-poor Nehemiah. The project of baptismal disguise required of Cotton Mather many pages. Of Hawthorne, the ironic deflation refutation just a few: a life in the day of a fool.

Least gripping of the three early historical efforts is the one of "Dr. Bullivant." Dr. Who? Well, history is like that: you can't remember everything. Understanding this, the sketch spends the bulk of its few pages explaining. You see, it's all pretty complicated.

Bullivant was a witty apothecary who kept shop in Boston in the years following the Restoration when, in the midst of New England's fabled and self-advertised "declension," sobriety was somehow more pronounced than ever. Being an Anglican, however, Bullivant saw no need to repress his satirical propensity; and apparently nothing could prevent this inveterate humorist from dispensing "hard, round dry jokes" (36) with every dose of pills; at which, some of the ailing Puritans laugh, unless they see a minister standing close-by. Too soon, however, the government of New England changes and, under a new charter, and especially within Governor Andross' ill-starred "Dominion of New England" (including, absurdly, New York), Bullivant, now a member of the ruling party, wreaks enough satire on the exacerbated native dullness to earn the "bitter and angry scorn" (39) of—that's right—Cotton Mather. And apparently the common people of New England have also stored up some resentment for, when the government changed again, in the New England version of the "Glorious Revolution," they get and they savor their counter-witty revenge.

Whew!—that took too long. Anyway, imagine now a "scene," exactly one paragraph in length: Bullivant alone, unhappy and in jail; now and then an unreconstructed Congregationalist peeps in at the one high window "to tickle poor Dr. Bullivant with a stinging sarcasm." Ha-ha, Dr. B. Or, as we might now say, neener, neener. The problem of course, is that no such sarcasm can be found in the archive—which Hawthorne has had to read in order to produce one little sketch, which lives, if at all, not for the moment of its (un-)dramatic turn, but as one of the most learnedly compressed accounts of the politics and sociology of the Puritan Declension ever written. Oh, dear; he knows way too much to please the passing fancy. What can follow from this seriocomic masquerade?

Which is to ask: how and when will Hawthorne get his self-deprecated but in fact remarkably professional knowledge of Puritan history in meaningful relation to his developing sense of scenic epitome? No one can possibly know enough to tell the whole story. And as these sketches clearly suggest, and as every practitioner of "historical criticism" will surely appreciate, it will be all too easy to tell an audience more than it wants to know about a subject not at the center of their attention. So we need to ask: will it yet be possible for someone well read in the archive to imply, in a very short space, some fact or view of the Puritan past which it were all but criminal for the descendants of such ancestors not to know? And in which even more remote audiences might well take an interest?

Not all at once, apparently, judging by the only tale we certainly know to have survived from Hawthorne's first, failed attempt to publish a collection of plausibly interconnected tales. Older than the *Salem Advertiser* sketches, the contents of the "Seven Tales of My Native Land" appear to date, in part at least, from Hawthorne's college days; and, surviving a manuscript burning some time after the collection failed to find a publisher in 1827, the tale in question evokes the lore of witchcraft, but it lacks anything like the historical placements that contextualize and/or burden the newspaper sketches. Nor is its witchcraft something we can readily identify with the infamous Salem episode of 1692. The setting is in fact quite vague: "those strange old times when fantastic dreams and madmen's fantasies were realized among the ordinary circumstances of life"; and the witch in question, quite possibly a fraud, appears to be a moderately competent fortune teller more than a mistress of spectral images. The young woman applying to her for privileged information wishes not for power to torment her small-town enemies—or even, Goodman Brown-like, to find out how the reprobates are faring—but only to learn the fate of those she has sinfully deserted. The witch-woman is a bad one indeed, relishing the tragic details she deliciously transmits or cruelly invents; and no doubt the remorseful young woman is guilty of trafficking with the Devil; but measured against the cynicism of her mediumistic accomplice, her guilt appears as not quite unpardonable. She may die not of guilt but of shame, when she learns that, one way or another, the witch-woman is in on her painful secrets but, sinful in the sentimental extreme, she still cares. Her guilt, that is to say, is serious but still on the human scale; not diabolical.

Over all, the "Hollow" is quite a good enough story for a college boy to have written, but it is not quite an act of history. Nor is "The Wives of the Dead," which could conceivably have been part of the *Seven Tales*: "witchcraft and the sea," as Hawthorne's sister reported on its contents and, set in a seaport, and involving at least one sailor, the "Wives" might qualify. An astonishingly subtle story for what it reveals about the (Emersonian) theme of privacy—two virtual sisters with the same (oxymoronic) "mutual and peculiar sorrows" and both entirely unable effectively to mourn nor yet rejoice with the other. But it offers itself as nothing like a contribution to our understanding of Puritan interiority as a fundamental chapter in the history of early modernism's discovery of the "subject."

Closer to the mark, very close indeed, is the curious case of "Alice Doane," as we are forced to imagine the ur-form of a tale that got reworked—and re-narrated by a very self-conscious "Story-Teller"—into something called "Alice Doane's Appeal," which appeared only in 1835, in the wake of the failure of Hawthorne's third and most ambitious ill-fated collection. There, surviving if not quite informing a self-embarrassed Narrator's self-confessed earlier indulgence in gratuitous reveling in the uber-gothic, the issue is "specter evidence" in precisely the form discovered by asking "What Happened in Salem?" The final scene, of diabolic celebration in a Puritanic burying ground, is said to involve revered saints and infamous felons alike: everyone, that is to say, very much in the manner of the witch-meeting in "Young Goodman Brown"; except that here the souls of the justly damned sinners are cavorting with "false specters of good men." Ah yes, we are forced to remember—or discover from a lucid David Levin (but not from a puzzled Hyatt Waggoner)—Satan could indeed weirdly impersonate persons who had *not* signed the book and gone over to the dark side. Which God might just decide to permit, to test (that's right) our Faith. And now we see the point of the otherwise tangled, tortuous and somewhat improbable narrative: twin brothers, with one sister, have for her the same sexual desire; a clever Wizard causes one twin to believe, erroneously, that the other has enacted that desire; then the one, having "trod out the accursed life" of his opposite number, learns too late the truth of the Wizard's diabolical deception. The crime, strictly enough, was to murder his "personified incest wish"; but his mistake was to take the Devil's word for it. The evidence, that is to say, was deeply suspicious. As well it was at Salem; as it was as well in the luminous beginning of Spenser's *Faerie Queene*: with Archimago's spectral assistance, Redcrosse dreams of sex with Una; oh dear, no; then he dreams he sees her act it out with his Squire. So he leaves in a huff—and only after many, many alexandrine-impeded cantos will he unite with his Una. Whose full name,

Hawthorne—naming that tune in no notes—will reveal to be Una Vera Fides. Even as he makes the point of it all quite explicit: with or without a personal devil, specter evidence is guilty projection.

Depth psychology is involved, no doubt, but history as well. And whether we like the marginal "Alice Doane's Appeal" or not, it turns on the same issue of funky evidence as the redundantly canonical "Young Goodman Brown"—of which it seems to be a sort of deconstructive explication. For the present purpose, however, the point is not to defend the practical wisdom of requiring quaint knowledge of a lapsed epistemology, but to look closely at the nature of the literary provocation to do so. Again, it seems, the method is largely static, not continuous or developmental. The storytelling narrator himself makes this emphatic: whatever was his story long ago, its retelling is almost entirely a matter of scenes—the climactic one in the graveyard, quite obviously, but also the "central scene," the "interview" between Leonard and the evil Wizard. More important almost, the re-telling is also self-consciously scenic: at the beginning, consciously composed, the teller and the unsuspecting girls, right there on Gallows Hill, which Salemites almost never visit, preferring to express their sense of the past in Guy Fawkes Day bonfires, once potent to keep away the Pope, now signifying nothing beyond the lurid display; and then, a careful setting of the "scene" of Salem in 1692. And again at the end: after confessing that he "dare not give the remainder of the [graveyard] scene, except in a very brief epitome."

Somewhere, it might have taken quite a long time to account for and trace out the relationship which, after the death of the parents in an Indian massacre, and in the gratuitous abstraction of his twin, grew up between Leonard and his unsuspecting sister; and even more, perhaps, to explain that, though sex is always sex, the epistemic world of this rampantly gothic fiction was not far from the time and place of the mad fantasies that tormented Salem. Happily, the decision has been to let a few moments speak for themselves: wishing sin, I find them guilty; so die, "mon semblable, mon frère"; oh God, I was deceived; they're not guilty; and all the devils run riot. Devils, that is, and their magic semblance. Of course this had been a lot to ask. And no wonder if, allowed to see print as first conceived, the tale would *not* in fact have got the writer cried out against as a witch: earlier, maybe; now, not so much. Evidently the re-telling was made to help us out: here, between present scenes lamenting the difficulty of bringing back the past, especially the guilty past, we encounter scenes suggested by the record of that very past. If you understand, then shudder for what our kind seems capable of. If not, better look a little deeper. Into the soul, of course, as "not to know [the Devil] argues thyself unknown"; but into the archive as well. And then, why not build a sort of Vietnam Wall at Salem? For, as Cotton Mather comes around to admitting, we lost that war too.

So much for a scenic re-telling which suggests that the project of adequate history in short fiction is not going to be easy. "Alice Doane's Appeal" exists partly to repent a failure to do it well enough—even as its frame challenges an audience not only to lend its imagination—which, years later, an audience of Main Street Salemites is still stubbornly withholding—but also to do their own contextualizing part. These stories happened not just in your haunted imagination, dear reader, but in some supposable time and place. Turn your mind to that and watch the scenes with awakened historical interest.

3

Separately published (in 1832) when a second collection of tales failed of corporate publication, "My Kinsman, Major Molineux," "Roger Malvin's Burial," and "The Gentle Boy" may well announce Hawthorne's full emergence into literary majority: it has made some sense to call the three-novels-in three-years period 1850–52 "Hawthorne's Major Phase," but he never did any better than in the early 1830s, and "Malvin" and "Molineux" at least are simply perfect, unmatched by anything in the English language. All set in the period between the 1660s and the 1730s, the method of these three "Provincial Tales" appears at first pretty much the same: all have rather copious historical head-notes, all name names (of places and events, if not always of persons), and all require of the serious reader a willingness to take from there—and from the body of a meticulously appointed text—some fairly subtle indications of the historical issues being pursued. But one of them is not quite like the others: far less ironic in its head-note, and quite a bit longer in its fictional disposition, "The Gentle Boy" is also less simply scenic in its balanced and largely unpleasant account of Puritans and Quakers. Surely the matter of the American Revolution and of the American "Indians" were complex and important, to require fiction-at-length, yet neither of them tempted Hawthorne into the experiment of narrative elongation. Yet somehow, early on, the painful and potent "Matter of the Puritans" seems to have done just that.

Unfortunately, however, the experiment was not entirely successful. More affective than learned, more nearly sentimental than ironic, "The Gentle Boy" is touching enough to have won the heart of Sophia Peabody—who drew a "portrait" of the nominal protagonist—but, one third longer than its provincial partners, it but goes on a little too long. The scenes themselves are vivid enough: the elderly not-quite-Puritan Tobias Pearson finding and rationalizing his pity for the orphan son of an executed heretic; the frenzied disturbance of a Puritan Congregation by Quaker Catherine, biological mother of the Gentle Boy, distracted by the Spirit; the tense covenant between her and Dorothy Pearson, "mother-woman" if there ever was one; the exchange between Tobias, drifting toward the morale of the Spiritists, and the (newly introduced) Elderly Quaker, whose chilling tale of leaving in triumph the bedside of his dying daughter represents something like the high-water mark of the rich neo-Puritan literature of "weaned affections," competing with the love-Jesus-more dialogue between mother and child in Susan Warner's *Wide, Wide World*, and capable of touching off a cult of sentiment all by itself; and finally, the sober admission by Quaker Catherine that a jealous God may have set the bar a little high for a woman to bear. Quite a lot of good scenes, actually—almost enough for a short novel; but requiring too much inter-textual explanation and assurance; and lingering long enough to leave a number of contextual questions unanswered.

For example: what precise sort of "refuge" was Tobias seeking in New England? Was he simply sick of the wars under Cromwell? Did he care *at all* that Puritans in New England—with Nehemiah on the Wall—were still building the Temple, in a Wilderness which God (and the Protestant ethic) had turned into a Garden? Which might yet come to figure as A City on a Hill. And what exactly explains his fiercely ambivalent drift towards the society of those doctrinally-repugnant Quakers? With what imaginable emotions had his wife agreed to follow his less-than enthusiastic Errand? In what supposable mood had she borne the deaths of "all the children" they transported from a veritable Homeland to a putative State of Grace? What insight or opening had turned Catherine from a Mother into a Seeker, in prosecution of a career of prophecy—less womanly, it appears, than authorship even? How do we explain Ilbrahim's unconscious "skill in physiognomy"? And—assuming that they do indeed "have to be carefully taught"—who taught the Puritan children the subtle tactics of gratuitous cruelty? All these and more, raised less by the emotional depth of the story than by its uncustomary length. And also, perhaps, its pace. Elsewhere, there is just enough time to raise the primary questions: look, quick; see what you can make of this act of ambivalent filial desertion, this ugly parade of controlled violence. Explanations may well reside in the implicated sources; but don't look for them in any vacant textual spaces. Here, however, they seem entailed, inescapably implied.

The tale is of course perfectly aware of its disregard for "the unities" and also, perhaps, of an epistemology too expansively narrative. The "scene" Catherine makes in church must wait for the "second Sabbath after Ilbrahim became a member" of the Pearson family; and the Narrator has time enough to tell us that their de facto adopted son is wearing "the new morning suit which Dorothy had wrought for him" (116). No one needs to know what the Isaac-like Cyrus Bourne was wearing the day his Abrahamic father gunned him down; and the patches on the clothes of Robin Molineux are more symbolic than verisimilar; nor has anyone thought their stories had wanted to grow up to be a novel. Here, the possibility awkwardly exists. We need to pass over a fairly lengthy "mean time" in which a Restoration in England would bring forth, though not immediately, an end to New England's open season on Quakers. Indeed the tale rather frankly announces—almost to the point of parody—its besetting problem with the narrative representation of historical change:

> And now the tale must stride forward over many months, leaving Pearson to encounter ignominy and misfortune; his wife to a firm endurance of thousand sorrows; poor Ilbrahim to pine and droop like a cankered rose-bud; his mother to wander on a mistaken errand, neglectful of the holiest trust which can be committed to a woman.

"Must"? Of course: it's just a tale, you know. Melville, in the throes of his own ambiguities, will take out his anger at the epistemology of fiction on his unsuspecting reader. Here there is only a semi-embarrassed apology—not for the possibility that criticism might one day make the author pay for his one-issue theory of gender, but for the equally evident fact that his imagination's reach has well exceeded the grasp of any fiction he yet knows how to write. To be sure, similar problems occur in *The Scarlet Letter*, which essays to cover seven historical years in a work just a bit longer than a "blest nouvelle" of Henry James, but there a method has been skillfully devised: denouement long since, principal scenes suggested by an earlier manuscript, the drama takes place in the imagination of a meditating narrator, who more than adequately declares that omniscient he cannot be—were such a thing ever anything but absurd when applied to history.

And so we find ourselves on the verge of a first, tentative conclusion: the hardest thing about history is "to make it move," and Hawthorne is no better at that than anybody else. His early historical fictions are not all one-day affairs in the paradigmatic manner of "Phips," or uni-scenic in the near-parodic case of "Bullivant"; but most of them work hard (if silently) to throw the bright light of thematic emphasis on visible moments of high drama, implying much that has gone before, and demanding a certain contextualizing work on the part of any serious reader. Pre-history, that is to say, there most assuredly is: "Phips" and "Bullivant" are preliminary advertisement of this; the architectonically dizzying "May-pole" its epitomizing instance. Gaps there unquestionably are, but not much pressure on us to fill them in.

"Young Goodman Brown" fiercely observes the rule of one day or less; "The Minister's Black Veil" does not; yet the tale of Hooper's less selfish version of that infamous Puritan "gloom" seems more implicational than developmental. Brown earns his Gloom in a single dream (or in none), and gloomy he goes on to death, and so in a sense does Hooper. The true sight of sin came on him all at once: I see something you don't see, and the color of it is black; but the congregation, the fiancée, and the neighboring minister all get their chance to guess. Time matters in the sense of defining when this all occurs; but the time it takes is all the same. In Brown's tale, life stops. In Hooper's, what stops is history: implication, not change; amplification, not development. The problem with the tale of Tobias and Dorothy and Ilbrahim and Catherine and the old Quaker enthusiast is that it has forced itself to go on, into matters too deep for scenic epitome.

Leaving, in the end, as many historical questions as it answers. Could the tragedy have been otherwise if "the person then at the head of the [Massachusetts] government" had not been the unnamed John Endicott, a man of "narrow mind and imperfect education, [...] [whose] uncompromising bigotry was made hot and mischievous by violent and hasty passions" (109)? Were the Quakers, who knew what to expect, in any sense asking for persecution and even death? And, more subtly, why has the deeply puritanic problem of "weaned affections" been given over, dramatically at least, to the Quakers? Hawthorne's Puritans hate their heretics, right enough, but they appear to love their own kind—even though much of their ample literature suggests that to love too well anything of one's "own" was to tempt their jealous God. Parson Hooper will appear to understand this: I need you, Elizabeth, but only God [...] something or other. So too will the Reverend Arthur Dimmesdale, who has to die to prove that he indeed loves God more. Issues for another time, perhaps. Here the lesson is simple: Hawthorne's "scenes" register pregnant historical moments, far easier to create and to justify than are credibly emplotted historical narratives. And even storytellers have to know their limitations.

4

Sufficient to the limited scope of this effort will be the observation, implied here all along, that eventually Hawthorne learns to make his method work. Brilliantly. No one ever bothers to ask what *else* Faith was wearing; or even, less parodically, where and when Goodman Brown made his secret date with the Devil. We know at once pretty well where we are: deep forest—unmarked as in a certain "Wood of Error," but familiar enough as one of those which, more literally than the famous Wall, surrounds every little Garden of a saintly community. Goody Cloyse sounds not so familiar, but once we hear the names of Goody Cory and Deacon Gookin (not to mention Martha Carrier) we know exactly: Salem Village, on or about 1692. Will it happen here again? And, apart from those names, will we require the further assistance of Cotton Mather's wonderful account? Maybe so. For unless we recognize the strong likelihood of spectral misrepresentation—lost souls, perhaps, but those appearing side-by-side with "fiends counterfeiting the likeness of [...] saints"—we may spend years wondering, with Melville, whether a too-knowing Hawthorne is not himself just a little of the Devil's party; or with James, what sort of allegorical game Hawthorne's fey imagination is playing this time.

But no: it's about history, stupid. Hysterical teenagers there may well have been; local quarrels without doubt; maybe even some rotten rye bread. Best worth remembering, however—and blame Cotton Mather if you must—is that the court cases often turned on testimony about "specters": "I saw him poison her cow." "Impossible: he was with us at the time." "Then it must have been his specter." Time out to consider—not (as in Robert Calef) specter, my foot; but far more subtly, can the Devil impersonate saints without their covenantal consent? No way; too weird; whom could you trust? All human intercourse would become tainted with ugly suspicion; surely God would never permit any such thing. No, wait: it says here the Devil has appeared as an angel of light. Well then, just maybe God would permit it—to test (that's right) our Faith. So there we are: the Court of Oyer and Terminer went right on taking spectral testimony, but we cannot. The question is not, how bad does Hawthorne think we are, but why is Brown so ready to take the Devil's word. Maybe, to paraphrase Sinatra, he's accusin' them of what he's doin' himself. Not the whole story of "What Happened in Salem," but a good part of it surely.

In the end we need the history to read the story. And knowing the history we learn something about the possible continuity between "their" superstitious psychology and "our" more enlightened beliefs. Bu as we know the morality of others only as we project ourselves, guilty suspicion lives. Diabolical evil may or may not exist, but until we know for sure, best idea is to keep a good thought.

What is this, a sermon? Well, OK, the more literary point. An enormous amount of Puritan intellectual distress has been packed into a fairly short story, but much of it we have had to discover and apply. All we are given is a brief scene of parting (of a man from his Faith), a short walk in the woods with an oddly familiar alien (no doubt compressing years of wondering if there are indeed sides and, if so, who all is on which), a mad moment of a doubter losing his Hope (which Calvin warned against), and then a truly spectacular display of memorable moral falsehood. Hawthorne had to know it all—and Spenser into the bargain. We have to recover at least some—without of course forgetting our Freud.

Who tells us rather less about Parson Hooper than about Goodman Brown—unless we decide that Hooper is just plain afraid of sex and Hawthorne is guilty of wasting his historical details. From the first we know two things. As the assembling worshipers are treating their Sabbath as a sort of innocent holiday (much like the parish Jonathan Edwards says he inherited from Solomon Stoddard) and, as they can think of their minister as a "Parson," Hooper's change of face evidently occurs rather late in the unfolding history of Puritan Piety. Then too, as the rediscovery of the immemorial Gloom has much to do with the protagonist himself, no doubt the question of sin is a little more subtle than the theological paranoia of Goodman Brown had made it seem. One day, all of a sudden, in the wake of some surprising conversion, a personable parish priest has made himself into a moral terror. Some people rationalize the uneasiness: "something must surely be amiss with Mr. Hooper's intellects" (374). Others, in the thoughtful wake of one morning's revelation, seem almost to get the point: I'm not OK, and neither perhaps are you.

So what next? A series of scenes which, for the Narrator at least, seem but to deepen the mystery. No more happy chats after church; no more cheer at weddings; no really *clear* word of explanation to the fiancée who, feeling entitled, broaches the topic lightly, comes then feels the darkness and yet turns away from a marriage; and only an oblique revelation in a final exchange with a neighboring minister who, recognizing a *symbol* when he sees one, is worried that people will infer that Hooper is a great sinner in *fact*. Only late in the tale does the Teller admit that the darkness of Hooper's new light has made many converts, admitting that, like it or not, their salvation had some unpleasant stages. And also, as if incidentally, that Hooper once preached an election sermon which all but turned the tide of Puritan history back to its gloomy beginnings. When was that? Well, some time during the rule of Governor Belcher. Oh, dear, are we supposed to read those old-time sermons? And discover, among the dozen or so that qualify, several that bewail the falling away and cry aloud for an awakening. Like the one about to be faithfully narrated by Jonathan Edwards? Or, worse for the project of fiction, its truly great and general follow-up? Long Treatises on that, fact and rumor, for and against. What's a mere Story-Teller to do—even if, at his distance and with his largely sentimental bias, he could get his facts all straight?

What indeed? Well, try this: somewhat histrionically announced, a local outbreak of piety divides a congregation in two: stunned into moral consciousness, one side turns back to the "gloom and piety" of the well-advertised past; the other marches right on into that self-assured morale of reason which recognizes profound piety as mental disturbance. How do we sympathize? Are we in fact meant to decide? Or is it enough to recognize that, when Hooper "forgets" to have Sunday dinner with a certain Squire who bears the famous pen name of Benjamin Franklin (i.e., Saunders), the New England Mind has come apart? Call the outcome too close to call. Then enlist Hawthorne in The Party of Irony. And notice how much complex, well-nigh un-summarizable history is epitomized into a single tale. Daring us, it seems, to not re-tell the local debate between Edwards and Chauncey nor yet re-invent the national myth of Edwards versus Franklin, but only to recognize that there came a time, almost a moment, in the eighteenth century when, like the town and the gown, perhaps, the Awakening and the Enlightenment stopped talking to each other.

In the long aftermath, we might like to know exactly what Elizabeth was thinking when this nice little Yankee girl next door began to weep before the veiled face of her lover. Or what measure of Byronism may infect Hooper's puzzling smile. Undoubtedly the Story-Teller, who clearly laments the sad life of a self-veiling minister—would tell us if he could. But evidently some facts are altogether too private to make it into history of any sort. On them, debate is permissible and thought is free. Enforced, however, is the need to refer these ambiguities as much to the events of the 1730s as to the vicissitudes of the Human Heart. No less than in simpler cases: like Hooper behind his veil, a certain archetypal Puritan named Digby will not come out of his cave. He too may be afraid of sex, but as the subject's own story matters, even in therapy, his issue appears to be the hysterical fear of praying with the possibly unregenerate. But that was earlier. And much simpler: Winthrop's reductive view of Williams; or, Separatism in a single scene. Hooper exists to suggest that sin separates de facto. And to prove the case at a single stroke. His life may go sadly on, but his history is momentary.

5

Overlapping at times with Hawthorne's evocation of the Puritans is his lively interest in The Matter of the Revolution, a fascinating subject all by itself. Worth mentioning here is the scenic economy with which Hawthorne handles some very early moments made to pre-enact or "typify" that complex, multiform event in itself. One, involving a certain people's "Champion" — elsewhere an absconded "King in the Mountain"— takes its leisurely narrative time to remind the distracted or instruct the uninformed what plentiful sources of historical sources say the latter-day Puritans had to suffer at the hands of the intrusive and largely incompetent agents of vicarious British rule. Elaborate preface, much in the manner of "Dr. Bullivant," but with ironies that suggest a strain of provincial paranoia. And then a scene: expecting the worst, but restrained by a sober pastoral voice, a New England multitude watches a Parade of British Horribles inexorably advancing—until an unrecognizable yet strangely familiar old man steps forward to tell the marchers "Stand." They do, and the provincial version of the Glorious Revolution against the Creeping Catholicism of James II is duly registered, and—antique regicide or political specter—the people's timely "Champion" is mythically established, and the wonderful story of "How the Puritans Won the American Revolution" is already pre-written in a single, well-researched but dauntingly economical stroke of fiction.

As it will be again, with just a little more complexity, in "Endicott and the Red Cross." It takes some time to figure out why Hawthorne does not follow Winthrop in identifying Roger Williams as the man who inspired Endicott to deface the flag of England; a little more, perhaps, to decide what level of irony taints the concluding salute to Endicott for provoking the question—still being discussed in the two opposing literary clubs at Hawthorne's Bowdoin—"What have we to do with England?"—and for suggesting that it will be far easier to cut a knot than to untie it; but, typology coming to the rescue once again, a couple of scenes are able to make both memorable and predictive a story that unfolds over many pages in the Journal of a cautious governor who left England with a very conciliatory speech and was constantly aware that Archbishop Laud, the Lion who "sought to devour" Thomas Shepard and so many faithful ministers of the gospel in England, might just send over an expeditionary force to capture and return with New England's precious charter. True, a simple patriot can read the tale with simple patriotism; but ripples of irony dare the more circumspect reader to look a little more closely into what is in and what has been left out of this tightly compressed, indeed explosive little tale.

Endicott appears again, more dynamically even, in the single most deeply learned and artfully crafted of Hawthorne's Puritan tales. The easy reading places it in the context of ill-fated *Story-Teller* where a self-ironic protagonist runs away from the sobriety of Puritan nurture in order to pursue a career in the entertainment business—a premise repeated again in "The Seven Vagabonds." Lots of luck: with Parson Thumpcushion behind and Endicott ahead, exit the possibility of all "fantastic foolery" in New England. But a less meta-political reading is required as well—presuming some degree of special knowledge but unavoidable after all. The William Bradford who ordered the arrest and deportation of the man who translated a Mount Wollaston into a veritable Merry Mount may not have known, but the John Endicott who cut down the maypole well after the fact of Morton's deportation certainly did: a certain royal edict—satirically known as "James' Book of Sports" had officially licensed maypole celebrations everywhere in his kingdom. To cut one down, therefore, whether or not anyone was still "dancing and frisking" about it, amounted to a denial that New England was indeed a part of that kingdom. As much a revolutionary as a "puritanic" gesture, the destruction of an Anglo-Pagan symbol amounts to an act of cultural differentiation and is every bit as "typic" as excision of the Anglo-Catholic Red Cross.

And, at the level of literary construction, the reader curious enough to ask about the utterly implausible presence of the Reverend Blackstone at the longest-day marriage of the totally fictional Edith and Edgar, will learn that as Hawthorne's big scene is totally invented, so Blackstone has been dragged in to replace Thomas Morton not just because Anglican nuptials require a priest more than a master of the revels, but more importantly to give Endicott the opportunity to "lay no reverent hand" upon his "surplice," a sign of English identity as technical as the Red Cross itself. Which is to say—whether we like the word or not—some of Hawthorne's best made and most learned scenes beg for an identification that amounts to a deconstruction.

Massively condensed and complex as well are the four tales of the American Revolution which make up the multiply narrated "Legends of the Province House" (1838). Very late in that long First Period of his tale-writing career, they reveal Hawthorne as a master of scenic manipulation in the service of historical epitome. Let's see: how *could* one make so long a story short? and how suggest that, along with (and perhaps deeper down than) the clichés of the Declaration, the ideology of Puritanism, surviving still or susceptible always of reawakening had a good bit to do with the American will to independence? Well, one way would be to tell the story backwards: begin with a scene in the midst of the war itself; retreat to the moment when mounting unrest public resistance (some of it staged) had seemed to require the presence of British troops; then retreating once again, as if from a proximate occasion to an ultimate cause, retreat one more time, to a moment when the cultural difference which had along divided two divergent peoples, began to show itself publicly— in the symbolic act of a single proleptic person, but in the actions of a mob that might yet become first a resistant army, then a separate people. Then, perhaps, the Puritans having won the Revolution, a view to the future: what indeed have we to do with England? Make it so. But realize the implication: history is always in a sense told backwards; and moments of high drama are more friendly to fiction than the long unfolding of historic differentiation.

For openers, a moment of past figuring as a sort of historical present. On the eve of General Washington's liberation of British-held Boston, "Howe's Masquerade" offers us, in one elongated scene, two conflicting representations of cultural identity: as if to divert their attention from the probability of their ouster from the symbolic and (so far) appropriately named Province House, the British occupiers amuse themselves with a performance in which a miscellany of maskers performing persons from all over British history and drama, admitting to their fanciful number even the figure of "Don Quixote with a bean-pole for a lance," and reaching across the Atlantic to include Washington and his generals dressed in tattered regimentals and looking like "scare crows." High comedy this: ha-ha-ha. But one guest at these promiscuous revels is not amused: Endicott-like, almost, this old man of "known Whig principles" scorns all this "mirth and buffoonery" and yet is said to be the best sustained character in the masquerade," representing as he does "the antique spirit of his native land" (630). And it is in his name—possibly under his direction—that a consciously devised anti-masque is appropriately presented. Not, this time, an imaginative miscellany but an historical "march": first the Governors of Massachusetts, from the Old-Charter rulers in their democratic dignity, then the "miserable men" who had the odd fortune to be appointed as "royal governors" (633), and finally the figure (or the specter) of Sir William Howe himself, first baffled, then increasingly angry at this performance of a Puritan March of History, ending with the prediction of his own defeat and inevitable departure, in "rage and sorrow." Elsewhere, "Don't tread on me." Here, without any visible snake, "Don't mess with Massachusetts."

Fair enough: invading forces will come in trailing clouds of an alien historical imagination; nor will they all at once appreciate the significance of the simpler, more provincial story their long-separated descendants have been learning to write. But—in the next set of scenes—what about quondam governor Thomas Hutchinson, native son and accomplished historian of this still-Puritan land? Surely he recognized the point of New England's monolithic narrative. Unless the enlightenment of this dyed-in-the-wool Loyalist chose to regard the fiction of Holy History as nothing but Superstition. Don't call for the troops, the American partisans duly warn him. Look at the blackened portrait above your desk, identified by your own researches as that of Edmund Randolph, who founded the Customs Service in Massachusetts and whose reports back home on mercantile and other matters resulted in the "repeal of [the] first charter," which earned him "the curse of the people" and, under providence, a blighted life and a horrible death. Silly tale, that second part, worthy of Cotton Mather. Yet perhaps the first part is penalty enough: what if, in their special version of history, you too will be blackened as an "arch-enemy of New England" (644)? Warning unheeded, Hutchinson signs the order to quarter troops in Boston—without which, no over-titled Massacre could possibly occur. All right, then, let the paranoid blackening begin: opposing God's people is opposing God. He should have known.

Perhaps he did, recognizing as he does that even outmoded beliefs have power to define identity and to motivate violence. Quieting a military man's not very veiled threat about the devil and his claws, a certain Selectman puts the Puritan-American case to a perfection rivaling the interpretative acumen of Perry Miller: "We will strive against the oppressor with prayer and fasting, as our forefathers would have done. Like them, moreover, we will submit to whatever lot a wise Providence may send us—always, after our own best exertions to amend it." Which is to say, we will fire at redcoats, but only after a ritual renewal of our Covenant Identity. "And there," the attentive historian Hutchinson observes—parting company with the "obtuse secularism" which treats the Jeremiads of the Revolution as mere "propaganda"—just "there peep forth the devil's claws" (648).

And now what? The ritual violence that seemed to make the troops necessary? Easy enough to rewrite from *Grandfather's Chair* "The Hutchinson Mob," explaining Hutchinson's exasperated "Would you have me wait till the mob sack the Province house, as they did my private mansion?" Or make something out of the Stamp Act crisis. Or look for the moment when Massachusetts Election Sermons began to suggest that proper citizenship did not entail "unlimited submission." None of these. Instead, strangely enough, the smallpox epidemic of 1721—and that without explicit mention of the famous inoculation controversy. Evidently Hawthorne well knew—as most of us do not—that in the year of Jeremiah Dummer's *Defense of the New England Charters*, and in the midst of an hysterical debate about whether this plague was proper punishment for the rash importation of foreign values, "New England was on the verge of revolution and everyone knew it." And a wild, scapegoating procession faithfully predicts many more to follow.

And so enough—except to return to the present. Or, to one historical moment after the one where we began. Up to the Province House marches a victorious John Hancock, spouting jejune formulas about a glorious future well sanitized of the colonial past. Old Esther Dudley has no idea what is going on, but in the scene of her unwitting transfer of the key to the restored American occupants, she raises the question of continuities deeper than political revolutions can touch. What indeed *do* we have to do with England? Which Hawthorne will still be asking in *Our Old Home* and the fascinating "American Claimant" manuscripts.

6

By one fairly plausible account, these static but strategically set "Legends" mark the end of Hawthorne's attempt to say the sense of "Puritan" within the scenic space of a short story, as the tales he wrote in the 1840s, at The Old Manse, come from a form of life completely different from the one that could be lived, more or less privately, in the Manning house in Salem. Concord meant that the lively example of Emerson and Thoreau might easily replace the memorial influence of Winthrop and Mather; nor is it wrong to think of the contents of the *Mosses from an Old Manse* as more "Transcendental" than Puritan in their inspiration. But evidently the past was not entirely dead: reprinted in an anthology called *The Scarlet Letter and Other Tales of the Puritans*. "The Birthmark" imagines an aspiring but incompetent scientist whose misguided cure for a faulty inheritance looks a lot like a parody of the Puritan attempt to replace nature with grace. More troubling still, with the oxymoronic reference to its scene as "the Eden of the present world," overseen by a brooding genius who might be God rather than Adam,

"Rappaccini's Daughter" looks alarmingly like an inquiry into the question of whether the "seminal" transmission of an original fall does not make God indeed the author if sin. Good God: what if the Shakers are right? And then there is, on the eve of *The Scarlet Letter*, the sad case of "Ethan Brand": "abortive romance" or not, someone's unrelenting search for the unpardonable sin can hardly be separated from the central, indeed the obsessive subject of Puritan casuistry. Hooker and Mather to the contrary, and even in some puritanic outskirt in Western Massachusetts, sooner or later some amateur Romantic Anti-hero will find the (Promethean) nerve to dare God himself to Pluck this self-declared Brand from the well-publicized Burning. A latter-day scene, to be sure, but not un-recognizable. Steady continuity seemed to elude Hawthorne, but evidently the scenes kept coming. In *The Scarlet Letter* they came in a flurry.

Of that revolutionary literary performance almost nothing has been more clear than the way its rather discontinuous narrative is structured by a series of vivid moments. Three "scaffold scenes" mark the exact beginning, middle and end—and have suggested, to Henry James, at least, that the book wants to be about Dimmesdale: first, he's on the balcony with the magistrates, not down on the scaffold where he belongs; then, years later, his guilty self-punishment pushes him up there, seeking relief, but it's the middle of the night and no one can see; then finally, in what can only be described as an astonishing *coup de théâtre*, he ascends the platform of punishment in broad daylight and tries to make visible the guilt he has tried again and again, ineffectively, hypocritically, to speak. To be sure, the historical moralist will be quick to point out that, marked by the highly questionable references to himself in the third person, his confession would probably not have passed the ordinary test for admission to a particular Puritan church; but the graphic point is also important: from one very strict point of view, the novel has been about getting Dimmesdale up on the scaffold, with Hester, where he belongs. Five "acts" have been pedantically identified, but no experience of Shakespeare is necessary to notice the three Big Scenes.

And others, just less strategically wrought: the early interview between Hester and Chillingworth, in which both admit some sort of guilt, and she, for pretty much the same reason she decides not to move away, agrees to keep Chillingworth's identity a secret too; the three-years-on interview with "Governor" Bellingham (just a little less hard to place than Blackstone), in which Hester appears to threaten Dimmesdale with exposure unless he defends her right to keep her Pearl of Great Price; the discussion about the psychology of confession carried on between Chillingworth and Dimmesdale, in which the cuckold effectively scorns the adulterer's usefulness-of-hypocrites theory that public confession can spoil a sinner's power to do good; and of course the famous forest-meeting between a confidently rebellious Hester and fecklessly remorseful Dimmesdale, she insisting that he "choose life," and he, justifying his decision to run away with the lame (pseudo-Calvinist) excuse that, having come to believe that he's damned anyway, he might as well seize the day. There are of course interstices, but these are filled largely with a Narrator's sober meditations—and also, perhaps, with the implication that it is unnecessary to narrate quotidian continuity and nearly impossible to imitate the pace of subtle change. And indeed the dramatic scenes have revealed enough that we could almost fill in the blanks ourselves. Which is what happens inevitably in anybody's reading of anybody else's writing of history.

In any case a fair amount of time is said to elapse between the first and the last scaffold scenes—enough, we are told, for Chillingworth to have turned himself from an aging intellectual into a monster; got his ministrations (including, no doubt, not-well-controlled doses of atropine) to have made an hallucinating Dimmesdale quite insane; and for public opinion to relent from its near-univocal view of the Fallen Woman; and for the woman herself, recognizably hypocritical in her own well-managed pretense of humble repentance, to have reasoned her way out of the seventeenth century altogether. Once persuaded she would like to spend eternity in hell with Dimmesdale, she comes to think, with Emerson, that what the wise physician needs to say, as the first condition of moral cure, is "Come out of that." Indeed, from the standpoint of change which is as much historical as personal, the most interesting thing about *The Scarlet Letter* is the utter dis-continuity of its presentation of Hester: instead of watching her slow growth from guilt-admitting, hell-deserving sinner to rebellious, quasi-antinomian speculator, the novel offers us instead the *fait accompli*—not a continuous or developmental but simply "*Another* View of Hester." And then, in the end, yet Another—as the Hester who returns to New England, years later, to take up her letter and counsel wounded women not to rebel but to wait, holding fast to the belief that the arrival of the prophet of the Day of Gender Equality is not far off—is one more advent of the same fascinating literary creation. Three scaffold scenes, doubtless, but then three Hesters as well.

In the end, what *The Scarlet Letter* confirms is that, for the most part, Hawthorne's history does not even try to imitate its movement. Characters live to suffer, in appropriate psychological time, the consequences of their actions; but this human inevitability is almost never made to stand for the changing state of worldly conditions or, more searchingly, epistemic shifts. Rather, what makes this "Puritan Love Story" ineluctably historical is that the characters all understand themselves in terms of premises somewhat alien to the reader. S/he might wish to intervene, to save them from their suffering in a world which Hawthorne's "Main-Street" had just characterized as "sinister to the intellect, and sinister to the heart"—to assure the Puritan Community that one case of what turned out to be adultery will not by itself bring down the wrath of heaven; to suggest to Dimmesdale that the more-than-ascetic effort to love God more than one loves a lover may be just too hard a task for carbon-based life; and even to hint to a finally-cautious Hester, who once convinced herself that "What [they] did had a consecration of its own," that stainless sexual purity may not be the distinguishing mark of the Feminist Redeemer—but s/he cannot. The characters live when and where they live, doomed to live out their lives within the premises available.

Somewhere in the archives of Boston's WGBH there exists a six-episode version of *The Scarlet Letter* in which an inspired and poetic screen writer tries to imagine the daily life of Hester Prynne in the months immediately after her brutal exposure on the scaffold; in one scene she struggles with the quite literal wolf she must keep away from her door. Professional consultants all said *no*: it's not Hawthorne. They meant, of course, that there's nothing like this in the text. But they may also have realized as well that this is not Hawthorne's métier. They might even have invoked the considerable authority of D. H. Lawrence: it's a "romance," stupid; no one even gets their feet muddy. But literary naturalism is not the only issue, as Hawthorne has also exempted from close investigation anything like a developmental account of Dimmesdale's relationship with Chillingworth, which some critics have suggested may have interested Hawthorne quite deeply. Comparative manhood might well be the issue, but the development of doctrine as well: was Calvinism the only available "Religion of Protestants"? More hypothetically still, one can easily imagine a novel in which Dimmesdale flees to Holland and falls in with a knot of Arminians, who have learned to define predestination in a completely different way; so that he might have found a ready and easy way to avoid the disastrous either/or of his forest scene. But Hawthorne did not write that novel. Sad to say, the best Dimmesdale can do is die of his premises. Hester, we are *told*, changes enough to avoid that truly gloomy outcome; but apparently no one was around to say, "dramatize, dramatize." And, had they been, Hawthorne might well have been wise enough to say, "This is already as much like a play as I can make it; I can help you picture difference, but you know I cannot make it move."

Or else, if I try, the effort will look a lot like parody—as when, in "Main-Street," the Showman who came alone to replace the Story-Teller, could do no better than flip his static cardboard cards and flatly assert the temporal dimension: "Pass onward, onward Time! Build up new houses here, and tear down thy works of yesterday, that have already the rusty moss upon them." The setting here is material and not moral, and the time frame quite long; moreover, the clunky scene-machine breaks down long before we get from the aboriginal then to the evanescent now; but the point survives: how well—in a sketch dramatizing just about all the objections one might raise against the epistemology of historical romance—how well Hawthorne knew his own limitations. If you lend both your imagination *and* a certain factual curiosity, he seems to say, I can let you picture an historical moment; but I am not the man to solve the subtle mystery of moment to moment.

Not in *The Scarlet Letter*, and not in the longer romances which follow. None quite so plainly "historical" as that paradigmatic example, but—in spite of a series of prefaces declaring the right of romance to float free of the binding concerns of the novel—all evincing a strong concern for the reality of time and place. There is no single *House* of the Seven Gables; and no attempt is made to fill in the long blank space between the prediction and the fulfillment of the curse made by the man who lost the house to a pious hypocrite; still, the setting can only be Puritan New England, and the narrative an explicit attempt to connect its sunny present with its darker past. Indeed, Phoebe appears to stand in for the two young ladies who, in "Alice Doane's Appeal," resist what they need to know about "What Happened." *The Blithedale Romance* requires about the same nine months which Hawthorne literally spent at Brook Farm but, from a distance, it exists to take a critical look at an aboriginal Puritan project, namely, the attempt to reform the world by separated example. Time intensely matters but, for reasons that may require abstruse explanation, it is severely distorted by a self-veiling Narrator reliving a set of epochal scenes from his own past. Finally, among the completed works, *The Marble Faun* requires us to think the history of Rome—from Etruscan, to Pagan, to Catholic. Oh, dear, we don't teach Western Civ. any more: can so much time really be revealed as archeology and as art? Maybe not, but Puritanism most certainly can be identified, even in its latter-day variety. Just arrange to send the innocent Phoebe-returned-as-the innocent-Hilda into a Catholic confessional. Or, better still, let a somewhat more worldly New England sculptor get caught up in a festive procession of rampant phallic figures and the difference appears at once. One hardly needs the example of James' "American."

In summary, then, the conclusion is not that Hawthorne could not learn to manage the kind of emplotment required of "continuous prose fiction." And certainly not that he outgrew his fascination with either the Matter of Puritanism or the method of scenic epitome. It is, much more simply, that in turning from tale to novel, he was willing to let fiction have its own way. As lives require time to unfold, so characters need narrative space in which to discover and explain themselves. Let it happen, even if the slow unfolding of character—the essence of that all-but-representative modern form we call *bildungsroman*—cannot be made to stand for the movement of human consciousness through historical time. A scene is emphatically not process. Nor can it perfectly represent an epoch or an episteme. But it is better than nothing, especially for an audience Hawthorne characterized early on as "a people of the present [with] no heartfelt interest in the olden time." And better, certainly, than assuming that, except for pockets of superstition, everyone has always thought the way we now think. History means difference (or why bother?), and Hawthorne's highly contrived but well instructed scenes challenge us to appreciate this simple fact. Unable quite to get us from there to here, he has instead the matchless ability to challenge us, for a moment at least, to look back then.

Chapter Four

"CERTAIN CIRCUMSTANCES": HAWTHORNE AND THE INTEREST OF HISTORY

Nothing would seem more obvious at first glance than the historical dimension of Hawthorne's literary art. His work of widest international reputation, *The Scarlet Letter*, is set squarely in the midst of the "Puritan" seventeenth century, and it shows all the signs of a determined inquiry into the moral circumstances of this relevant and specifiable past. The settings of his tales turn out to be quite various, but from among them a modest number set in colonial New England have attracted a disproportionate share of attention, as if in recognition that such "local history" were somehow his true metier. And compared to the universalism of contemporaries like Emerson and Thoreau, Hawthorne's bookish curiosity about historical particularities would certainly seem a distinguishing mark. So it might appear irresponsible to ignore the problems which arise when our literary present is constituted as an imitation of an historical past: This is now, as always, whenever anyone reads; but that was then. What if it was all different?

At the same time, however, few readers appear to relish the suggestion that what they read as "literature" may require an effort of historical reconstruction—and even of something like research. Perhaps we all begin by defining "the literary" so as to preclude that exact possibility: now for something on my own terms; or else, with a little more finesse, something complete in itself, something which invents and deploys its own world of fact and assumption. Granted, all acts of writing are past to the reader; and *the further* past of historical fiction may well compound the problem of possible human difference. But all acts of reading are present; nor does literature properly speaking occur until someone actually reads. So most readers are inclined to trust their own instincts: That was then, but this is now; and life is short.

Nor have the institutions of academic criticism always opposed these readerly assumptions.[1] True, many Professors of Literature appear duty-bound to lecture their

---

1. The assumptions I ascribe to "most readers" would find support in at least two important modern schools of critical opinion: in the so-called New Criticism, which insists that literary meaning is entirely "internal" to the text; and also (more recently) in the variety of "Reader Response" theories, which stress the extent to which literary meaning is a production of the individual reader. For a brief exposition of these positions, see M. H. Abrams, *A Glossary of Literary Terms* (New York: Holt, Rinehart, and Winston, 1985), pp. 223–24, 231–34. For more

classes on something called background or context; and many of them are known to lament that teaching grows more difficult every year, as each new class seems less well informed about the history of the world where literature has been written and read.[2] But most students prove immune to this preprofessional embarrassment: They have, after all, only so much time for each course; nor did they enroll in "English" with the same factual expectations as in history or sociology. And professors usually concede the point in the end: When the push of class discussion comes to the shove of a take-home paper, any fair comment on theme or style will usually suffice. A more complex approach—more worldly or more "intertextual"—must wait till graduate school. Or for some "New Historicism," to point a way outside the well-enclosed garden of literary study.[3]

Meanwhile, of the explicit "approaches" that have retarded the interest of history, one may count the discrediting effect of "source studies." In these, a scholar persuaded of the obvious—that the "Puritanism" of "Young Goodman Brown" or the revolutionary lore of "My Kinsman, Major Molineux" surely implies some special historical knowledge—sets out to locate the very books from which Hawthorne has derived his facts. Such studies have been successful in certifying an impressive number of works Hawthorne *must* have read. Often enough, however, historical consideration ends with the thrill of the discovery, truly electric to the investigator, but hard to communicate to the less fortunate audience. A "fact" is added to the lore of "literary history"; but the avid reader, lured to the library by the promise of insight, almost always asks, "So what?" Or else she or he is soberly instructed that, though Hawthorne has read something which *happened* to spur the creative process, he has of course gone on to "use history" for his own literary end—implying, always, that we need not trouble ourselves much about the issues of the sources themselves.[4] We honor thus the artist's creativity, but we also empower our own autonomous reading. Imagination transmutes every difficulty of worldly fact into the "textual" condition of rhetoric. A most convenient system, truly.

But another form of criticism has also acted to counter the interest of history in Hawthorne—one so habitual as to appear inevitable. Psychology may or may not appear

---

extensive discussion of the theory of internalism, see Murray Krieger, *The New Apologists for Poetry* (Minneapolis: University of Minnesota Press, 1956); *Theory of Criticism* (Baltimore, MD: Johns Hopkins University Press, 1976); and Vincent B. Leitch, *American Literary Criticism* (New York: Columbia University Press, 1988), pp. 24–59. And for a sample of the theories that empower the reader, see Jane P. Tompkins, ed., *Reader-Response Criticism* (Baltimore, MD: Johns Hopkins University Press, 1980).

2. For professional complaint about the unpreparedness of the American student, see Allan Bloom, *The Closing of the American Mind* (New York: Simon and Schuster, 1987); and E. D. Hirsch, *Cultural Literacy* (Boston, MA: Houghton Mifflin, 1987).
3. For a brief introduction to the incipient theory and practice of the "New Historicism," see Ross C. Murfin, "What Is the New Historicism?," in Murfin, ed., *The Scarlet Letter* (Boston, MA: St. Martin's Press, 1991), pp. 333–44. For fuller treatments, see H. Aram Veeser, ed., *The New Historicism* (New York: Routledge, 1989); and Brook Thomas, *The New Historicism* (Princeton, NJ: Princeton University Press, 1991).
4. For an epitome of the achievement of Hawthorne "source studies," see Neal Frank Doubleday, *Hawthorne's Early Tales* (Durham, NC: Duke University Press, 1972).

to us as Queen of the Sciences, but whenever we sit down to read for more than mere diversion, we usually find ourselves within its quietly extensive domain; for, as serious readers, we imagine we are looking for insight into something like "the human condition"—glorious or pitiful, yet pretty much unchanged over time. Long since persuaded that the pursuit of wisdom begins nowhere but in self- knowledge, we go on to decide that literature shall be our primary aid to that reflection. Conscientiously secured and arranged by our colleges, the corpus of canonized texts represents, to us, a preserve of all the more important traits of our own curious species. Thus literature continues, without fail, to appear "more philosophical than history": It looks for evidences of things that are *always* true, about ourselves.

In loyalty to this complex of assumptions we steadfastly resist the suggestion that historical change may be real and radical—that "the self" may be largely the creation of modern ideology, and that the notion of an essential human psyche may be only a narcissistic illusion. Accordingly, in the case of Hawthorne, we seize some fragment of his language to insist that his true interest can be nothing but the profounder workings of "our common nature."[5] His characters may be Puritans or other awkward provincials but his real interests, we are sure, are timeless: not historical but human.

Predictably, therefore, critics concerned to assemble the evidence of Hawthorne's anticipations of modern psychology have worked with an agreeable sense of their own inevitability; and, happily persuaded of the primacy of their project, they have tended to mock the interest of history as merely academic.[6] Argued out in full, however, their case might demand great philosophical acumen indeed. How did we become *so* sure of the network of propositions that underlies our belief in "the literary" as an infallible index of "the human"? And what are the practical implications of this complex faith? May not imagination look to the condition of an historic community as well as to the structure of the psyche or the state of the soul? Must literature treat even politics as but a department of psychology?

Of course the "historicist" position is not without its own difficulties. If change is so radical a fact of human experience, how can we recover a meaningful sense of the past at all? Perhaps, on this "Heraclitan" view, its patterns of experience were *so* different as to escape present categories altogether. Or, to state the problem from the opposite perspective, surely we would not read *any* text if we expected to encounter an alien mentality, one that utterly eluded the scope of our own concepts. Thus a radical skepticism, very hard to reconcile with the nature of intellectual inquiry as we understand it, may lie in wait for those who would reject "essentialism" altogether. The river of thought in which we step had better be *somewhat* the same. Yet even as we are forced to accept some version

---

5. In context, Hawthorne's remark about "burrowing [...] into the depths of our common nature, for the purposes of psychological romance" reads not as a rejection of history but as a defense against "egotism"; see Hawthorne's Preface to *The Snow-Image*, in *Hawthorne: Tales and Sketches* (New York: Library of America, 1982), p. 1154.
6. See, for example, Frederick Crews, *The Sins of the Fathers* (New York: Oxford University Press, 1966), especially chap. 2, "The Sense of the Past," pp. 27–43.

of Emerson's dictum that "there is only *one mind*,"[7] we may yet resist the conclusion that psychological theory (or psychoanalytic practice) has yielded up a science of all its various moods and behaviors. And we can maintain, quite apart from questions of structure, that shifts of attention and varieties of expression are significant enough to arouse and satisfy a curiosity about human difference over time, that the writings we preserve as literature are competent to inscribe difference as well as sameness, that these two may be about equal as possible reasons to read literature.

And, finally, since readers always will, we may as well premise that they may, judge for themselves: can a modest familiarity with the issues of America's colonial history offer any useful hypotheses for the interpretation of Hawthorne's early tales? If not, why have they made themselves so pedantically correct about such matters? Or if so, how may the construction of this "American Studies Hawthorne" come to modify our sense of "Hawthorne's Psychological Themes"? Perhaps these tales are trying to force us to learn something. And once we recover from the shock to our literary sensibility, we might come to like that fact.

2

One is always tempted to begin with a "Puritan" tale—the sort we associate with the "solitary" Hawthorne who, just after college, spent twelve or so years living in the home of his mother's family, reading his way through the Salem subscription library and trying (unsuccessfully) to put together several collections of tales of his "Native Land" which, however "Provincial," must yet have its own "Story."[8] From among that group, it is almost irresistibly tempting to select the widely discussed "Young Goodman Brown," which clearly invokes the (mis-)deeds of some of Hawthorne's Puritan ancestors, but also suggests other, more "profound" considerations. Yet even this prime exemplum may need to be placed within the range of Hawthorne's interest as a writer of historical fiction.

Published in 1835, after the breakup of the collection for which it was intended—and which may well have provided it with an important narrative setting—it is by no means Hawthorne's first meditation on the question of New England "witchcraft." Earlier

---

7. For Emerson's most famous defense of the proposition "There is one mind common to all individual men," see "History," in Alfred R. Ferguson and Jean Ferguson Carr, eds., *The Collected Works of Ralph Waldo Emerson*, vol. 2 (Cambridge, MA: Harvard University Press, 1979), pp. 3–23. This essay compresses the argument of his lecture series on "The Philosophy of History"; see *The Early Lectures of Ralph Waldo Emerson*, vol. 2, Stephen E. Whicher, Robert E. Spiller, and Wallace E. Williams, eds. (Cambridge, MA: Harvard University Press, 1964), pp. 1–188.
8. The story of Hawthorne's early career as a writer of tales involves his serious but failed attempts to publish collections of tales which might answer the widespread complaint that America was not a "storied" nation: "Seven Tales of My Native Land," ca. 1825–27; "Provincial Tales," ca. 1828–29; and "The Story Teller," 1831–34. For discussion, see Nelson F. Adkins, "The Early Projected Works of Nathaniel Hawthorne," *Papers of the Bibliographical Society of America* 39 (1945), pp. 119–55; Nina Baym, *The Shape of Hawthorne's Career* (Ithaca, NY: Cornell University Press, 1976), pp. 15–52; and Michael J. Colacurcio, Introduction to *Nathaniel Hawthorne: Selected Tales and Sketches* (New York: Penguin, 1987), esp. pp. vii–xxv.

treatments date back to his first projected collection (of 1827 or earlier) and reveal a more Gothic literary style. Clearly Hawthorne's concern was a developing one. Nor does it in any way epitomize his interest in "The Matter of Puritanism."[9] The dark mood which concludes the fictional life of Goodman Brown has often suggested some psychic kinship with the somber and solitary experience of Parson Hooper in "The Minister's Black Veil" (1836); but as Hooper's revival of Puritan gloom seems much more deliberately self-cultivated, his tale may involve other issues altogether; particularly when we learn to date its action well into the eighteenth century.[10] And elsewhere the terms are noticeably different. "The Gentle Boy" (1832) tells a sad enough story—of family disruption in the midst of sectarian dispute—but it dwells at some length on the domestic issues so popular in the fiction of the period. And a fair number of Hawthorne's Puritan tales seem not moodily spiritual at all but quite frankly *political*.

"The Gray Champion" (1835) and "Endicott and the Red Cross" (1838) both profess to find predictions of the American Revolution in acts of resistance of the most local and Puritanic sort; and even "The May-Pole of Merry Mount" (1836), often treated as a moral allegory, may fit this typological model as well as any other. When John Endicott cuts down "the only maypole in New England" (368),[11] his action may seem less political than when he rends "the Red Cross completely out of the banner" (548) of the realm of England; but only until one learns the current status of this immemorial or mythic symbol. Legitimized—even recommended—by the King himself, maypole ceremonies had become, by the late 1620s, an important symbol by which England's civil religion distinguished itself from its Puritan antagonist.[12] In both cases, therefore, Endicott implies the disestablishment of an "Anglican" religion in the transatlantic territories of *New* England. And most fully evincing this care for ancestral politics, the four tales of the Revolution known as "Legends of the Province House" (1838) discover the legacy of Puritanism at work not in experiences of dark moral privacy but in a rhetoric of resistance and destiny.

The distinguishing mark of "My Kinsman, Major Molineux" (1832), in this context, is that it is frankly political without being very noticeably "Puritan." Few readers can resist its implication of interest in the American Revolution, but its point of literal reference

---

9. The other early "witchcraft" tales are "The Hollow of the Three Hills" (1830), originally intended for "Seven Tales," and "Alice Doane's Appeal" (1835), apparently a reworking of an earlier "Alice Doane," probably intended for that same volume. For "The Matter of Puritanism" as but one subject of importance to the interest of an American literature, see Rufus Choate's 1833 Salem lecture on "The Importance of Illustrating New England History by a Series of Romances Like the Waverley Novels," in *Works*, vol. 1 (Boston, MA: Little, Brown, 1862), pp. 319–46. For discussion, see Doubleday, *Early Tales*, pp. 24–26.
10. For the significance of the dating of "The Minister's Black Veil," see Michael J. Colacurcio, *The Province of Piety* (Cambridge, MA: Harvard University Press, 1984), pp. 312–85.
11. All citations of the text of Hawthorne's tales, given in parentheses, are from *Hawthorne: Tales and Sketches* (New York: Library of America, 1982).
12. For the English background of the "The May-Pole of Merry Mount," see Doubleday, *Early Tales*, pp. 97–99; and J. Gary Williams, "History in Hawthorne's 'May-Pole of Merry Mount,'" *Essex Institute Historical Collections* 108 (1972), pp. 3–30.

is in fact the 1730s. And its way of being "proleptic" is not quite like that of "The Gray Champion" or "Endicott": what it offers is not some mysterious prefiguration, in a minor historical event, of a major religious apocalypse, but only the more ragged sense that what happens in a well forgotten episode of mob violence is not *so* different from the Event which everyone has agreed to remember. Evidently Hawthorne's interest in "The Matter of the Revolution" was not limited to the terms of Puritan typology. What this suggests, further, is that Hawthorne's reading in colonial history may have been more purposive than is sometimes assumed.[13]

Especially instructive, in this regard, are the terms of the unresolved critical debate on the "Molineux" problem. A rare case in the annals of Hawthorne criticism, the tale was given its first professional sponsorship by "historicists," powerfully persuaded that Hawthorne's account of the violent expulsion of a Tory leader was meant to prefigure the loss and gain—or the imputed guilt—of America's separation from England. Psychoanalytic readers protested, almost at once, that the true interest in the story is the *personal* one, of Robin's ambivalent search for some indulgent paternal influence, and that the "revolutionary" violence which engulfs him is itself best understood as a resistance to "the father"; thus all historical readings unduly particularize the tale. Yet the discovery of names and faces and issues sharply relevant to America's provincial circumstances has caused the particularist reading to remain strong, encouraging a sort of polite compromise: In this story, perhaps, political revolution and oedipal overthrow simply figure one another, endlessly, without subordination or primacy of interest.[14]

On this supple premise, the American Revolution comes to seem just like the act or process of growing up—painful and even violent, as the overthrow of paternal authority must always be, whether literal or figurative; yet not less inevitable for that reason, as nations, just like young men, must surely assume their own "separate and equal station." Still, the scrupulous reader may observe that this conciliatory view quietly elides the one consideration the tale tries hardest to problematize: the intriguing but not always attractive question of "conspiracy."

Quite obviously, most of the story's broad humor and all its irony about "shrewdness" depend on the fact that Robin is the only character in the story who does not know what

---

13. In an 1837 letter to former classmate Longfellow, Hawthorne admits he has "turned over a good many books," but only, he protests, "in so desultory a way that it cannot be called study"; see *Nathaniel Hawthorne: The Letters, 1813–1843*, Thomas Woodson, L. Neal Smith, and Norman Holmes Pearson, eds. (Columbus: Ohio State University Press, 1984), p. 252. For discussion, see Colacurcio, *Province*, pp. 71–78.
14. For the historicist view of "My Kinsman, Major Molineux" (MKMM), see Q. D. Leavis, "Hawthorne as Poet," *Sewanee Review*, 50 (1951), pp. 198–205; and Roy Harvey Pearce, "Hawthorne and the Sense of the Past," *ELH*, 21 (1954), 327–34. For the psychological response, see Hyatt H. Waggoner, *Hawthorne* (Cambridge, MA: Harvard University Press, 1955), pp. 46–53; and Seymour Gross, "Hawthorne's MKMM: History as Moral Adventure," *Nineteenth-Century Fiction*, 12 (1957), pp. 97–109. For the attempt at reconciliation, see Robert H. Fossum, *Hawthorne's Inviolable Circle* (Deland, FL: Everett/Edwards, 1972), pp. 26–31; and Peter Shaw, "Fathers, Sons, and the Ambiguities of Revolution in MKMM," *New England Quarterly*, 49 (1976), pp. 559–76.

the local politicos have in store for his kinsman, that very evening. Robin has stumbled into something, well over his head, and its planned events take place in total disregard for his own psychic case. He is forced to grow up, we might say, *just when* some other men are plotting the ouster of an obnoxious local authority, but the logic of the two events is separate enough. It may flatter some theorists to observe that he does, momentarily at least, join in with the general will to revolt. But plots and cabals are entirely alien to his countrified adolescence. And—as it would be naive to suppose that a tar-and-feather procession has come about in a purely natural "course of human events"—we are left with an important reminder: Revolutions are plotted in a way that maturation never is. To imply that the one is as natural and inevitable as the other is to obscure the question of political responsibility.[15]

Some of the tale's best ironies touch just this question of conspiratorial difference. At a moment of potential clarification, Robin asks the stranger who joins him at the meetinghouse if he "happen [s] to know" the fellow with the face painted half-red and half-black. "Not intimately," comes the reply, "but I chanced to meet him a little time previous [...] [and] you may trust his word [...] that the Major will very shortly pass through this street" (82). Obviously the stranger *knows*. And surely his answer is as ironical as Robin's question is innocent: Needing to be in just the right place at just the right time, he has met with the man (of a lower social order) delegated to head the parade which he and other, more powerful but less conspicuous leaders have carefully arranged. Evidently nothing like "chance" was in any way involved. Clearly it is only Robin himself who just happens to be there, where the Molineux procession is duly scheduled to pass in review.

Not coincidentally, perhaps, the same sort of irony is playing about the tale's curious headnote. After rehearsing some arcane materials from the "annals of Massachusetts," an obviously learned narrator seems suddenly anxious to spare us a "long and dry detail of colonial affairs"; but when his forgiving formula suggests that "the following adventures [...] *chanced* upon a summer night, not far from a hundred years ago" (68, my italics), we recognize a first version of the forget-real-politics fallacy the tale itself exists to identify and undo. For only in pure romance would all this ritual activity just "happen" to provide the context for an aspiring hero's *rite de passage*. The American Revolution was nothing such. And not even Shakespeare's "Dream" reads this way any more.

Most readers can appreciate the pace and the pathos of Robin's "evening of ambiguity and weariness" (80) without knowing the cause and extent of the rum riots of the 1730s. They may even get along without recalling that a certain kind of nepotistic politics had once acquired the name of a "Robinocracy." But the story of American political resistance in the eighteenth century is no longer credible without reference to the mob actions that were thoroughly stage-managed by the respectable leaders of colonial

---

15. For Jefferson's attempt to "naturalize" the coming of the American Revolution, see Garry Wills, *Inventing America* (Garden City, NY: Doubleday, 1978), pp. 93–110. For an account of Americans' self-forgiving view of their "Coming of Age," see Michael Kammen, *A Season of Youth* (New York: Knopf, 1978), pp. 186–220.

society.¹⁶ And what is most noteworthy about Robin's psychic adventure is that absolutely nothing in his growing resistance to figures of paternal authority has quite prepared him for this encounter with the politics of "controlled" and "ritual" violence. Adrift in the city, balked at every turn, cudgel in hand, ready to club anyone you please, Robin may seem ripe for a wider rebellion. But his enduring naivete—a type of our own apolitical criticism, perhaps—has no way of coping with the art of overthrow; evidently some other, more circumstantial initiation is yet to be faced.¹⁷

Yet the logic of "Roger Malvin's Burial" may offer an even more severe education in the competing claims of general principle and historical circumstance. It is, on the one hand, the tale most boldly claimed by the psychoanalytic science of Frederick Crews; and indeed the experience of its protagonist seems compulsed and nightmarish even after Crews has recanted his systematic Freudianism.¹⁸ On the other hand, however, it attaches itself to an event far more obscure than the American Revolution or even the Salem Witchcraft. For—apart from the tale's own headnote—what modem reader has even *heard* of "Lovell's Fight"?

Innocent of all such concerns, Crews opposed instead certain orthodox approaches to the case of Reuben Bourne: Unless one were extremely wary about the ending of this disturbing tale, one had better not venture a religious interpretation at all. What happens there is more barbarous than pious or at any rate, more psychologically elemental than rationally moral. Reuben Bourne may feel that "his sin was expiated" (107) in the killing

---

16. On the question of "Robinocracy," see James Duban, "Robins and Robinarchs in MKMM," *Nineteenth-Century Fiction*, 38 (1983), pp. 271–88. For the management of mobs in eighteenth-century America, see Arthur M. Schlesinger, "Political Mobs and the American Revolution," *Massachusetts Historical Society Proceedings*, 99 (1955), esp. pp. 244–50; Edmund S. and Helen M. Morgan, *The Stamp Act Crisis* (Chapel Hill: University of North Carolina Press, 1953), pp. 159–68, 231–40; G. B. Warden, *Boston 1689–1776* (Boston, MA: Little Brown, 1970), pp. 92–101; Gary B. Nash, *Urban Crucible* (Cambridge, MA: Harvard University Press, 1979), pp. 292–311; and Peter Shaw, *American Patriots and the Rituals of Revolution* (Cambridge, MA: Harvard University Press, 1981), pp. 5–47. For application of these matters to MKMM, see Shaw, "Hawthorne's Ritual Typology of the American Revolution," *Prospects*, 3 (1977), pp. 483–98; and Colacurcio, *Province*, pp. 130–53 (bibliography, pp. 562–71).
17. For readings which resist the conclusion that Robin has learned his needful lessons—"or will have when apprehension becomes knowledge" (Gross, "Moral Adventure," p. 108)—see John P. McWilliams Jr., *Hawthorne, Melville and the American Character* (Cambridge: Cambridge University Press, 1984), pp. 85–88; Frederick Newberry, *Hawthorne's Divided Loyalties* (Rutherford, NJ: Fairleigh Dickinson University Press, 1987), pp. 62–65. And for an emerging emphasis on Robin's problems of manhood in a new, urban environment, see David Leverenz, *Manhood and the American Renaissance* (Ithaca, NY: Cornell University Press, 1989), pp. 231–39; and T. Walter Herbert, "Doing Cultural Work: MKMM and the Construction of the Self-Made Man," *Studies in the Novel*, 23 (1991), pp. 20–27.
18. For Crews's strictly Freudian reading of "Roger Malvin's Burial" (RMB), see "The Logic of Compulsion in RMB," *PMLA*, 79 (1964), pp. 457–65; and cp. *Sins*, pp. 80–95. A more distanced attitude toward Freud is expressed, *passim*, in *Out of My System* (New York: Oxford University Press, 1975); and explicitly revisionary remarks on Hawthorne are offered in *Skeptical Engagements* (New York: Oxford University Press, 1986), pp. xiii–xiv.

of his son, but (unless one posits a "teleological suspension of the ethical")[19] the issue is not salvation but psychic survival. The plot of which is clear enough: Ineffectually remorseful ever since his abandonment of his prospective father-in-law, Reuben has thwarted himself in business, poisoned his social relations, then wandered compulsively back to the spot where it all began, to expiate in slaughter what began in grief. Obscurely guilty of the death of a figurative father, he frees his tormented soul by killing—not *quite* accidentally—his literal son. "Regeneration through Violence"[20] with a vengeance.

Chastened, the moralist may protest that it requires less than oedipal theory to notice that Reuben will suffer great distress at the decision he seems forced to make: Heroically, he would like to remain beside his dying companion in arms; as a Christian, perhaps, he would like to "lay down his life for his friend"; yet he is utilitarian enough to realize the greatest good of the greatest number; and he *would* like to save his own skin. He sees at once the truth of Malvin's prediction: Dorcas will be upset at first, but she will come around; things will be awkward in the meantime, but they must be endured. Yet it is this very meantime that Reuben fears he cannot endure: He knows that Dorcas's eyes, if not her voice, will accuse him of cowardice; and he cannot face this refracted version of himself. This is why he allows a tough and ruefully smiling Malvin to persuade him that his real project is to go off and seek a means of rescue. Only thus can he save his life and still maintain the standard of heroism objectified in the glance of Dorcas.

Clearly, this old-fashioned psychology is as relevant as Freud. Source critics might even observe that Reuben's moral dilemma is constructed as a traditional "case of conscience," the very sort of problem treated in one of Hawthorne's favorite seventeenth-century authors.[21] Indeed this older style of motive analysis—pressing rational analysis to the point of disappearance—may even explain why Reuben feels guilty in the first place: not for refusing "the gratuitous sacrifice of his own life," but for "concealment" (98), of both fact and motive, from all concerned. Including himself.

What draws Reuben back, compulsively, to the spot where he left Malvin is the memory of his unredeemed vow. Baffled by his options, Reuben had promised to return,

---

19. Thus Soren Kierkegaard has described the "existential" demand of Genesis 22, as a transcendent God requires Abraham (consciously) to sacrifice his son Isaac (but intervenes to provide an animal substitute). For readings which take this religious paradigm as seriously as possible, see Ely Stock, "History and Bible in Hawthorne's RMB," *Essex Institute Historical Collections*, 100 (1964), pp. 279–96; and Emily Miller Budick, *Fiction and Historical Consciousness* (New Haven, CT: Yale University Press, 1989), pp. 36–54.
20. Richard Slotkin reads the ending of RMB as an explicit critique of frontier mythology; see *Regeneration through Violence* (Middletown, CT: Wesleyan University Press, 1973), pp. 477–78, 483–84. On the issue of the frontier in RMB, see also Edwin Fussell, *Frontier* (Princeton, NJ: Princeton University Press, 1965), pp. 75–77; Ann Ronald, "Roger Malvin's Grandson," *Studies in American Fiction*, 12 (1984), pp. 71–77; and James McIntosh, "Nature and Frontier in RMB," *American Literature*, 60 (1988), pp. 188–204.
21. The importance to Hawthorne of the seventeenth-century "casuist" Jeremy Taylor was first established by Neal F. Doubleday, "The Theme of Hawthorne's 'Fancy's Show Box,'" *American Literature*, 10 (1938), pp. 431–33. For a full account of Taylor's influence on RMB, see Colacurcio, *Province*, pp. 109–14.

if not to rescue Malvin, then at least to bury him. Yet this becomes impossible the moment he is less than honest with Dorcas: She inquires for her father and, as he rambles on about the terrible complexity of his forest scene, she falsely infers that her father died with Reuben nearby and was buried by him. Reuben merely holds back the truth; yet when she spreads the tale of his wonderful "courage and fidelity" (97), he is trapped in his own deceptive silence. Nor is this "mental reservation" unrelated to his original mixture of motive. The situation turns out exactly as he had imagined: She expects heroism and he cannot bear to confess ordinariness; he lets her conclude exactly what he, looking at himself through her eyes, had himself wished to believe. And the whole problem had arisen, some old-time casuist might observe, because Reuben has failed to be clear about his real intentions, to "settle his own motives."

Yet the possible application of moral categories is not at all the main problem with the psychological approach to this tale. The more crucial question, surely, is where either of these analyses leaves the reader who happens to wonder what any of this could have to do with an incident of "Indian warfare" (88). Generalists may prefer to see the tale's headnote as written under a kind of polite erasure. Yet one could also read it as a picque to historical curiosity; and surely no one can *forbid* an inquiry into the possible relevance of "Lovell's Fight."

Source hunters long ago traced a number of the story's symbolic details—Reuben's bloody handkerchief, most famously—to various accounts of what transpired when Lovewell's raiders went out to meet the Natives on a mission of protective retaliation. More recently, a truly inspired sleuth finally discovered the obvious: The oak tree to which Reuben ties that handkerchief looks exactly like the Charter Oak from the flag of Connecticut, held sacred by colonials ever since they hid, in the original, the land titles they meant to protect from the King of England.[22] Evidently the question of bloody wars for territory is supposed to occur to somebody, not utterly distracted by the strife or the delicacy of Reuben's after-the-fact dilemma. For it is after one of the most curious facts in the entire provincial period of New England.

We can—if we think about "The Matter of the Indians" at all—easily imagine that "Lovell's Fight" was probably not a very grand affair, whatever "its consequences to the country"; no doubt its historian can achieve "romance" only by "casting certain circumstances judiciously into the shade" (88). Indeed, Lovewell's men were bounty hunters, seeking Indians at the astonishing value of one hundred pounds per scalp; among other ventures, none very glorious to either side, they managed to kill a small party of Indians while they slept, then got themselves ambushed in pursuit of a single Indian who appeared unarmed but who may have been a decoy. Many of their number

---

22. For the *realpolitik of* Hawthorne's "symbolic" tree, see John Samson, "Hawthorne's Oak Tree," *American Literature*, 52 (1980), pp. 457–61. Earlier source studies include G. Harrison Orians, "The Source of Hawthorne's RMB," *American Literature*, 10 (1938), pp. 313–18; David S. Lovejoy, "Lovewell's Fight and Hawthorne's RMB," *New England Quarterly*, 27 (1954), pp. 527–30; and Stock, "History and Bible." For fullscale thematic uses of these materials, see Robert J. Daly, "History and Chivalric Myth in RMB," *Essex Institute Historical Collections*, 109 (1973), pp. 99–115; and Colacurcio, *Province*, pp. 107–30 (bibliography, pp. 556–62).

were killed outright; some stragglers died in the attempt to return to the settlements; a few escaped to tell the tale.[23] By which tale hangs Hawthorne's own, though this plot might require a little cynicism to predict.

Evidently the first returning witness misrepresented certain circumstances of the expedition—not to his fiancee (though in fact he had been scalping Indians for money to get married), but to his minister who, not unlike the Dorcas of our tale, immediately turned the affair into a ballad of chivalry. His story took hold and was widely republished and rewritten, even after many in Lovewell's town had come to know the less heroic version. With the result that, a hundred years later, just as Hawthorne was graduating from college and preparing to enter the solemn career of making an original American literature out of authentic American materials, a whole culture was preparing to celebrate the centenary of that famous "Fight." One of Hawthorne's professors produced a hymn for the occasion; so did his classmate Longfellow. A Salem newspaper even ran a front-page story on just how and when to hold the celebration.[24] Historical science having recovered the exact date, a pious and grateful people might recall the deeds by which their ancestors had secured the land they now occupied. And—in the midst of a national policy of "Indian Removal"—they would renew their "covenantal" dedication to the same historic values.

The ironies are mostly self-evident. One need not romanticize the Indians to notice that a local embarrassment had been turned into a National Cultural Treasure. People made pilgrimages to a monument erected near "Lovewell's Pond." For the moment, at least, "Lovewell's Rock" was better known than the one filiopietism had tried to drag from the seacoast to the center of Plymouth. And both these monuments—with many others, in fact and literature—expressed the same sense as the famous one at Bunker Hill, the elective destiny of America. Given these circumstances, might one not expect a writer who once suggested building a monument to the supposed witches on the Gallows Hill of Salem Village[25] to mark the occasion in some unorthodox way? And how better than with the story of a would-be hero who spoils life and prevents posterity with an historical lie about the ragged facts of the sad provincial case? For Reuben indeed operates as an historian; and Dorcas too, after she has functioned first as his imagined and then his literal audience. Together they fashion a tale in which, though there is undeniable tragedy, yet everyone acts as nobly as possible and all things turn out for the best. And yet there

---

23. For the factual account of the Lovewell affair, see Fanny Hardy Eckstorm, "Pigwacket and Parson Symmes," *New England Quarterly*, 9 (1936), pp. 378–402; and Gail Bickford, "Lovewell's Fight, 1725–1958," *American Quarterly*, 10 (1958), pp. 358–66. But for a reading of RMB which insists we not romanticize the Natives—and which challenges the ironic reading of Hawthorne's headnote—see David Levin, "Modern Misjudgements of Racial Imperialism in Hawthorne and Parkman," *Yearbook of English Studies*, 13 (1983), pp. 145–58.
24. *Salem Gazette* (April 15, 1825), p. 30; for analysis, see Colacurcio, *Province*, pp. 128–30.
25. Near the end of "Alice Doane's Appeal," the narrator suggests that as we "build the memorial column on the height which our fathers made sacred with their blood," so "here"—on the Gallows Hill—"should arise another monument, sadly commemorative of the errors of an earlier race, and not to be cast down, while the human heart has one infirmity which may result in crime" *(Tales,* p. 216).

is, well advertised in the headnote to their fateful little romance, the memory of "certain circumstances" which the interest of history had better not repress. True, it requires a certain determined provincialism to read the tale this way; but the alternative may be just as unsettling. For it may be a good deal easier to rehearse the structure of the psyche than to recover the unlovely actualities of the colonial past. And, as we have yet to suggest, even Hawthorne's Puritan tales may look to circumstances as much as to the soul.

3

The outline of "Young Goodman Brown" is quite simple; but the account it provides seems almost too compressed. A noticeably unsuspecting young man spends a single night in a suspicious-looking forest and returns to spend the rest of an unhappy life suspecting everyone. At one moment this still-resisting protagonist is loudly proclaiming that he "will yet stand firm" (282); but then, in the fluttering of a few pink ribbons, his "Faith is gone." By which he means, shockingly, that "There is no good on earth; and sin is but a name" (283). He may as well give *himself* over to the Devil. It all happens so fast: we seem to have missed something. What power in the world could have utterly overset the painful teaching and sober practice of a whole pious lifetime—transforming a moment of moral panic into a studied and lethal blasphemy? And with such violence?

The narrator suggests, as Brown goes tearing into "the heart of the dark wilderness," that he is simply following "the instinct that guides mortal man to evil" (283). Yet this "Calvinistic" law can account for the direction but not the pace or the timing of Brown's sudden moral collapse: Why had he not been following that path all along? Nor can it quite explain the overdetermination of his new-found despair: Is nihilism the proper opposite of "faith"? Nor does it at all predict the fact that Brown will try to pull himself back from the precipice toward which he is rushing: is it an *evil* instinct which prompts him to cry out to Faith, at the lurid climax of the witch meeting, "Look up to Heaven, and resist the Wicked One!" (288)? Evidently something more is at stake than Melville's suspicion of "innate depravity and original sin."[26]

Something altogether more primal, the psychoanalytic reader is sure to suggest: Brown's readiness to overthrow all authority is instantaneous because it is a given of adolescent experience. And if Brown is a little old for this onset of oedipal hostility, that fact may well account for the rage in his response. His "manhood" has been pent up and smoldering too long; not wisely socialized but too well inhibited by fathers and ministers and even a prim little wife, it will not go forever without finding its moment of eruption. The story merely gives us that moment. As Brown's Devil is nothing more than the emergence of his most unpuritanical unconscious, so the witch meeting in the forest is pure fantasy—for Brown as surely as for his creator. It is not insistently sexual for nothing.

---

26. For Melville's response to "Young Goodman Brown" (YGB), see "Hawthorne and his Mosses," conveniently reprinted in the Norton Critical Edition of *Moby-Dick*, Harrison Hayford and Hershel Parker, eds. (New York: W. W. Norton, 1967), pp. 535–51.

And no one should be surprised if Hawthorne chooses the moralistic world of latter-day Puritanism to stand for the problem Freud called "Civilization and its Discontents."[27]

"Be it so, if you will" (288), as the narrator says in response to his own proposed reduction of Brown's twilight-zone experience: There is no reason to suppose Hawthorne believed in the Devil any more literally than do we ourselves; nor need we resist according him a certain prescience about the silent power of sexuality in controlling our motives and centering our identity. Yet Hawthorne's Puritan sources were very much concerned with the question of diabolical agency, and perhaps this provides some other clue to the violence and speed of Brown's rebellious outburst.

It may be only a rare historical joke that the tale evokes Brown's visit to the forest in one of Puritanism's most famous self-descriptions—an "errand" (276) into the "wilderness" (283),[28] but elsewhere the language is as apt as it is official. What it insists is that, however we describe the Devil that erupts from Goodman Brown at the moment of his "horrid blasphemy" (284), another Devil has been conjured well in advance; and that, for all our sense that Brown gets more than he has bargained for, there has indeed been a bargain. From which Goodman Brown tries, at first, to back out: "Friend, [...] having kept covenant by meeting thee here, it is my purpose now to return whence I came" (278).

Brown could hardly have used a more telling and technical word to describe his agreement with the figure who leads him along the forest path. In his world, "covenant" named not only the pact the Calvinist God had made with Christ, by which his obedient sacrifice came to count as reparation for the sins of mankind, but also the agreement by which the saints accepted this vicarious atonement. It served, further, as a mystic substitute for terms like contract or compact in the Puritan's consensual theory of government. And most pointedly, it named the origin and essence of the particular church or congregation. Other churches might claim to exist on some a priori or "catholic" basis, but Puritan churches came into being only when self-professing saints enacted a covenant, among themselves and with God, to walk in His ways. Thus, as historians of witchcraft have pointed out, it could serve to name that unspeakable agreement by which reprobates might swear to walk, antithetically, in the ways of His Archenemy.[29] Well may Goodman Brown hope *this* covenant is not yet sealed.

---

27. For more or less Freudian readings of YGB, see Crews, *Sins*, pp. 98–106; Reginald Cook, "The Forest of Goodman Brown's Night," *New England Quarterly*, 43 (1970), pp. 473–81; and Edward Jayne, "Pray Tarry with Me Young Goodman Brown," *Literature and Psychology*, 29 (1979), pp. 100–113. For a newer style of (Lacanian) analysis, see Elizabeth Wright, "The New Psychoanalysis and Literary Criticism," *Poetics Today*, 3 (1982), pp. 89–105.

28. "Errand into the Wilderness" titles an election sermon delivered in Massachusetts in 1670 by Samuel Danforth; in after years, that much referenced sermon lent its title to one of Perry Miller's most probing inquiries into the Puritans' original motive and latter-day morale. For a brief application, see Bill Christopherson, "YGB as Historical Allegory," *Studies in Short Fiction*, 23 (1986), pp. 202–4.

29. For the full *valeur* of "covenant" in the Puritan world, see Perry Miller, *The New England Mind: The Seventeenth Century* (Cambridge, MA: Harvard University Press, 1939), pp. 365–462. As Miller notes elsewhere, "the heinousness of [the] crime [of witchcraft] was the fact that

The fact that Brown manages to avoid parodic baptism *in nomine diaboli* suggests that it is not. And indeed the initial intention of his "errand" seems more tentative than simply to "go over." In the more easily supposable case, someone still failing, after a long and anxious time, to discover any trustworthy signs of election by God might grow desperate; in this mood he might get word that, though God's was surely the only covenant *in town*, there was another, inverted one, off in the forest. The reader of *The Scarlet Letter* will recall that Mistress Hibbins appeals to a despairing Hester Prynne in just such terms; and though Hester resists, the appeal might be very strong indeed. Orthodoxy stoutly held that whole lives might have to be lived out with no assurance beyond that of hope itself, but imagination inferred that here and there some "Ishmael" might despair of ever being recognized as one of God's adopted—declaring, in the formula Emerson made bold to appropriate, "If I am the Devil's child, I will live then from the Devil"; and most suitably, perhaps, if that tortured "I" could share the misery Dickinson called that "white sustenance, despair." A terrible prospect, yet perhaps "a guilty identity [...] was better than none."[30]

But the story of Goodman Brown is a turn more subtle. Setting out for the forest, Brown feels guilty enough about his purposes, yet feels confident that he can make his little visit with impunity: After this one short venture into the Devil's territory, he can safely come back to town, to Faith, to everything as it was. His experiment appears to prove this impossible, but it also suggests, to him at least, that his sense of salvation may have been an illusion all along. And it is this "discovery" which turns his curiosity about the Invisible World into an express confession of diabolical loyalty. Which he then tries to take back.

Brown's wife—Faith, "aptly named," but not yet an allegory we can quite construe—entreats him to "tarry" with her on this "of all nights in the year"; perhaps it is October 31, when evil influences were known to be abroad. But he converts concern into suspicion: "dost thou doubt me already, and we but three months married!" And this curious mood of moral dis-ease continues. His heart smites him, understandably, for leaving his wife "on such an errand!" He even wonders whether "a dream had warned her what work is to be done to-night." But as there is no evidence of this, we infer that Brown's guilt is nervously imagining things. Then, the moment after this recognizable attack of guilty projection,[31] Brown goes on to settle his conscience and compose our allegory: "Well, she's a blessed angel on earth; and after this one night, I'll cling to her skirts and follow her to heaven" (276).

There is a question of gender here, of course, as Brown imagines his wife as a different sort of moral being. But—as it is "with this excellent resolve for the future [that]

---

it, like regeneration, took the form of a covenant"; see *The New England Mind: From Colony to Province* (Cambridge, MA: Harvard University Press, 1953), p. 193.

30. For the theology of Ishmael (and Isaac), see Thomas Werge, "*Moby-Dick* and the Calvinist Tradition," *Studies in the Novel*, 1 (1969), pp. 484–506. The Emerson quotation is from "Self-Reliance," the Dickinson from "I cannot live with you" (640). The verdict about a "guilty identity" is adapted from that of Crews on Hawthorne himself (*Sins*, p. 38).

31. For the psychology of projection in Hawthorne, see Crews, *Sins, esp.* pp. 53–60.

Goodman Brown felt himself justified in making more haste on his present evil purpose" (276)—there is also the problem theologians have called "presumption," the act of declaring one's salvation already certain, whatever might occur in the rest of one's mortal life. Earlier theorists called it an "unpardonable sin," not because it was the most heinous act or thought they could imagine, but because it made nonsense out of their notion of life, all of it, as a period of testing, during which one might, at any moment, turn one's mind toward or away from the will of God.[32] And not surprisingly, Calvinist thinkers kept having to explain that their idea of eternal predestination, based not on merit, but bestowed as the gift of faith, was not just the latest invitation to this familiar moral evasion. Feeling "justified"—the technical word for one's gratuitous acceptance by God—was scarcely an excuse for laxity or experimentation. For one thing, individual assurance could never be perfect; and for another, it needed to be read from the quality of one's ethical dispositions.[33] Certainly, therefore, the Calvinists did not intend a moral holiday. Yet they may have opened a crack in the wall of perfect behavior. And Goodman Brown appears to be creeping out at that crack, suspending the ordinary rules for a brief period, but trusting in his safety after all; assuming salvation, it appears, in spite of his devilish transgression. "Presuming on Faith," the conscience of official Puritanism might angrily declare; and invalidating the mystical "Marriage" into the bargain. "I told you so," the older system might smugly observe, and deepen its sense of triumph when Goodman Brown goes on to "despair," the only *other* unpardonable sin; the other way, that is, of nullifying the moral life at a stroke.

Yet Brown's despair is scarcely the normative case. Typically, an individual became aware of sins too great to be forgiven by God himself; this looked like an extreme of humility, but was really a bizarre form of pride, as its anatomists never tired of pointing out. Or else, as we have suggested, a Puritan might simply crack under the strain and accept the worst-case scenario. But Brown's problem is not at all a matter of such gloomy introspection; rather, with the help of his Devil, he comes to suspect the settled appearance of virtue in all his most familiar acquaintances. Then, undone by this challenge to the assumptions of his whole life, he despairs of the possibility of goodness in the world.

---

32. For a review of the traditional theology of presumption and despair as applied to YBG, see Joseph T. McCullen, "YGB: Presumption and Despair," *Discourse*, 2 (1959), pp. 145–57.
33. The so-called Antinomian Controversy (of 1636–38)—subtly evoked by Hawthorne's sketch of "Mrs. Hutchinson" (1830)—settled the point that, despite the public objections of Ann Hutchinson and the fine distinctions of John Cotton, "sanctification" (the observable ability to obey divine law) would clearly follow as a proper effect of "justification" (the private revelation of a person's acceptance by God); see Miller, *Seventeenth Century*, pp. 389–92; Edmund S. Morgan, *Puritan Dilemma* (Boston, MA: Little Brown, 1958), pp. 134–54; and William K. B. Stoever, *A Faire and Easie Way to Heaven* (Middletown, CT: Wesleyan University Press, 1978), esp. pp. 21–33. For application of these concerns to YGB, see James W. Matthews, "Antinomianism in YGB," *Studies in Short Fiction*, 3 (1965), pp. 73–75; Claudia G. Johnson, "YGB and Puritan Justification," *Studies in Short Fiction*, 11 (1974), pp. 200–203; and Jane Donahue Eberwein, "'My Faith Is Gone': YGB and Puritan Conversion," *Christianity and Literature*, 32 (1982), pp. 23–32.

And so fast that his logic—and our explanation—must be embedded in the terms of Puritan history.

Most simply, perhaps, in the doctrine of "visible sanctity." No fool and no mad zealot, the Puritan knew there were "hypocrites" in the churches of New England. These churches had as their explicit aim to be the purest the world had seen since the Savior had elected His own handpicked disciples. Even He had got one "Judas," and so even the most careful of men in these latter days could hardly fail to make mistakes. But members of Puritan churches who were not Saints—who dissembled or who were simply mistaken about their call from God—were to be the exception. Formally so, since by rule one had to give a public account of this call in order to be taken into "communing" membership. Elsewhere, churches might exist to *produce* saints, little by little; but in the New World Order, churches existed to identify, with all human precision, those whom God *called* to be saints, and to bring them together, visibly, into an exemplary order of holy community.[34]

Trained by their system to recognize one another, the Saints came to rely on one another for support of all kinds. Particularly, perhaps, for mutual sanction: One could *hardly* be sure of one's own election, all by oneself, particularly when the evidences of faith were so much more subtle than the older standard of behavior; then too, if one thought about it, there was the whole Anglo-Catholic world one had left behind, scorning the Calvinist theology of total depravity and irresistible grace as an insult to moral sense, and spurning as utopian the doctrine of visible sanctity. But if the whole group held together in these beliefs, the faith of all might stand. Forswearing the intermediation of priest and sacrament, the Puritan might yet find himself comparing notes: our *nature* is evil, as witness our former lives, but has not God's *grace* introduced a principle of goodness? Truly so? In my *own* case? Well, other people might recognize the grace shining forth from one's halting profession more surely than oneself; and *their* conviction—necessary to admit the would-be saint to the bosom of Faith in any event—might become the surest basis of one's own.

What this interdependency implies is the irreducibly social dimension of Puritan faith, even in so private a fact as one's election.[35] For what if an unhappy Puritan found

---

34. For the uniqueness of the "congregational" polity, see Miller, *Seventeenth Century*, pp. 432–62; and Edmund S. Morgan, *Visible Saints* (Ithaca, NY: Cornell University Press, 1963), pp. 1–112. The remnants of this system lasted well into Hawthorne's own century, but the basis of his scholarly knowledge of the problem may well have been Book 5 ("Acts and Monuments of the Faith and Order in the Churches of New England") of Cotton Mather's *Magnalia Christi Americana* (London: Thomas Parkhurst, 1702).

35. Though Miller implies that the Puritans' "subjective insight" and "obsession with individuality" *(Seventeenth Century*, p. 22) are balanced by their sense of the particular church as "the center of a communal system" where "the fraternity was made one by their mutual and irrevocable pledge" (p. 443), we still lack a convincing account of the overwhelming commitment to community we sense in the pages of Bradford's *Plymouth Plantation* and Winthrop's "Model of Christian Charity." For the best available study of the social dynamics of the profession of "saving faith"—made for the judgment and edification of the entire congregation—see Patricia Caldwell, *The Puritan Conversion Narrative* (Cambridge: Cambridge University Press, 1983), esp. pp. 45–116.

occasion to doubt the good faith of those very individuals whose assurance of salvation had become so entwined with his own? Honestly explored, these doubts might go straight to the source of his own assurance. Even less radically applied, however, they would amount to a suspicion that the covenanting procedures of the particular church had been an empty formality, unable to discover any appreciable difference between the persons one "had met at the communion table" and those seen "rioting at the tavern" (283). Would this experience not threaten all one believed? Might it not bring on, with only some hyperbole, the nihilistic rejection of everything?

So it turns out for Goodman Brown. And so his particular Devil seems to have foreknown, as the climax of his commencement address only confirms the sense of Brown's mid-forest outburst: Evil is indeed "the nature of mankind," as Calvin's theory of depravity has prepared you to discover; and now, as there *is* no such thing as regenerating grace, "Evil must be your only happiness." But the Devil's word to the initiates has another note as well. His welcome to the Community of Evil is, before all else, a farewell to the covenantal delusion: "Depending on one another's hearts, ye had hoped, that virtue were not all a dream. Now are ye undeceived!" (287). And—among all the losses of faith that are possible—this "congregational" circumstance contributes powerfully to making Brown's loss a particularly memorable instance.

Equally important, however, is the logic which effects that undeception. We follow well enough the steps by which Brown comes to feel that he and Faith are "the only pair . . . yet hesitating on the verge of wickedness" (287). If all these trusted and familiar Saints turn out to be the Devil's own, then so must the rest of this wretched world as well. But what *of* those supposed Saints? Has Goodman Brown been reliably informed about their true allegiance? Are they indeed all in league with the Prince of Darkness? Or is there reason to suppose that Brown has been deceived? Could there be something wrong with his evidence, even where plain sight has supplied an ocular proof?

We might begin by recalling that not all that evidence has been visible. The process begins, in fact, with hearsay, a couple of stories about the misdeeds of Brown's ancestors; and though it moves on from there, to the sight of the irreverent Goody Cloyse and the lascivious church officers, there seems no marked change of mood or conviction. The Devil is prosecuting his proper case, and Brown's responses are perfectly continuous: sad business, but no rule for the likes of a "simple husbandman" (279) like me; and besides, there's always "My Faith." Then come the pink ribbons, and it's all over but the blasphemous shouting. Yet not even these most material objects can quite disturb the reader's sense of a single shape and direction—a single epistemology—of the whole sequence. If there is a climax, it involves the ordering of the persons charged rather than the evidence presented. It is as if the line between imagination and being, perception and conviction, suspicion and proof had entirely disappeared; as if one had merely to lead Brown's attention from one fantastic projection to another.

Certainly this impression will be strongest in the reader who notices that none of the characters Brown meets on the forest path seems to cast a shadow, and that they appear and disappear in the most remarkably convenient manner, as if conjured by the Companion's "snakelike staff" (279). Curiosity about this magical quality ought to be enhanced by the observation that each of these exemplary apparitions is referred to as a "figure" or a "shape," as if to reserve judgment on their proper mode of existence. And it is precisely in this mood that a reader may profit to discover—in a learned article by David Levin—the antique doctrine of "specters," those mysterious simulacra of physical appearance which made it possible for persons to appear in places remote from their locus of true and substantial being. And to learn, too, of the controversy, in Brown's own (third-generation) New England, about the Devil's power to manipulate these spectral appearances.[36]

Most authorities taught that the Devil regularly did assume the shape of his sworn disciples—whenever he went abroad to carry out their guilty wishes. And this understanding made it possible for the witch accusers to maintain their allegations against persons who could otherwise account for their whereabouts: I must have seen their *specters*. The crisis arose when someone thought to ask whether the Devil had the power to assume the shape of a person who had *not* freely chosen his covenant, to cause a Saint to appear in the most compromising of places and postures. The magistrates appointed to conduct the proceedings against the accused witches thought a just God would never permit the exercise of a power so fatal to the cause of human faith. But a panel of experts returned the opinion that the Devil might well enjoy that very power: What else could Scripture mean by declaring that "the Devil has appeared as an Angel of Light"?

The story of the events which followed the proclamation of this unsettling possibility has held a terrible fascination for those who have pursued the historical record—including Arthur Miller, whose dramatic rendition (in *The Crucible*) has caused the metaphor of "witch hunt" to stand for all sorts of accusations which admit no refutation. Here, however, there are no courtroom recriminations; and no hint of that general breakdown of faith Hawthorne elsewhere refers to as a "Universal Madness riot in the Main-street" (1047). Only the possibility that Brown may be witnessing not the real activities of his fellow congregationalists but only the meretricious antics of their spectral shapes. We cannot be sure.[37]

In his running contest with the Devil, Goodman Brown has tried to make it all depend on his "Faith"; and so in the end it does, though in a way his presumptuous confidence had little prepared him to expect. Did Faith indeed "look up to heaven and resist the Wicked One"? Was she in fact even there? Or was it her specter, stolen by the Devil for

---

36. See "Shadows of Doubt: Specter Evidence in Hawthorne's YGB," *American Literature*, 34 (1962), pp. 344–52. Levin provides an extremely useful collection of texts and documents related to the "spectral" question of 1692 in *What Happened in Salem* (New York: Harcourt, Brace & World, 1960). For a full-scale account of YGB as a crisis in the Puritan theory of evidence, see Colacurcio, *Province*, pp. 283–313 (bibliography, pp. 610–17). And for an attempt to generalize the notion of spectrality to cover the question of history, see Budick, *Historical Consciousness*, pp. 79–97.

37. This "undecidability" lends some credence to a "postmodern" reading; see, for example, Christopher D. Morris, "Deconstructing YGB," *American Transcendental Quarterly*, 2 (1988), pp. 22–33. And yet, as Goodman Brown is forced to make *some* decision, the story appears to concern faith more properly than signifiers. Clearly (in any case) it is shortsighted to claim that the issue of specter evidence causes us to blame the Devil and excuse Goodman Brown; see Paul J. Hurley, "YGB's 'Heart of Darkness,'" *New England Quarterly*, 37 (1966), pp. 410–19.

the express purpose of tempting the faith of Goodman Brown? He never can know. She may well be as innocent as Shakespeare's Desdemona—whose innocence, as a modern reading has observed, can never be known by Othello in the same way that *she herself* knows it.[38] Nor can the story itself inform us without entirely compromising its own epistemology: We never do know the intentions of others, not as they themselves know them. As intentional reality is hidden, so all moral appearances are in an important sense spectral: We observe the shape but do not behold the substance. Best to reserve judgment, therefore, ascribing to others, always, the same degree of good faith we habitually discern in ourselves; best to assume that others' resistance to Evil is about equal to our own.

Doubt, in this sense, becomes the source of, even participates in, the nature of faith: The negative term signifies only our unhappiness about the fact that we cannot know certain things for sure; the positive one, our recognition that we have nevertheless to make up our minds and act. All Goodman Brown can know, in the end, is that, after keeping his initial covenant, he recoiled from the Devil's baptism; he flirted with the power of Evil, so to speak, but did not in the end espouse it. Might he not suppose that the wishes of his wife have been equally hypothetical? Failing this sort of ascriptive trust, his final gloom reveals nothing so plainly as the lasting effect of his initial bad faith: The guilty self-knowledge which caused him to suspect Faith of suspecting him assumes its settled form in doubting the victory of her virtue. The problem has its "psychoanalytic" side, of course, but it requires less than a full course of "analysis." For if Brown's bad faith puts forth, from the beginning, the textbook traits of "guilty projection," the same must be said of Spenser's Red Cross Knight, whose deception by the "dreamy" machinations of Archimago had long since suggested that specter evidence is but a curious name for the shameless tendency to discover in others, as fact, the guilty wish we repress in ourselves.[39] And more important, in any case, may be Hawthorne's historical re-application of this Spenserian principle – to a set of theological circumstances that matter as much as the more political ones in "Molineux" and "Malvin."

Not that Hawthorne has solved the question of "What Happened in Salem." It is worth noting that, where his contemporaries tried to rationalize the problem of witchcraft—by invoking the quasimedical notion of "hysteria," or by appealing to the pseudo-historical idea of "superstition"—Hawthorne is careful to let this limit phenomenon retain something of its terrible wonder.[40] We learn to suspect that people who discover witches are telling us more about themselves than about the persons they accuse; but "Young Goodman Brown" has nothing to say about what persons did and did not indulge this self-betraying behavior.

---

38. See Stanley Cavell, *In Quest of the Ordinary* (Chicago: University of Chicago Press, 1988), p. 55.
39. For Spenser's influence on Hawthorne's theme of specter evidence, see John Schroeder, "Alice Doane's Story: An Essay on Hawthorne and Spenser," *Nathaniel Hawthorne Journal*, 4 (1974), pp. 129–34; and Colacurcio, *Province*, pp. 84–85, 295–97.
40. For the inceptive version of the nineteenth-century view of the Salem witchcraft as a combination of outmoded superstition and the deleterious influence of Cotton Mather, see Charles W. Upham, *Lectures on Witchcraft* (Boston: Carter, Hender, and Babock, 1831).

What this taut little tale observes, instead, is that the discovery of Saints and the detection of witches were parts of the same problem, that specter evidence was simply the negative test case of visible sanctity. In morally opposite but epistemologically identical instances, certain official persons needed to make reliable judgments about the soul *in extremis*. Beyond actions, which are various; beyond even intentions, which may be fleeting and even whimsical; the Puritan had to identify the deep spiritual orientation of another person. Here is a soul, solemnly requesting admission to the sacrament which sets the seal on the mystery of salvation: Is it sworn to God, finally, beyond all possibility of change or mistake? Or, as the curiously unfolding historical plot suddenly reversed itself, has it perhaps made that other oath? Sooner or later, in the latter, parodic instance if not in the former, normative one, this dedicated group of religionists would surely discover that their most important judgments were all more or less projective. Needing to know what cannot certainly be known—the true spiritual estate of another person—such judges must put in the place where literal "in-sight" is denied a hypothetical version of their own relevant experience.

In the matter of Puritan church admissions, the official insistence that everyone exercise the "judgment of charity" came close to recognizing the peril: judge the faith of others, always, by the light of one's own best faith. But then, by a reversal of logic and a lapse of sympathy one notes without quite understanding, the witchcraft proceedings of 1692 seemed to invert their own rule: Saints are known by faith but witches by suspicion. Indeed, Brown's swift progress—from believing in those who have believed in him, to doubting all virtue but his own—seems invented to mimic the outline of this definitive Puritan dilemma. And though we can learn to state this problem in some remarkably general ways, the story itself seems remarkably loyal to its very own circumstances. By its logic, the history of the lapsed Faith of Puritanism remains a capital way of learning the benefit of doubt.

Chapter Five

"LIFE WITHIN THE LIFE": SIN AND SELF IN HAWTHORNE'S NEW ENGLAND

Few critics have been as enthusiastic about the interpretative possibilities of Hawthorne's two "Allegories of the Heart" as Melville's famous review of "Hawthorne and His Mosses" suggested they ought to be. The assertion of a "mystical blackness" has become famous enough; so has the premise of a lurking sense of "Puritanic gloom." Even the ascription of something *like* a "Calvinistic sense of Innate Depravity and Original Sin" has generated its fair share of critical responses. But these suggestions have been easier to associate with "Young Goodman Brown," which overwhelms the emphasis of the second installment of Melville's famous review, than with "Egotism; or the Bosom Serpent" and "The Christmas Banquet," the curious pair of stories that actually inspired these famous remarks.[1] "Egotism" has seemed prime evidence that the "historical" premises of Hawthorne's earlier tales generate more plausible fictions than those odd maxims floating free in his notebooks: "A man to swallow a small snake—and it to be a symbol of a cherished sin"; and the "Banquet" which follows, more sketch than tale, more list than either, seems chiefly to demonstrate that the earliest of Hawthorne's brief imaginings, in the 1820s and 30s, are uniformly more powerful than those produced in his "Old Manse Period."[2]

The first, more gothic and grotesque member of this deliberate pairing has compelled an energetic corps of source-hunters, who have discovered, among other things, that Roderick Elliston's curious disease is but one case in a veritable epidemic of snakes and worms in the bosom, breast, or stomach; and also, more surprisingly, that the plight of Hawthorne's victim owes more than a little to the real-life career of fellow Salemite, Jones Very; but neither these worldly facts nor the barely repressed hint of an available Spenserian moral has prompted its commentators to emphasize and sponsor its thematic

---

1. See Herman Melville, "Hawthorne and His Mosses," in Herschel Parker and Harrison Hayford, eds., *Moby-Dick* (New York: Norton, 2002), pp. 521–22. For the early critical history of Melville's suggestions, see my own *Province of Piety* (Durham, NC: Duke University Press, 1994), pp. 5–36.
2. For the allegorical germ of "Egotism; or The Bosom Serpent" (EBS), see Hawthorne's *American Notebooks* (Columbus: Ohio State University Press, 1972), p. 228; and for the earlier formulation—"a type of envy or some other evil passion"—p. 22. For a sense of Hawthorne's distinct "periods" of tale writing, see R. P. Adams, "Hawthorne: The Old Manse Period," *Tulane Studies in English*, 8 (1958), pp. 114–51; John J. McDonald, "The Old Manse Period Canon," *Nathaniel Hawthorne Journal*, 2 (1972), pp. 13–40; also "'The Old Manse' and Its Mosses," *Texas Studies in Language and Literature*, 16 (1974), pp. 77–108; and Nina Baym, *The Shape of Hawthorne's Career* (Ithaca, NY: Cornell University Press, 1976), esp. pp. 84–122.

teaching. Its companion piece, though intriguingly the narrative product of the man just cured of his snaky plague, and authorized somehow by that curious fact, has attracted very few professional readers of any sort. Nor—in a world where only the most uninhibited Freudians have cared to defy the widespread rumor of Hawthorne's all-but-perfect "negative capability"—has criticism rushed in to take up the suggestion that these two tales "would be fine subjects for a curious and elaborate analysis, touching the conjectural parts of the mind that produced them."[3] A modest but mannered little diptych, our classic criticism appears to conclude, re-inscribing Hawthorne's unvarying loyalty to "the heart," trusted (if not quite theorized) as the center of vital personality, which many an inward voyager has sought and never found.

Even our best nouvelle critique, aware that we are in the near neighborhood of the encompassing modern subject of "the subject," has made less of the two tales—and of the subtle "story" of their interrelation—than Melville's excited suspicions would seem to authorize. Strangely enough, a masterful account of Hawthorne's not-always-blissful relation to the "Dearest Beloved" of his love letters makes no use of this suggestive twosome, though written in the first years of the Hawthorne's exemplary marriage, and though the two together appear first to honor and then to challenge the love-cure nineteenth-century men were increasingly required both to undergo and to confess. And our more philosophical readings have declined to investigate either the ambiguous nature of the cure proposed in "Egotism" or the odd light thrown back upon it by the tale this reformed egotist feels authorized to propose. Evidently some embarrassment remains, some tasteful unwillingness to inquire too closely into the personal source or the thematic outcome of a symbolic donnee that cannot overcome its literal self-embarrassment.[4]

Yet it remains hard to dismiss altogether Melville's suspicion that the always self-protective Hawthorne had woven a kind of ironic self-portrait of his isolated and

---

3. Melville, "Hawthorne and His Mosses," p. 540. Curiously, EBS gets only the briefest mention in the analysis of Frederick Crews, as one more instance of Hawthorne's "'matrimonial fears'"; see *Sins of the Fathers* (New York: Oxford University Press, 1966), p. 111. Gloria C. Erlich's psychoanalytic study makes no mention of the tale whatsoever; see *Family Themes and Hawthorne's Fiction* (New Brunswick, NJ: Rutgers University Press, 1984). And Edwin Haviland Miller mentions it only to quote the call for a "curious and elaborate analysis" and to observe that "What Melville intuited he kept to himself"; see *Salem Is My Dwelling Place* (Iowa City: Iowa University Press, 1991), p. 248. Relevant source studies include John W. Schroeder, "Hawthorne's 'Egotism,'" *American Literature*, 31 (1959), pp. 150–62; Robert D. Arner, "Hawthorne and Jones Very," *New England Quarterly*, 42 (1969), pp. 267–75; Sargent Bush, "Bosom Serpents before Hawthorne," *American Literature*, 43 (1971), pp. 181–99; Thomas Werge, "Thomas Shepard and Crevecoeur," *Nathaniel Hawthorne Journal*, 4 (1974), pp. 236–39; and David Van Leer, "Roderick's Other Serpent," *ESQ*, 27 (1981), pp. 73–85.
4. For an account of the personal setting in which Hawthorne might *well* have wished to speak back to the sentimental transcendentalism of his wife, see T. Walter Herbert, *Dearest Beloved* (Berkeley: University of California, 1993), esp. pp. 33–87. Modern studies of Hawthorne's sense of "the subject"—in EBS and elsewhere—include James A Wohlpart, "Allegories of Art, Allegories of the Heart," *Studies in Short Fiction*, 31 (1994), pp. 449–60; Alice Easton, *The Making of a Hawthorne Subject* (Columbia: University of Missouri, 1996), esp. pp. 136–54; Joseph Alkana, *The Social Self* (Lexington: University of Kentucky, 1997), Chapter Two; and Harvey Gable, *Liquid Fire* (Bern: Peter Lang, 1998), esp. pp. 1–70.

gloom-writing "Puritan" self into the fabric of "Egotism"—a self that needed to be redeemed, perhaps, by some sunnier female sensibility, but which might go on from the point of that rosy redemption to propose other cases of diseased selfhood that woman's love alone might fail to cure. Surely Roderick Elliston *too* required someone to open for him "an intercourse with the world" more normal than that achieved by accosting it with intimations of the depth and breadth of its guilty secrets. But clearly he as well as Hawthorne was never quite induced to turn his talent to a constant focus on the "Indian-summer sunlight" so evident on the "hither side" of many a complex soul. Beyond this, there is something insistently personal about the strategic resistance of the sequel. As modestly proposed as any tale in which the colors of real life have been sacrificed to the demands of allegory or any other ideal loyalty, "The Christmas Banquet" is more than just a proof that a soul once trapped among the dated and gloomy materials of an ancestral faith has acquired power to write the history of a soul divested of all such symbols. A loving Rosina declares the puritanically obsessed Roderick Elliston cured and, for the moment at least, the part of love can but accept the gift. But life goes on, including the life of writing. And when, one narrative instant later, Roderick rouses himself to offer for consideration the subtle outlines of a character not obsessed with but rather dissociated from himself, a certain oppositional energy is impossible to dismiss. As if the former patient should turn to the author of his cure and say, with all due respect, "cure this."

2

The first thing to notice about Elliston's snaky disease is that, though its exact psycho-biographical cause has been deliberately made hard to determine, its intellectual origin seems indeed "Puritanic." To be sure, Thomas Shepard is not the only "source" for the idea that a snake in the bosom—which "gnaws"—is an all but intuitive sign of the activity of a guilty conscience. Nor is Elliston's favorite reading matter, the seventeenth century's massive and perhaps definitive piece of "casuistry," the *Ductor Dubitantum* of Jeremy Taylor, to be reassigned from the Anglican to the Puritan column. Yet this well-known Hawthorne source accords well enough with the recognizable Puritan tendency to "make conscience" of much that others might let slide.[5] Further, the idea—the cliché, so to speak—of a snaky obsession suggests the proper domain of the Puritan, and Elliston's summary remark that "there is poisonous stuff in any man's heart, sufficient to generate a brood of serpents" (793)[6] might be taken as a slogan of the New England Puritans down to Edward Taylor. Then too, the argument about whether Elliston's snake could somehow have been inherited or must be regarded as his very "own snake, and no man

---

5. For Hawthorne's early fascination with the "casuistry" of Jeremy Taylor, see Neal Frank Doubleday, "The Theme of Hawthorne's 'Fancy's Show Box,'" *AL*, 10 (1938), pp. 431–33; also *Hawthorne's Early Tales* (Durham, NC: Duke University Press, 1972), pp. 151, 155–57. And for a more general treatment of Hawthorne and the diseases of conscience, see Austin Warren, *The New England Conscience* (Ann Arbor: University of Michigan Press, 1966), pp. 132–42; and cp. my own *Province*, pp. 107–14.
6. All citations of EBS and CB refer to *Hawthorne: Tales and Sketches* (New York: Library of America, 1996).

else's" sounds a lot like an ironic reference to New England's self-baffling arguments about original sin, from Edwards' austere identity-philosophy down to the more recent, more sentimental "Wood 'n Ware Controversy" of the 1820s. Indeed it is just possible to suspect that Elliston's reading in the "natural history of the serpent tribe" (792) refers obliquely to a book like Mather's *Magnalia*, a "tribalist" history, in all historical conscience, and of a people who knew how to give the serpent his due.[7]

More generally, however, it is easy to see that Roderick Elliston, an exemplary victim, has become obsessed with "himself," and that under the aspect of sin and guilt, like someone who has had the spiritual misfortune to get stuck in the preparatory or "true sight of sin" phase of the Puritan morphology of conversion—predictably, perhaps, and exactly as Sacvan Bercovitch has suggested in his classic derivation of the "Puritan Origins of the American Self."[8] The locus of all sin, the particular, self-interested (fallen) self, is exactly the thing the would-be saint needs to be rid of; but evidently it is possible to settle in and work on the problem just there, day and night, with all the might and main an aroused consciousness can muster, only to find one has dug a hole one cannot climb out of; or, less metaphorically, fabricated a discourse so powerfully descriptive of the soul's first spiritual awareness that it comes to seem the very substance of that notoriously occult entity. And so one goes about, noxiously bewailing but also thereby emphasizing, even advertising one's unhappy plight and grimly ascribing it to all the less conscience-stricken souls one happens to meet. Even down to the nineteenth century. There, it appears, as audience unskilled in the discrimination of self-reference—and anxious, as it appears, to avoid all hint of guilty self-knowledge—can see nothing in such extravagant behavior except an egotism maddened to the point of monstrosity; and no solution except to call the police. Nothing like the impolite idea of sin to disturb the peace of Vanity Fair.[9]

A fictional century earlier, the histrionic and somewhat aggressive gestures of a certain Parson Hooper, similarly driven to make public his "awakened" Puritan vision of the sin we are, provoked, in the jargon of emergent medical enlightenment, the minority opinion that "'Something must surely be amiss with [his] intellects.'" Yet not even the local

---

7. Significantly, Mather's *Magnalia* has been identified as one of Hawthorne's bosom-serpent sources; see Morton L. Ross, "Hawthorne's Bosom Serpent and Mather's *Magnalia*," *ESQ*, 47 (1967), p. 13. For the ironies of the "Wood 'n Ware Controversy"—including the "owning" of original sin—see Joseph Haroutunian, *Piety Versus Moralism* (New York: Henry Holt, 1932), pp. 208–16; and cp. H. Shelton Smith, *Changing Conceptions of Original Sin* (New York: Scribner's, 1955), pp. 60–85. For a fair sample of the liberal logic, see the selection from Henry Ware in Sydney E. Ahlstrom and Jonathan S. Carey, eds., *An American Reformation* (Middleton, CT: Wesleyan University Press, 1985), pp. 199–209. All citations of "Egotism; or The Bosom Serpent" (EBS) and "The Christmas Banquet" (CB) refer to the Library of America edition of *Hawthorne: Tales and Sketches* (1996).
8. Observing that Puritan "humility is coextensive with personal assertion" (p. 18), Bercovitch argues that the first authentic version of American selfhood was a product of a language that expressed an ineluctable and (old-)self-defining sinfulness; see *Puritan Origins of the American Self* (New Haven, CT: Yale University Press, 1975), pp. 1–34.
9. According to "The Celestial Rail-road," Liberal Religion needs to avoid not only the mythology of hell but also the entire psychology of sin, guilt, repentance, and atonement; only so can it avoid giving "shock" to the modern "sensibility": see *Tales and Sketches*, p. 810.

physician was altogether immune to the unsettling moral implications of the minister's veiled suggestions; and, delivered from the sanction of the regular pulpit, the religious insult to common sense called forth only a deputation from the less comprehending half of his congregation—who, in the baffled failure of their reasonable attempts to get their "good parson" to say his meaning without recourse to symbol, could look for relief only to the consensual determinations of a "general synod."[10] Here, however, in a more self-assured age of Hawthorne's peculiar province of piety, where moral disturbance is easier to recognize as social deviance, Elliston is roundly declared a "pest to the city" (789), and—after several quackish and unsuccessful attempts to get him to eliminate some literal snake—is sent off, temporarily at least, to nourish his snaky guilt in the local hospital for the civilly insane.

In the footsteps of Jones Very, as we have been suitably instructed: detecting and delivering one's neighbors of their "bosom idol," that conversion-blocking trait of natural selfhood with which they most identify and so will *not* agree to surrender, not even to the power of God's very spirit—might seem a curious and interesting game when played quietly and among good friends but probably not when loudly obtruded upon the notice of one's Classics Professor.[11] And all that keeps the author of "The Minister's Black Veil" himself from suffering a similar fate, particularly with our modern students who have managed to outlive the sense of sin, is the fact that the setting of his insistence on the *moral* truth of the black veil's ambiguous evocation of "sin or sorrow" is fiction and not social practice.

Or is it also because Hawthorne allowed himself to be cured of the obsessions nourished so fatally in the "dismal and squalid" upper chamber of his mother's family home, which came to stand not only for effective imagination but also for the solipsistic sort of art which understood only the world of its own creation? There, by his own estimate, "fame was won" but relational identity, as he also confessed, was all but lost. So that if the publication, in 1837, of the *Twice-Told Tales* did manage to "open an intercourse" between the world and "the obscurest man of letters in America," it did so in large part because it identified the author of anonymous and pseudonymous magazine tales—this failure to publish at least three earlier "projected collections"—to the citizens of his native Salem, to the Peabody family not the least, from among whom he would eventually find his way to his proper (perhaps too proper) wife. And so that, even if we blush to translate Hawthorne's "squalid" as Hyatt Waggoner's "masturbatory,"[12] we know that

---

10. See "The Minister's Black Veil," in *Tales and Sketches*, pp. 374, 377. For a full reading of MBV in this historical spirit, see my *Province*, pp. 314–85.
11. For the curious career of Salem's self-appointed diagnostician of the all-but-universal disease of the "bosom idol," see Edwin Gittleman, *Jones Very: The Effective Years, 1833-1840* (New York: Columbia University Press, 1967), pp. 215–87.
12. For commentary on Sophia Hawthorne's editing the word "squalid" out of this famous self-analysis in the Notebooks, see Hyatt H. Waggoner, *The Presence of Hawthorne* (Lafayette: Louisiana State University Press, 1979), pp. 98–118; see also Crews, *Sins*, p. 113. For the claim that collected publication ended both his obscurity and his unhealthy solitariness, see Hawthorne's Preface to the 1851 edition of *Twice-Told Tales* (Columbus: Ohio State University Press, 1974), pp. 6, 3.

the love letters are not just begging for sex when they thank Sophia for saving him from the self-enclosing fate he seemed so long to have been courting.

Shall we not say, in short, that he let himself be led, down from a too curious and lonely meditation on the self-analyses and indeed the sins of the fathers and out into the "refulgent" summer-world of New England in the days just before the death of Emerson's glorious son and Thoreau's beloved brother? For what but some Rosina-like cure for his quasi-puritanic ailment is Hawthorne confessing when he ascribes to the self-awakening of Sophia, the new created beginning of his own "real life"? Without which, he passionately confesses, his best self-knowledge "would have been merely to know my own shadow—to watch it flickering on the wall."[13] Historical criticism will un-forget the essential Plato, far behind, but Sophia's present-day transcendentalism would recognize her own idiom on the instant. The only question, really, is whether she would recognize its re-inscription in the ironic epithalamium her husband was yet to write.

Sophia is both more and less than the women who show up in the proper "tales" of the Old Manse Period: more capable of appreciating her husband's complex relation to "the beautiful" than the simple-hearted Annie Hovenden-Danforth, who loves a blacksmith's baby much better than The Artist's mechanical butterfly; worshipful, in fact, of her transcendently wonderful artist-husband, but too sensible—too pious, in fact—to allow herself to be objectified by any experiment in fastidious perfectionism; and, pale and semi-invalid that she was, never unconscious of the power of female sexuality. She is more than enough to account for the idyllic side of "The New Adam and Eve"; and to inspire, by the swelling size of her pregnant belly, the delight taken in the "vegetable progeny" of the garden at the Old Manse and insistence (by the somewhat less biographical narrator of "The Hall of Fantasy") on a "great round solid" world that is more real to the touch than in their idea.[14] No doubt her regimen of headaches prevents *The Scarlet Letter* from being more monochromatically gray than it is; and the delicacy of her esthetic determines that the masterwork of Puritan gloom will be followed by a book that is both "sunnier" and "more proper" for a happily married man to write.[15]

Yet not even that magnificent (if delayed) tribute is without a certain backstroke of resistance. In debt to and in honor of the luminous innocence and spiritual potency of the "Dove" of the Love Letters, this most slender Pyncheon-protagonist of *The House of the Seven Gables* manages, in a series of chapters devoted to her relation to each of the

---

13. In what is probably the most famous of all his hyperbolic yet painfully self-revelatory "love letters" to Sophia Peabody (October 4, 1840), Hawthorne credits his beloved fiancée (already called "wife") with—hardly less than the salvation of his soul—the recovery, or perhaps even the creation, of his "real" identity. The "lonely chamber" expressed youth and literary vision but also a solitude and seclusion deep enough to be called an imprisonment. Then the heart was touched and that "touch" created his real being. How odd, therefore, to hear someone call this touch of loving otherness an "idea."
14. See *Tales and Sketches*, pp. 1131–33, 744.
15. For Sophia's "grievous" response to Hawthorne's reading of the ending of *The Scarlet Letter*, see David Leverenz, *Manhood and the American Renaissance* (Ithaca, NY: Cornell University Press, 1989), pp. 259–78; and cp. Herbert, *Beloved*, pp. 208–9. For Hawthorne's determination to produce a "sunnier book," see Baym, *Shape*, pp. 152–54.

other main characters, to begin the redemption of each and all of the other occupants of the ancestral mansion; and the formal indication of her talismanic power lies in the fact that the ugliest Pyncheon of the present cannot force his plans to their depraved conclusion as long as she remains within the house that embodies their unhappy inheritance. Surely this new, more fictional Phoebe is the prettiest compliment a sick-souled artist ever paid to a "once-born" wife.[16] But as her innocence needs to be instructed, in the public and social manifestation of "something, somehow like original sin," it becomes the part of Holgrave to keep showing her pictures she does not wish to see—daguerreotypes which, seeing only what the sun sees, manage nevertheless to suggest that natural joy and a New England instinct for neatness are not the only inheritances of the human spirit. "A girl learns many things in New England," to be sure, but without the proper artist-historian as husband, not enough about the darker underside of the sprightly New England soul. Phoebe's "cheerful little body" may be the slender grace that redeems both her lover and her lineage, but without being forced to face the unpleasant facts of life and death and history. As if Hawthorne had insisted on marrying the resistant audience he plainly gendered female as early as "Alice Doane's Appeal."[17]

Just so, it makes some sense here to look closely at the cure that Rosina so confidently pronounces. It may seem mean-spirited, even in the wake of the deconstruction of the Hawthornes' ideal middle-class marriage, to notice the family reference of the Narrator's observation—in the name of morphological completeness, as it otherwise seems—that "All persons, chronically diseased, are egotists, whether the disease be of the mind or body" (785): where is it written that chronic headaches serve to efface the ego of the sufferer?[18] But surely it is necessary to ask why, when Elliston asserts that, in order to be saved from his "diseased self-contemplation," he would need to "forget [him]self," Rosina bids him, so earnestly, to "forget [him]self in the *idea* of another" (793, emphasis added). The famous letter to Sophia had thanked, at least metaphorically, her "touch." Literary sentiment might here have said the *arms* of another; philosophy, the *being*; the story's own repeated language, the *life*. But no: the idea. Surely this curious displacement is meant to suggest some systematic overdetermination, some warp or bias in the optimistic thought of Rosina that places it within a discourse more specialized than the pseudo-universal realm of "woman's love." Surely we have here a clue to the problem of Gervayse Hastings who, in "The Christmas Banquet," can neither enjoy nor suffer

---

16. The evident suffering involved in the chronic headaches of Sophia Peabody may make it hard for us to identify her with the "once-born" of William James classic analysis; yet her mind seems to have been incurably "healthy." The real problem with James's "Varieties" is that there are only two, leaving no place for the really interesting cases—of Hawthorne, Melville, Dickinson, and (perhaps) his own literary brother—the sick soul who never does become "twice-born."
17. *House of the Seven Gables*, in *Hawthorne: Novels* (New York: Library of America, 1983), pp. 415–16. For Hawthorne and Audience in ADA, see my *Province*, pp. 78–98.
18. The local application of this reference to the "chronically diseased" was first suggested to me, years ago, by a remarkable graduate named Bruce Jorgensen; and his Cornell dissertation—"The True Madmen of This Nineteenth Century: Cases of Consciousness in Concord" (1978) has provided more than one important suggestion for the present essay.

the works and days—indeed the persons—of his life because they seem to him shadowy, representational rather than real. And also a spur to Roderick Elliston himself, to tell the story of that unhappy personage as a way of suggesting, even to the beloved Rosina, while love may be potent to cure the grosser forms of solipsism, yet, once the insight of the idealist has occurred, "Marriage (in what is called the spiritual world)" becomes simply "impossible."[19]

Nor is Rosina's "idealism" limited to the curious use of a single world. When Herkimer, Elliston's well-meaning but none-too-perspicacious sculptor-friend, wonders prosily whether a "breast" so long inhabited by "as fearful a fiend as ever stole into the human heart" can ever really "be purified," Rosina goes on to sing the top note of her idealistic revisionism:

> "Oh, yes!" said Rosina, with a heavenly smile.
> The Serpent was but a dark fantasy, and what it typified was as shadowy as itself. The past, dismal as it seems, shall fling no gloom upon the future. To give it its due importance, we must think of it as but an anecdote in our Eternity. (794)

Now we know why those gloomy old Puritan portraits came down the day the Hawthorne couple moved into the "Old Manse." But we can only imagine what significance Melville may have attached to this gloom-denial, this happy bundling of sin and history into the capitalization of Eternity. For here, presumably, one finds not somewhat less but very much more than a "ray of his light for every shade of his dark." Why take just this occasion—of an optimism all but expressly transcendental—to assert of Hawthorne that "the black conceit pervades him, through and through"?[20] Unless he had noticed that some irony of structure serves to situate and qualify, if not expressly deny, Rosina's moment of ideal victory and joy.

Such an ironic end-effect would be very far from unique, particularly in Hawthorne's post-nuptial Old Manse Period, where tales and sketches alike have capitalized endings that satisfy themselves better than they do many readers. Asleep at the switch, for once, Melville himself misquotes the ending of "The Artist of the Beautiful" in order to enhance the Narrator's manic sense that Owen Warland was in the business of art exclusively for the transcendent thrill of "The Beautiful" and so grieved not at all for the destruction of the art-object that had absorbed his very life.[21] More ominously, the Narrator of "Earth's Holocaust" detects in an age's lust for universal reform the obvious

---

19. See Ralph Waldo Emerson, "Experience," in *Essays and Lectures* (New York: Library of America, 1983), p. 486. Correctly intuiting Emerson, James A. Wohlpart nevertheless blames Roderick for introducing the question of "idea"; see "Allegories of Art," pp. 449–51. To me, CB reads better as resisting the cure proposed in EBS. For a face-value acceptance of the love-cure, see Baym, *Shape*, p. 109.
20. Melville, "Hawthorne and His Mosses," p. 521.
21. Changing the tense of the tale's expression of its concluding observations from past to present tense—from "rose" to "rises," for example—Melville universalizes Hawthorne's thoroughly specified (indeed overdetermined) "Artist," implying that all true creators always care for the process and not the product, the private intuition and not the public reception or social effect; see *Tales and Sketches*, pp. 930–31; and cp. Melville, "Hawthorne and His Mosses," p. 517. For

moral danger of neglecting the reform of the all-engendering heart of man but overlooks the quiet but insistent implication, luridly evident in modern science fiction, that the ideal standard of a perfect world will tell a little hard against carbon-based life. And most shockingly, perhaps, the Narrator of "The Birthmark" laments that some avoidable philosophical mistake has caused Aylmer to lose the happiness he might well have enjoyed—leaving it to other, more ironic interpreters to observe his wife is still quite dead and that the Platonic zeal of a scientific amateur is no defense.

Most instructive, however, may be the ending of "The Hall of Fantasy" where, after defending the substance of the world as vigorously as he can, in terms that make him sound to his Transcendental companion like "the very spirit of earth," a philosophically distressed Narrator finally allows himself to be convinced that in the end-time, post-human, post-historical state of things "Idea shall be all in all."[22] Apocalyptic fantasies are of course quite free—or are, at very most, a dime-a-dozen—but this one calls attention to itself by its difference from its Pauline paradigm, which imagines that not Idea but God shall be "all in all." Nor does it sound much like the familiar New Heavens and New Earth predicted by the prophecy of "Father Miller," whose last-day time predictions the sketch's two amateur theorists of history have been considering as epitome and *reductio* of the various perfection-fantasies they have dutifully been listing. Most of all, perhaps, it sounds like the "Prospects" Emerson has imagined in the last, secular-apocalyptic chapter of *Nature*. There, we need to recall, Emerson's "Orphic Poet" proposes that Man, whose roots are "not in matter, but in spirit," but who now stands "a god in ruins" and a "dwarf of himself," timidly adoring a Nature that is in fact "his own work," will recover the secret by which in the beginning he "made for himself this huge shell." All of which inspires this Poet's editor to propose that, having built already our own house, we begin even now to build our "own world," in conformity to "the pure idea in [our] mind." Surely, then, it is some faithful disciple of Emerson who, with only a little slippage, tries to assure his earthier companion in "The Hall of Fantasy" that, when all else is said and done, "man's disembodied spirit may recreate Time and the World for itself."[23] Every man's mind will be its own holodeck.

Surely Rosina is even closer to the Emersonian Idea when she bids her remarkably restored husband to dismiss at once all the "gloom" of his "dismal" past—haunted, solipsistic chamber and all—and, fact or symbol merely, to regard his "serpent [as] but a dark fantasy." Something like "the soul's mumps, and measles, and whooping cough,"[24] we easily infer: part and parcel of those "disagreeable appearances" the concluding paragraph of *Nature* assures us are bound to disappear, as the intimations of Man's true relation to spirit begin more and more to assert themselves. Farewell not only to "swine,

---

the ironies embedded in the emerging discourse of the artist-as-such," see M. H. Abrams, *Doing Things with Texts* (New York: Norton, 1989), pp. 113–87.
22. *Tales and Sketches*, p. 745. For a survey of Hawthorne's various versions of apocalyptic fantasy in the Old Manse Period, see Jonathan A. Cook, "New Heavens, Poor Old Earth," *ESQ* 39 (1993), pp. 209–51.
23. Emerson, "Nature," in *Essays and Lectures*, pp. 45–49.
24. Emerson, "Spiritual Laws," in *Essays and Lectures*, p. 305.

spiders, snakes, pests" (even of the social order, perhaps), but also to the "madhouses, prisons, [and] enemies," of which Elliston has known his share.[25] Not woman's love alone, it appears, but a good stiff dose of Idealism, administered by her own loving hand: together these two cannot fail to oust the last snaky remnants from the mind of the man who studies the guilty conscience and reads Cotton Mather. Not an inevitable cure, perhaps, but then neither was the disease. So that, given an accurate historical diagnosis, of a lingering "touch of Puritanic gloom," what better historical remedy? Sentimental Woman bearing, as a literary gift, the "pure tone" of Emerson.[26]

So we are permitted to imagine, the world into which Sophia had led Hawthorne was a world of feminine Conversations and transcendental Lectures. The letters and journals record some of the redeemed captive's astonishment at—and some of his resistance to—the radical change of psycho-religious atmosphere. But not as well, perhaps, as some passages of the fiction itself. Noticing the altogether polite tone of a Christianity liberal enough to be freed from the doctrinal encumbrance known as a "substitutionary atonement," and leaving behind (or at least repressing) the fear of Hell, "The Celestial Railroad" looks back to the hard sayings of John Bunyan (if not to the compromised Faith of Goodman Brown) with something like nostalgia: once upon a time religion offered an actual challenge to human sensibility and culture. Indeed something of the same is intimated by the religious reflections of the rainy days at the Old Manse. And not the least part of the unsettling effects of "perfectionist" sketches like "Earth's Holocaust" and "The Hall of Fantasy" is the sense that only the Devil of History, in the one case, and Father Miller, in the other, sees any reason to doubt the spreading meliorist expectation. The Narrator of "The Birthmark" may translate the protagonist's fastidious obsession with his wife's physical imperfection into something somehow like the language of the fall, but this fact does not at all hinder Aylmer's disastrous attempt to destroy the enmity between the best and the good, which the Narrator himself regards, at last, as less an arrant blasphemy than an unfortunate conceptual error. Introducing a disaster at least as flagrant, the head-note to "Rappaccini's Daughter" notices, with some sense of resistance, that "the Transcendentalists [...] have their share in all the current literature of the world"; and, by way of introducing all these curious works of latter-day New England sensibility, "The Old Manse" tries to convey the bewildered sense of what it might be like to live "at the opposite extremity of the village" in which the beacon light of Emerson attracted its fair share of "bats and owls."[27]

---

25. Emerson, "Nature," in *Essays and Lectures*, p. 48.
26. As Randall Stewart long ago suggested, Hawthorne never did quite share Sophia's belief that "Mr. Emerson is the greatest man—the most complete man—the ever lived"; quoted from *Nathaniel Hawthorne: A Biography* (rpt. New Haven, CT: Yale University Press, 1961), p. 58. More recently, T. Walter Herbert has suggested that "If Elizabeth had succeeded in publishing the Cuba Journal in 1833, Sophia Peabody would be numbered among the earliest exponents of transcendentalist spirituality" (*Beloved*, p. 51). For Hawthorne's "personal rivalry with Emerson"—including his attempt to "replace Emerson as the greatest man in Sophia's life"—as a unifying concern of the Old Manse Period, see Larry J. Reynolds, "Hawthorne and Emerson in 'The Old Manse,'" *Studies in the Novel*, 23 (1991), pp. 60–81.
27. *Tales and Sketches*, pp. 975, 1146.

Not that this climate of Transcendentalism was all Sophia's fault: Hawthorne would at least have had to approve the plan to move his writing into the study "where Emerson wrote *Nature*." Yet as he looked back, a decade later, on the life that followed his marriage, it seemed not at all his own world. Except for the restful, indeed sleepy life at the Manse, his real self never really inhabited that world, any more than it ever went to and got calluses and muscles at Brook Farm, where his readings—of Emerson's *Essays*, the *Dial*, Carlyle's works, George Sand's romances—all suggested the cry of some "solitary sentinel," whose cadre had got "considerably farther into the waste of chaos than any mortal army of crusaders had ever marched before."[28] Then too, it is far from inevitable that the patron of "idea" should be a woman. So the effect seems deliberate indeed: love—and a dash of Emerson's idealism—as a cure for the neo-Puritan self-absorption of the man who had read too much Cotton Mather and lived too long in his mother's family's attic. Unless the cure should prove worse than the disease. For the issue is less the transcendental tension between Hawthorne and Sophia and more the play and the place of "Idealism as it appears in 1842."[29] And clearly, the instance which Rosina's optimism cannot quite understand is a fairly elaborate case of exactly that.

3

Except for the stewards charged with arranging the annual counter-Christmas Banquet, of all the wretched and disconsolate of the earth, none of the attendees can see any reason for Gervayse Hastings to be in attendance. The idea of assembling, on the anniversary of our salvation, all those who appear to have some fairly advanced Quarrel with God—a blasphemy straight out of Voltaire[30]—appears to leave no room for a person marked by worldly success and unfamiliar with the usual occasions of grief, a person whose "soul has never been shaken" (306). Students who have felt the force of Emerson's "Experience" have some intimation of the problem: Gervayse Hasting never quite *says* "I grieve that grief can teach me nothing," but he comes close enough for what Melville might call a "shock of recognition." Seated in the midst of the assembled grievous, trying to catch some hint of their feelings yet terribly calm in the face of the sudden death of a fellow guest, his only response bespeaks a perfect Emersonian composure: "Would that he could teach me somewhat!" (860). So compelling is the feeling of connection that students are discouraged at first to learn that Hawthorne's twin "Allegories" antedate the publication of Emerson "Experience" by almost a year.[31]

Yet the similarity seems worth pursuing, even in the New Historicist mode of the uncanny. Perhaps the Emerson of "Experience" was not the only resident of Concord suffering, in the 1840s, from an all but undiagnosed case of the soul's failure to thrive

---

28. *Blithedale Romance*, in *Novels*, p. 677.
29. Emerson, "The Transcendentalist," in *Essays and Lectures*, p. 193.
30. See Frank Davidson, "Voltaire and Hawthorne's CB," *Boston Public Library Quarterly*, 3 (1951), pp. 244–46.
31. Emerson, "Experience," in *Essays and Lectures*, p. 473. CB was first published in the *Democratic Review* for January, 1844; Emerson's "Experience," never given as a lecture, first appeared in *Essays, Second Series* in October, 1844.

for the lack of "any burden of real grief" (849) or who appeared to lack the "powerful characteristics of a nature that had been developed by suffering" (856). To be sure, only Emerson ever wrote in his Journal "I have never suffered" but, before the death of his mother, Hawthorne himself may have had life pretty easy.[32] Perhaps the man who seemed always to doubt his own real presence at the important events of his life—the man in whom Jones Very could detect no "bosom idol" whatsoever— might himself have experienced, now and then, a touch of artistic dissociation. Certainly Hawthorne's prefaces, letters, and notebooks regularly deny that his real self is on display in and of his works, often enough for us to detect the suspicion that, behind his uniform and never-failing negative capability there might lurk just nothing at all.[33] No doubt some such suspicion governs the creation and deployment of the exemplary and self-admonishing character of Coverdale, that pseudo-authorial emptiness who only imagines he sympathizes, and of whom Gervayse Hastings is the partial precursor. But it is also possible that Hawthorne *knew* the sense of idealism and emptiness from Emerson's very own journals. This precise possibility was explicitly suggested, long ago but cogently, in the remarkable (though unpublished) dissertation of Bruce Jorgensen. What else can we so suitably infer from Emerson's remark, in the aftermath of a long and congenial walk with Hawthorne to the famous Shaker Community at Harvard, that the "two old collectors [...] had never

---

32. Though Hawthorne may occasionally represent himself as something of a Sybarite, there is nothing in his Notebooks to compare with Emerson's early confession that—though "suffering [...] is the law of our condition" (*Journals and Miscellaneous Notebooks*, II, 131), he himself had "never suffered" (JMN, VII, p. 132). For Hawthorne's agitated, indeed nearly hysterical response to his mother's approaching death, see *American Notebooks*, pp. 429–33; for analysis, see Herbert, *Beloved*, pp. 167–70.

33. Priding himself on his ability to intuit the feelings of others—just where they thought he might be revealing his inmost self—Hawthorne must have been stunned by Jones Very's discovery that the bosom of Hawthorne alone possessed no dominating trait that needing to be sacrificed, for that would imply a lack of stable self-image; see Gittleman, *Very*, p. 282. Applying the confession of a fictional character to the author himself, T. Walter Herbert observes that the lament of growing up "alone" and "without a root" is "spectacularly at odds with the story of Hawthorne's boyhood," particularly that spent running free in the wilds of Maine; and the subsequent "horror" of feeling that "there is no reality in the life and fortunes, good or bad, of a being so unconnected" he ascribes to the "ontological emptiness" involved, necessarily, in the project of self-making (*Beloved*, pp. 59, 85). Less speculative would be the observation that, from the 1837 letter to Longfellow, complaining of the "witchcraft" that carried him "apart from the main current of life," causing him somehow to make "a captive" of himself and "put me in a dungeon," down (at least) to the 1851 preface, in which a certain "enchantment" has set him down by "the wayside of life," Hawthorne's self-story is pretty consistently that of an all but involuntary self-isolation that brought with it an odd feeling of un-self-identity, of not being where or indeed *who* he was supposed to be; see *The Letters*, 1813–1843 (Columbus: Ohio State University Press, 1984), p. 251; and cp. *The Snow Image* (Columbus: Ohio State University Press, 1974), p. 5. Haunting the letters and notebooks as well as the fiction, this self-dissociation—of being an observer merely, of sympathizing with others rather than asserting his own real self, of not being capable of adult male friendship, of never really being in either Custom House or at Brook Farm—is the disorder set out for analysis in "The Christmas Banquet." And it is one for which neither Sophia nor Emerson could quite imagine a cure.

had opportunity before to show each other our cabinets."[34] What better way, after all, to establish or cement a transcendental friendship?

Supposing the two really did exchange journals, Hawthorne may well have read, here and there, in any number of the scattered passages that Emerson's peculiar knack of "composition" would press together into his single most ambitious and telling essay, the dull realization that not even the death of his son Waldo could introduce him to that "reality, for contact with which" he at least was willing to "pay the costly price of sons and lovers." The poignant addition to *Nature's* comprehensive list—the fateful discovery that "Grief *too* will make us idealists"—will have to wait for the published text, but already Emerson is learning that in all disaster "we fall soft on a thought," that grief, "like all the rest, plays about the surface" and teaches us only "how shallow it is."[35] Neither the woman Rosina nor the sculptor Herkimer is quite able, in the end, to grasp the idea of the strangely anaesthetized protagonist of "The Christmas Banquet," but one way or another Emerson has characterized him well enough: in "Experience," in the journals from which it is drawn, and quite possibly in conversation with the Hawthorne who had newly arrived in Concord. For what else could have been so heavily on his mind in the fall of 1842 when, some months after Waldo's death, the text of his terrifying memorial was beginning to take shape? And if we should ask ourselves why Gervayse Hastings, though under no obligation, continues to attend the yearly convocation of all the miserable of the earth, the readiest answer is simply that he continues to perform Emerson's grief test—to see, that is, whether the congregated and self-magnified experience of human suffering might give him the sense of a "reality" he is just aware enough repeatedly to "seek."

Of course it does not. If the language of his repeated, baffled denial of any real interest in the "shadows, flickering on the wall" before him implies the archetypal idealism of Plato more pointedly than the vernacular version one discovers in and about Concord in 1842, the point not only survives but is actually heightened thereby. For the issue is not the curious personality of Emerson but the sense of unreality that might be felt by any person perceptive enough to identify his perceptions as exactly that: structural and yet idiosyncratic representations of a possible thing-in-itself that nevertheless defies our wish to know it as such. Subjective idealism, that is: skepticism about the being of the figures flickering on the wall without any possibility of getting out of the cave to look upon the real and to reason the relation.[36] Rather like a knowledge of the Fall without

---

34. Not recorded in Hawthorne's *American Notebooks*, the incident appears in Emerson's Journals for September (or October) 1842; see William H. Gilman, ed., *The Journals of Ralph Waldo Emerson*, vol. VIII (Cambridge, MA: Harvard University Press, 1970), pp. 272–73. For the original suggestion, see Jorgensen, "True Madmen."
35. "Experience," in *Essays and Lectures*, pp. 472–73.
36. Perhaps this is the place to suggest that—though Hawthorne could not have known it—Emerson's investigation of the connection between idealism and solipsism would eventually produce, in "Illusions," the essay that concludes *The Conduct of Life*, a pretty self-conscious and effective rewriting of Plato's famous "Allegory of the Cave"—suggesting that the prison-house of sensation (and Kant's categories) amount to a cave not even the philosopher escapes.

the hope of Grace. We may seem to recognize the fate of an unhappy Lidian Emerson in the figure of Hastings' wife, who "wept secretly [...] because she shivered in the chill of his bosom," (862) but there is no reason to suppose that Hawthorne is writing *nouvelle a clef*. The really uncanny thing about "The Christmas Banquet," that is to say, is not the confident certainty with which Hawthorne recognizes the disease Emerson would call the fall into "subjectiveness" as a sort of skeptical Platonism, but the ease with which he grants his own 'reformed egotist the privilege of telling this tale of this subtle and well-nigh incurable separation from reality. As if both conditions were deformations of what we have come, in place of the "subject," to call the "ego."

As assuredly they are. Gervayse Hastings may be, first of all, impervious to grief and next, in order of human defect, unable to believe in—or, what amounts to the same thing—to form any affective relation with the fellow-beings we often think of as fellow-sufferers, but in his final, old-age formulation he reveals that his own being has become every bit as remote, as representational, as "ideal" as that of any thing or anyone else:

> All things—all persons—as was truly said to me at this table long and long ago—have been like shadows flickering on the wall. It was so with my wife and children—with those who seemed my friends: it is so with yourselves whom I see now before me. Neither have I myself any real existence, but am a shadow like the rest! (866)

Just here both Hawthorne and Emerson seem to be treading very deep philosophical water. For in the theory of consciousness at issue, which Jacques Derrida has called, rather scornfully, "the philosopheme of the subject," the self, considered as a conscious knower, is supposed to enjoy everywhere the unique valeur of the really real.[37]

So it was at the beginning of Descartes' *Philosophical Meditations*, where the cogitating or, minimally, the doubting mind was itself un-doubtable because self-evidently self-present: deception or illusion might attach to the experience of the human body and that of all the world beside, but self-consciousness was immediate, a given of individual experience as such.[38] So also in the formulation of the Introduction to Emerson's *Nature*, where it becomes clearer than in Descartes that, given the standard of "subjective" self-knowledge, other persons, however intimately familiar may be their voice, can count no more than anything else in the world of natural objects "thrown up against" the self-certain experience of the knowing subject. "Strictly speaking," Emerson assures us, "all that is separate from us, both nature and art, all other men and my own body, must be ranked under [the] name, Nature." The "us" is, of course, polite; or, in the language

---

37. I recall the phrase from a lecture delivered at UCLA in the late 1980s, but the (anti-Cartesian) point is implied almost everywhere in Derrida's argument against "presence"; but see, for example, "'Eating Well,' or the Calculation of the Subject," in Eduardo Cadava, ed., *Who Comes after the Subject* (Abingdon-on-Thames: Routledge, 1991), pp. 96–119.
38. Students of Emerson's "Idealism" need to know not only Plato and Plotinus, and Malebranche and Berkeley, but Descartes at least equally—as his first three *Meditations* constitute the founding scene of modern epistemology; see *Discourse on Method and The Meditations* (rpt. London: Penguin, 1968), pp. 95–131.

of "Experience," it is an act of "ascription": the self-certain subject generously imagines that the same subjective privilege is enjoyed by all other beings who appear in the human form. The strictness of the difference between any subject's knowledge of itself and any other "object" of its knowledge, is made emphatically clear in the chapter on "Spirit": the value of "Idealism," Emerson proposes, is that it

> acquaints us with the total disparity between the evidence of our own being and the evidence of the world's being. The one is perfect; the other incapable of any assurance.[39]

And the same foundational certainty lasts at least as long as the essay "Friendship," in *Essays, First Series*, which Hawthorne's Coverdale confesses himself to have read. There, the Cartesian Subject has steeled his nerves to announce, in defiance of "all the muses and love and religion" that "In strictness, the soul does not respect men as it respects itself" and that, "In strict science all persons underlie the same condition of an infinite remoteness"; and, from a position of perfect ontological safety, to remind the friend that "the vast shadow of the Phenomenal includes thee also in its pied and painted immensity."[40]

But the same shadow has never yet fallen on the self. So that, in a story that implies Emerson, as clearly as anything else written in a manse located "at the opposite extremity" of the village of Concord, in that "most delightful little nook of a study" where in fact "Emerson wrote 'Nature,'"[41] it comes as a surprise when the protagonist, suffering the unlooked-for effect of idealist philosophy, a sort of Cartesian Schizophrenia, finds that his very self has come to seem as unreal as everything else. Yet something very like that is being confessed in "Experience," which begins not with the bold claim that "Undoubtedly we have no questions to ask which are unanswerable," but with the puzzled interrogative, "Where do we find ourselves?"[42] As if he had asked, "How, again, do we go about locating that noumenal self?" Placed luminously beyond—or, rather, prior to—all doubt by Descartes, then indubitably doubted by Hume, it threatens to become as phenomenal as everything else in Emerson's discovery that consciousness too obeys the Heraclitan law of "succession," reducing the self to a river of moods never twice the same. *Moral* selfhood may remain—from the "Address" given to the Divinity School on the duty to make religion a subjective fact to the one calling on the citizens of Concord to break the Fugitive Slave Law—but the speculative necessity of this norm of practical reason appears to have disappeared and, along with it, the possibility of confirming its existence, at need, by simple introspection. In all ordinary experience, that is to say, when no exemplary act of moral defiance is being demanded, we hardly know ourselves except as the scene of flickering shadows.[43]

---

39. Emerson, "Nature," in *Essays and Lectures*, pp. 8, 40–41.
40. "Friendship," in *Essays and Lectures*, pp. 343–44.
41. "The Old Manse," in *Tales and Sketches*, pp. 1145, 1124.
42. "Nature," p. 7; "Experience," p. 471; both in *Essays and Lectures*.
43. For Hume's as-if casual rejection of Descartes foundational certitude, see *A Treatise of Human Nature* (rpt. New York: Oxford University Press, 1978), pp. 251–63. Where Descartes found, in

On Emerson's account—in which objects, including persons, are known only by their ideal representations—it seems inevitable that, here or there, some poor soul might discover certain unhappy consequences. Berkeley and Edwards had both declared that their transference of reality from the scene of the world to the mind of God was not as fraught with insane consequences as many seemed to fear: absent Locke's dogmatic trust in the extra-mental reality of the "primary" or *touch* qualities available in all experience, practical life goes on just as before. In Edwards' famous formulation, it is all just *as if* "God in the beginning, created such a certain number of atoms, of such a determinate bulk and figure, which they yet maintain and always will."[44] Early on, Emerson himself repeats the same sort of reassurance: "The frivolous make themselves merry with the Ideal Theory," but "God never jests"; and, as long as God makes the mind "the receiver of a certain number of congruent sensations, [...] what difference does it make, whether Orion is up there in the heavens, or some god paints the image in the firmament of the soul?" Only this uplifting difference: "Idealism sees the world in God."[45]

To be sure, there is some slippage between the "God" left over from Berkeley and Emerson's less committal, less theistic "some god." Idealism—knowledge by impressions whose representational veracity we "cannot try"—may be a compelling account of human epistemology even if Berkeley's theology of an idea-supplying God should become as outmoded as Plato's ontology of pure forms. And though the possibility of being trapped in the "splendid labyrinth"[46] of his own perceptions does not seem to worry Emerson very much in *Nature*, it is precisely that possibility that has come to haunt him in "Experience." Hawthorne may have seen the problem as early as his own reading of Emerson's famous "ground plan." Absent God, or given the suspicion that the subject may know him as "but one of its ideas," the world begins to look a little lonely. Perhaps there are, in addition to the inestimable religious advantage of Idealism, some unhappy consequences as well. Emerson might rejoice in his power to make "the selectmen of Concord and the Reverend Doctor Poundmedown himself [begin] to look unstable and vaporous," but elsewhere certain exemplary idealists have already been experiencing a certain "nostalgia for the object."[47] Should we be *so* surprised to find, even in a tale by the relentlessly unsystematic Hawthorne, an advanced case of what an inspired student

---

the "cogito," his very "self"—clear, distinct, and irreducible—Hume's inquiry found in that place only "some particular perception or other" (p. 252).

44. Jonathan Edwards, "The Mind," in Wallace E. Anderson, ed., *Scientific and Philosophical Writings* (New Haven, CT: Yale University Press, 1980), pp. 353–54. Berkeley makes the same point, more elaborately, in Part I of his *Principles of Human Knowledge*; see Isaiah Berlin, ed., *The Age of Enlightenment* (rpt. New York: Meridian, 1984), pp. 138–43.

45. "Nature," in *Essays and Lectures*, pp. 32, 39,

46. "Nature," in *Essays and Lectures*, p. 41.

47. Apropos of romantic thought and poetry, "Nostalgia for the object" is the memorable phrase of Paul de Man; see "Intentional Structure of the Romantic image," in Harold Bloom, ed., *Romanticism and Consciousness* (New York: Norton, 1970), p. 70. "Transcendental subjectivity blues" is the department lounge formulation of Bruce Jorgensen; I trust he will accept "Cartesian Schizophrenia" as the appropriate inflation of philosophic diction.

once called "them old transcendental subjectivity blues"? Perhaps they come along as part of the cure for the "measles, mumps, and whooping cough of the soul." An ironic outcome in every way. For if indeed the loss of affective selfhood were somehow implied in Rosina's innocent little dose of "Idea," then the guilty identity might indeed have been better than none.[48]

4

Of course Hawthorne nowhere presents Gervayse Hastings as an idealist, or indeed as any sort of philosopher at all. But then neither does "Egotism" say in so many words that Roderick Elliston's is somehow neo-Puritan. Some things may well be left to inference. Even so, the point would not be that Hastings, like Emerson, has lived to suffer the un-looked-for consequences of a strange, self-dissociating theory, but that if Emerson's analysis of the fall into "subjectiveness" is anything like *true*, then its consequences may be felt not only by professional philosophers but by ordinary people as well—by Hastings, for example; or by Hawthorne. From this perspective, the purpose of "The Christmas Banquet" would be less to get the drop on Emerson's difficulty and more to rue the unhappy implication of his truth. For surely it would be frivolous to deny that stories like "Young Goodman Brown" and "The Minister's Black Veil"—along with many another evocation of "The Haunted Mind"—are innocent of the intimation of the mind's terrible solitude.

And if this much, why not one degree more? What if there is indeed a fatal link between the loss of our primitive certainty about the co-equal existence of "others" and the impairment of the ordinary ego? For if the subject necessarily implies an object, and if "a subject and an object" are indeed all that is required "to make the galvanic circuit complete," then we should not be too surprised if some merely phenomenal sense of the experience of the object begins to infect the morale of the subject as well. By the time all objects—including all persons—have fallen "successively into the subject," that subject can scarcely feel enhanced by the addition of so much lack of substance. "Cryptic might" would have to lie elsewhere.[49] Descartes to the contrary notwithstanding, real objects may complete or validate our own real existence in about the same degree as, in another idiom, persons answer our need for love. Perhaps Hawthorne meant something like this when he had the semi-competent narrator of "The Hall of Fantasy" insist on the importance of the world, not as will and idea, but as a "great round solid self."[50] That would be, after all, only a modest expansion of what he meant when he declared that it was only Sophia's love that had made him "real." Reality is a condition of mutuality and not at all of subjective *valeur* and polite ascription. Perhaps the philosophical failure

---

48. The formula—remembered, but from where I cannot now recall—might unite observers as unlike as Frederick Crews and Sacvan Bercovitch.
49. "Experience," in *Essays and Lectures*, pp. 489, 488.
50. *Tales and Sketches*, p. 744.

Hawthorne confesses at the end of "The Old Manse" is not as complete as his modesty would imply.[51]

Yet our attention must fall, finally, not on Hawthorne's implied philosophy of "interpersonalism" but on the relation between the two halves of his curious diptych, and on the implication that the snaky sufferings of Roderick Elliston have somehow prepared him to tell the chilly story of Gervayse Hastings' altogether less gothic predicament. That task involves, at the simplest level, a comparative interpretation of the phrase "the life within the life." More subtly, however, it may force us to posit some connection between Puritan and the Cartesian/Transcendental identity that is more than a curious accident of New England moral history. About Puritans we can almost imagine Hawthorne himself saying, with the Showman he contrived to narrate his "Main-street," that "Such a life was sinister to the intellect, and sinister to the heart." Written even closer to the authorial first person, "The Old Manse" risks much less about the likely tendency of Emersonian Transcendentalism—only that its rare light caused a number of "bats and owls" to collect in the vicinity of Concord and that, happy for the first time in his life, he himself "sought nothing from [Emerson] as a philosopher."[52] But perhaps the fiction reveals more than the biographical prose.

As for the "life within the life" (786), to Roderick Elliston it signifies a self-consciousness that has grown so pronounced that, like all obsessions, it appears to have a life of its own. Under the aspect of sin and guilt, the inward-looking or reflexive experience of self seems to have taken over from that more innocent sense, automatic in all normal function, of being the same percipient and volitional person from moment to moment. In-look having become compulsive and nearly continuous, the ordinary out-look has all but disappeared so that, instead of savoring each new experience for its own sake, the mind cannot keep from reflecting on the sort of person who is having that experience. Existentially speaking, Elliston has become a *for-itself* almost without interruption; and with a Puritan vengeance.[53]

Hastings' condition is in some sense the opposite: his complaint is that there is, for him, *no* "life within the life," which he identifies not as a reduplication of consciousness but as the "the deep, warm secret" (863) of human existence. Evidently Elliston recognizes and is intrigued by the condition as a sort of inverse of his own. Never stirred by an Emersonian sense that "He ought," Hastings remains trapped in what Kierkegaard might call life's "aesthetic stage": the world exists as an imaginative arrangement to which his own relation remains altogether hypothetical; no experience

---

51. Named among the things Hawthorne failed to produce in his Old Manse years are, along with a proper novel, a "profound treatise of ethics" and some appropriate "philosophic history" (*Tales and Sketches*, p. 1148). Someone may yet think to dispute his claim.
52. "Main Street," p. 1038; "The Old Manse," p. 1146; both in *Tales and Sketches*.
53. For an "Existentialist" (and contra-Cartesian) account of human being as a "*pour-soi*," emerging from a confrontation with "*le neant*," see Jean Paul Sartre, *Being and Nothingness*, Hazel Barnes, trans. (New York: Philosophical Library, 1956), pp. 73–218. Sartre might well recognize Hawthorne's Hastings—and perhaps Emerson himself—as a "shameless" failure of "Being for Others."

comes close enough to arouse—or even to hurt—and thus to identify the self as anything but a more or less scene of perception.[54] He knows the rumor: life is suffered as a "vale of soul-making," and so he returns, year after year, to the place where the miserable know themselves in their suffering and in their resentment: here, surely, are Emerson's "sharp peaks and edges of truth." But no: "It turns out to be scene-painting and counterfeit,"[55] one more production of the omnigenous human imagination. The world is an assortment of impressions he cannot own as *his*; and thus, not surprisingly, the "self" that should underlie or support or simply *have* these experiences begins to flicker on the wall like everything else. Evidently the self is the reflex of an experience powerful enough to force "ownership"—pain, for example; or else, in the next, just less philosophical case, what Hawthorne repeatedly calls "sorrow" (including, it may be noted, sorrow for sin).

As both the narrator and the audience of the story imply, there may be—prior to Freud—no satisfactory explanation for the failure of ego-function at this level, only examples that never quite define themselves: Emerson in the mood of "Experience"; Hawthorne, equally a post-Puritan, in his repeated moments of aesthetic dissociation. At one level, of course, the cause would seem to be modern idealism's special view of subject and object, into which Rosina's cure had offered to lead Roderick Elliston. Yet the intellectual woods are filled with idealist philosophers of one sort or another and, out of that mostly well adjusted group, only Emerson wrote "Experience"; and when Hawthorne encountered the "entire subjectivity" of Jones Very he thought first of a personage no more philosophical than the character his Story-Teller project had named "Eliakim Abbott."[56] What this suggests is that Emerson's self-challenged yet unflinching "idealism," though very close to the surface of Hawthorne's mind throughout the entire "Old Manse Period," was less the cause of Hastings' existential dissociation and more an idiom in which this failure of a lively inter-personalism could best be expressed. As if all the world were indeed a play performed on one's own private stage.[57]

---

54. Hastings seems trapped in the kind of despair which, in one analysis, results from seeing life "in terms of possibility and not of action," and could be cured only "by a leap into a higher stage of existence"; see Ronald Grimsley, *Existentialist Thought* (Cardiff: University of Wales, 1955), p. 20. For Kierkegaard's various and elaborate evocation of life's "aesthetic stage," see the first part of *Either/Or*, David and Lillian Swenson, trans. (Princeton, J: Princeton University Press, 1959), esp. pp. 165–296; and *Stages on Life's Way*, Walter Lowrie, trans. (New York: Schocken Books, 1967), esp. pp. 27–93.
55. "Experience," in *Essays and Lectures*, p. 472.
56. For Hawthorne's association of the "entire subjectivity" of Jones Very with his own, early (and now irrecoverable) conception of Eliakim Abbot, see Gittleman, *Very*, pp. 282–85. For the significance of what we have lost in this "Very-esque" conception, see my *Province*, pp. 496–522.
57. Beginning—one may yet live to argue—in a journal-based sermon on the philosophical significance of "Conversation," Emerson's determination to inhabit the question of solipsism reaches a sobering climax in a journal entry of June-Aug. 1845: "Men go through the world," he observes, "each musing on a great fable"; their first impulse is to try to make first "their brothers" and then "their wives, acquainted with what is going forward in their private theatre." But sooner or later they give up, "and all parties acquiesce at last in a private box with the whole play performed before himself *solus*" JMN, IX, p. 236.

What Hawthorne offers instead of an ultimate cause is a certain proximate continuity. Placing his protagonist in the "analytic" place where he himself once stood, Elliston invites us to consider Hastings as himself a possible case of "egotism." No longer the puritanic sort, of course, and otherwise abstruse enough to be difficult to recognize as such, his disease is nevertheless one the sufferer-turned-narrator considers himself specially entitled to propound. Of course we notice at once his signal failure to sympathize: where Elliston was driven to intuit or imagine, everywhere, analogues of his own guilty sick-soul, Hastings appears to have nothing to confess; nor, in a life-long series of deliberate exposure to resentful expressions of "woe," can he discover anything that reminds him in the slightest of his own experience of natural or civilized discontent. No wonder if the other banquet guests should find his lack of sympathy more than a little self-centered. And probably we should be correct in supposing that eventually Hastings' endless search for the solution to his own problem of dissociation from reality becomes the predominant form of his self-awareness.

But the case is slightly more subtle than that. For Hastings' special sort of egotism is one in which the ego is reduced to the reflexive status of the search for itself. As if David Hume, failing to find the substantial self that underlay his myriad "perceptions," went right on with the search, relentlessly, instead of playing a little backgammon with his friends.[58] Where *do* we find the self if it fails to appear in any of the ordinary places? Parson Hooper's confident universalization to the contrary, Hastings has neither sin *nor* sorrow—so that Romantic theories of deep identity are precluded along with the Puritan. Nor, in his long life of waiting for something to happen, like some protagonist in the later Henry James, has he ever felt the call to necessary moral action. Lacking, therefore, the sort of identity that is forged in pain or forced in self-assertion, Hastings' identity amounts to little more than a routine of social relationships—parodied, it may be, by the identity of his appearance at the same yearly banquet. A construct of whatever you please, evidently a stable identity, once lost, is not so easy to replace.[59]

Absent from all this speculative psychology, we ought to note, is any hint that some Christian "new birth" might make either Elliston or Hastings an entirely "new man." This converted or "Christic" identity is, of course, the one which, on Puritan theory, was supposed to come along to replace the sinful identity so deeply entrenched and so hard to leave behind. But Rosina's "idea of another" carries no suggestion of that divine "Other" whose reception transposes the problem of selfhood into a completely different register. Rosina may declare Elliston saved from gloomy introspection by some mix of womanly love and idealist metaphysics, but to the skeptical reader he

---

58. Admitting that his "skeptical philosophy" left the intellectual landscape a little barren, Hume confessed in the "Conclusion" of his book *En Enquiry Concerning Human Understanding* that he was content to "dine, [...] play a game of back-gammon, and [make] merry with my friends" (p. 269).
59. Alison Easton argues that in his Concord Period Hawthorne moved away from an older, socialized sense of identity toward a more romantic conception based on "desire"; see *Hawthorne Subject*, esp. pp. 131–66. On this account, what Gervayse Hastings lacks is, regressively, the desire for desire.

continues to look like that old-time case of the true sight of sin without an authentic experience of grace. And Elliston looks like a case of a man, enlightened well beyond or otherwise immune to the ancestral doctrine, to whom the older sensibility might come as something of a relief. What Melville may have sensed is that, happily married since his middle years, and never one of the authentic Puritans himself, Hawthorne remained indeed glad to have had "such ancestors." Perhaps his very identity—despite the best Sophia could do—depended on the lively memory, at least, of the puritanic self-constitution.

Melville himself is, of course, our prime theorist of what "The Christmas Banquet" dares to name as "the philosophy of evil" (855), repeatedly assembling and meditating upon such "griefs" as are "worthy to stand as indicators of the mass of human suffering" (850). As his 1850 review of "Hawthorne and His Mosses" makes abundantly clear, he thought of Hawthorne as a powerful precursor, whose work stood to his own as both inspiration and as "sanction."[60] Nor will it be any surprise to see the two of them ranked together, over and against Emerson, who publicly taught that "Evil is merely privative," that "Saints" suffer a "confusion of thought" when they allow "conscience" to persuade "intellect" to regard sin as "essence, essential evil"; and whose strong and consistent philosophical "optimism" privately regarded any attempt to divide the world into good and evil as everywhere the work of the "wicked Manichee."[61] But what "The Christmas Banquet" actually suggests, paradoxically perhaps, is that Hawthorne may have had more sympathy for Emerson than either he or ourselves might have suspected. For though this curious tale is as far as possible from celebrating Hastings' version of Emerson's idealist dissociation, it nevertheless recognizes it as a real and haunting possibility: not quite the Fall of Man in a new key, perhaps, but in the tale's own logic, as serious a mishap as may befall a self-conscious being; a positive disaster of consciousness, but without the humanizing effect of sin or sorrow.

However that may be, it seems sufficient to conclude with the safer observation that Hawthorne is at least as penetrating a commentator on the question of selfhood as Emerson himself. Surely the author of "Main-street" prided himself on being more thoroughly post-Puritan than Melville might be willing to allow. Yet he also recognized the extent to which the literary identity of the West depended on the allied experiences of sin and sorrow. Observing in Liberal Christianity a ratification of a more widespread loss of the sense—and the symbols—of sin, he was far from certain what new fact of mentality or of discourse might come along to replace it. Sophia need not be expected to provide the answer. And, whatever one's expectation, Emerson seemed to be admitting that he himself did not know. Compared with "the Sinner" or "the Sufferer," "the Artist"

---

60. What Melville admired (and envied) most about Hawthorne is his "Shakespearian" ability to say—dramatically, fictionally—his negative, even blasphemous things and get away with it": to remain popular, that is to say, but also not to run amok, Ahab-like, and destroy his own will to go on thinking about just how bad things might actually be; see "Hawthorne and His Mosses," pp. 541–43.
61. Emerson, "Divinity School Address," p. 77 and "Experience," p. 489, in *Essays and Lectures*; and JMN, V, pp. 536–37.

is patently too specialized a notion. Besides, it only repeated the "subjective" problem in another idiom: the artist was a self whose life was sustained by the sins and sorrows of other people; even if the sorrow of one of them was the lack of sorrow. Perhaps, in the recognizable contest between Sin and Self, it was still a moment too soon to surrender the older identity.

Chapter Six

THE TELLER AND THE TALE: A NOTE ON HAWTHORNE'S NARRATORS

As I have tried to suggest more than once, the 1835 break-up of the third of Hawthorne's early collections—"The Story Teller"—is a sadly significant event in the literary history of America in the nineteenth century.[1] And beyond. In the historic moment, it almost certainly contributed to the author's growing discouragement about the viability of a literary career: how long could one go on writing anonymously (or pseudonymously) for magazines and yearbooks? Surely we are not to understand the year (1836) spent editing *The American Magazine of Useful and Entertaining Knowledge* as anything but a last resort. To be sure, the quality of the editing, and of Hawthorne's own contributions, is fairly high. Then too, the literary enterprise appeared to be rescued when a former classmate subvented the publication of the *Twice-Told Tales*. Yet the rescue was hardly complete. That collection may have opened an "intercourse with the world" for this "obscurest man of letters in America," but it was far from the *kind* of thing the author originally had in mind.[2]

Essentially a miscellany—pairing "Wakefield" with "A Rill from the Town Pump," "Endicott and the Red Cross" with "The Lily's Quest"—it altogether lacks the kind of formal and thematic unity Hawthorne had clearly aimed at in his out-setting "Seven Tales of My Native Land," which seemed to be experimenting with the enforced combination of gothic and domestic sentiment, and the astonishingly sophisticated "Provincial Tales," in which Hawthorne's ironic patriotism might frighten Oliver Stone.[3] And it published most of the tales intended for "The Story-Teller" quite apart from the scenes of their local performance, whose "frames" their narrator had modestly suggested might

---

1. See my *Province of Piety* (Cambridge, MA: Harvard University Press, 1984), 515. And cp. my more recent "Supernal Loveliness and Fantastic Foolery," *Nathaniel Hawthorne Review*, 44.1–2 (2018), pp. 1–13.
2. The 1851 preface—to the third edition of *Twice-Told Tales*—both laments an obscurity which lasted "for a good many years," but also protests that the early tales were not the product of "solitary mind" conversing with itself, but rather an attempt to "open an intercourse with the world." He might have added that the 1837 *Tales*, bearing the author's name for the first time, introduced him to the Peabody sisters of Salem, one who helped get him his first real job and the other who became his "Dearest Beloved."
3. The "bitter patriotism" of Hawthorne's early tales is best sensed in "Roger Malvin's Burial" and "My Kinsman, Major Molineux"; cf. *Province*, pp. 107–53.

be "more valuable than the pictures themselves";[4] and, significantly for this study, without benefit of their fully characterized Narrator—an orphan in the care of a puritanic minister, then a run-away, committed to story-telling against all New England odds, the traveling companion of one Eliakim Abbott, who looks to the Story-Teller somewhat like an "unfledged divine from Andover" (180), and whose memory Hawthorne called to mind when he first came to understand Jones Very.[5] Nothing else remotely like this in the early years of a tenuously emergent American *belles lettres*. An experiment complex enough to warrant its own chapter in Anybody's History of Narratology.

But no. The Tales Themselves, each with a Teller doomed to be identified as Hawthorne Himself. Whoever the hell that was. Let's see: his remote ancestor (spelled Hathorne) helped condemn the Salem witches; his father was a ship's captain who died abroad when his son was young; he lived with his mother's family, mostly women, but two uncles who ran a stage-coach line; he was shy; he had private tutors rather than ordinary schools; he hurt his foot one summer, and this made him more shy; he avoided church service at a cut-rate country college with a Harvard-like curriculum; after that, he spent a lot of time brooding in a "dismal and squalid" chamber—but he did take long walks in the summer, and sometimes played cards with friends.[6] A full, rich, and interesting life, no doubt. Lots of luck with that.

Of course one can locate certain "narrator" issues in earlier tales, not written for inclusion in "The Story-Teller." Not in "Wives of the Dead," perhaps, where—unless one chooses to vex the reference of the "she" (67) in the last paragraph—the complexifying interest lies in the dramatization (and the symbolism) of sameness and difference the drama of the tale concerns.[7] But maybe just a little in "The Hollow of the Three Hills," where one is tempted to wonder whether the author, who seems to have been reading eighteenth-century fiction, quite agrees with the narrator's implication that "madman's fantasies" could occur only in "those strange old Times" (7). And somewhat more in the longer stories intended for the "Provincial Tales." Not so much in "The Gentle Boy,"

---

4. "Passages from a Relinquished Work," in Roy Harvey Pearce, ed., *Hawthorne: Tales and Sketches* (New York: Library of America, 1996), p. 177. Unless otherwise identified, all Hawthorne quotations refer to this edition.
5. See Edwin Gittleman, *Jones Very* (New York: Columbia University Press, 1967), p. 2183. And for the figure of Very behind the protagonist of Hawthorne's "Egotism; or, The Bosom Serpent," see Robert D. Arner, "Hawthorne and Jones Very," *New England Quarterly* 42.2 (1969), pp. 267–75.
6. For a full and un-ironic account of Hawthorne's early life, one may consult and compare, Randall Stewart, *Nathaniel Hawthorne* (New Haven, CT: Yale University Press, 1948), pp. 1–74; Robert Cantwell, *Nathaniel Hawthorne: The American Years* (New York: Holt, Rinehart, and Winston, 1948; rpt. Octagon, 1971), pp. 3–264; Hubert H. Hoeltje, *Inward Sky* (Durham, NC: Duke University Press, 1962), pp. 3–128; Arlin Turner, *Hawthorne* (New York: Oxford University Press, 1980), pp. 3–129; James R. Mellow, *Nathaniel Hawthorne in His Times* (Boston: Houghton Mifflin, 1980), pp. 3–198; and Edwin H. Miller, *Salem Is My Dwelling Place* (Iowa City: Iowa University Press, 1991), pp. 3–186.
7. For the theory that the action of "Wives" is *all* a dream, see Hans-Joachim Lang, "How Ambiguous Is Hawthorne?" in A. N. Kaul, ed. (Hoboken, NJ: Prentice-Hall, 1966), pp. 82–84; for my counter-reading, see *Province*, pp. 102–7.

where morality and sentiment have to have everything pretty much their own way. But, clearly, in the headnote to "Roger Malvin's Burial," somebody is expected to know (or go and discover) more than the narrator is saying about the "well-remembered" event called "Lovell's Fight" (88). And no one in their right, suspicious mind can be expected to believe that the ritualistic and well-orchestrated events of "My Uncle Molineux" merely "chanced" to happen "upon a summer night, not far from a hundred years ago"—any more than the man who appears to befriend Robin Molineux had "chanced" (68/82) to meet the man with the painted face of red and black. Here, and with astonishing effect later, in "The May-Pole of Merry Mount," the personage graciously offering us some "authentic passages from history" (366) is seldom to be given entire credit. History, it appears, is a story. And so is a story: lots of tellers, not all to be trusted.

To be sure, the assembled twice-told tales—some of them—are incomparably wonderful, all by themselves: "The Minister's Black Veil," "The May-Pole of Merry Mount," even the less precisely historical "Prophetic Pictures" and "Ambitious Guest." From the same period, "Young Goodman Brown" missed the cut but, famously, it leaves one to wonder who exactly thinks Brown's traumatic adventure in the forest may really be a nightmare, but leaves readers of Cotton Mather to imagine that experiences of "specter evidence" may be dream-enough to cover the case? Who, in the case of "The Minister's Black Veil," thinks it sufficient to tell us that Parsons Hooper's scary new sermon "*had reference* to secret sin" (373, my italics); or who is obtuse enough to suggest that his "awful power, over souls that were in agony for sin" has "no other apparent cause" (381) than the histrionic black veil. And was it the cancelled "Story-Teller" or the enduring Author who inserted into the text of "The May-Pole of Merry Mount" the curiously indirect footnote about Blackstone? Not to mention the self-cancelling political ironies of "The Gray Champion" and "Endicott and the Red Cross."[8] To be sure, all these questions can be dealt with internally, so to speak, but all would be more than a little different if (what Emily Dickinson called) a "supposed person"[9] were explicitly given as the nearest source of these complexities; and he, standing in a place with a local habitation and a name. Even as originally intended.

Then too, if you happen to pick up the second (1851) edition of *Twice-Told Tales*, there will be the four dazzling "Legends of the Province House," written just after the 1837 *Tales* and—as if to compensate for what was lost in "The Story-Teller"—employing a carefully specified Narrator who, with a nostalgic (and boozy) interest in his country's past, tells the tales he hears from two other tellers, one an incorrigible old Tory, and both given to a fondness for myth and legend. All this in a bar that used to be part of the Province House, a pivotal place in the history of American trade and taxation. Narrated thus obliquely are four well-specified but not chronologically arranged episodes, the "present" moment of initial hostility, the provocative decision to quarter troops in Boston, then—by virtue

---

8. For the problem of patriotism and irony in Hawthorne's "typological" anticipations of the Revolution, see my *Province*, pp. 208–38.
9. Dickinson's apparent denial of simple first-personhood was made in an 1862 letter to her informal adviser and sometime patron Thomas Wentworth Higginson; see L268 in Thomas H. Johnson, *Selected Letters of ED* (Cambridge, MA: Harvard University Press, 1986), p. 176.

of some way-back machine—the social unrest associated with the smallpox epidemic of 1721, and then, back to the more-than-present moment of civil restoration. Read all by itself or in tandem with the reassuringly linear account of historian George Bancroft, the effect of all this is more than a little disconcerting. As if we were meant to be reminded that history is after all a tale, told by somebody or other, and that its form is far from inevitable.[10]

But then, another story: the happy interruption of ordinary reality. The nameless author of this or that tale published in some place or other turns out to be none other than Nathaniel Hawthorne, part-time recluse of Salem. One Peabody sister helps him get a low-level political job; another, amicably connected with educator Horace Mann, enables the writing of some intriguing tales for children; a third, imperfectly distracted by chronic headaches, becomes his very inamorata, writing and receiving urgent love letters to and from Boston, where the newly identified author—who "never cared much for those blue diamond rings"—had gone to work in Uncle Sam's revenue service. Open intercourse indeed. Before you know it, this newly awakened worldling will be investing $500 in a communal experiment: where cooperation aspires to replace competition, perhaps two can live as cheap as one. No? Can't write there? Well, some further (and remarkable) stories for children, but nothing all grown up. Turns out, the Soul can be buried under a dung heap as easily as under a pile of money.

So—duly married anyway—off to the Old Manse at Concord; Emersonville, in very fact, an entirely new scene, offering an irresistible temptation to write, down from the attic, a moral history of his own remarkable time. But in what form? And requiring what sort of narrative persona? That is to say, who would you have to be in order to register a timely critique of the various ideal aspirations in evidence there without admitting that you were, after all, a practical materialist? An after-the-fact Preface might assert that the *real* you—about which there remained in your own mind considerable doubt—was decently concealed behind some sort of veil, but the real problem is that your stories, many of them, end with strong interpretative instructions, some of which are borderline insane and almost none of which come close to covering the issues raised by a new set of themes and characters. Who speaks, in the tales of Hawthorne's Old Manse Period? And how consistently? Unlike the tales of the 1830s, the specified story-telling Narrator is absent by design; so that, unless we can identify one that is merely implied, there is now no one to praise or blame but the author himself. Even if we say these cunningly wrought tales were written by language.

2

From the Concord period, the only tales that seem designed for a collection are "Egotism; or The Bosom Serpent" and "The Christmas Banquet," identified, both of them, as belonging to a set called the "Unpublished Allegories of the Heart," of which there

---

10. For the ordering of the four "Legends of the Province House"—and for the significance of their appearing in O'Sullivan's *Democratic Review*—see *Province*, pp. 389–457.

are, so far as we know, no other members. But the first is interesting enough to have provoked interpretative psycho-theological comment from Melville; and together they require at least a certain amount of narratological acumen. Linked, internally, by the repeated but widely differing use of the phrase "life within a/the life" (786/863), they more significantly require the reader to notice that the second tale ("Banquet") is told by the protagonist of the first ("Egotism"); cured, presumably, by the suggestion of his estranged wife that he try to lose diseased self-awareness in "the idea of another" (793), he turns to posit a case of more-than-clinical identity formation that may not be so easy to cure. What but his own disease, we are strongly invited to ask, gives the once insanely self-involved Roderick Elliston the right to puzzle us with the case of the hopelessly dissociated Gervayse Hastings, to whom everything Emerson would call the "not me"—and then even his very own "me"—is as a shadow "flickering on the wall" (856/860/866).

Allegorically, as I have argued elsewhere, it might be not Jones Very recalling Eliakim Abbott, but a preternaturally ingrown Hawthorne propounding the case of a conscientiously apathetic Emerson.[11] But however we handle the key to this curious *moins de roman*, our attention has been turned to the question of who tells what; and why. The snaky and sin-obsessed discourse of the first tale is clearly puritanical; of the second, Emersonian and in the end Platonic; but we need to know the situational source and interpersonal function of this peculiar but clearly deliberate pairing of philosophical idioms. What follows from the fact that a character cured of a self-involvement clearly related to somebody's idea of "the true sight of sin," turns on his wife and friend with a puzzling tale about what might be called "them old transcendental subjectivity blues"[12] or else, more generally, Platonic or Cartesian schizophrenia.

So alerted, we may even, plausibly enough, ask about the narrator of the original story—George Herkimer, the sculptor, who demands to know the "origin" of Elliston's rare and remarkable disease and who solemnly pronounces it "an awful affliction, whether it be actual or imaginary" (793). For which relief, some small thanks perhaps; but less than a competent criticism might eventually require. As almost everywhere in the mini-canon we have designated, somebody in the story, named or not, is only too ready to tell us less than we need to know. Or worse, something we are supposed to know is dead wrong. As in the case of Aylmer and Georgina: yes, this compulsive purist has indeed lost his best chance for worldly happiness, but she's the one who gets dead. More of this anon. For the moment, call this the technique of flagrant but flawed self-interpretation: put your yellow marker back in your school bag and move along.

Backing up to the very beginning of the Old Manse Period, we encounter, in an under-investigated tale called "The Virtuoso's Collection," a Narrator perceptive enough to identify the learned and voluble guide of his tour through a museum of reified literary

---

11. See my "Life within the Life," *Nathaniel Hawthorne Review*, 30 (2004), pp. 1–31.
12. I own the phrase to Bruce Jorgensen, now professor of English at BYU but who, as a graduate student at Cornell University, first noticed that, as a sign of their mutual good wishes, Hawthorne and Emerson had exchanged journals; see "These True Madmen of the Nineteenth Century," Doctoral Dissertation (Cornell University, 1978).

symbols none other than the Wandering Jew, which legendary personage will reappear more than once between here and "Ethan Brand." More than that—and stuff written about "the elixir of life" to the contrary—he is wise enough to suspect that earthly immortality might not be good for the mortal man, that without some hope for what Poe would call certain "glories beyond the grave," all wish for the better, all aspiration might in due time disappear. And, though he is perceptive enough to recognize that the Virtuoso who leads him through his encompassing collection has made some odd pairings, he never even tries to figure out what game this proto-encyclopedist may be playing. Leaving the reader to wonder what might be wrong with pairing Una's lamb with "Alexander's steed Bucephalus" or the "very dove [...] that brought to message of peace and hope to the tempest-beaten passengers of the ark" to the raven—not of sacred scripture and, for reasons of chronology, no doubt, not of Poe—but of Barnaby Rudge (698/700). Or, more crucially still, what might be wrong with reducing the full semantic range of a complex dialogic text to its symbols. Or, what mythographer might be reductively identifying any one myth with any other? And why? Or, again, just who in the course of Hawthorne's omnivorous reading might be guilty of any such procedure? Don't say P. T. Barnum. Please.[13]

Similar instances of deliberate but inadequate self-interpretation occur in "The Hall of Fantasy" (1843) and "Earth's Holocaust" (1844), both of which also touch the theme of ideal aspiration and loyal earthliness. In the one, an interested but cautious and skeptical Narrator moralizes, for and against the theories of a whole gallery of poets, prophets, reformers, projectors, and other fantasts: good to keep alive the idea of the better, but very bad to get lost somewhere in cloud land. A Christian, perhaps, he will yet have no part of Father Miller's Adventist wish for the near appearance of God's last put-out-the-light. Aroused, he even breaks out into a hymn to the peculiar, matchless, indeed unreplaceable pleasures of this very earth altogether worthy of Thoreau, or, closer to the sketch's own system of reference, of Channing's poem, "The Earth Spirit."[14] But in the end, a final, well-elaborated moral rings a little hollow. Indeed, its overtone and specific allusion may betray the entire force of his studied naturalism.

Offered the chance to share the "vegetable diet" of his tour guide (organic, free-range, grass-fed sprouts, as I imagine it), he produces—unconsciously, or at least without emphatic comment—one of Hawthorne's most telling philosophical puns: this invitation to dinner, even when the fare was to be nothing very "*substantial*" (my italics) "compelled us forthwith to remove from the Hall of Fantasy" (745). Talk, talk, talk; when do we eat? Or, as Emerson's self-satire has it, "Children, eat your vittles and say no more of it."[15] And then, an ending that overtly references Emerson—when "the Idea shall be all in

---

13. For the minimally helpful suggestion of the relevance of Barnum to Hawthorne's VC, see Gregory Green, "Show-Man," *Journal of Popular Culture*, 14.3 (1980), 385–92.
14. The text of Channing's "Earth Spirit"—which first appeared in the *Dial* for 1843—is conveniently anthologized in Perry Miller, *The American Transcendentalists* (Baltimore, MD: Johns Hopkins University Press, 1957), pp. 248–50.
15. Emerson, "Experience," in Joel Porte, ed., *Emerson: Essays and Lectures* (New York: Library of America, 1983), p. 478.

all" (745)—suggesting that the Narrator is unaware that he has been withholding from us somebody's knowledge that Emersonian idealism is fundamentally connected with the morale of this exhaustive (and, in the original magazine version, fully specified list of eager dissatisfactionists.[16] Blasphemously parodying St. Paul—"the Idea shall be all in all"—but clearly invoking the apocalyptic conclusion of Emerson's *Nature*, it is this ending which clearly informs the structural meaning of this otherwise prosy sketch: the pre-millennial Adventism of Father Miller may seem the epitome and *reductio* of all plans to make it new, but the logic of immaterialism may register an even deeper unhappiness with the way things are. Plotinus either did or did not hate his body, and Emerson worries that his denial of real being to the world of matter implies an insult to Mother Earth;[17] but while an inadequate Narrator mouths a pseudo-Christian platitude, a suspicious Hawthorne may be inviting his readers to wonder.

Equally explicit and equally incompetent is the Narrator of "Earth's Holocaust," a sketch which imagines a secular approximation of Father Miller's end-time bonfire but without a perfect courage of its conviction: What if a Bonfire of the Vanities got out of control? Or, in the radical logic of a relevant "Star Trek" episode, what if the crusade against imperfection entails the elimination of all created being? At one point the Narrator wonders out loud, what next? "Unless we set fire to the earth itself, and leap boldly off into infinite space, I see not that we can carry reform to any further point" (901). Or else, as *someone* might have said, now we devoutly await its Millerite consummation, a mighty conflagration to consume the earth and, in it, all who are not among the blessed. As if the title implied a Holocaust not *in* or *on* but *of* the earth.

All along, destruction by destruction, the Narrator is, alternately, enthusiast and skeptic: at one time, on the occasion of the elimination of the death penalty, "That was well done" (897); at another, upon the burning of the Bible, "This is terrible" (904)—requiring, in both cases, the words of a certain "grave observer" (889) to suggest that the process involves somewhat less of good and evil than might at first appear. Tempting one to say to the unsteady Narrator: "Oh foolish Mortal, ever blind to fate;/ Too soon dejected and too soon elate."[17] And in any case, to doubt the adequacy of this unstable observer's final, explicit, elaborate moral: how sad if, playing into the hands of the Devil himself, we discarded things and reformed institutions but left unreformed—untouched by the fire of true religion—"that inward sphere" (906) from which it all proceeds. True enough, as any card-carrying Awakener could surely observe, and as even the logic of Emerson's "Self-Reliance" might imply. But what if the point is that, Christian and Secular Radicalism to the contrary notwithstanding, the human heart is subject to education but not perfect transformation? What if, in the name of ridding the universe of imperfection, the Great Fire would have to consume rather than merely purify the

---

16. Published in John Russell's magazine, *The Pioneer* for February 1843, the initial version of "The Hall of Fantasy" contained no fewer than twenty-seven brief recognitions of American writers, including contemporaries; see Harold P. Miller, "Hawthorne Surveys His Contemporaries," *AL*, XII (1940), pp. 228–35.
17. Almost a quotation from Pope's "Rape of the Lock": too heavy for that comic context, perhaps, but memorable enough to guide the way of wisdom elsewhere.

all-engendering heart of man? What if carbon-based life turns out to be as imperfect as it is expensive"? Fear death by perfection, Georgiana. But not quite yet—as "The Celestial Rail-road" offers us yet another case of a Narrator not quite sure what his tale is supposed to mean.

A slightly more complicated instance: the Narrator is aware that he is living out and retelling the most famous not-quite-biblical story of the seventeenth century, but he seems not entirely sure why. And, though he is aware that the liberal guru who instructs him in all the improvements made to religion since the time of poor old John Bunyan is not entirely to be trusted, he appears to have no knowledge that this (plainly allegorical) Mr. Smooth-it-away has an important literary predecessor—the "Smooth Divine" who, in the mock epic of Timothy Dwight, relishes Charles Chauncy's amazing discovery that the assembled Jewish/Christian scripture does *not* in fact hold forth the doctrine of hell. And his responses to the specifics of the new liberalism is decidedly mixed.

On the one hand, he notices that the new bridge vibrates rather dangerously as they pass over the old Slough of Despond—which "cartloads of wholesome instructions" (808) had failed to fill and make solid; and he slyly declines to say whether he believes the "Evangelist" who sells tickets may be in fact an impostor, or whether they will be accepted at "the gate of the Celestial City" (809). On the other hand, however, he supposes that "it would have done Bunyan's heart good to see" that his rag-tag assortment of sorrowful souls traveling on foot had been replaced by "parties of the first gentry and most respectable people in the neighborhood" (809–10). We can say, of course, that this praise sounds like a little insincere; but then that is the besetting problem of satire: when do we understand a dramatic speaker to be less enlightened than the author, and when do we hear the author himself "being ironic"?

And the problem continues: conversations on "religion," though "indubitably the main thing at heart, was thrown tastefully into the background"; so that "Even an infidel would have heard little or nothing to shock his sensibility" (810). Clearly Hawthorne has read that "pattern American" who arranged a religion that would "satisfy the professors of all religions and shock none";[18] is *he* being ironic, or is the Narrator simply deluded? Same with the "great convenience" of removing one's burden from one's back into the "baggage car" (810) and of employing "Apollyon, Christian's old enemy" as the engineer of this train to perdition. But it seems a bit much to have the now-and-then perceptive Narrator break forth into absurd excitement:

> "Bravo, bravo!" exclaimed I, with irrepressible enthusiasm. "This shows the liberality of the age; this proves, if anything can, that all musty prejudices are in a fair way to be obliterated. And how will Christian rejoice to hear of this happy transformation. (811)

---

18. Thus, in his *Studies in Classic American Literature* (rpt. London: Penguin, 1971), p. 16, does D. H. Lawrence represent Franklin's eclectic, irenic, comparatist Deism, which purported to be the "Essentials of every known Religion, and being free of anything that might shock the Professor of any Religion"; see *Autobiography* (New York: Norton, 2012), p. 90.

Too heavy, this. And, partly at least, it is the not-quite-Swiftian management of ironic narration which makes "The Celestial Rail-road" seem somehow more clever than profound.

The Narrator is not so foolish as to imagine a permanent residence in Vanity Fair. And, unlike so many others, he does not respond to the sudden disappearance of persons from that familiar delusion, "as if nothing had happened" (821). But in the end, when a pleasant ride on the modern road of a plausible Christianity delivers him, with his cargo of unforgiven sins still in the baggage car, at the very gates of hell, he relieves himself of the obligation of adequate interpretation with the discovery that, after all, "Thank heaven, it was a Dream" (824). Convincing the reader that the Narrator himself was, all along, being mildly, inadequately satirical—suspecting something blithely amiss, but unable to penetrate to the heart of a design fairly called Satanic. Yet leaving that same reader to wonder exactly where Hawthorne himself might stand on the doctrine of Atonement. Clearly, the tone seems to say, one is less hysterical now than was the grandson of Jonathan Edwards, who thought the Universalism of Charles Chauncey might speak the world back into biblical and poetic (Pope-like) darkness;[19] but is it after all just a matter of tone? And causing one to wonder, perhaps, whether Hawthorne's not-smart-enough Narrators might be some form of self-protection. Where exactly did he stand—on the matter of The Protest? On the reality of the spiritual world? On the credibility of historical Christianity? Perhaps he thought it quite enough to wonder.

Yet wise skepticism is not everywhere the answer—as in the desperate case referred to earlier. Having shut up his (weirdly) beloved in an angular chamber—with curtains borrowed from Poe's "Ligeia" to make it appear circular—a Mad Scientist (with a Neoplatonic backstory) does his level worst to make his beloved appear perfect. No mention of her character, except as a learned echo of the source, in which an experimental amateur named Sir Kenelm Digby poisons his wife with freckle-curing viper wine *and*, in an attempt to repress the knowledge of her career as courtesan, changes her name from Venetia to Stelliana.[20] Two stories there, but here only one: hating her freckle-turned-tiny-hand, and, if the barely hidden truth were known, fearing the power of her sexuality, a fastidious pseudo-spiritualist named Aylmer, having already, in a gross external parody of conversion, "administered agents powerful enough to do aught except to change your entire physical system" (777), the final step. With her desperate approval: how can she love life if there is something in her he hates? Even if my one-time graduate student was right: what he gives her is the psycho-moral equivalent of a cliterodectomy.

She dies of course. But unlike Beatrice in "Rappaccini's Daughter," who manages to discern more resident evil in her lover than in herself, Georgiana, who might well be Georgina, except for the four-letter allusion to Stell***iana***—that's right, pedantry strikes again—completely absolves her experimental but incompetent (and no doubt impotent)

---

19. For the connection between Dwight's "Triumph of Infidelity" and Hawthorne's "Celestial Rail-road," see my "Cosmopolitan and Provincial," *Studies in the Novel*, 23.1 (1991), pp. 4–6.
20. For the figure of Sir Kenelm Digby behind the character and career of Hawthorne's Aylmer, see Alfred S. Reid, "Hawthorne's Humanism," *American Literature*, 38 (1966), pp. 337–51.

lover of all guilt. She consented, *and*, after all, did he not mean well? Was it not all done in the name of spiritual aspiration? So far, so bad. Read this cautionary tale, all you young women starving yourselves into anorexia because the magazines convince you that men hate fat. But then the Narrator appears to agree. At least as to the name and nature of Aylmer's crime.

Apparently convinced that he has a sort of Faust tale on his hands—that Aylmer's strong claim is that he refused ever to say something like, "Stay this moment, thou art so fair"—he consoles rather than blames his death-dealing aspirations. Poor Aylmer, he as good as concludes, he meant well but he made an identifiable philosophic mistake, learning to his infinite sadness, how "the gross Fatality of Earth exult[s] in its invariable triumph over the immortal essence" (780). Along with the absurd thematic capitals, the self-parodic "Thus ever" makes it clear to all but the most convinced literalists that they must, in the words of D. H. Lawrence, in a famous essay on Hawthorne's indirection, "Never trust the teller. Trust the tale."[21] The tale says Aylmer is crazy and dangerous. It well implies that we emphasize the hand print he leaves on the arm of the "prying woman" (776) who would dare suggest that her interest in her body, herself could in any way bear on the import of his experiment is the symbol of moment. Sexual obsession aside, the rest is just freckles. And the Narrator's forced conclusion—that Aylmer "failed to look beyond the shadowy scope of Time, and living once for all eternity, to find the perfect Future in the present" (780) reads less hard-won insight than like a recited lesson in Transcendentalist grammar.

"The Artist of the Beautiful," offers a similar (if less tragic) case of artfully authorized misprision. Comfortable all along with the *topos*—about to become a cliché—of sensitive artist suffering at the hands of bourgeois audience, he makes nothing of the fact that, from the outset, while Owen Warland is still misemployed as a watchmaker's apprentice, he has turned all the clocks in his shop window face-inward—as if to suggest that the Artist owes his Audience not so much as the time of day. Like certain modernist poetry, perhaps. (Who started this?) Nor does he bother to thematize the fact that, once at least, Owen performed the rare service of repairing the clock on the church tower. Dear me, what if one function of art were to suggest, from time to time, an adjustment to the conscience of official religion? But absent-minded omission is one thing, thematic pontification quite another.

So there we are: finally successful at the much-interrupted and often-thwarted attempt to produce a thing of absolutely no use other than to imitate, mechanically, the graceful beauty of nature, the Artist presents his Object to his hopelessly ill-prepared Audience. With no one by to suggest that "a poem should not mean but mean but be," they are curious but plainly uncomprehending: Is it alive? What is it for? Equally puzzled, the poor butterfly cannot find a place to land. Not on Peter Hovenden, who cordially hates

---

21. See *Studies in Classic American literature* (1923; rpt. London: Penguin, 1977), p. 8. Though the remark occurs in the introductory chapter ("The Spirit of Place"), it applies pretty well to the chapter on *The Scarlet Letter*, which applauds the "absolute duplicity of that blue-eyed *Wunderkind* of a Nathaniel" (106).

"The Beautiful" even if it does not exist. Not on Danforth the blacksmith, whose strong natural presence makes the tale—in a line started by "The Legend of Sleepy Hollow"—a memorable moment in the story of The Jock and the Nerd. Nor is this magical new thing "For Annie," even if Owen's obsessive minimalism suggests Poe's decision that poems must be short. Back to the Artist? No way. Like the Robert Frost I once heard, avoiding the intentional fallacy by refusing in public to parse his own poem. So it tends to the chubby Child, with or without a "most knowing eye": perhaps the "shades of the prison house have not entirely closed." But no. In what modern professors can only take to be an allegory of teaching poetry to freshmen, crunch! Oh well, Owen did his level best.

And the Narrator thinks it's all OK. In so ponderous a thematic pronouncement that so sensitive a reader as Herman Melville misquotes it as a General Truth, missing in the process a string of historic and philosophical ironies long enough to keep criticism off the streets for a whole weekend. The passage is remarkable enough to address in its entirety. Determined at one moment to show them all, to make them "know, and see, and touch, and possess" (925) the fleeting secret of Beauty here ably reified, he then, in the moment of fat and clumsy—one had almost said "retarded"—refusal, Owen suddenly finds himself the site of entire transcendence. Or so the Narrator would have us believe. For had this Artist not caught "a far other butterfly"? Archetypal, no doubt, and if the truth were known, imitable only at some steep Platonic discount. Was he not in it all along for the thrill of aspiration itself? Then learn the lesson:

> When the artist rose high enough to achieve the Beautiful, the symbol by which he made perceptible to mortal senses became of little value in his eyes, while his spirit possessed itself in the enjoyment of the Reality. (931)

Was not the process always more important than the product? How could this ideal artist care at all for the thing he gave the best part of his life to create? Or mind what anybody else might happen to think of it? Art is aspiration. Its "object" not some beautiful thing but Beauty Itself. How could John or Jonathan know about that?

One finds it said that this is the story Emerson would have written, had he chosen a literary kind more fictional than the essay.[22] One hopes not. For surely literary solipsism can go no further; and the man who in maturity despaired of ever making plain to brothers or wives the nature of the drama "forward on his private boards"[23] never stopped writing and polishing essays designed to teach, rather than privately cherish, the

---

22. Quoting from the *Edinburgh Review* of 1855, Millicent Bell cites the following: "If the Sage of Concord had sat down to write a short story, he would surely have produced 'The Artist of the Beautiful'"; see *Hawthorne's View of the Artist* (Albany: SUNY, 1962), p. 94. For a more balanced and discerning view of the Hawthorne/Emerson question, see Frederick Newberry, "'The Artist of the Beautiful': Crossing the Transcendent Divide in Hawthorne's Fiction," *Nineteenth Century Literature*, 50.1 (1995), pp. 78–96.
23. Properly included in Stephen Whicher, *Selections from Ralph Waldo Emerson* (Boston: Riverside, 1957), p. 281, this epitome of Emerson's firm grasp on the nature of human "privacy" occurs in his *Journal* for June (?), 1845.

life of the Spirit. And can we seriously imagine the Hawthorne who kept writing needy prefaces was any less concerned with connecting himself to a proper audience? Had "My Uncle Molineux" and "Roger Malvin's Burial" been written in the name of ideal self-possession? How do the sufferings of Hester and Dimmesdale lend their parts to the soul of the Beautiful? Rather, Hawthorne is the one who, quite as much as Emerson, mends the clock on the church tower. And both wish us to notice.

Of course there is a less inflated, indeed ironic sense in which the Narrator's remarks make some practical sense. Devoutly we wish to believe that Owen Warland got some higher pleasure out of the worldly deprivation and pain involved in his long process of making his idea real—because, in the end, that was about all he got. The artist had better *like* what he is doing or it could be all a waste of time. And life. Perhaps we may charitably imagine that this is something like what Melville meant when, in his famous essay on "Hawthorne and His *Mosses*," he misquotes the Narrator's blatant pseudo-Platonic moral.[24] Changing all the tenses from past to present, he effectively translates what the Narrator affirms about *this artist* into a universal claim about *The Artist* as such, forcing us to ask ourselves whether such really is the nature of the general case: Artists live for the pleasure of the creative process. Period. Maybe so. Maybe Melville didn't care whether *Moby-Dick* ever got published or not; or if it did, whether it sold a single copy. But if this is indeed the rule, then Hawthorne is the capital exception. He cared.

And while we are asking, we may need to remember that the concept of *the artist as such* is not an ancient and venerable concept; indeed, as the researches of M. H. Abrams have admirably demonstrated, this all-embracing concept was less than a century old when Hawthorne thought to inquire of it. To be sure, Plato had enough of a general concept of "the poet" to propose banishment from the universe of critical discourse; but prior to about 1750 one had to speak of the poet, the painter, the singer, the dancer, the landscape gardener, the fake butterfly-maker, one by one—and apply to separate publications for the rules governing each.[25] That is to say, it is necessary to notice that "The Artist" in Hawthorne's title is every bit as overdetermined as is "The Beautiful"—the latter pointing to the long shadow of Plato's otherworldly ontology, the former a modern invention designed to unify in one inflated conceptual family all those who try to make something pleasing rather than practical. So that, today, we can without irony speak of this or that "Rap Artist." Appropriately deflated, the plot concerns "The Guy Who Hated Trains So Much He Manufactured a Small Mechanical Butterfly."[26]

---

24. "Hawthorne and His Mosses" (1850) is conveniently available in the Norton Critical Edition of *Moby-Dick* (2018), pp. 544–58.
25. Implicit in the eighteenth-century invention of "Art" as a specialized form of human experience is the generalized idea of "the Artist" as one who, regardless of the particular medium and its supposed rules, aims at the production of esthetic effect; see M. H. Abrams, "Art-as-Such: The Sociology of Modern Aesthetics," in *Doing Things with Texts* (New York: Norton, 1989), pp. 135–58.
26. For the foundation of an ironic, counter-Romantic reading of "The Artist of the Beautiful", see Millicent Bell, *Hawthorne's View of the Artist* (Albany: SUNY, 1962), pp. 94–113.

The story is—indeed and provocatively—about art and society, but not in the way the Narrator thinks.

Crowning the achievements of the Old Manse Period, but establishing itself as something of a special case, is the must-discussed and still-elusive "Rappaccini's Daughter," which sometimes appears with a not-very-witty headnote identifying its author as M. le l'Aubepine, naming his tales as tomes, translating some of Hawthorne's former works into plausible-enough French, and entitling the present offering as "*Beatrice; ou, la Belle Empoisonneuse*" (976). We can locate the biographical source of this unusual foreplay,[27] but its narrative function is somewhat harder to determine. With the ascribing most of the day's serious literature to "the Transcendentalists," "under one name or another" (975), one might expect the reference to be German. Unless some French writer, like Eugene Sue, be taken as the *beau idéal* of the sort of writer whose "brilliant success" (976) owes to the rare ability to work just in between the "spiritual or metaphysical" interest of the Transcendentalists and "the great body of pen-and-ink men who address the intellect and sympathies of the multitude" (975). Clear enough, however, is the almost-mock modesty by which Hawthorne is learning to satirize himself in advance—as if, as Adam Gordon has well argued, he felt safe only if he anticipated the insensitive criticism he most feared.[28]

Accordingly, Aubepine's works are just as fatally allegorical, just as devoid of ordinary "human warmth" as Hawthorne's own. The Hawthorne who will soon express envy of the under-the-glass realism of Trollope[29] is here confessing "a very slight embroidery of outward manners—the faintest possible counterfeit of real life." And, anticipating the major self-attack-defense of "Main-street," he concedes that unless "the reader chance to take them in precisely the proper point of view…they can hardly fail to look excessively like nonsense" (975). Poor Hawthorne—who read Spenser and Bunyan at an impressionably early age and, given the ready availability of romance, failed to become a novelist in any proper sense.

But it is also clear, from the first line of this headnote growing toward the rank of a preface, is the not-very-veiled allusion to the sometime Transcendentalist who, after standing in for Emerson in the "Infidelity" controversy with the Pope-like head of the Harvard Divinity School, set about editing and introducing to a provincial American reading public, in fourteen volumes, certain selected "Specimens of Foreign Standard

---

27. Evidently it was a half-German French teacher named Schaeffer—whom Hawthorne met at the home of his friend Horatio Bridge—who in July of 1837 conferred on Hawthorne the name of Monsieur de l'Aubepine, even as he named Bridge Monsieur du Pont. The fact was recalled to me by the talk of Leonardo Buonono at the Hawthorne and Poe Conference in Kyoto in 2018, "In a Foreign Land: Estrangement in 'Rappaccini's Daughter'"; but see also Robert Cantwell, *Nathaniel Hawthorne: The American Years* (London: Octagon, 1971), pp. 202–5.
28. See Adam Gordon, "The Critic on Main Street," in Carol M. Bensick, ed., in *A Passion for Getting It Right* (Bern: Peter Lang, 2016), pp. 223–40.
29. In an 1860 letter to Fields, Hawthorne writes of the "solid and substantial" virtues of Anthony Trollope: it is "as if some giant had hewn a great lump out of the earth and put it under a glass case."; see the Centenary Edition of *The Works of Nathaniel Hawthorne* (Columbus: Ohio State University Press, 1987), p. 229.

Literature." Almost certainly Hawthorne had Ripley in mind, as the very first sentence begins, "We do not to have seen any translated *specimens*" (975) of Aubepine's voluminous but not too popular output. Clearly Hawthorne knew Ripley well from his months at Brook Farm, and earlier he could scarcely have been unaware of Ripley's part in the so-called Miracles Controversy, which found its way, absurdly, into the daily papers. At one level, the reference reinforces our sense that he wishes to talk about his contemporaries—as about himself—in some sort of code: consider the thinly veiled and faintly meretricious reference, in the last line, to George Bancroft, whose boyishly patriotic theory of the American Revolution had been subtly undermined in the four "Legends of the Province," and whom a letter to John Louis O'Sullivan refers to as "the blatant beast."[30] No egotism here, but no chance of mistake either. The magazine version of "The Hall of Fantasy" named all the names. The collected version took them all out. Why should a perilously placed writer go out of his way to make enemies?

But the Ripley reference also alerts the contextual reader to the necessary question of an *evidence*—relating Ripley's "better mode" of verifying the truth of scripture to the "better evidence" (999) to which the Narrator ascribes Giovanni's weak and failing faith in Beatrice. Some allegory here: what if the woman who, hearing the healing words of the divine savior and faithfully touching the hem of his garment, shriveled up like a spider held too long over the fire?[31] And thus the deep Narrator problem in "Rappaccini's Daughter," whether or not we follow the rare pleasure of Carol Bensick's long and winding "Road to Padua."[32]

Clearly Beatrice is speaking metaphorically—possibly for the first time in her socially innocent life—when she poses her final, rhetorical, accusatory question to her would-be lover: "Oh, was there not, from the first, more poison in thy nature than in mine" (1005)? Probably so. We easily spot the "vile empiric" (998) problem of Giovanni's "decisive test" (999): he must know "whether there were those dreadful peculiarities in her physical nature, which could not be held to exist without some corresponding monstrosity of soul" (999). And the Narrator is absolutely unforgiving at just this point, convicting Giovanni, but exposing at length a spiritual creed that may carry the Reader beyond her own credence. Of course there had been signs of some terrible poison, but

> These incidents [...] dissolving in the pure light of her character, had no longer the efficacy of facts, but were acknowledged as mistaken fantasies, by whatever testimony of the senses they might appear to be substantiated. There is something truer and more real, than we can see with the eyes and touch with the finger. On such better evidence had Giovanni founded his confidence in Beatrice, though rather by the force of her high attributes than by any deep

---

30. See Centenary Edition, *Vol. XVI, The Letters 1843–1853*, William Charvat, ed. (Columbus: Ohio State University Press, 1985), p. 114.
31. For a precocious, almost whimsical statement of the case for RD as, in part, a response to New England's contemporary Miracles Controversy, see my "Better Mode of Evidence," *ESQ*, 54.1 (1969), pp. 12–22.
32. See Carol Marie Bensick, *La Nouvelle Beatrice* (New Brunswick, NJ: Rutgers University Press, 1985), esp. pp. 29–43.

and generous faith, on his part. But now, his spirit was incapable of sustaining itself at the height to which the early enthusiasm of passion had exalted it; he fell down, groveling among earthly doubts, and defiled therewith the pure whiteness of Beatrice's image. (999)

A lot going on here. Time, in another context, for another hand, to go very slow.

Not just the Narrator's evident (and rather simple) Platonism, but the difference between faith and "confidence," a technical term in Locke and, after him, in the carefully crafted apologetics of "Pope" Andrews Norton—not quite scientific proof, but highly convincing probability of the truth of historical Christianity.[33] Then too, "enthusiasm," a very bad word for old Charles Chauncey but not for Jonathan Edwards.[34] And "passion": does that play any part in the drama which will come to be called "the fixation of belief"?[35]

But much more simply, for the moment, the Narrator expects Giovanni to embrace Beatrice, whether in literal twilight-zone fact her father has poisoned her or not. Of course she may be morally quite innocent, not at all privy to her father's plan to secure her a poisoned partner in the dangerous dance of earthly life among the Borgias; but on some crazy-ass premise she may be quite lethal. Poisoned body, pure spirit? *Whose* premise? If Hawthorne's very own, then let the feminists have at that spiteful sonofabitch. Giovanni could not be more afraid of her (sexuality) than if she had some social disease. But maybe she does, inherited from her sickly-looking father. Or else, why the reference to those little vials which Benvenuto Cellini was known to provide for the doctor who had syphilitic friends? Ben Who? We all know about Dante and his Beatrice, in which national epic Giovanni was "not unstudied" (976). Maybe even about Shelley's "Beatrice Cenci," who murdered the father who had raped her. But Benvenuto Cellini? It's like asking the reader to consider Cotton Mather when reading "Young Goodman Brown." But then, "Whose Hawthorne" is it anyway?[36]

Yet the simple point is telling enough: the more-than-transcendental Narrator, having found his protagonist shallow in the Neapolitan manner, now convicts him of a faith

---

33. For the rare epistemology of "confidence," see James Duban, *Melville's Major Fiction* (DeKalb: Northern Illinois University Press, 1983), pp. 196–202.
34. Provoking various responses by Jonathan Edwards—ultimately his magisterial *Treatise Concerning Religious Affections* (1746)—Harvard Professor Charles Chauncy identified and defined "enthusiasm" as a sort of mental disease in which "people are truly beside themselves, acting as truly by the blind impetus of a wild fancy, as though they had neither reason nor understanding"; quoted from David Levin, ed., *America in Literature* (Hoboken: Wiley, 1978), p. 361.
35. The memorable phrase rehearses the title of an important essay by Charles Sanders Peirce, but it is to the less academic thought of William James that we look for the never quite conscious and rational factors in the formation of our deepest-held beliefs; see, for example, his 1896 essay "The Will to Believe." Both essays are conveniently anthologized in Perry Miller, ed., *American Thought:Civil War to World War I* (New York: Holt, Rinehart and Winston, 1954), pp. 121–39; 142–65.
36. Glancing back toward Lionel Trilling's classic essay "Our Hawthorne," Gordon Hutner raises the question of whether that author may be quite so available as once it seemed; see Richard H. Millington, ed., *Cambridge Companion to Nathaniel Hawthorne* (Cambridge: Cambridge University Press, 2004), pp. 251–65.

weaker than that of his ancestor, Goodman Brown, just because he cannot live on "the words of Beatrice Rappaccini's lips" alone (992). Plainly it is a vulgar error to believe that a deadly soul can be inferred from diseased body, but C'mon, Man, the chick could be toxic. So that, once again, an elaborately intrusive and annoyingly moralistic Narrator may not know what-the-fuck he is talking about. Hawthorne, is reported to have said he never knew whether Beatrice was beautiful or deadly or both.[37] And the reader can't know either. Unless we discover some allegory deeper than Male Horror—like, according to some theology, original sin is a sexually transmitted disease—we need to experience the puzzle without solution. One more turn of the screw since "Young Goodman Brown": Giovanni's evidence is indeed a little funky, but in this tale there seems no easy way to make it go away.

3

Then of course there is "The Old Manse," after-the-fact introduction to the things Hawthorne wrote in Concord between 1842 and 1845. Neither tale nor sketch, this pleasant but evasive preface is, like all self-writing, in some sense a fiction: a linguistic construct designed to offer some created representation of the human person whose name is on the cover. Call it *persona* rather than narrator, the writer's problem is pretty much the same: "Who am I this time?"[38]

And the Hawthorne who appears is only a little less self-effacing than the other voice someone describes in French. By the end the Hawthorne impersonator is offering one professional apology and one persona. On the one hand, given the rich intellectual context, there should have been a novel, if not a "profound treatise of ethics" or a "philosophic history." Some sympathetic reader may yet tease out from the tales and sketches gathered here together something not unlike both of these. But the voice of the apologetic author authorizes only these "few tales and essays" ("sketches," we have learned to call them), all of which "had blossomed out like flowers in the calm summer of my heart and mind" (1148). Nothing here about their blooming it "too retired a shade," to be sure but, oh dear, "my heart and mind": it really is Hawthorne talking to us, right?

Well, *some* Hawthorne. And, before we get too excited about the possibility of honest, authorial self-revelation, we need to recall that the self-same heart and mind has just patiently explained, in one rather long paragraph, that, deliberately at least, nothing very personal had been in fact revealed. Having collapsed three summers

---

37. On the account of his son, Hawthorne "read the as yet unfinished manuscript [of RFD] to his wife. 'But how will it end?' she asked him, when he laid down the paper; 'is Beatrice to be a demon or an angel?' 'I have no idea!' was Hawthorne's reply, spoken with some emotion"; see Julian Hawthorne, *Hawthorne and His Wife*, Vol. 1 (Boston: Osgood, 1884), p. 360. Feminist or not, the modern reader is of course free to evade (or deconstruct) this too-familiar binary.
38. Evoked here is the title of a richly suggestive book by Jay Martin which, though it pays greatest attention to "the darker side" of the problem, is nevertheless an essential work on the question of authorial self-invention; see *Who Am I this Time?* (New York: Norton, 1988).

into one—anticipating and outdoing the self-inventing strategy of *Walden*—this here Hawthorne stipulates that, unlike his second-most famous neighbor, he neither expects nor means to provide "a simple and sincere account of his own life."[39] In fact,

> How little have I told!—and, of that, how almost nothing is even tinctured with any quality that makes it exclusively my own! Has the reader gone wandering, hand in hand, through the inner passages of my being, and have we groped together into all its chambers, and examined their treasures or their rubbish? (1147)

Like Parson Hooper, perhaps, the author of the humbly estimated *Mosses from an Old Manse* is determined to "veil [his] face" (1147).

More than that, the author who earlier had assured his wife that, given his "involuntary reserve" and, in consequence, "the objectivity of [his] writings," "people are wrong when they think I am pouring myself out in a tale or an essay"[40]—and who may well have suspected that his great gift of negative capability came at the expense of any proper selfhood—now professes, with comic hyperbole, that he is not, nor ever has been, "one of those supremely hospitable people, who serve up their own hearts delicately fried, with brain sauce, as a tid-bit for their beloved public" (1147). Shy he most certainly was. And modest. Yet hardly unconcerned with audience: his "public" may have been more distrusted than "beloved," but no writer of his generation—not even Melville—suffered more anxiety on their account. Who were they, exactly? What would they have him produce? Could they recognize any reality in his rare form of neo-allegoric mimesis? Soon enough, in preface after preface, for romance after romance, the personal would become a prime literary project.

In the interim between the self-protective "Old Manse" and the less guarded but equally fictional "Custom-House," two quite different cases present themselves: the sober fiction of "Ethan Brand," which declares itself—and leaves referent-less references to reinforce the point—but "A Chapter from an Abortive Romance" and the serio-comic sketch called "Main-street," equally abortive as it turns out, breaking off well short of the date proposed to a well-dramatized audience. Abortive or not, the disturbing tale of the Brand that would *not* be plucked from the burning is told by one of the most neutral and simply efficient narrators in all of Hawthorne's short fiction. Within the fiction itself, it seems, there is character enough to underestimate the seriousness of the issue at stake: Ethan Brand scares the hell out of Bartram *fils*, but his less percipient father is sure he can recognize superstition when he sees it. The most we can say is that the Narrator does not bother to emphasize what is supposed to be obvious: only the very smoothest of divines can be got to teach that "Tophet has not even a metaphorical existence" (815). And that his friendly greeting to the sunlit day after the defiant suicide of a man once

---

39. In the space of something like an "authorization," the first page of *Walden and Civil Disobedience* (3rd ed. (New York: Norton, 2008)) stipulates that its author absolutely requires—and presumably feels himself bound to furnish.
40. The letter of 2/27/42 continues: "I am merely telling what is common to human nature, not what is peculiar to myself. I sympathize with them—not they with me"; see the Centenary Edition, *Vol. XV, The Letters, 1813–1843* (Columbus: Ohio State University Press, 1984), pp. 612–13.

"simple and loving" (1063) was convincing enough to deceive, for a while at least, the competitive intelligence of Melville.[41]

"Main-street," on the other hand, exposes a somewhat less existential threat, but its emphasis is primarily on the Narrator himself. And on his audience. Once again, it appears, the committed but unassured Moral Historian is determined to get out in front of the moral and the historical criticisms he expects to encounter. Or *would* encounter, if anyone were paying close enough attention.

OK, so some spirited amateur is, with the aid of the pictures historically arranged in his showbox—just a "passing fancy," but "our love is here to stay"—going to tell his fellow Salemites the whole history of their originary but thereafter infamous town, whose main street just happens to be laid "over the red man's grave" (1028). In the narrative, some Red Men look on as local leadership passes from Roger Conant to a more militant—and *energetic*—John Endicott, and as more and more Puritans with hobnail boots make a deeper track in the wilderness than would thousands of moccasins, even if their wearers had not been decimated by white men's disease. Secure at first in the thought that "their own system of things will endure forever" (1025), they look on at first with curiosity, then with growing concern, as they "become aware" that the path-turned-street "is no longer free to them" (10323); and then they disappear.[42] But all this is merely subtext, and the Showman, sort of dumb-it-down Hawthorne, appears to accord it no special emphasis, as he portrays the gradual, perhaps inevitably destined, transformation of a wilderness into a proper town.

Yet his story is by no means flattering to the Salem audience—characterized much earlier in Hawthorne's career as not knowing where to find Gallows Hill, making them fit descendants of the ancestors who set bonfires on Powder Treason Day to scare away the Pope.[43] The audience will have to face up to their, well, unfriendly treatment of the Quakers; they will have to hear that all the generations after the first were narrower and less attractive souls, and they will have to experience the infamous Salem Witchcraft as a "Universal Madness run riot in the Main-street" (1047) a scene left on the cutting floor of an otherwise perfect "Young Goodman Brown." And none of this they really can dispute. But some other things they do, and rather vigorously.

Even before anything bad has happened, one captious critic in the audience protests the art of the performance: "The trees look more like weeds in a garden, than a primitive forest." To which the showman replies—nearly ironic even in his dumbed-down persona—"Human art has its limits." And then, in language familiar from the headnote to "Rappaccini," "we must now and then ask a little aid from the spectator's imagination."

---

41. For a word about the Bartrams in EB, see my "Artificial Fire," *Nathaniel Hawthorne Review*, 33.1 (2007), esp. pp. 11–12, 20–21.
42. See my "Red Man's Grave," *Nathaniel Hawthorne Review*, 31.2 (2005), pp. 1–18.
43. The Narrator of "Alice Doane's Appeal"—quite probably Hawthorne's fictive "Story Teller"—takes note of the stunning lack of historical awareness in his (Salem) audience: almost no one comes "on pilgrimage to [the] famous spot" where the witches were executed, and "Every fifth of November" the young men build a bonfire "without an idea beyond the momentary blaze"; see *Tales and Sketches*, pp. 205, 206.

To which, "You will get no such aid from mine. [...] I make it a point to see things precisely as they are" (1029). Peter Hovenden, we think. Or Tom Tristram, in case we have read *The American* in the wake of Hawthorne. And on it goes: responding to the suggestion of the rose-like beauty of "the lady who leans on the arm of Endicott," the same critic protests:

> Here is a pasteboard figure, such as a child would cut out of a card, with a pair of very dull scissors; and the fellow modestly requests us to see in it the prototype of hereditary beauty.

Matter of perspective perhaps, the Showman faintly suggests; matter of "light and shadow"; try sitting further back. Nope: "I want no other light and shade. I have already told you, that it is my business to see things just as they are" (1029). No further self-defense. But goodbye to "History as Romantic Art."[44]

Wait. Another objection, somewhat more sophisticated, from a "gentlemanly person" who seems to know a bit about the subject the Showman would now lightly, now darkly imagine. Modestly, but with authority,

> I would suggest to the author of this ingenious exhibition [...] that Anna Gower, the first wife of Governor Endicott, and who came with him from England, left no posterity; and that, consequently, we cannot be indebted to that honorable lady for any specimens of feminine loveliness, now extant among us. (1029–30)

It matters not whether any *other* Salemite would have these biographical facts ready to hand: the objection is Hawthorne's own, manufactured to anticipate a possible criticism, sometime, somewhere, from some "professor of biographical exactness," unhappy with anything like poetic license (not to say metaphor) in the text of history. And if the objection is a hopeless misprision, so the answer is a modest but ironic apology: "Having nothing to allege against this genealogical objection, the showman points again to the scene" (1030).

But the irony comes sharply into focus in the very next paragraph: the showman noticing the re-forming effects of "Anglo-Saxon energy—as the phrase now goes" (1030), the reader grasps at once the real subject: Anglo-Saxon energy as polite code for Manifest Destiny, and the representative determination of Endicott himself as a symptom and symbol of just that. The word "prototype" having been used, one is invited to regard Endicott as the "type" of the forces that tamed the wilderness and at the same time caused the native population to, well, not quite disappear, but to recede to the invisible margins. Typological prediction being not the same as precise historical causation, the objection against Anna Gower disappears in a cloud of epistemic misprision.

And on it goes. Even as the historical literalist protests the "anachronism" of the Showman's assembling together a number of personages who, though they "probably

---

44. Evoked here is the seminal book in which David Levin explains the special, Romantic, Walter Scott-inspired epistemology of most American historical writing in mid-nineteenth century, see *History as Romantic Art* (Palo Alto, CA: Stanford University Press, 1959), esp. pp. 3–23.

did all visit our town at one time or another," "could not possibly have met together in the Main-street" (1034), the "realist" critic once again refuses the suggestion that he "take another point of view" (1035). Later he loudly observes that the Showman's "mettled steed looks like a pig" but, for the moment at least, refuses to leave with a refund, preferring instead to offer one of Hawthorne's best-made self-criticisms. Realizing too well that the historian's prime difficulty is to "make it move," his Showman hopefully intones, "Pass onward, onward, Time." To which the critic, "Turn your crank" (1043). But the point has already been made. Sensitive to the problems of his craft, Hawthorne is deeply suspicious of his probable audience: history is story, and stories are fictions, and only the most primitive (or unimaginably sophisticated) can do without tropes. So here it is: apologia as plea for latitude. What if he were yet to find some old manuscripts? Who would believe that? Who would you invent to tell that story?

4

"Who speaks?" Virtual mantra of the once-vital movement called "The New Criticism"—which, temporarily at least, rescued the classroom teaching of literature from learned but not always pointed lectures on biography and "backgrounds"—the question marks a well-considered determination to keep the meaning of meaning "personal," what some imaginable somebody tried to say to somebody else.[45] *Language itself* may be thought to have an all-engendering life of its own, but not unless and until somebody speaks. Nor can it ever quite account for the appearance of those "monuments of undying intellect" which stubbornly refuse to lapse into the background of this or that "discourse." The personalization of speech—author or narrator or character, trustworthy or not, sincere or ironic—creates the drama of competing and conflicting meanings we used to call "literature," which opposes itself the sentences undergraduates underline with a yellow magic marker or else, more professionally, to the criticism which discovers that specialized groups have a diction, a grammar and even a syntax we can learn to identify as such. Like, doctors talk funny.

The endurance of classical lore (and certain emergent conditions of the Irish Renaissance) may well *enable* "Leda and the Swan," but W. B. Yeats assembled and styled the rhythmic sentences. And, closer home, that same lore, falling into the hands of an orphan who made poems instead of ordinary sexual love, is well required to explain why a "weary way-worn wanderer" is going *home* to Helen; but in the whole history of *langue* and *parole*, who but Edgar Poe could have written of "Nicean barks"? Or, intruding into a competing discourse, who else would think to redefine a wandering comet as a Muslim limbo turned into an aesthete's paradise? Or felt compelled to compete with a Persian

---

45. In the memorable words of Wayne C. Booth, "Though it is most evident when a narrator tells the story of his own adventures, we react to all narrators as persons"; see *The Rhetoric of Fiction* (Chicago: University of Chicago Press, 1961), p. 273. More general (and more self-consciously philosophical) is the view strongly advanced by E. D. Hirsch Jr., namely, that for literary purposes the only coherent sense of meaning is what somebody tried to say to someone else; see *Validity in Interpretation* (New Haven, CT: Yale University Press, 1973, esp. pp. 24–31.

poet he knew to be fictional? What is an author, indeed? The one who, turning the generally available into astonishingly precise, manages to make language precise and memorable. For a literary critic to say anything less is either inattentive or ungrateful.[46]

Once I tried to explain to my engineer father how "language" was coming to replace the "author function" in the spiffiest sort of academic criticism. He thought a minute, then told me this story. Making the rounds of his rural parish, a minister noticed that a long-neglected property was showing signs of human habitation and interest. Spotting the owner, he said, "I must compliment on the wonderful garden you and the Lord have conspired to produce." Pausing a moment, the new owner replied, "I know where you're coming from, Reverend, but when the Lord had it by himself, it was all weeds." Language is weeds. Authorship is gardening.

Once upon a time, when all this went pretty much without saying—when literature was understood as a stylized kind of human saying—the problem was always to characterize the human speaker. Who's telling us this? The author *in propria persona*? Or some invented *persona*? If the first, then—understanding that literary self-presentation involves some degree of self-invention—how is he representing himself this time? Ok: I never said it was going to be easy. If the second, what sort of person has the author invented to do the work of narration?

For example, we may, in the wake of "The Custom House," wish to say that the Narrator of *The Scarlet Letter* is obviously Nathaniel Hawthorne. But then we need to ask, who does that person appear to be here? The vengeful bastard who tried to get even with the political hacks who fired him for publishing a literary review in an opposition newspaper? Or the inveterate dreamer in the attic, who imagined what it would be like to find some old manuscripts and decided to obey the summons of the past as directed by a ghost? And would either of these Hawthornes explain the critical fact that *somebody* in a position of authorship is trying very hard to keep the redundant sexuality of Hester Prynne in careful check? And which one is hinting that Chillingworth, clearly dosing Dimmesdale with something or other, may have got the dosage wrong and inadvertently poisoned the man he lived to torment?[47] I, Nathaniel Hawthorne, former dependent of

---

46. For the history of this patent ingratitude—smarter-sounding in French than in English—see, first, Roland A. Barthes, "*Le Mort de l'auteur*," first published in *Aspen*, 5–6 (1967); next, less allusively, Michel Foucault, "Qu'est-ce-qu'un auteur?" delivered as a lecture at the College de France on February 22, 1969, then published the same year in the *Bulletin de la Societe francaise de philosophie*; then, better late than never (but happily avoiding the what-is-it-which-is construction), Jacques Derrida, in a memorial of Roland Barthes. The best one can say is that this particular version of THEORY—Continental Philosophy Taken Out of Context—has not really caught on in the Anglophone world. One reason, well explained by Jeanne Willete, on line, is that we have become rather sensitive to the question of subaltern speech; see "Michel Foucault: 'What Is an Author?'" *art history unstuffed* (1/24/14). "What does it matter who speaks?" Ask Frederick Douglass. More cogently, when will the French get over their hysterical disowning of the Cartesian subject?

47. For the (disputed) theory that Chillingworth actually poisoned Dimmesdale, see Jemshed A. Khan, "Atropine Poisoning in Hawthorne's *The Scarlet Letter*," *New England Journal of Medicine*, 311 (1984), pp. 414–16. In my view he probably did: not intentionally, of course, for his obvious purpose was to keep him alive and in pain; so that, when Dimmesdale dies,

Uncle Sam, about-to-be-Citizen of Somewhere Else. But once pen is in hand, who am I this time?

Then, on the other hand, one Miles Coverdale—who, speaking words from Hawthorne's own letters and notebook, was long and confidently taken to be none other than our blue-eyed darling Nathaniel, incompetently hiding his "inmost me" behind an all-but-transparent gauzy veil. Until, undeterred by the biographical facts, literary critics, discovered that this subtle representation of incompetent (or meretricious) narration could not possibly be an authorial self-portrait. To the point where a couple of literary super-sleuths proposed that Coverdale, whose story does not quite hang together, who was the last to see Zenobia alive, and who knows exactly where to find her body, may be in fact less a quasi-Hawthornean Paul Pry and more a murderer. Leaving others to debate whether Hawthorne's most mature character-narrator is an incompetent literary amateur or a brilliant sociopath. Or somehow, weirdly—as it has seemed to me—both.[48]

To be sure, all this epistemological curiosity defers the necessary question of exactly what real person Hawthorne was, in either case, trying to say to what supposable audience, real-historical, or formal-imagined. But on the personalist premises of the old New Criticism, neither the metaphor-system of Puritan salvation theory nor the real politics of early socialism can quite speak for themselves. Nor can, in either case, the "Woman Question."[49] Views are held by people, not as authorities, to be sure, but as the very condition of existence. And so we ascribe to the wide-reading Hawthorne, and no one else, the linguistic messages precisely if ambiguously arranged in his tales and romances. Language may well be said to have a life of its own, but quite like many monkeys at many typewriters (or computer terminals), it sends nothing to the publisher. And, unlike young scholars, it does not perish thereby.

Of course there is a non-trivial sense in which language is the last discovery of all literary criticism—as if David Hume had said, I go looking for the author and find always some words. But so it is with all human interaction: bodies can touch and be variously penetrated, but "souls never touch their object"; and no degree of passion can make "consciousness and a script ion equal." Language is as close as one human consciousness ("subject") can get to another. And even if we come to believe that the Self is elevator music, this "privacy" remains true: I simply cannot hear your raging guitars or rampant raps; not you, my own, more sophisticated, jazz-inflected lines: flatted fifths and minor ninths. Call this Epistemology 101–then read my book on "Emerson and Other Minds."[50]

So we live with the paradox: meaningful literary criticism—as opposed to discourse analysis or even old-fashioned intellectual history—absolutely requires a personal, even

---

Chillingworth simply dries up and blows away. I guess he got the dosage wrong: after all, it's the seventeenth century, who knew about titration? Still, as I have suggested elsewhere, "A minister thin/ Was sure It was sin/ But actually he died of surreptitious atropine poisoning."

48. See my "Nobody's Protest Novel," *Nathaniel Hawthorne Review*, 42 (2008), pp. 1–31.
49. See my Introduction to the John Harvard Library Edition of *The Scarlet Letter* (Cambridge, MA: Harvard University Press, 2009), esp. pp. xxxi–xlvi.
50. Michael J. Colacurcio, *Emerson and Other Minds*, 2 Vols. (Waco, TX: Baylor University Press, 2020).

an intentional model of meaning; yet no sort of analysis, not even the most subtle psycho biography, can render the authentic authorial subject. Language conceals as much as it connects. Yet we also live with the simple fact that real language acts are infinitely various: not everybody uses the same words in the same order. Poe wrote *Eureka* and not *Nature*. Hawthorne wrote *The Blithedale Romance* and not *Uncle Tom's Cabin*. Melville invented the word *Isolatoes* and not Whitman: *he* invented *Camerados*. And, creative as we wish the act of our own act of reading to appear, we did not entirely *make* the texts we are privileged to consider. So that, at the very least, the author function is a form of politeness and, one might say, honesty. Credit where credit is due. The rare Form we call Basketball enables the astonishing achievements of Michael Jordan and LeBron James; but, disembodied as it is, it never sank a single three.

Chapter Seven

A BETTER MODE OF EVIDENCE: THE TRANSCENDENTAL PROBLEM OF FAITH AND SPIRIT

Concentrating on the context of the story's composition—New England in the 1840's—this early essay is blissfully insensitive to the problem of its setting in early modern Padua. What it might well have noticed, however, is the glancing allusion to George Ripley the very first line, where "translated 'specimens' of the productions of M. de l'Aubepine" must surely recall Ripley's famous <u>Specimens of Foreign Standard Literature</u>.

From beginning to end the nineteenth century was a period of crisis for historical Christianity. No doubt God had been disappearing from men's actual experience for quite some time before that, and certainly the previous century had produced a significant amount of very articulate disbelief; but the nineteenth century has its own peculiar tone and atmosphere. The further we go, the less we are confronted by a wide separation between affirmation and denial, the more we hear the painful modern voice of doubt on all sides. If the eighteenth century is Paley against Hume, Bishop Butler against the Deists, Yale University against Tom Paine, the nineteenth century is Tennyson, Arnold, Melville. Similarly, apologetics becomes less and less the defense of specific doctrines and more and more an inquiry into what-William James would boldly come to call man's "will" or "right" to believe. In an atmosphere of widespread doubt—when argument has countered argument and proof stalemated proof—there yet remain many reasons for believing. But none of the reasons is any longer "pure" and faith is everywhere felt as a "risky" business.

True, the sense of faith one sees emerging in the nineteenth century is, though not precisely new, quite unlike the fading medieval sense. "Reason and Faith" could never again be the sort of problem it was for the scholastics. How could faith simply seek understanding when the very nature of faith had itself become the central epistemological question of the day? And more fundamentally, perhaps, how could a "faith" based on a set of preliminary "proofs" be other than a self-contradictory notion? Ironic as it seems, only when the higher criticism had cast substantial doubt on the Christian "evidences" did many people begin to feel such evidences were irrelevant even if they were perfectly trustworthy. How could propositions about reality or conduct based on the infallible authority of a prophet who had proved himself either God or at least a unique divine intermediary amount to more than words put into a person's mouth? Evangelical Protestantism might argue that this sort of *"mere* historical faith" was after all only a debased Catholic notion and no part of Christianity as such, but it would be hard to show that the faith-as-saving-experience school was less concerned to uphold the absolute authority of the Christian Scripture than others. Indeed, evangelism and fundamentalism often went together. The medieval conception of faith simply could not be maintained intact into the nineteenth century; attempts to do so could produce only the blindest sorts of "fideism." Obviously, however, the modern, "pragmatic" sense of faith did not emerge full formed and at once: To us, the line from Kant's second *Critique* to James' "Will to Believe" must seem fairly direct; so too must that from the higher criticism to Newman's undisguisedly voluntaristic "illative sense." But real historical developments do not always follow the most direct lines of implication. And thus between the fading medieval idea of faith as unproven propositions accepted on proven authority and the equally straightforward modern idea of faith as an inevitable condition of psychic health lies the vastly more problematic "idealist" conception of faith as direct spiritual insight. In Kant, the data of the practical reason become—in another, separate act—a significant part of the (steadily dwindling) content of Christian faith. In some of his transcendental successors (Jacobi, early Hegel, Coleridge, for example) there seems to be only one. Rejoicing in the threatened bankruptcy of the empirical proofs of natural theology and of the historical Christian evidences, the "Saturnalia of Faith" declared that in the higher Reason the mind has its own eyes; with them the spirit intuitively recognizes its own objects of truth and goodness. Not only are certain ontological truths (like Kant's God, freedom, and immortality) immediately evident to consciousness as such, but more importantly, perhaps, the soul's eyes can recognize the truth of any genuinely divine revelation by its consonance with the soul itself. Christianity is true not because the confirming evidence of miracles supports it, but because the soul recognizes it as its own proper good. Or, more carefully, we can distinguish between the transient and the permanent in Christianity through the active and immediate exercise of our own moral consciousness.

What I wish to suggest in this essay is that certain arguments about insightful faith and miraculous evidences, recognizably related to the situation I have just outlined, constitute a theme of considerable importance in the American Renaissance; that, specifically, the so-called "miracles controversy" of the late 1830s and early 1840s is a good deal more than a technical debate between the Unitarian "Pope" Andrews Norton and his former Divinity School students, and more than the scarcely veiled argument about democracy which it seemed to Perry Miller. Emerson, as everyone knows, declined to enter the debate in any polemical way, preferring simply to "speak his thought" in the "Divinity School Address" and then professing inability to explain or give "reasons." But his deepest beliefs—and his idealism is clearly a faith—are intelligible only in terms of the larger debate about faith in general. Hawthorne might write off all theological controversy as a "stupendous impertinence" which seldom really touched its ostensible subject, but not before spending certain rainy days at the Old Manse with some *very* significant volumes of the *Christian Examiner*, and not without embedding in "Rappaccini's Daughter" a logic which looks very suspiciously like the one Ripley employed against Norton. And it is hard to imagine how the crucial decision of Melville's Pierre is to be adequately understood without some reference to the historic question of faith and evidence. Obviously the argument becomes more generalized as we move into fiction, concentrating less on any specific faith and more on faith as such; but even the technical debate itself shows this same tendency towards epistemological generality. And given the transcendental logic, the difference between believing the words of Jesus and believing those of Beatrice or Isabel is not nearly so great as might first appear.

2

The impulse towards a transcendental conception of faith within New England comes, as we might suspect, from William Ellery Channing. To be sure, Channing wrote several fairly standard defenses of the Christian "evidences": "The Evidences of Revealed Religion" and the two parts of the "Evidences of Christianity" purport to demonstrate the truth of Christianity on grounds largely other than the inherent satisfactoriness of its doctrines. All of the accepted "external" evidences are there, as they were in Paley and as they would be, with a vengeance, in Andrews Norton. But whereas Norton would make such evidences the subject of a lifetime of study and of a three-volume opus, Channing chose to treat the subject far more casually. The evidences were important to him, but they were not quite a *sine qua non;* and they were only one of the many important subjects to which the "pastoral theologian" had to address himself.

More significant than Channing's obvious freedom from obsession on the subject of evidences, however, is the whole direction and emphasis of his thought on the subject. His "Evidences of Revealed Religion" moves surely from a defense of miracles as external evidence to an explanation and substantiation of his claim that "Christianity is not only confirmed by miracles, but is in itself, in its very essence, a miraculous religion"; it grows more enthusiastic on the subject of the "internal proofs which the books of the New Testament carry with them"; and it reaches its climax with "another evidence of Christianity still more internal, [...] an evidence to be felt rather than described."

> I refer to that conviction of the divine original of our religion which springs up and continually gains strength in those who habitually apply it to their tempers and lives, and who imbibe its spirit and hopes. In such men there is a consciousness of the adaptation of Christianity to their noblest faculties [...] This is the evidence which sustained the faith of thousands who never read and cannot understand the learned books of Christian apologists, who want, perhaps, words to explain the ground of their belief, but whose faith is of adamantine firmness, who hold the gospel with a conviction more intimate and unwavering than mere argument ever produced.

At first glance the argument seems frankly pragmatic: habitual application proves Christianity perfectly applicable, hence true. But if the form of the argument is pragmatic, the content is potentially transcendental. The "noblest faculties" will become the substance of man's "Likeness to God," the ground of his ability to be perfect in imitation of Christ's perfect character. The "application" Channing speaks of is an application by the Soul, and in this sense Christianity is proved by the agreement between Christ and the Soul.

The same doctrine is clear even earlier, in "Unitarian Christianity" and "The Moral Argument Against Calvinism." One knows that the Unitarian view of God and man is true and the "orthodox" Calvinist view false because the former agrees with the moral Reason whereas the latter shocks and affronts it. All we have to go on, Channing strenuously insists, is this noblest of our faculties; this we may never second-guess or undercut. Thus the last test of a supposed divine revelation is its consonance with the highest perceptions of the Soul. Ripley, Brownson, and Parker would scarcely say more.

But though Channing is quite willing, quite early, to admit nearly all that Norton's opponents would eventually claim, he never gives up his commitment to the appropriateness of miracles as an external validation of an inner response. In "The Essence of the Christian Religion" he maintains that "miracles are most appropriate proofs of a religion which announces the elevation of man to spiritual perfection."

> For what are miracles? They are the acts and manifestations of a spiritual power in the universe, superior to the powers and laws of matter. [...] And on the existence of such a power, the triumph of our spiritual nature over death and material influences must depend [...] I prize [miracles] not because they satisfy the passion for the wonderful. [...] but as discovering in a way which all can comprehend that there is some real being mightier than nature.

Clearly the question of immortality is central for Channing, and for this reason he clings to a more-thanphenomenological notion of spirit-as-substance-and-power which many minds, otherwise predisposed to be perfectly loyal to his thought, will very soon declare irrelevant to the life of faith. At this point it is sufficient to notice his eclecticism. He hopes for a faith which supports itself but which is not without trustworthy external supports as well.

Emerson's relation to Channing is, on this point at least, fairly easy to grasp. He simply draws out the implications of Channing's logic of the "noblest faculties." One sees it happening in the *Journals*. An entry for 1826 suggests that every man has moments of revelation which "touch all the springs of wonder, and startle the sleeper consciousness in the deepest cell of his repose" and which cause the mind to stand "forth in alarm with all her faculties, suspicious of a Presence which it deeply behooves her to respect." These moments of revelation in the soul are not "the state reasons" which support religion but they usually constitute, Emerson judges, "the body of evidence on which private conviction is built." The similarity of this to Channing's sense of an internal evidence which "sustains the faith of thousands who never read and cannot understand the learned books of Christian apologists" is perfectly obvious. Emerson is more responsive to one paragraph in Channing than to his whole Divinity School training.

But Emerson does not stop here. The leap beyond an historical Christianity endorsed both by miracles and by the soul's evidences is clearest in a journal passage for 1832, a passage which seems to answer Channing's eclectic position fairly directly. No one, Emerson observes, is quite willing to preach the full implications of "man's moral nature"; everyone ends his plea for some great human truth by a cautious suggestion of its agreeableness with the life and teachings of Jesus. This, he insists, deprives the truth of more than half its force, "by representing it as something secondary that can't stand alone."

> The truth of truth consists in this, that it is self-evident, self-subsistent. It is light. You don't get a candle to see the sun rise. Instead of making Christianity a vehicle for truth, you make the truth only a horse for Christianity. It is a very operose way of making people good. You must be humble because Christ says "Be humble." "But why must I obey Christ?" "Because God sent him." But how do I know God sent him? Because your own heart teaches the same thing he taught. Why then shall I not go to my own heart at first?

Why indeed? If the soul's insights are trustworthy and final, let us trust them directly. And if they are thus crucial, they prove far more (or less) than Christianity as such. Channing's faculties recognize and endorse Christian Scripture; Emerson's faculties, liberated from all such "operose" indirection, become aware of their own ideal authority. When this happens Idealism subsumes Christianity, and the rest of Emerson's religious teaching follows naturally enough.

To be sure, Emerson did not get over a certain interest in miracles immediately. The last chapter of *Nature* suggests that the Ideal or Spiritual Faith itself might draw some support from miraculous evidences:

> the traditions of miracles in the earliest antiquity of all nations; the history of Jesus Christ; the achievements of principle [...] ; the miracles of enthusiasm [...] ; many obscure and yet contested facts, now arranged under the name of animal magnetism; prayer; eloquence; self-healing; and the wisdom of children.

This odd little mix is probably the worst thing in the whole essay; surely it is far worse than the justly infamous transparent eyeball passage. It rests on a set of assumptions about the meaning of "spirit" far more open to objection than Channing's theory of miracles. But conceptions which could serve a mesmerist or a Mary Baker Eddy do not last long in Emerson. *Nature* itself contains the more fundamental suggestion that the truest support for the Ideal Faith is the fact that it "presents the world in precisely that view which is most desirable to the mind"—and this places the argument in the area of perception rather than of "power." The "Divinity School Address" goes on not only to reject any sort of miracle which is "not one with the blowing clover and the falling rain" but also to affirm the primacy of the moral faculties in the area of faith. And "Experience" seems to repudiate the paragraph of pseudo-spirituality in *Nature* rather directly:

> The physicians say they are not materialists; but they are :—Spirit is matter reduced to an extreme thinness; O so thin!—But the definition of the *spiritual* should be, *that which is its own evidence*. What notions do they attach to love? What to religion?

Here, no doubt, is Emerson's truest voice: the area of spirit is that of love and religious feeling, not that of power to suspend the ordinary workings of nature. To say that spirit is its own evidence is to say that spirit is accessible only through that "faith" which is the soul's ability to recognize and embrace its proper good with intuitive immediacy. It is to have rejected the last remnant of conventional connection between miracles of power and a salutary life of the soul.

3

Once we grasp the implications of Emerson's break with the position of Channing, much of the miracles controversy proper may seem anticlimactic—as Ripley struggles to make it plain that he is neither mystic nor infidel and Norton finally admits he has nothing against the religious sentiment. But this first impression is not entirely valid. A fundamental question is being faced head-on: what valid relationship can possibly obtain between the idea of a miracle as a temporary suspension of the ordinary workings of nature and that of faith as an insightful but ultimately unforced operation of the human mind? It seems entirely possible that Ripley's insights on this question forced Emerson to correct the spiritualism of *Nature* with the faith of "Experience"; and it seems evident that they lie behind the problem and the language of "Rappaccini's Daughter."

Ripley's doctrine is not at first absolutely pure. His 1835 review of Herder's *Spirit of Hebrew Poetry* expresses a certain hesitancy about that author's "mysticism" but, like the early Emerson, Ripley is anxious to approve any mind in touch with more of reality than could be dreamed of in the Lockean philosophy. Thus Herder's mind, he tells us, was in a "constant state of communion with the invisible world."

> Organic forces of nature were always a favorite subject of investigation. He wished to penetrate into her secret laboratory, in order, if possible, to discover the laws of her spiritual activity. On this account, he took a deep interest in [...] Galvanism [...] Electricity and Magnetism, the geological system of Werner, the investigations of Camper and Sommering in physiology, the theories of Dr. Gall on the brain.

This defense—which may have provided Hawthorne with a clue for the character of Aylmer in "The Birthmark"—reveals that Ripley is still thinking of "spiritual activity" at least partly in terms of a fairly crude sort of "super-naturalism," involving occult or "obscure and yet contested" phenomena. But although Ripley's mature definition of divine revelation as an advanced degree of natural knowledge is quite similar to the one he ascribes to Herder, he swiftly rejects the conception of the spiritual as a function of scientific "mysteries."

Ripley rejects such a conception because its application to the question of Scripture proves it valueless and possibly misleading. Jesus worked miracles. Fine. But so, for all the state of our science can tell us, did and do scores of false prophets. How is "a true miracle to be distinguished from a false one?" Only by a *prior* belief in the truly holy character of the wonderworker and the truly salutary content of his teaching. If the spectacle of the Pharisees accusing Jesus of "casting out devils by the Prince of Devils" is not sufficiently instructive, then one has only to consider the "phenomena of electricity and magnetism" (now uncapitalized) which seemed, upon their first discovery, to be quite miraculous "wonders surpassing the ordinary agencies of nature." Clearly, then, Jesus was and is known by his "witness to the truth" and not by any exercise of marvelous power. Faith, therefore, is rightly understood as our direct, immediate, intuitive, unproven recognition of the Truth of Jesus and the spiritual salutariness of his doctrine. Spirit in this context names not substance or power but the dimension of consciousness in which the highest cognitive and moral faculties of man operate.

Theodore Parker brilliantly elaborates Ripley's insight about the *priority* of faith in persons to that in miraculous evidences with his reductive suggestion that miracles would be useful only in support of a doctrine "contrary and repugnant" to man's native moral sensibilities. Kierkegaard might have something to say on this point but (unless it was Hawthorne) New England had no Kierkegaard. At any rate, however, it was Ripley who gave the new doctrine of faith its fullest and most impassioned expression.

Without denying the propriety of trying to determine the probability of the Christian miracles by all the appropriate historical means, he continued to espouse a "better mode of examining the evidences of Christianity than that which is usually pursued in the study of theology." The higher theology would be neither historical nor, in the ordinary sense of the word, empirical; it would begin with "the Image of God in the soul of man." With this beginning, and "if our inward eye is unsealed, we shall discern the Glory of God in the Person of his Son." Without denying the physical, he continued to stress the higher reality of that spirit which was its own evidence. At his most conventional he can make use of an "Edwardsian" sense of the material universe as an "expression of an Invisible Wisdom and Power" or an "Emersonian" doctrine of the dependence of things on our souls; he can make all the standard transcendentalist appeals to Reason, Duty, Disinterested Love, The Ideal. But always his most fundamental question concerns the new definition of faith: "Does the body see and is the spirit blind?"

The dominant note in Ripley, then, is that of "recognition": the unsealed inward eye recognizes the Person and the doctrine of Jesus because there is a fundamental correspondence between that historic incarnation of divine truth and something inherent in the soul as such. Crucial to man's recognition of the Christian Revelation is the "coincidence" of Christianity "with the higher nature of man."

> As the image of God is displayed in the divine elements of our nature, a similar image is presented in the revelations of the gospel. Shall we not recognize the likeness? Are not the spirit which breathes in the human soul and the spirit which breathes in the religion of Christ brother spirits that have come down from their native heaven to conduct the creatures of earth to their home with God? Yes they are of kindred origin, they know and love each other, and as soon as the spirit of man becomes conscious of its affinity with God, and beholds the same image in Jesus Christ, it utters what it cannot but feel. By this we know thou comest forth from God.

The result of this "brotherly" recognition is for Ripley the only faith worthy of the name—a faith that is not "merely a form of lifeless words," but rather one "that will satisfy the soul."

If there is one other note to attend to in Ripley—i.e., beyond his stress on faith as a *personal* recognition that takes place between two corresponding *personal* incarnations of divine truth—it is his less insistent but still discernible emphasis on "voice." Most of his language about recognition is, by transcendentalist necessity, visual; but not all of it. Embodied in Ripley's argument is the inchoate realization that personal recognition of whatever kind depends far more essentially on vocal than on visual encounter. In discussing the appeal of Jesus to his immediate historic audience, a matter of "witness to the truth" rather than of "wonders and prodigies," Ripley. suggests that the truly salutary experience for those who "cherished the love of truth in pure hearts" would be to "bear his voice and acknowledge his sovereignty." And far more climactically—in his last letter to Andrews Norton—he insists that to demand the evidence of miracles, ultimately visual in character, is to put out of court not only "the prophets and the divine messengers of old who *uttered* the burden of the Lord" but "even the glorious Gospel of the blessed God, which, in every *word* of its promises, every *tone* of its rebuke, every *expression* of its truth, exhibits the power of God, and the wisdom of God to salvation" (my italics). Ultimately one "sees" miracles and "reads" the lifeless words of Norton's scholarship but, as always, he must "hear" the Word of God. Miracles are irrelevant, finally, because the ultimate recognition is vocal.

What Ripley and his sympathizers seem to be saying to Norton—on every page, if between the lines—is that all the scholarship and all the miracles in the world cannot help a person deaf to the divine tonalities to hear the Word of God. The ultimate spiritual bankruptcy is the empiricist's inability to hear God when he talks. The charge against Norton may seem to be that his Lockeanism has blinded or sealed his inner eye; and we are entitled to feel that the quasi-mystical language of vision is a species of false transcendence. But deeper than this lies the suggestion that the faculty of faith is, by synaesthetic paradox, more like the bodily ear than the bodily eye. In heaven or in the mystical experience one sees; the result is not faith but knowledge: one knows as one is known. On earth one may see miracles, but that experience does not result in faith either. Properly speaking, faith is the result of a personal encounter with the Incarnated Word and, like any personal encounter, it is essentially vocal. Spirit means voice. On earth we see body and its permutations; we hear spirit. To recognize an Incarnation is to hear a Sovereign Voice.

4

Hawthorne, one must immediately admit, did not "discover" the general theme of faith in Emerson or Ripley. His movements from Salem to Boston to Roxbury to Concord expanded his horizons to include the figures and ideas of his own contemporary, Transcendental New England, but he had needed no more than Spenser and the records of Puritan witchcraft to inspire the story of Goodman Brown. From one point of view, "Rappaccini's Daughter" is simply a retelling of that earlier story; the two were appropriately placed back-to-back in the *Mosses*. Giovanni loses his Beatrice for many of the same reasons Brown loses his Faith: in both cases an unenlightened use of certain problematic evidences deprives the protagonist of the only "beatific" possibilities offered. But there are also, obviously, many important differences; and "Rappaccini's Daughter" seems to depend for its specific conception as directly on the transcendental understanding of faith as "Young Goodman Brown" does on the Puritan problem of spectral evidence.

With his concern for witchcraft and mesmerism, Hawthorne was admirably prepared to understand the problem of "supernaturalism" or debased spirituality as raised and solved by Emerson and Ripley. Indeed it would be surprising if this concern had not produced some fictional consideration of the relation between miracles and the true spirituality of faith. That consideration is the very substance of the tale of Giovanni's encounter with Beatrice. Giovanni fails his test of faith precisely because he attaches more weight to certain outwardly visible wonders than, according to the transcendental logic of Ripley or Emerson, a proper understanding of the nature of spirit can possibly justify.

Evidently Hawthorne intends us to recognize Beatrice's problematic ability to kill flowers and insects as some parodic form of miracle. From his "distance," of course, Giovanni can never be absolutely certain that Beatrice in fact *has* such powers, though his empirical observations establish roughly the same degree of probability the Transcendentalists were willing to grant to the researches of Norton. But in a sense this is trivial: even absolute certainty on his point will not settle questions about her spirit. Again we have, quite directly, the recognition of a radical discontinuity between wonder-working power (of whatever kind) and spiritual salutariness. Different orders of reality are involved; different orders of perception are required for the recognition of each. Granted Ripley's assertion of the non-relation between faith and wondrous evidence, and granted Emerson's revolutionary definition of the spiritual as its own evidence, what possible connection can exist between Beatrice's "spirit" and her ability to kill insects with her "breath"? The brother-spirits described by Ripley breathe in an entirely different medium. Only Emerson's crassly pseudo-spiritualistic, materialist "physicians" (or Hawthorne's Westervelt) would conclude that bad breath is an infallible sign of innate depravity. ·

Nor is Giovanni without Ripley's better mode of evidence. When he is with Beatrice, when he confronts her personally; when she talks to him, when "her spirit gushes out before him" like the sparkling water from the fountain which impresses Giovanni as an "immortal spirit" singing its song; at such times Giovanni is convinced that his Beatrice is, like Dante's, absolutely pure, completely worthy to be loved. In these moments something in Giovanni—something which ultimately proves too weak—recognizes and responds to her immediately: "the effect of her character was too real not to make itself familiar at once." Although this incipient faith "strikes no deep root into the heart" of Giovanni, the seed and the possibility are clearly there. "There is something truer and more real than we can see with the eye and touch with the finger," the narrator's simple Platonism instructs us, and it is "on such better evidence" that Giovanni had, temporarily, "founded his confidence in Beatrice."

The source of Giovanni's inability to sustain this sort of "deep and generous faith" is not among the story's famous ambiguities. A basic "shallowness of feeling and insincerity of character," a certain "vanity" not incompatible with his "quick fancy" and "ardent southern temper" make him incapable of a "true lover's perfect faith." Beatrice's "high attributes" may have excited his imagination (or some other "ardent" faculty), but his shallow spirit is never really able to hear the sovereign authority of her voice. Giovanni fails his test of faith because he lacks soul.

Under the fatal influence of the murderous rationalist Baglioni (whose slogan is "the limits of ordinary nature"), his empirical instincts triumph. Already possessed of the only evidences of spirituality which can possibly be valid, he yet grovels among his earthly doubts and demands a final proof in support of faith.

> He resolved to institute some decisive test that should satisfy him once and for all, whether there were those dreadful peculiarities in her physical nature which could not be supposed to exist without some corresponding monstrosity of soul. His eyes, gazing down from afar, might have deceived him as to the lizard, the insect, the flowers; but if he could witness, at the distance of a few paces, the sudden blight of one fresh and healthful flower in Beatrice's hand, there would be room for no further question.

If he could just be sure about her wonder-working powers: that, he thinks, would solve *all* questions. Just one more miracle, Beatrice, please.

In the paragraph which immediately precedes this desperately reductive logic, Baglioni has accused Rappaccini of being a "vile empiric." But, as every reader now senses, the story is really about Giovanni and, clearly—whatever may be the truth of the argument in "black letter tracts" between the two physicians—the really vile empiricism is that of Giovanni. The only "upshot of [his] experiment" is the discovery that he can wilt flowers and kill insects. But this poison is not the one which Beatrice ruefully discovers was *there* in his nature "from the first." In this story there are (to paraphrase Emerson) two poisons, discrete, not reconciled, poison for man and poison for thing. Beatrice may be poisoned in so far as she is a thing, and that poison may be discovered empirically; but as a person or spirit, all the valid evidence points to her purity. Beatrice is not a shrub; her spirit is not an odorous exhalation. Giovanni, on the other hand, is poisoned in *both* ways; and we fall into a vile empiricism like his own if we decide there is any real connection between the two. Poisonous things and poisonous people are known in different ways. Spirit is its own evidence. Our mental eye—or ear—must be able to recognize and detest Giovanni's final blasphemies apart from his poisoned breath—just as Giovanni himself was asked to recognize and love "the outgush of Beatrice's heart, when the pure fountain had been unsealed from its depths," in spite of her inverted miracles.

Read at this level, then, "Rappaccini's Daughter" seems an eccentric but recognizable version of the Transcendental-Christian argument. Looking for pitfalls, one might assume, Hawthorne has decided to provide a critical, negative test case of Ripley's logic about the discontinuity of wonder-working power and true spirituality by offering us a case of parodic anti-miracles. If the ability to raise Lazarus from the dead has, by itself, no spiritual significance, then what spiritual significance might be attached to an opposite kind of power? If miracles have no meaning apart from the character of the performer (to be known independently and on its own personal, spiritual, or vocal terms), then there ought to be no problem. In the case of Jesus, of course, there seemed to be none: all sides agreed that the miracles were perfectly in keeping with a truly spiritual character;

all evidences, it was happily observed, pointed toward a heavenly agency. But what if?—asks Hawthorne, *grasping* the problematic instance lurking in the logic being employed; what if a truly spiritual character should be seen to work death-dealing suspensions of the ordinary laws of nature? What if all empirical evidence worked not with but against the soul's instinctive perceptions? What then might become of the faith of the average sensual man?

Beyond this introduction of a crucial if somewhat gothic hypothesis into an otherwise tidy little argument, Hawthorne might at first seem to have extended the idea of a personal or spiritual or vocal encounter with Jesus to include personal encounter as such, possibly extending the logic beyond its proper limits. But as we have seen, Ripley's account of the divinity in man recognizing the divinity in Jesus has already suggested that one detects spiritual truth and goodness in *all* persons in the same way: incarnation speaketh unto incarnation. And once we advert to the full Dantesque symbolism of Beatrice it becomes apparent that Hawthorne has not "extended" the logic at all.

As in Dante, Hawthorne's Beatrice is offered as a genuine incarnation of divine truth and goodness. Both as a human person and as a symbol of Revelation she embodies the presence of the Word in the flesh. Realizing that the Transcendentalists are affirming—what no Puritan could affirm—that God is incarnated to some degree in every human person, Hawthorne is able to let Beatrice stand as a test of Giovanni's faith in all possible senses and to assert that all the instances, both human and divine, are somehow alike. Faith in the literal and in the symbolic Beatrice is alike a recognition of the Incarnated Word; in both cases the recognition must be purely spiritual, unmediated by evidences of any other kind. In both cases only a direct vocal encounter can have significance.

The dramatically climactic encounter between Giovanni and Beatrice makes the latter point unmistakably clear. Beatrice instructs Giovanni to discount all the "idle rumors" he may have heard about *her*, especially Baglioni's misguided "stories about [her] science." (The rationalist's empirical decision about the Christian miracles or about Biblical science generally is irrelevant to the "new views" of the autonomy of spirit.) Nor, as it turns out, should he believe "all that [he] has seen with [his] own eyes." Giovanni's stated wish to believe "nothing save what comes from [Beatrice's] own lips" may be filled with sexual innuendo not lost on Beatrice, but her answer clearly comes from another level of understanding—and our understanding is expected to be beyond hers.

> Forget whatever you may have fancied in regard to me. If true to the outward senses, still it may be false in its essence; but the words of Beatrice Rappaccini are true from the depths of the heart outward. Those you may believe.

Should he believe this? Should we? It is part of the greatness of the story and of the adequacy of Hawthorne's understanding of the nature of faith that we are never told "authoritatively," just as there is no one to explain to Goodman Brown about the pitfalls of specter evidence. In all cases all one has to go on are one's own perceptions. And in all significant cases, faith must always be *in spite of* certain problematic evidences.

But though neither we nor Giovanni can ever know the final truth about Beatrice, it is quite clear that she claims sovereign authority for her "words" *and demands* complete and unconditional acceptance; without this no further relationship with her can possibly be meaningful. The situation is parallel to that of Theodore and the Veiled Lady in *Blithedale*: a commitment must come before final revelations are made. And surely the whole encounter here ends in a way that is meant to recall many of Dante's experiences with Beatrice in the *Paradiso*: "A fervor glowed.in her whole aspect and beamed upon Giovanni's consciousness like the light of truth itself." The "light of truth itself": that would seem to be, at once, a capsule summary of Emerson and Ripley and the very definition of Dante's Beatrice.

This, of course, is not the whole story. Hawthorne's Beatrice may be as much Beatrice Cenci as she is the Beatrice of Dante. The curious fragrance in the atmosphere around her has no analogue in the *Divine Comedy* and the insoluble "ambiguity" or "paradox" of her apparently dual nature measures the distance between Hawthorne's ironic and Dante's romantic mode as surely as it measures the tonal difference between the affirmations of Hawthorne and those of the Transcendentalists. However one interprets, allegorically, the Manichean premise of poisoned body/pure spirit, the central fact is that Giovanni's test of faith takes place not in any "Paradiso," and not in either of the two realms distinctly graded down from there; for Hawthorne's sadly representative Giovanni, there is only the one fallen, historical "Eden of the present world." His whole experience may seem like a dream, but that fact does not guarantee its ideal authority.

But let Giovanni's test be however much more difficult than Dante's, the basic logic of the tale is clear: if Emerson and Ripley are correct about faith and evidence, then man should be able to recognize his Faith, his Beatrice, his corresponding spiritual good when presented, under *whatever* empirical conditions, to his own properly spiritual apprehension. If he fails to recognize the incarnated Word of Beatrice, the fault can be charged only to his own spiritual deficiencies.

5

If Hawthorne pressed the transcendental argument into some highly problematic and ambiguous realms, it remained for Melville (one might suggest by way of conclusion) to subject the contemporary logic of faith and evidence to its most telling scrutiny. Melville was no less well prepared for the general theme of faith than Hawthorne: the problem of masked doubt in *Msrdi's* Maramma, the question of the relevance of the hereditary guidebook in *Redburn*, the study of Starbuck's too-easy faith in *Moby-Dick* all prepared Melville to respond creatively to Hawthorne's investigations in the *Mosses*. And, of course, Melville goes on with the theme, almost obsessively. "Bartleby" seems to test the "proof" of pure Biblical Christianity from its perfect applicability; *The Confidence Man* exhaustively catalogues all the "brother spirits" which cry out for immediate and unquestioning recognition; and *Clarel* is a virtual handbook of faith-stances in the nineteenth century. But it is *Pierre* which, with certain differences of emphasis, takes up the question of faith and evidence exactly where "Rappaccini's Daughter" had left it. Where Hawthorne's narrative, in spite of all sort of difficulties, convicts Giovanni of "vile empiricism" for demanding some external, reductive, non-spiritual test of Beatrice's truth and salutariness, Melville has his young hero (fool?) of faith explicitly reject the temptation of "evidences." He decides to accept and love the tragic truth (or is it the body?) of Isabel on the strength of her voice and spiritual presence (or is it her hair?) alone. At the crisis of his career, he believes exactly what Giovanni doubts.

The case for Isabel's truth is not without a whole array of problematic evidences: the mysterious suggestions of the private portrait and of certain dim family rumors on the one hand, and the more "miraculous" implications of the lettered handkerchief and guitar on the other. All these suggest a wondrous but maddeningly inconclusive probability. At one point Pierre is moved to ask for a clear miracle. Let the Memnon stone fall on him if he is about to invest *his* belief in an illusion. Solomon the Wise could have warned him of the vanity of this expectation in an ironic and naturalistic universe, and the logic of "Rappaccini's Daughter" would be equally cogent. Faith is not confirmed by any event extrinsic to the spiritual process of faith itself. The natural world is spiritually silent; revelation is by persons, and commitment precedes assurance. The rock does not fall and Pierre is left with the conclusion that faith must be its own evidence. He accepts it.

Even before he has heard the second half of Isabel's curious gospel, he senses the insoluble problems connected with her history. Short of a lifetime investigation, the ambiguities are not to be cleared up; perhaps not even then. Meanwhile, as the Transcendentalists asked Norton, what of the call of the spirit? Cannot Pierre recognize the tragic truth of Isabel's sisterhood by the same clarity of correspondence with which Ripley's soul recognizes Jesus? If spirit does not speak directly unto spirit, then spirit is deaf, dumb, and blind indeed. In what seems an open allusion to the contemporary faith-problem, Pierre heroically decides to take Isabel's at its word, rejecting all other evidences.

> By posting about hither and thither among the reminiscences of his family, and craftily interrogating his remaining relatives on *his* father's side, he might possibly rake forth some few small grains of dubious and unsatisfying things, which, were he that way strongly bent, would only serve the more hopelessly to cripple him in *his* present resolves. He determined to pry not at all into this sacred problem.

Miraculous external evidences and the consultation of historical witnesses are, it turns out, methods equally empirical and equally irrelevant when the spirit has its own evidences, the heart its own reasons.

And here, of course, in Pierre's "prior" heart-reasons, we touch the source of all the ambiguities—and, we measure Melville's distance from Hawthorne. "Rappaccini's Daughter" and *Pierre* are different stories not merely because Pierre believes where Giovanni doubts; and not principally because Melville takes the problem further, into an exploration of the results of the young man's faith-decision (the weakest part of the novel). We might like to know what the rest of Giovanni's life was like or, better, what it would have been like if he had trusted and loved "La Belle Empoisonneuse"; but these questions lie without the bounds of Hawthorne's *allegory*, and we go behind the donnee if we worry about them too much. Giovanni lost what little soul he had, period. But Melville's real addition to the argument is his elaboration of Hawthorne's hint that somehow Giovanni's poisonous, empirical decision was made "from the first." Where Hawthorne merely suggests that Giovanni's failure is temperamental, a matter of constitutional shallowness or lack of soul, Melville makes it unmistakably clear that Pierre's recognition of Isabel and his decision to accept her is so aboriginal as to be instinctual.

The entire first half of the novel carefully explores the nature of Pierre's "prior" and "from the first" heart-reasons, so unlike the "baths and holy writ proofs" demanded by the "dull head" in the "cold courts" of justice; it clearly concludes that his worry about miraculous and/or historical evidences is little more than after-the-fact rationalization, a rather desperate search for confirmation of a decision already somehow "there." He knows what he is going to do from his first sight and hearing of Isabel; she is the sister for whom *his* whole soul has for so long been longing, the one thing needful to his complete earthly happiness. At bottom, Pierre's "recognition" is far less a matter of transcendental truth seen or sovereign voice heard than of a deep arid instinctual need fulfilled. His sexual embrace of Isabel figures his adoption of faith out of some hidden and instinctual need; the embrace is incestuous because the believer and his object have become more closely related than would seem quite healthy.

The orthodox might predictably complain that Ripley's view of man recognizing Christ as a "kindred spirit" threatened to reduce Christianity to a species of brotherly love, but Melville stated the problem in an allegory as shocking in substance as in figure. To say that in faith man's faculties recognize their spiritual sibling may be merely to admit that man posits a kindred object of faith and invests it with the qualities he most needs to believe in and worship. Just so, Pierre "recognizes" Isabel's meanings because they are largely the creation of his own needs. She is not "himself," but an aspect or a projection of himself, allegorically a "sister." The proper figure of this too-close relationship between faith and its object would seem to be incest.

With Melville, then, the transcendental argument has come in a full and self-defeating circle. The transcendental definition of faith ultimately reduces to the pragmatic. The idea of faith as recognition, Melville seems to discover, was only a temporary and rather desperate attempt to avoid the conclusion that faith *is* the creation of the individual psyche, according to the complexity of individual physic need. Judging from his later works, Melville—who got as far into the problem as anyone in the American Renaissance—was not fully prepared to accept this outcome. He did not exactly wish to retreat into the old morass of evidences, but he continued to study the higher criticism. He struggled with the ambiguities of the problem as the nineteenth century had presented it to him. For good or ill, the full endorsement of the pragmatic view of faith would have to wait for William James.

Chapter Eight

"ARTIFICIAL FIRE": READING MELVILLE (RE-)READING HAWTHORNE

Melville, we mostly agree, is our first strong reader of Hawthorne: our blue-eyed Nathaniel really does have the power greatly to deceive the "superficial skimmer of pages"; and the premise of "blackness" endures, even if troubled by our evolved sense of racial discourse.[1] But this is not to say that Melville always gets it right. The discovery that "Young Goodman Brown" is no "Goody Two-Shoes" seems to record a perfect shock of recognition: someone (else) is taking the premise of Evil pretty seriously. But given what we have learned about "specter evidence," we may hesitate to address the author in his very own words: "It is yours to penetrate, in every bosom, the deep mystery of sin." The words are in fact those of the Devil, and Melville's own energetic will-to-blasphemy seems everywhere to shorten up the distance between Hawthorne's doubtful drama and Satan's subtle plot. Then too, the premise of "blackness" is founded not here, but in certain biographical suggestions about "Egotism; Or, The Bosom Serpent" and "The Christmas Banquet"; and these, as I have suggested elsewhere, have not always been taken quite seriously.[2] "Strong" readings are, as we have learned, not always meticulous; and this may be particularly true in the case of a literary competitor, who may well have a critical agenda all his own.

No harm would be done in trying to share—with Melville's "Virginian Spending July in Vermont"—a certain enthusiasm for the fine touches of "The Old Apple Dealer" or "Fire Worship." One could even, at a discount, permit Melville to read more of Hawthorne than of his own readerly self into the Truth-seeker of "The Intelligence Office." It would take a determined skeptic to conclude that Melville errs in simply paraphrasing the too explicit moral of the excitable and inconstant narrator of "Earth's Holocaust": the danger may well be that "the all-engendering heart of man" might itself be consumed by a blaze whose purpose is to rid the world of imperfection. But even the most ardent devotee needs to be reminded that Melville significantly misquotes the conclusion of "The Artist of the Beautiful":

---

1. See "Hawthorne and His Mosses," in Herschel Parker and Harrison Hayford, eds., *Moby-Dick* (New York: Norton, 2002), pp. 530, 521–22. Cited hereafter, in the text, as HHM.
2. See my essay "The Life within the Life," *Nathaniel Hawthorne Review*, 30 (2004), pp. 1–31.

> When the Artist rises [rose] high enough to achieve the Beautiful, the symbol by which he makes [made] it perceptible to mortal senses becomes [became] of little value in his eyes, while his spirit possesses [possessed] itself in the enjoyment of the Reality. (HHM, 517)

Changing all the narrator's historical past tenses to the generalizing present, Melville ascribes to Hawthorne the virtually solipsist view that the true artist cares for neither object nor audience—for nothing beyond the pleasure in the process of artistic aspiration itself. Surely Hawthorne had satirized this view on his very first page, where Own Warland appeared in the midst of all sorts of watches, "all with their faces turned from the street, as if churlishly disinclined to inform the wayfarers what o'clock it was."[3]

Artists there are, we surely recognize, so purely bent on realizing the blessed dream of their private world or the complex interplay of their arcane reference that they decline to offer their reader so much as the time of day: Poe, in *Al Aaraaf*, in Hawthorne's own day; or else, for many readers, Eliot in *The Wasteland*. Hawthorne's text is full of learned allusion, to be sure, but he expects them to be found out. And surely the final sentence of his "Artist" contains enough historical overdetermination to suggest that the subject is one oddly Platonic practitioner and not art-as-such.[4] What Hawthorne may well have felt—and no one was in a better position to underline the point than Melville—is that, given the reality of a marketplace literary economy, the serious writer had better be prepared to live without the reward of great public adulation, at least in the present. Thoreau would, in the first chapter of *Walden*, make the same discovery—studying to "avoid the necessity of selling" the intricate baskets no one wished to buy.[5] And no doubt many professors can be got to agree: you'd better like what you're doing, with or without the offer from Yale, hoping always that someone else will like it too. Never quite thinking of himself as "unacknowledged lawgiver," Hawthorne could easily have identified with the Owen Warland who did, one time at least, repair the clock on the church steeple—helping to keep, that is to say, the conscience-keeper's conscience.[6]

---

3. See "The Artist of the Beautiful," in *Hawthorne: Tales and Sketches* (New York: Library of America, 1996), p. 907. Cited hereafter as *Tales*.
4. Ironic readings of Hawthorne's AB begin with Millicent Bell, *Hawthorne's View of the Artist* (New York: State University of New York, 1962), pp. 94–113. The Platonism (and Poe-ism) implied in the notion of "The Beautiful" as the end of artistic activity ought to be self-evident. Less obvious and equally important is the fact that the generalizing idea of "The Artist" is, in Hawthorne's day, a recent and problematic formation; see M. H. Abrams, "Art-as-Such" and "From Addison to Kant," in *Doing Things with Texts* (New York: Norton, 1989), pp. 135–87.
5. For the context of Thoreau's famous complaint about supreme artistic dedication versus market reality, see Michael T. Gilmore, *American Romanticism and the Marketplace* (Chicago: University of Chicago, 1985), pp. 35–51; and cp. Stephen Railton, *Authorship and Audience* (Princeton, NJ: Princeton University, 1991), pp. 50–73.
6. The prominent use of time-pieces to represent conscience in both Emerson's "The Transcendentalist" and Melville's *Pierre* suggests the general availability of the conceit—possibly deriving from Coleridge; see *Aids to Reflection* (rpt. Port Washington: Kennikat, 1971), p. 219.

Yet none of this local quibbling takes us to the heart of the problem of "Hawthorne and His Mosses." Nor will it help if we dispute the question of Hawthorne's greatness as compared to that of Shakespeare—who quickly takes over the essay as soon as Melville touches the question of dangerous things obliquely said. Hawthorne may or may not be the American literary "Shiloh," but he appears to have suggested to Melville that a local writer too could take daring chances—blaspheme, even—and get away with it: tell the whole of some forbidden truth and yet not alienate one's audience; and, more important perhaps, not let life's worst possible meanings drive oneself to madness. Shakespeare uses his "frantic" Lear to tear away the "mask" of order and goodness, and Hawthorne knows the devilish trick as well. Surely "it were all but madness for any good man, in his own proper character, to utter, or even hint" that "There is no good on earth, and sin is but a name";[7] but the cautious Nathaniel had trained up his Goodman Brown to the purpose. And hence the structure of the Hawthorne-inspired *Moby-Dick*: Ahab, his crew assisting, has to bear the problem of absurd Evil to the throne of God in his own blighted person; Ishmael—"one of that crew" (152)[8]—has the noticeable advantage of being able to watch him do it; and Melville (and the reader) have the doubled, literary security of watching them both. There certainly is, as Melville will come to word the warning, the problem of dwelling too long with the Devil's inverted point of view, of looking "too long in the face of the fire." But, as the "glorious, golden, glad sun" cannot hide Virginia's Dismal Swamp, nor [...] the millions of miles of deserts and of griefs beneath the moon" (MD 328), sooner or later you do have to look. Or else, at very least, you have to look at some literary character taking his own long look.

2

No wonder, then, if Melville's critical notice should fall, sooner or later, on the fire-born vision of Ethan Brand, whose story he read under the initial, over-determining title of "The Unpardonable Sin."[9] Not in "Hawthorne and His Mosses," to be sure, which offers itself, in the summer of 1850, as a belated "review" of a collection that appeared in the spring of 1846, but first of all in one of the letters an aroused Melville could not keep from writing to Hawthorne after he too had moved into the Berkshires. Wonderfully hyperbolic yet not very subtly competitive, the letters continue the delicate task of balancing ingratiating flattery and prodigious self-announcement. And nominally at least, the process of "review" continues, omitting *The Scarlet Letter*, dwelling instead on the less demanding *House of the Seven Gables*, and getting around to the sadly but ambiguously instructive career of Ethan Brand in its own good time.

---

7. See "Young Goodman Brown," in *Tales*, p. 283.
8. All citations of *Moby-Dick* refer to the Parker-Hayford edition (see "Hawthorne and His Mosses," in Herschel Parker and Harrison Hayford, eds., *Moby-Dick* (New York: Norton, 2002)).
9. For the somewhat complex publication history of "Ethan Brand," see Lea Bersani Vozar Newman, *Reader's Guide to the Short Fiction of Nathaniel Hawthorne* (Boston, MA: G. K. Hall, 1979), pp. 95–101.

The letter of April, 1851, offers a curiously off-center response to the "sunnier" novel which followed Hawthorne's much-discussed *Scarlet Letter*. One could well argue that a more telling review is offered a year later, in *Pierre*—which presents itself as a sort of Goodman Brown in the House of the Seven Gables, and which self-consciously refuses to pretend that a little heterosexual romance can atone for age-long sins of caste and class. Here, however, an odd indirection is the only sign of resistance, which may not recognize itself as such. Metaphors of aristocratic furnishings give way to the conceit of an imaginary book left upon a table: "Hawthorne: A Problem"; and to an excited but unconvincing praise of the character of Clifford: no "caricature," but simply "Clifford." And then, finally, to the evocation of a Hawthorne who "declares himself a sovereign nature" and "insists upon treating with all Powers upon an equal basis" (L 536–37).[10] Evidently Hawthorne has helped Melville shed the pious mask he imagines himself to have been wearing since the blind-guide episode of *Mardi*.[11] Yet most readers suspect a dramatic displacement: busy at revision, Melville is inventing the openly blasphemous Ahab and blaming him on the covertly impious Hawthorne.

As interesting as the moral overstatement, however, is the not very veiled attempt to confess himself as the author of the recent, anonymous review of the "Mosses"; for, did "circumstances permit," he would "like nothing better than to devote an elaborate and careful paper to the full consideration and analysis of the purport and significance of what so strongly characterizes all of this author's writings" (L 537). The appropriate "circumstances" would have to wait for the enforced leisure of modern criticism, but surely Melville's recent review must count as something like a down payment on this noticeably academic project. Redundant verbiage and all. And it would not have taken much imagination to connect the "Calvinistic sense of Innate Depravity and Original Sin" of the review with the "NO! in thunder" of his letter (HHM 521; L 537). Evidently Melville wants Hawthorne to recognize him as the kindred spirit who has already praised his genius so generously, and in so special a manner; to sympathize with him in the project of telling some "grand truth" their liberal and enlightened age does not wish to hear; and to praise him, in return, as a literary equal. At least.

Nowhere, however, is this plot of recognition, revision, compliment, and competition more curiously revealing than in the logic that leads from the short-shrift and somewhat patronizing review of "The Unpardonable Sin," in a letter of May, 1851, to the deconstructed re-presentation of its moral problematic in the "The Try-Works" chapter (96) of *Moby-Dick*. In the first instance Melville simply misreads the tale, in a perfectly predictable way: heart, yes; head, no. But then he seems to have thought better of the

---

10. Melville's letters to Hawthorne are quoted from the Parker-Hayford edition of MD and cited as L.
11. Nowhere is Melville's plea for permission to produce a literature of honest doubt than in chapter 109 of *Mardi*: in conventionally pious Maramma, a blind guide named Pani wishes for an un-asked discussion of dark and difficult issues, that he "might know what warranty of fellowship with others, my own thoughts possess." Until he remembers his public role: "But those pilgrims; that trusting girl.—What, if they saw me as I am? Peace, peace, my soul; on, mask again."

question, as in what we may call Ishmael's "fire sermon"—his third and final attempt to tell us exactly how far we need to go with Ahab[12]—he furnishes a complex and cogent, if competitive, theme summary of "Ethan Brand." As if he had come to recognize that, allowing for differences of source and motivation, he was writing a version of the same God-defying story.

A certain line of connection has long appeared obvious: if the electrified masts of "The Candles" (Ch. 119) seem to have been lighted at the blazing pine trees in Goodman Brown's forest, then surely it is all but self-evident that "the flame into which Ishmael stares resembles the lime-kiln fire into which Ethan Brand [...] had too long gazed and by which he was destroyed." It may seem a little dated to pronounce, with psychoanalytic glee, that both fires represent "the demonic and irrational forces to which Freud gave the name 'Id.'"[13] But intuitively, the connection seems strong before any critical language is applied: two fires, two fierce confrontations with the nighttime negative, two heroes of defiance, two destructions that seem both plausibly motivated and inevitably fatal. One almost imagines that Melville is assuring Hawthorne that he did after all get the subtler point of "Ethan Brand": a man may begin the search for the secret of cosmic justice full of "love and sympathy for mankind" and yet end up a "fiend" (EB 1064)[14]—a monstrous egoist, forgetting the humane origin and rationale of the quest. Ahab too had "his humanities"; and was it not the hateful sufferings of "the whole race from Adam down" (MD 156) that he set out to redress? What happens? What fiery vision turns the dark wisdom of requiring "something somehow like original sin" (HHM 521) to the deadly madness of seeking to treat "with all Powers upon an equal basis"? (L 537)

That is to say: if Melville is, consciously or unconsciously, re-writing Hawthorne's most unabashedly Promethean story,[15] he is also revising his earlier critique—re-valuing the strength of the literary effort made in "The Unpardonable Sin" and, more

---

12. Ishmael's first two general instructions—on the attraction and then on the danger of Ahab-ism—are chapter 23 ("better it is to perish") and chapter 28 ("Push not off").
13. Howard P. Vincent, *The Trying-Out of Moby-Dick* (Carbondale: Southern Illinois University, 1949), pp. 333–36. Oddly enough, the learned notes of Luther S. Mansfield and Howard P. Vincent gloss not Hawthorne but Emerson, who warned, in "Experience," that we not "stay too long at the spark"; see their (once standard) edition of *Moby-Dick* (New York: Hendricks House, 1962), p. 798. Closer to the mark might have been Emerson's (later) injunction, in "Fate," to "go face the fire at sea"; see *Essays and Lectures* (New York: Library of America, 1983), p. 954. The connection of "The Candles" to the flaming pine trees of "Young Goodman Brown" was made by Nathalia Wright in "'Mosses from an Old Manse' and *Moby-Dick*," MLN 67 (1952), 387–92.
14. All citations of "Ethan Brand" refer to the Library of America *Tales*.
15. The relevance to EB of the career of Faust has been well recognized; see, for early example, William Bysshe Stein, *Hawthorne's Faust* (Gainesville: University of Florida, 1953); and cp. J. Lasley Dameron, "Hawthorne and Blackwood's Review of Goethe's *Faust*," *ESQ* 19 (1960); and Joan E. Klingel, "EB as Hawthorne's Faust," *Studies in Short Fiction* 19 (1982), pp. 74–76. The example of Prometheus has been, despite the central image of the civilizing fire, more difficult to recognize, but the critical suggestion about "the overthrow of Uranus by Chromus" might not be entirely beside the mark; see Richard Kelley, "Hawthorne's EB," *Explicator* 28 (1970), p. 47.

significantly, changing the very terms of response and analysis. The letter in question concedes that this recent story, with its hell-fire suggestions, was probably "responsible for many a shake and tremor of the tribe of 'general readers.'" And it duly notices the "frightful poetical creed that the cultivation of the brain eats out the heart" (L 540)—thus placing the thematic emphasis on the idea that Ethan Brand had produced in himself the unpardonable sin the moment when, basking in the "star-lit eminence" of an intellectual preeminence that remains, in this "abortive" effort, entirely putative, his heart "had ceased to partake of the universal throb" (EB 1064). Such a reading may fairly appeal to Hawthorne's *Notebooks* for support; and it will flatter all those readers who continue to treasure the well-worn thematic of the head and the heart.[16] But it does not take us very far into the question of what it was Ethan Brand saw (and saw too much) in the artificial fire; nor does it provide any but the most general connection between Brand and Ahab, who at the outset all but devastated the ego of the not-so-fragile Stubb—and who mostly forgot to say goodnight to his crew.

Moreover, it is a reading whose general applicability Melville immediately goes on to reject. Momentarily at least. "Poetical creed" is one thing, but his own "*prose* opinion" remains fixed:

> in most cases, in those men who have fine brains and work them well, the heart extends down to the hams. And though you smoke them with the fire of tribulation, yet, like veritable hams, the head only gives the richer and the better flavor. (L 540)

Then, not wanting to break the mood of writerly affinity—and sensing perhaps that he is defending the nature of the "vast intellectual development" that began when he moved from the Yale College and the Harvard that was his whaling ship to the greater riches of Evert's Duykinck's remarkable library[17]—he drops all opposition to the anti-intellectual theme his partial reading has precipitated: "I stand for the heart. To the dogs with the

---

16. As Lea Newman has pointed out, the *American Notebooks* actually propose more than one thematic center for EB: the early evocation of a "cold and hard-hearted man" whose "body will petrify" at death survives "The Man of Adamant" for reuse in EB; and then, in 1844, the formal suggestion of "the investigator for the Unpardonable Sin" who "finds it in his own heart and practice" competes with the thematic hypothesis that "The Unpardonable Sin might consist in a want of love and reverence for the Human Soul," implying "the separation of the intellect from the heart"; see *Guide*, pp. 98, 100. To any or all of which we go at our own risk: Hyatt Waggoner (*Hawthorne* (Cambridge, MA: Harvard University Press, 1955), p. 58) warned long ago that almost all of Hawthorne's valuable thinking was done in fiction, where a priori moral premises are ambiguated almost beyond recognition; and—failing to take this point—the thematic doggerel produced in the name of the head and the heart has been, all by itself, more than sufficient to motivate the theoretic rejection of semantic criticism altogether. For a learned but somewhat overwrought attempt to translate Hawthorne's problem of self and other into the discourse of the (post-)existential, see John Dolis, *The Style of Hawthorne's Gaze* (Tuscaloosa: University of Alabama, 1993), pp. 151–58.
17. For the beginning of Melville's massive and unflagging attempt to catch up with the literature and philosophy of non-whaling world, see Merrill R. Davis, *Melville's Mardi: A Chartless Voyage* (rpt. New York: Anchor Books, 1967), pp. 62–64.

head! I had rather be a fool with a heart, than Jupiter Olympus with his head" (L 540). And on the other side of the Hawthorne-inspired revisions of *Moby-Dick*, *Pierre* will be preaching something of the same sermon: head-and-heart together, if the rare combination is maturely possible; but heart alone, if choice has to be made.

In all of this there is only a slight hint of the terms in which "The Try-Works" would re-engage the moral anthology that is "Ethan Brand"—the fire that smokes the brainy hams to manly wisdom and the "tribulation" that fire might symbolize. The symbol system is quite different, of course: transplanted from lonely lime-kiln to domestic smoke-house, the fire—borrowed no doubt from Hawthorne's "Fire-Worship"[18]—seems a lot less hellish; seems friendly, even. Implied, at least, is the sense that the thought-provoking fire might have affected Ethan Brand in a way far other than it did. Thus the criticism of the ostensible moral seems not entirely withdrawn: "plus heart, minus head" makes Jack—or Charlie Millthorpe, in fact—a rather dull boy. And so perhaps it is not altogether surprising that, when Melville again took up the matter of the fire, the terms of his exploration were somewhat more complex.

And that his (implied) address to Hawthorne was more heartily sympathetic at the outset. Prose of head and heart to one side, they share a poetical creed in common: "look not too long in the face of the fire"; doing so has destroyed both Ethan Brand and Captain Ahab and, as Ishmael now gives us his last general reflection, it came damn near destroying him as well. Complexities and distractions arise almost at once, as if to defer the exact definition of the fire. Partly, it appears, the Ishmael problem is the quite general one of looking when one is supposed to be acting: "Never dream with thy hand on the helm"; as soon drift dangerously into the Oversoul while up on the masthead to spy whales. Closer to the issue, he may be staring at one symbolic thing too long and too intensely. This surely is the second sense of Pip's crazy-witty discovery that "when aught's nailed to the mast it's a sign that things grow desperate" (MD 335); life, after all, has many images, and the "slippery Proteus" is never to be caught in a single figure.[19] Finally, taking the full force of the figure into account, it's a bad idea to fix one's stare on a lively, deadly metaphor when the management of a ship requires life-and-death attention to the literal. And so the excited thematic prose comes back to its Hawthornean center: "Give not thyself up [...] to the fire." Look, presumably, but not too long, or it will "invert" and "deaden," as for a time it did Ishmael himself. Some "wisdom" burns at the center of this fire, no doubt; but a "wisdom that is woe." And near it burns as well a "woe that is madness" (MD 328). Searching for the secret of the fire is a deadly business: don't try this at home.

But what, aside from the ever-present "Id," has Ishmael seen in the fire? And what exactly does Melville imagine Ethan Brand to have seen? Neither Brand nor his daring creator can yet know anything of the "monomaniac commander's soul," which seems

---

18. In HHM Melville emphasizes the "domestic kindness" of Hawthorne's fire, despite its capacity for "mad destruction" (pp. 519–20).
19. Thus Emerson (finally) protests the easy and uniform symbolism of his one-time hero Swedenborg; see "Swedenborg; or the Mystic," in *Essays*, p. 676.

to Ishmael the spiritual counterpart of "the rushing *Pequod*, freighted with savages, and laden with fire, and burning a corpse, and plunging into that blackness of darkness" (MD 327). That, surely, were but one memorable but fantastically over-determined version of life as hell; or, more aptly, perhaps, of life lived against the knowledge that savagery is its only law and hell its only reward. Yet hell is indeed the word proposed by Ishmael to cover the case and, racism to one side, what else could he possibly be imagining as he watched "the Tartarean shapes of the pagan harpooneers' stoke the fire of the *Pequod's* try-works with their three-pronged poles? Or as he listened to their "tales of terror told in words of mirth?" A "red hell" midst "the blackness of the sea" (MD 327).

Some less graphic version of hell must have teased, then tortured the inland imagination of Ethan Brand. Michael Wigglesworth, let us suppose, if not Herman Melville. And something less philosophical as well. Nowhere, at the outset of his intellectual career, has Brand been able to read that "There is no good on earth, and sin is but a name." And that itself might be nothing but the head putting too fine a point upon the heart's rebellion; something like this a youngish Pierre will have to learn in trying, prematurely, to write a mature book. Nor can lonely, meditating Brand be assumed to appreciate the full significance of his suggestive surname. The brand of Cain, a simple man in his position might know, well before he himself becomes a "vagabond on the face of the earth";[20] but it will take more than a little quaint and curious lore to discover the relevance of Thomas Hooker's *Firebrand*, which told the story of his and others' nearly unsuccessful attempt to convince the prolific and multiform despair of a certain Joanna Drake that she had in all likelihood not committed the unpardonable sin; and of Cotton Mather's more recent *Brand Pluck'd out of the Burning*, which told of his own therapies in the same arcane genre.[21]

Not Brand but clearly somebody is supposed to have these old-time casuistic texts in mind, or we lose the full force of Brand's momentary panic at the "painful" (EB 1059) thought that perhaps he has NOT discovered in himself the unpardonable sin; and of the precise significance of his final earthly gesture, suicide in a moment of cosmic blasphemy. As if his rebellion had meant to say, to some pious Puritan or other, "Pluck this." But such is hardly his mood at the beginning. Ending as a would-be hero of the Transcendental Negative—and then, abortively, as a bushel of fertilizer—he surely began by looking into the question of that very hell which the Calvinistic yokels of the

---

20. For Hawthorne's negative hero as bearing the "brand" of Cain, see Eli Stock, "The Biblical Context of EB," *American Literature*, 37 (1965), pp. 115–34. Unlike Ahab and Ishmael, Brand is born with a suggestive name; Ahab has a crazy mother to thank, and Ishmael is self-(un-)christened. Name-wise, the received French translation of *Moby-Dick* begins with a problem: "Je m'appelle Ishmael" works only if we insist on the literal, "I call myself Ishmael"; certainly *not* "My name is Ishmael."

21. For a commentary on Thomas Hooker's casuistical debate with Joanna Drake, see Frank Shuffleton, *Thomas Hooker* (Princeton, NJ: Princeton University Press, 1977), pp. 29–66. For Mather's therapeutic success with the would-be witch Mercy Short—and then with Margaret Rule, "Another Brand Plucked"—see David Levin, *Cotton Mather* (Cambridge, MA: Harvard University Press, 1978), pp. 223–49. And cp. Kenneth Silverman, *The Life and Times of Cotton Mather* (New York: Harper and Row, 1970), pp. 120–22; in Silverman's words, the Mercy Short case had allowed Mather to behold "the very state of the damned itself" (122).

hill country of Western Massachusetts know all too well. And fear. Unless of course they have been reading Brand's other namesake, Ethan Allen, that hill-born prophet whose Oracle of Reason had no use for that particular hypothesis.[22]

Obviously Ahab needs to believe himself a representative man, bringing the unspoken resentment of his crew—and the baffled suffering of all humanity—to the throne of God, or to the bar of those gods who kill us for their sport; and surely Brand, a partial precursor, begins with some kindred mission in mind. What exactly would it mean to go off and search for the unpardonable sin in a spirit of love and tenderness and pity? Quite evidently: to discover and then to publicize that precise sin "which could neither be atoned for, nor forgiven" (EB 1056). For after centuries of Scholastic and then Reformed inquiry, its exact name and nature remained a mystery still.[23] A liberal theorist like Charles Chauncy (who figures prominently in the disputed theodicy of Hawthorne's "Celestial Rail-road")[24] might refer to the non-existence of hell as "the mystery hid" from all the Christian generations so far, but the scene of Brand's out-setting quest is altogether orthodox; and in his world the name of the unforgivable sin retained its primacy as the hidden mystery. Hell is altogether real; and full it is of unpardoned—doubtless unpardonable—sinners. If only we could learn the terrible secret. Probably, if Calvin's predestinarian account should prove correct, there might be no way for a reprobated man or woman to avoid this last-last crime against the light, but at least one could know. If one had not yet in fact committed this hell-requiring sin, then hope might spring up and even flourish. And if in fact one had—well, there remained at last the option of joining the Devil's party. At all events, no distracted mother need ever again throw her very own child down a well, just to be sure at least which side she was on.[25]

Surely we need to posit some such train of (Melvillean) thought in the mind of Ethan Brand as he stared, night after night, into the flames of his lonely, lime-kiln fire. Until the face of the fire became the face of Satan himself, with whom, as legend told the tale,

---

22. Widely maligned for his "deistic" rejection of the premise of supernatural revelation, Allen was also notorious for his belief in the salvation of all men—which earned him a place, as the "Great Clodhopping oracle of Man," in Timothy Dwight's "Triumph of Infidelity"; see Collin Wells, *The Devil and Doctor Dwight* (Chapel Hill: University of North Carolina, 2002), pp. 68–73.
23. For the competing—Catholic and Protestant—theories of the unpardonable sin, see Joseph McCullen and John Guilds, "The Unpardonable Sin in Hawthorne," NCF, 15 (1960), pp. 221–37. Scholastic theorists had settled for twin gestures presumption and despair—both sins against the cardinal virtue of "hope," and both, accordingly, in defiance of the latter-day teaching that "it ain't over till it's over." Closer to Hawthorne's moment lay the various attempts of Protestants to interpret the crucial text of Matthew 12:31–32: "All manner of sin and blasphemy shall be forgiven unto men but the blasphemy against the Holy Ghost shall not be forgiven unto men." For essays in pursuit of this theme, see Newman, *Guide*, p. 101.
24. For Hawthorne's response to the Universalist controversy between Dwight and Chauncy, see my essay "The Cosmopolitan and the Provincial," in *Studies in the Novel*, 23 (1991), pp. 1–19.
25. As Michael Dunne puts the positive case, "Brand could show others that they were innocent of [the unpardonable sin] and that they could therefore anticipate divine forgiveness"; see *Hawthorne's Narrative Strategies* (Jackson: University of Mississippi, 1995), p. 150. For the grotesque (and of courses illogical) incident of attempted child-murder, see John Winthrop's *Journal*: Richard S. Dunn, ed. (Cambridge, MA: Harvard University, 1996), pp. 229–30.

Brand began to hold steady and sober converse. As if the Archenemy himself aspired to know the substance of God's final lore. The fireside scene of Brand's impious meditation is extremely significant. For daily use by ordinary mortals, the fire itself required a deed of god-defiance. And, while somewhere a bound Prometheus lives to feel the vultures eat away his human liver, Ethan Brand here turns a resistant rock into the substances that will fertilize fields and seal the homes of men against the hostile elements. Advancing the cause of that very civilization which the stolen fire set irresistibly in motion, and that against the will of an array of jealous deities, Ethan Brand ponders the secret which they—or their monotheistic yet oddly schizophrenic replacement[26]—may treasure yet in godly privacy and guard against the swelling pride of aspiring man. If the final fact were known, God might still be God. But just barely. One might still need to own, repeatedly, the "speechless, placeless power" (MD, 382, 383), but morally, the secret would be out.

3

Of course it all goes terribly wrong, this heroic act of inverted piety. And though Brand never has the luck to take a ship down with him, he well establishes the futility of all such would-be-heroic quarreling with God. Essaying to treat "with all Powers"—"would they let [him]" (MD 22)—he manages to lose the very humanity he sets out to justify, destroying (as we are told) the psyche of some hapless "Esther" along the way, and mercilessly scorning the "half-way sinners" (EB 1056) he left behind, in some god-forsaken town, on his way to reaching that philosophical peak of nihilistic defiance in which he wishes not so much to discover as to commit the unpardonable sin.[27] And all this at a length much less than the average philosophical romance. As if to leave room for a writer more highly charged with negative energy, less willing to notice and to emphasize the "abortive" nature of the project from the outset.[28] For if Hawthorne had rehearsed a good bit of the Melvillean meaning in prescient prediction, still the thing might bear repeating, once more, with greater feeling. And even if Hawthorne had named the tune of Negative Transcendence in almost no notes—the all-defying Superhero as a pail of useful stuff—perhaps he was a little too generous in his praise of the Nature that endures; for she seems quite happy to reabsorb the body of the Rebel, whatever shall

---

26. One waits for a reference to Melville throughout the entire course of Jack Miles' provocative account of divine schizophrenia as a replacement for the available polytheism, but it never comes; as with Melville himself, Shakespeare is still being asked to do all the theosophical heavy lifting; see *God: A Biography* (New York: Vintage, 1996).
27. See Nina Baym, "The Head, the Heart, and the Unpardonable Sin," *New England Quarterly*, 40 (1967), pp. 31–37; and cp. *The Shape of Hawthorne's Career* (Ithaca, NY: Cornell University, 1976), p. 117.
28. Biographical evidence indicates that the eventual subtitle of EB—"A Chapter from Abortive Romance"—has some basis in Hawthorne's actual literary intention; see Newman, *Guide*, pp. 95–111. My own view is that, after the publication of his *Mosses*, Hawthorne was intending to move to a longer form; nor would he have set out deliberately to use up all the rich and curiously observed North Adams material in his *American Notebooks* on a single tale. Yet there is merit in the suggestion that Brand's project is inherently abortive; see Kermit Vanderbilt, "The Unity of Hawthorne's EB," *College English*, 24 (1963), pp. 453–56.

have happened to his soul, and she smiles benignly, as if to reassure the Bartrams (on behalf of the tribe of "general readers") that Peace and Justice reign in heaven after all; and that horrible things happen only to deeply crazy people. And never in the light of day.

When Ishmael's fire-sermon stipulates that his world and ours will look very different in the morning, when "the artificial fire" of lonely meditation has been replaced by "the natural sun" of ordinary perception, his creator is surely thinking of—and endorsing, momentarily—the gloriously reassuring morning after the nighttime self-immolation of Ethan Brand. Suspend all such will to disbelieve, we are told; wait for "the glorious, golden, glad sun, the only true lamp" (MD 328). Little Joe Bartram has been suitably terrified by the last moments in the life of this tender man gone wrong; perhaps his less percipient father too; subliminally, at least, both have heard the "fearful peal of laughter" (EB 1065) with which Brand had ended his abortive life. But now, by the light of day, all seems changed, utterly.

> The early sunshine was already pouring its gold upon the mountain tops, and though the valleys were still in shadow, they smiled cheerfully in the promise of the bright day that was hastening onward. [...] Old Graylock was glorified with a golden cloud upon his head.

In the midst of this "golden radiance," a "mortal man" might almost step from cloud to cloud and thus "ascend into the heavenly regions" (EB 1066). Here is Hawthorne giving us somewhat more than "a ray of his light for every shade of his dark" (HHM 522); but after giving us so much darkness he seems to have earned the right. And the recognition: "believe not the artificial fire"; believe only the "natural sun"—all other lamps "but liars" (MD 328). "Night Thoughts" (so to speak) are false: write theology in the light of day.

But then, the not unexpected turn from validation to critique. Believe the reassuring sun, right enough, but note as well—a whole list of things the glad and glorious sun "hides not." Notice, that is to say, that if the sun shines on the good and the evil alike, it requires a lot less than a maniac's nighttime hallucination to see the natural evil on which it does so equitably shine. "Rome's accursed Campagna" may be no more than an ill report until the dose of Roman Fever that nearly extinguished the young life of Una Hawthorne. Even then, Hawthorne might not complain, accusing God; and neither would Henry James in his "study" of Daisy Miller. But Henry Adams would make up for them both; and Melville would issue his own protest in advance.[29] Similarly, "wide Sahara" may be singled out to stand for "all the millions of miles of deserts and of griefs beneath the moon" (MD 328) without reference to the Hawthorne problem. But the very first item in Ishmael's list of Nature's nasty insults, "Virginia's Dismal Swamp," has special relevance to the reader of "Ethan Brand." For two of the prominent naturalists

---

29. Watching his sister die the horrible death of lockjaw under the smiling Roman sun, Adams concludes that "God might be, as the Church said, a Substance, but He could not be a Person": see *The Education of Henry Adams* (rpt. Boston, MA: Riverside, 1961), p. 289.

associated with that sun-bathed blight on the landscape of natural theology were named, *pere et fils*, Bartram.

Readers who reject the image of a "pedantic" Hawthorne will wish to believe that Hawthorne's naming of the businesslike father and the significantly more sensitive son who watch at the site of Brand's initial—deadening, inverting—misconception was entirely arbitrary and accidental; and it must be admitted the limestone hills of Western Massachusetts are singularly un-swampy. Still, we may be expected to remember that the famous patron of middle-landscape gardening, William Bartram, follows a long tradition in making his experience in the swamps of the American Southeast sound a lot like a naturalistic hell. And in no case can we mistake Melville's responsive intention: no one matching light against dark, sunlight against shadow, in the perilous game of trying to establish the balance of Nature's symbolic meaning, could afford to leave out the gloomy and forbidding landscape hinted at in the naturalistic writings of the two men who had done so much of their original work in and around a region which offered itself as yet another problematic instance in what had come to be called the "Sacred Theory of the Earth."[30] If not the swamps themselves, with their own dismal beauty; or even the snakes, which neither Bartram feels the compulsive need to kill; then surely the alligator, which fights with others of its kind with the awesome strength of a "monster," with "clouds of smoke issu[ing] from his dilated nostrils"; which could, with violent ease, turn his attention upon the mild-mannered and curiously empirical "botanist," who expects at every moment to be "seized and dragged [...] into the river": and which in fact does, with a few of its fellows, devour "thousands, I may say hundreds of

---

30. John Bartram, explicitly, and his son William, by evident implication, were admirers of the idiosyncratic work of Bishop Thomas Burnet, whose *Telluris Theoria Sacra* (1681–89) agreed with the familiar proposition that the earth "furnishes enough evidence of design to prove a deity" yet held that the world as we know it, after the flood, is in fact "a mighty ruin"; see Basil Willey, Introduction, *The Sacred Theory of the Earth* (rpt. London: Centaur, 1965), p. 5. What mountains and excessive, irregular oceans were to Burnet (and Cotton Mather), swamps may well have been to the Bartrams: susceptible to redemption as the sublime, perhaps, yet prima facie a problem. For a history of the swamp's redemption, from the status as "a place of evil, a land of the dead," see David C. Miller, *Dark Eden* (Cambridge: Cambridge University, 1989), pp. 47–76. As to the widely known *Travels* of William Bartram, in and about the swamplands of the Carolinas and Florida, we may choose to value the "romantic qualities" of his verbal and pictorial evocations, but cannot overlook the fact that some of them are "natural 'representations' or approximations of hell" (201, 199); see Thomas P. Slaughter, *The Natures of John and William Bartram* (New York: Knopf, 1996), esp. pp. 197–204. It seems likely that Melville knew of the elder Bartram from the pages of Crevecoeur's famous *Letters from an American Farmer* in which (in Letter XI) this Quaker Botanist and paragon of practical farming is seen draining all the swampland on his Pennsylvania farm and wishing his neighbors to the south could be got to do the same—unaware, as it seems, that when all swamps are drained, all original life is gone from the land Clearly, some of the more brutal cetology in Crevecoeur's heavily ironic account of whaling off Martha's Vineyard demands to be called "Melvillean"; and one can only wonder what thought the fierceness of Crevecoeur's little humming-bird might have inspired in a so pacific a botanist: "Where *do* passions find room in so diminutive a body?" See *Letters* (rpt. New York: Penguin, 1987), pp. 187–99, 184.

thousands" of fish in a single engagement, to the accompaniment of the "horrid noise of their closing jaws."[31]

One could make too much of all this, of course: perhaps there was no "mighty secret" (L 537); perhaps there was in fact "naught beyond" (MD 140) the maddeningly variable face of the natural world. But had Hawthorne's natural sun not conceded too much to the premise of a universal benevolence? Had not his terrifying story retreated too far in the direction of reassuring its "general reader"? Did not his final vision of the daylight's radiant transformation of a terrain of terror into a landscape of reconciliation suggest that Brand's entire career—of sounding the depths of evil in the name of a good that failed to appear—had been nothing but a bad dream? Once upon a darkness it seemed man might have reason to quarrel with God. But now, in vision at least, a wondrously enlightened "Earth was so mingled with sky that it was a daydream to look at it" (EB 1066).

Unless of course the Hawthorne who had resisted the Universalist Charles Chauncy in the name of the Edwardsean Timothy Dwight had meant to suggest that this vision of a peaceful, accessible ascent from earth to heaven was indeed a "daydream," as partial and misleading in its way as anything one might see burning in the fires of hell. Enceladus had found it so but failed to inform Pierre of his finding. And so—consciously or unconsciously, and with a signal almost too subtle to detect—Melville's Ishmael seems to allow for this possibility as well. For, sunup or sundown, there remains the question of books: what is one supposed to read on the subject of how sanely to live in a world where the sun fails to hide so much? "Unchristian Solomon's wisdom" might almost go without saying: "Ecclesiastes is the fine hammered steel of woe," whether Hawthorne has gone to school there or not. But other books by implication: not Rabelais, though he might be judged "passing wise, and therefore jolly" by those who would "rather talk of operas than hell": but "Cowper, Young, Pascal, Rousseau," even though passing wisdom may call them "poor devils all of sick men" (MD 328).

An interesting list, without the daring Shakespeare of "Hawthorne and His Mosses" and the Dante of the more infernal *Pierre*. And yet scarcely unintelligible: Rousseau for the sense, clear as early as *Typee*, that Western Rationality has left a lot of biological life to be desired; Pascal to acquaint the head with the reasons of the heart; Young to swear that "night thoughts" can be as true as any others; and Cowper—whose metaphoric "Castaway" has lent its name to Chapter 93—to prove, in the case of his own once-born sick soul, that Calvin's creed applies to quite a few who cannot find their way to saving grace.[32] Four arrayed against one, we presume, to "strike the uneven balance" (HHM

---

31. *Travels*, 114–18. Once upon a time, on a golf course in South Carolina, an alligator seized and thrashed a small dog, playing beside some casual water. Before being dragged under, the dog seemed quite surprised, with an expression that seemed to say, "I did not think we were part of the same food chain." The pious Bartrams know we are—but the exemplum will not be on the final.

32. Cowper's lines upon "The Sofa" are part of a long poem called *The Task*, set by a female friend who, without the therapeutic expertise of Thomas Hooker or Cotton Mather (and unaware of the gender reversal implied), sought to distract the melancholy poet from his settled conviction of reprobation. "The Castaway" briefly relates the tale of a sailor fallen overboard and

521); but if we were to let Cowper stand alone against Rabelais, the opposition would be familiar indeed. And it would amount to a sort of final endorsement of Hawthorne's "Calvinistic" sense of literary history. Not in "Ethan Brand," to be sure, but back in a very curious item in the *Mosses*—which Melville had omitted to mention but not failed to notice.

Emerging from the museum of literary symbols that supplies the conceit of "The Virtuoso's Collection," the oddly neglected sketch with which Hawthorne chose to end his collection of 1846, a familiar if not terribly percipient Narrator, "feeling somewhat weary from the survey of so many novelties and antiquities," looks for a place to sit and rest. His host, the same. "I sat down upon Cowper's sofa, while the Virtuoso threw himself carelessly into Rabelais' easy-chair" (VC 711). It would require an ideal reader with a more than ideal insomnia to explain all the details of an encyclopedic collection in which the literature of the world is being identified by its leading symbol, and then reduced to its material counterpart: clearly Hawthorne remembered more in *The Faerie Queene* than Una's lamb; or in Dr. Johnson than his "cat Hodge": and somebody or other is supposed to protest the analogy which links the dove of Noah's ark with the raven that "belonged to one Barnaby Rudge" (VC 700).

Literature is as "material" as one is pleased to insist, yet its value may be thought to present another sort of issue. But the point of the final pairing is perfectly clear: the Virtuoso, who has been rewarded for learning "to despise all things" (VC 704), who believes that "Life—earthly life—is the only good" (VC 708), and who is at last identified as "the Wandering Jew" (VC 713), can no doubt rest comfortably enough in the jollity and worldly wisdom of Rabelais; his guest—Hawthorne in ironic reduction, perhaps—settles far more comfortably into the symbolic sofa of sick-soul Calvinist Cowper. And it seems quite likely that this is the symbolic opposition that Melville, honoring Hawthorne, is permitting Ishmael to reproduce and embellish. Hawthorne might not agree to talk as frankly and freely and volubly as Melville would have liked, about "all the things that lie beyond human ken,"[33] but no one would accuse him of "dodg[ing] hospitals and jails" and of liking better to "talk of operas than hell" (MD 328).

---

abandoned by his helpless mates. It concludes in a Melvillean "misery" that still delights to trace the "semblance in another's case": "No voice divine the storm allayed,/ No light propitious shone,/ When, snatched from all effectual aid,/ We perished, each alone;/ But I beneath a rougher sea,/ And whelmed in deeper gulfs than he." Evidently Pip is not the only Castaway associated with the Pequod. For further commentary, see Gordon H. Mills, "'The Castaway' in *Moby-Dick*," *University of Texas Studies in English*, 29 (1950), pp. 231–48.

33. Hawthorne's full response to Melville's incessant wish to engage him in "ontological heroics" is nowhere preserved; but one finds it easy enough to infer backwards from Hawthorne's account of their last meeting, in Liverpool, where Melville stopped (in 1856) on his way to the Holy Land: "Melville, as he always does, began to reason of Providence and futurity, and of everything that lies beyond human ken. [...] It is strange how he persists—and has persisted ever since I knew him, and probably long before—in wandering to-and-fro over these deserts, as dismal and monotonous as the sand hills amid which we were sitting": see *The English Notebooks*, in the Centenary Edition of *The Works of Nathaniel Hawthorne* (Columbus: Ohio State University Press, 1997), Vol. XXII, p. 163.

So perhaps it all comes out even in the end. Plus heart, minus head was *not* a fair reading of "Ethan Brand": that, surely, were but a superficial skimming of pages, the result of which could only be some thematic doggerel. The motive to defiance and the likely career of the accomplished blasphemer were much closer to the mark. This way madness lay, to be sure, but this way someone had to walk: Hawthorne discreetly, perhaps, with ample opportunity for the unfit audience to misunderstand; Melville boldly, emphatically, so no one half-alert could duck the blow. Was the sunny Hawthorne ending too faithful, too pious? Or was it just a hair too subtle? No matter: they both agree—and without benefit of William James, either one—that sick souls are more nearly wise.[34] So much so, in fact, that when the reviewer of Hawthorne got back Hawthorne's own review of *Moby-Dick*, well might he ask: "Whence come you, Hawthorne?" (L 545).

4

It might require a separate paper to distinguish between the *contemptus mundi* which won Hawthorne's Virtuoso "the golden vase of Bias, with its inscription: 'TO THE WISEST'" (VC 704) and the "unchristian wisdom" (MD 328) Melville read out of Solomon's unvarnished, unedited evocation of life as a vanity. But this may be the place to notice that the figure of Wandering Jew, who is evoked more than once in Hawthorne's later tales and sketches, and who makes a brief but significant appearance in "Ethan Brand,"[35] is no part of the inspiration Melville appears to have taken from that tale or any of the others. Or if that ambiguous figure of loss and/or rejection does matter to *Moby-Dick*, it is only in the negative: that is precisely who Ahab is NOT going to turn out to be; or Ishmael either. Better in either case "to perish in [the] howling infinite" (MD 97) than to wander around, "ingloriously," a vagabond upon the earth, waiting in vain for something that never happens, or that happened once, long ago, in a landscape so strange and an idiom so local that only the eye and ear of the elect could discern its true import. If the Wandering Jew is the "Christian" figure of the chance that was wasted—as suggested by the "statue of opportunity" (VC 697) that stands at the entrance to the Virtuoso's museum—then Ishmael is the spiteful Calvinist reminder of the chance that never came: Call me bastard outcast of the universe; call me—not "Gansevoort's

---

34. Though William James fails to invent a category for Melville, Hawthorne, and Dickinson—the "sick souls" who never do get "twice born"—his impatience with the placid happiness of the once-born seems everywhere apparent; see *Varieties of Religious Experience* (rpt. New York: Modern Library, n.d.), esp. pp. 77–162.
35. Also well recognized in EB, in the person of the German Jew with the diorama, the Wandering Jew is a familiar figure in the literature of that "Negative Romanticism" which takes its (anti-) heroes from the ranks of the failed or the excluded; see G. K. Andersen, *The Legend of the Wandering Jew* (Providence: Brown University, 1965). The Wandering Jew also appears, for comic purposes, in "A Select Party": "This personage [...] had latterly grown so common, by mingling in all sorts of society, and appearing at the beck of very entertainer, that he could hardly be deemed a proper guest in a very exclusive circle": so off he goes "on a ramble towards Oregon"; see *Tales*, p. 949.

younger brother" but—the guy who came *that* close to the covenant of redemption, but who just happened to have the wrong tribal mother.[36]

Nor will Ethan Brand agree to spend his life wandering. Unpardonable sin or not, it ends here. More softly than we might expect, perhaps, as the blasphemy of Brand's final address to Mother Earth, "who art no more my Mother" (EB 1065), seems a little deficient in Melvillean energy. And no doubt this is one reason why Ahab, gone all the way into the world of the artificial fire, has need to "breathe it back" at heaven's show of power—at a "fiery father" who seems to have done something to hide the "sweet mother" (MD 382–83). Unlike Brand, however, Ahab does not perish in and by the fire. Because, unlike Brand, he has conceived an object beyond the fire. Or beyond himself, the place where Brand's quest comes at last to rest. Crazier than Brand, Ahab has still the whale to pursue. Not the unpardonable sin, in his case, but the unbearable insult, the "wall, shoved near" (MD 140).

And this is one reason, no doubt, why Melville could write the story of the new, heaven-defying Prometheus to the length of 500 pages. Ishmael knows, from the example of Narcissus, that "the key to it all" lies within the self (MD 20); and he says it all again in warning us to "push not off" from our one sane "insular Tahiti" (MD 225). But the warning comes too late, for we have all already pushed off into the "howling infinite" (MD 97), as if there were in fact some scene outside the self in which to seek: the furious ocean any more than the tedious land? Or some being to attack: "Vengeance on a dumb brute?" (MD 139)—the voice might well be that of Hawthorne, the extent of whose contribution to *Moby-Dick* we will probably never know. No man has wished the novel longer, but few would be satisfied to see the *Pequod* turn about at just this point. Ethan Brand does not witness the scene of the dog chasing its own tail but, in the strictness of Hawthorne's theology, he comes to learn the lesson all the same. Though it may say something about our own more tempered will-to-blasphemy, we're mostly glad that Hawthorne left his friend the room. And no doubt Melville's re-review of "Ethan Brand" is his own conflicted vote of thanks.

---

36. For the psychoanalytic replacement of Isaac by Gansevoort, see James Haviland Miller, *Melville* (New York: Braziller, 1975), pp. 90–117.

Chapter Nine

"RED MAN'S GRAVE": ART AND DESTINY IN HAWTHORNE'S "MAIN-STREET"

Let me confess at the outset: I remain a little ashamed of having chosen for this paper the most aggressively correct title my material could conscientiously justify. And that for a captive audience—whose presence at an anniversary occasion surely signals a dedication to the life and works of Nathaniel Hawthorne that can survive ever so many discoveries of an ingrained resistance to the sacred causes of the modern academy. Of which there may be more than just one.

An ambivalent feminist at best, Hawthorne deeply sympathizes with the travails of Hester and Zenobia, but he does damn the mob of the "scribbling" female competitors he recognized as early as his sketch of "Mrs. Hutchinson";[1] and he did not wish his daughter to become a writer. He allows the traduction of his fair Priscilla to remind the suspicious reader of a certain class of fugitive slave transactions, but he defended the compromising policies of Franklin Pierce and, when the push of theory came to the shove of war, he seemed more concerned about the fate of poor southern whites than about the enslaved blacks.[2] And, in the matter closest to hand, he did far less with the American Encounter than with the other subjects singled out—by Rufus Choate and

---

1. The sketch of "Mrs. Hutchinson" (1830) asks us to notice "how much of the texture and body of cis-atlantic literature is the work of those slender fingers, from which only a light and fanciful embroidery has heretofore been required" and—warning Dimmesdale well in advance—suggests that "Woman's intellect must never give the tone to that of man, and even her morality is not exactly the material for masculine virtue"; see *Hawthorne: Tales and Sketches* (New York: Library of America, 1996), p. 18. The more familiar reference, to the "d——d mob of scribbling women," occurs much later, in a (January 19, 1855) letter to William D. Ticknor, his publisher; see Vol. XVII of the Centenary Edition of *The Works of Nathaniel Hawthorne* (Columbus: Ohio State University Press, 1987), p. 304. Hawthorne partly recovers himself when, in his next letter (pp. 307–8), he writes admiringly of *Ruth Hall* and enquires about the identity of "Fanny Fern" (Sara Payson Willis Parton).
2. Famous for its observation that "No human effort on a grand scale, has ever yet resulted according to the purpose of its projectors" and for the less empirical claim that "Man's accidents are God's Purposes" (431); infamous for representing Southern Blacks as creatures "akin to the fauns and rustic deities of olden times" (420), "Chiefly about War Matters" (1862) also looks to the war to free a certain class of Southern "peasants" (429) "from a thralldom in which they scarcely begin to be responsible beings" (430). See Vol. XXIII of the Centenary Edition of the *Works of Nathaniel Hawthorne* (Columbus: Ohio State University Press, 1994).

others—for treatment in the project of building up a respectable American literature out of authentic American materials.

"Hannah Duston" will scarcely help the cause; and though "Roger Malvin's Burial" can certainly be read in this important canonic sub-category, the thematic significance of "Lovell's Fight" was for a long time easy to miss. There, in the best case, the interest of the Native Americans had figured as a narrative pretext; and elsewhere, as in *The Scarlet Letter*, their presence can seem something of an historical prop. The itinerant "Story-Teller" probably overstated his creator's case in confessing that he did "abhor an Indian story," but there seems not much injustice in agreeing that Hawthorne's historical imagination was never altogether energized by "the matter of the Indians."[3] Puritanism almost everywhere, by cultural necessity if not by familiar bias; and Revolution too, much more than we often recognize; but the aboriginal aspect and cultural significance of America's Red Men, not so much.

So the fact of their emphatic representation in Hawthorne's stylized history of Main Street, Salem, Massachusetts, New England, USA seems remarkable enough as a simple fact. Significantly, the Indians of "Main-street" do not speak, but they do appear—to puzzle over and then begin to rue the "march" of a new civilization, appropriately symbolized by the artifice of a straight and purposeful street in the space where their own paths had seemed merely to meander. And if they gradually disappear from the text, in prediction of that later time when politics would seek to accomplish what theory of culture could only presume, the image of their fundamental and somehow poetic reality has been insistent enough to sink into the narrative unconscious of this remarkable (and noticeably under-interpreted) sketch. The puritanic force that overcomes—which the automatic exponent of progress can be counted on to praise and perhaps to naturalize—is complex enough to offer us much to admire but somewhat to dread as well; and to leave us wondering what Providence has arranged this unambiguous triumph of Purpose over Nature. The strangers seem strong and stern, warlike and religious, but not overly given to the pleasures of the imagination. And, as the Natives disappear, well may we wonder: what cultural gain to repay this demographic loss? Will the astonished muse of New England indeed find thousands at her side?

---

3. The word "abhor" is technically that of "The Story-Teller," as that narrative personage expresses himself in "Sketches from Memory"—which ought to have been a frame for "The Great Carbuncle"; see my *Province of Piety* (Cambridge, MA: Harvard University Press, 1984), pp. 310–13. Yet the full text may well contain a touch of the confessional:

> The habits and sentiments of that departed people ["the red men"] were too distinct from those of their successors to find much real sympathy. It has often been a matter of regret to me that I was shut out from the most peculiar field of American fiction, by an inability any romance, or poetry, or grandeur, or beauty in the Indian character, at least, till such traits were pointed out by others. (*Tales and Sketches*, p. 343)

For the influence of Rufus Choate's identifying the three principal "matters" of interest to American followers of Sir Walter Scott, see Michael Davitt Bell, *Hawthorne and the Historical Romance of New England* (Princeton, NJ: Princeton University Press, 1971), pp. 3–14.

Clearly the Showman-Narrator of "Main-street" has some such hope. He knows of course that he is not a tragedian nor even a proper novelist; only a local entertainer, he operates the clumsy contrivance that changes the scene of Salem life, from day to day and year to year, with only the pictorial—and of course the historical—imagination to compensate for the flat un-sophistication of his mechanical medium. Hawthorne himself may know all that post-enlightenment theorists of the Imagination might claim; and surely he trades, elsewhere, on some fairly well developed theory of "History as Romantic Art."[4] But it is the distinguishing mark of this self-effacing piece of literary self-defense that, while putting a certain burden of imaginative cooperation on an audience not entirely prepared to assist in its own edification, it claims for its own artistry as little as possible. "Turn your crank" (1043),[5] a resistant member of the audience cries out at one point. And the showman, silently acknowledging his creator's understanding of the performative and indeed the mechanical nature of all literary production, can only comply without protest. Oh, yes, much might be said about the creative intuition behind or the vitalizing spirit within the performance; or about the organic unity of the product; but it's still some slightly pedantic misfit patching stuff together, trying to make a buck like anyone else. Better concede the worst at once: the vaunted Romantic Imagination is "Fancy's Show Box" still.

2

Before any critical voice from the audience interrupts the performance, however, a certain preview of Salem's early history has already been presented—in a way that appears to resist its recounting in the local history of Joseph Felt, the second edition of whose *Annals of Salem* had just recently appeared. Earlier in his career Hawthorne learned to keep his eye on the way George Bancroft wove the providential thesis of the Puritans into the heroic tale of national destiny;[6] now, as a stage-managed persona rehearses the tale of his own native place, even his eye seems to catch more of irony than of innocence. The Showman premises nothing overtly to oppose Felt's claim that the settlement of Salem was "planned and commenced on the noblest principles of human action" and so preserved from the "baneful irregularities" that have marked the history of communities "begun and continued in motives of vicious ambition and debased selfishness."[7] But

---

4. For the Scott-inspired belief that history can and should avail itself of not only of imagination and but of even certain devices of literary invention as well, see David Levin, *History as Romantic Art* (rpt. Oakland, CA: Harbinger, 1963), pp. 3–23.
5. All citations of the text of "Main-street" refer to *Hawthorne: Tales and Sketches* (New York: Library of America, 1996).
6. For Hawthorne's resistance to the ideology of American Destiny—and to the rhetoric of George Bancroft in particular—see my *Province of Piety* (Cambridge, MA: Harvard University Press, 1984), esp. pp. 207–8, 453–57.
7. Joseph B. Felt, *Annals of Salem*, Vol. I (S. B. Ives, 1845), p. 11. This is a second edition of Felt's *Annals*, the second volume of which was published in 1849; the first (one-volume) edition of 1827 Hawthorne borrowed twice in the 1830s and again in 1849; see Marion L. Kesselring, *Hawthorne's Reading: A Transcription and Identification of Titles Recorded in the Charge-Books of the Salem Athenaeum* (New York: New York Public Library, 1949), p. 50.

the growth of Hawthorne's Salem seems more random than planned. And, at the same time, the baneful possibilities seem buried in the very regularities being introduced into a world with an entirely different set of rules. Where Felt presents a complex transaction of cultural negotiation and fair exchange, Hawthorne's Showman merely notices some surprising alterations of habitat and of manners.

The "ancient and primitive wood" has, at our first glimpse, not yet felt a single blow of "the white man's axe," and his "footstep," which comes to figure as an insistent motif, has not yet "crumpled" a single withered leaf; yet "already a faintly-traced" Indian path "running nearly east and west" and ever "Onward"—to Parkman's Oregon, no doubt, or Bancroft's California--seems but the "prophecy or foreboding of the future street stolen into the heart of the solemn old wood" (1024). As if both Nature and Indian culture had little business other than to predict a certain westward destiny just waiting to be made manifest. Conjured up by the Showman's historic art, the "great Squaw Sachem" has no reason to suspect the end of her earthly sway, yet we easily imagine that, if her necromancer husband could see, "mirrored in the pool of water at his feet," a glimpse of the "stone-front of a stately hall which shall cast its shadow over [the] very spot" where now he stands, his fright might be greater than all that his midnight "incantations" produced in the hearts of the early white settlers. And what if he could know that this "destined" edifice would contain a "noble Museum" where, among "countless curiosities of earth and sea, a few Indian arrow-heads shall be treasure up as memorials of a vanished race"? But as the scene is entirely the product of a white man's retrospect—victorious in the fact, and inevitablized in the construct—its effect is entirely lost on Wappacowet and his wife, who innocently "imagine [...] that their own system of affairs will last forever." A squirrel, a deer, a partridge, a wolf, an Indian queen and an Indian Priest: "Can it be that the thronged street of a city will ever pass into this twilight solitude?" "Wilderness from the creation, must it not be a wilderness forever?" (1024–25).

Just now, at this retrospective moment of prophetic pathos, comes the first voice of critical interruption, protesting not the curious conflation of "will" and "must"—this tendentious evocation of effect before cause, of purpose before intention—but merely of the deficient skill of its representation. An "acidulous-looking gentlemen in blue glasses" (borrowed, no doubt, from a certain skeptical realist in "The Artist of the Beautiful") boldly declares the entire performance a "manifest catch-penny": because, as he closely observes, the stiff-jointed figures in the scene "move with all the grace of a child's wooden monkey, sliding up and down on a stick." "Human art has its limits," the Showman admits with comic generality; and, more to the local point, it now and then requires "a little aid from the spectator's imagination." Well it will get none here, for this "critic" must "make it a point to see things precisely as they are" (1025). The American-ness of this view will still be amusing Henry James but, without the advantages of expatriation or the international perspective, the Showman can only bear up and go on against the local odds.

Another glance of retrospect reveals that "Strangers have [now] found their way into this solitary place." The showman does not indicate what motives have led "Roger Conant, the first settler in Naumkeag," to build his rude dwelling in the midst of a "leaf-strewn forest-land"; he merely accords a certain amount of respect to a "man of thoughtful strength" who has in fact "planted the germ of a city." Yet from the first we detect both an exaggeration and an opposition that take this suitable praise very close to the precinct of irony. Striding so sturdily "onward," this "stalwart figure" projects such an "an air of physical force and energy" that heroic poetry might well "expect the very trees to stand aside, and give him room to pass." But a different tone, even a different system of value, is implied when the trees around the space that Conant's mythological axe has cleared begin to wonder at "the breadth of sunshine which the white man spreads around him." No surprise, then, to learn that "An Indian, half hidden in the dusky shade, is gazing and wondering too" (1026): the strangers bring light, perhaps, into the shade of the forest, but must they cut down quite so many trees?

And—now that Conant is beginning to have neighbors—what are they wearing on their feet? Observe:

> The forest-track, trodden more and more by the hob-nailed shoes of these sturdy and ponderous Englishmen, has now a distinctness which it could never have acquired from the light tread of a hundred times as many Indian moccasins. (1027)

Clearly, "it *will* be a street" (emphasis added), meandering no more, but pushing ever "onward." It may plunge, here and there, into a "shadowy strip of woods," but already it shows "a decided line, along which human interests have begun to hold their career." Children happily "trip along the path" (1027) without stumbling; and the hoofs of the deer are being replaced by those of cows and goats. It's called the march of civilization. But—naturally adaptive if not ecologically self-conscious—the Indians can only

> marvel at the deep track [the white man] makes, and perhaps [be] saddened by a flitting presentiment, that this heavy tread will find its way all over the land; and that the wild woods, the wild wolf, and the wild Indian will alike be trampled beneath it. (1027–28)

"Even so it shall be," the Showman solemnly pronounces in retrospective prolepsis; but the discourse of destiny suddenly implies the imputation of guilt when he goes on to observe that "The pavements of the Main-street must be laid over the red man's grave" (1028). Not here exclusively, of course, but everywhere in the steady movement West. And so much the worse if, arguing special exception, local history wishes to take original credit. The Puritans of New England may or may not be part of God's grand design, but these "Strangers" will be a lot harder on the land than the natives had been; and the shoes that tread the main-traveled road of Holy History will trample the lives of other, more original men.

But no such thought disturbs the great arrival scene that now ensues: advance man for the Great Migration, Endicott enters and the trees which made way for Conant "unite their branches high above his head" in a sort of "triumphal arch." (1028). A touch of historical fantasy, no doubt, but well prepared for by a similar moment of solemn entrance in Felt;[8] and as no one protests this spontaneous tribute, the Showman proceeds to the

---

8. Featuring a portrait of Endicott on his title page, Felt's account marks the new governor's arrival with a long set piece—which only a painful lack of talent keeps from being literary. Old

politics of the moment: the historical Conant is known to have resented Endicott's appointment, but in this generalized account the "old settlers" see and approve the man the English planners have sent over to govern, pro tem, the first well-appointed congregational outpost in the New World. They like his "resolute, grave, and thoughtful" visage; pronouncing that the Old World planners "have chosen [...] a man out of a thousand," they all "toss up their hats, and salute their new governor and captain with a hearty English shout of welcome." Even the Showman is impressed: recognizing on behalf of his creator the authentic signs of historic legitimacy, he declares that the very "aspect" of Endicott is "better warrant for the ruler's office, than the parchment commission which he bears" (1028–29). So in one sense at least the civil history of Salem seems well begun: you get the ruler you deserve.

Flush with the reflected glow of this triumphal endorsement, the Showman presses his audience to recognize, in the rose-like beauty of Mrs. Endicott, "the model of features which still beam" in their own busy streets: are not our women, he wants to know, all "flowers of the same race"? "Ridiculous," "insufferable," mutters the critic we have heard before—"a pasteboard figure, such as a child might cut out of a card, with a pair of very dull scissors," is offered as "the prototype of hereditary beauty." Again the self-effacing self-defense: Sir, you "sit altogether too near" to get the proper effect of my "light and shadow." And again the anti-illusionist insistence: "I want no other light and shade; [...] it is my business to see things just the way they are" (1029). Then, before the Showman can so much as shuffle his feet, a second, less impressionistic critic weighs in:

> I would suggest to the author of this ingenious exhibition [...] that Anna Gower, the first wife of Governor Endicott, left no posterity; and that consequently, we cannot be indebted to that honorable lady any specimens of feminine loveliness, now extant among us. (1029–30)

And now, we think, the battle is fairly joined—a criticism of history from the venue of history itself.

And so it is. The Showman, confessing that he has "nothing to allege against this genealogical objection," merely points again to his scene; but his very next sentence reveals the game he (or perhaps only his cunning creator) has been playing from the outset. Some time has passed during this "little interruption," and now we see that "Anglo-Saxon energy—as the phrase now goes—has been at work in the spectacle before us" (1030). That phrase, as the original work of David Levin long ago taught us to recognize, names the best reason America's "Romantic Historians" could give to explain why

---

planters on one side, Indians on the other, all "gaze intently" at Endicott and his wife as they approach.

> Everyone receives a silent impression of the stranger, as he looks upon his face. The thoughts and feelings of the whole company are out of the common course. The doings and emotions of that day were never effaced from memory. It was no ordinary theme for the pencil of an artist. Its well drawn sketch would deserve to be classed with that of the pilgrims at Plymouth rock. (43)

Wonder only that the trees do *not* form an arch.

the restless English and not the lazy Spanish or the polite French won out in extended contest for North American empire; and why the nomadic Natives, never very anxious about *vacuum domicilium*, proved so easy to supplant.[9] Anglo-Saxon, it readily appears, is the race manifestly destined to spread out from sea to shining sea. Already in the portrait of Conant we have seen it: endorsed and indeed apotheosized in Endicott, we recognize the temperament—and the feet—of those Pilgrims whose "stern impassioned stress/ A thoroughfare for freedom beat/ Across the wilderness." The hymn comes much later, of course, but its sentiment was all too familiar.

And so this lesson in historical continuity has less to do with the genetics of Anna Gower than with the representative identity of John Endicott, that "Puritan of Puritans," whose portrait appears on the frontispiece of Felt's volume of 1845, and whom even the cautious epistemology of Hawthorne dares to offer as the type and genius of his land. The beauty of the wife is dead and buried if you insist, but the morale of the husband lives on. At issue, then, in the profile of the man sent to replace the man who would end the rule of the "great Squaw Sachem," is some pre-figuration of a nation's mature ideology and political practice. English symbols well behind, a straight road to western empire all before. Starting at Salem, if local history should think to dignify itself in just that way.

Leaving this inference at the mercy of our own typology, however, the Showman notices only that even Saxon energy does not produce its full effect at once, and that its noble constructions do not always surpass the loveliness of the nature they replace. Smoking chimneys everywhere now present "the aspect of a village, yet everything is "so inartificial and inceptive" as to suggest that "one returning wave of the wild nature might overwhelm it all" (1030). And, while we are puzzling over the significance of this curiously Ramistic diction,[10] the promise of permanence is more credibly offered by the centralized placement of a Puritan meeting-house: obdurate and durable it appears, though "a meaner temple was never consecrated to the worship of the Deity." And if we should wonder, with our showman-instructor, how the separatist meeting-house could possibly replace an open-air worship "under the awful vault of the firmament" or a solemn communion within the precinct of "carved altar-work" and "pictured windows," the answer is not far to seek: the Puritan house of worship could afford to be "naked, simple, and severe" because "the zeal of a recovered faith burned like a lamp within their

---

9. See Levin. *Romantic Art*, pp. 79–92.
10. "Inceptive" can mean simply "initial," but in grammar and logic it also has the specialized meaning of initiating or generating; and it suggests the public "inceptio" or "commencement" of an academic career. Similarly, "inartificial" has the (now rare) meaning of "not resulting from art or artifice," hence "constructed without art or skill, rude, clumsy, inartistic" (and indeed it has just this meaning in Cooper's *The Pioneers*), but in the logic of Peter Ramus it refers to "arguments" whose "invention" is from received authority rather than ordinary experience; see Perry Miller, "The Instrument of Reason," in *The New England Mind: The Seventeenth Century* (Cambridge, MA: Harvard University Press, 1939), esp. pp. 123–39. An insomnia more nearly ideal than my own may yet discover a learned source lurking here; meanwhile, it suffices to observe that we are dealing with the inception of an argument as well as the founding of a town.

hearts." Lovers of religious art these early Salemites may not have been, but exemplars of a living faith they undeniably were. And no doubt it was chiefly the dimming of this original faith, "whether in their time or their children's," that has caused some in these later generations to exclaim—with texts of both Bunyan and Winthrop in mind—"how like an iron cage was that which they called Liberty" (1030–31).[11]

But as *The Scarlet Letter* is not yet, the Showman returns from this explicit moralism to the scene of early town development. But to assure us that the great theme of Manifest Destiny is indeed the subtext of this otherwise unassuming little pageant, he refers us again to the operation of "Anglo-Saxon energy"; and again, the word for its heavy tread is "trampling," as if its self-same march along the main street of American progress could not avoid stepping on the lives of others. Even Holy History has its losers, as it readily appears. For now, as the forest and the wild-flowers are seen to be "shrinking back," as "Gardens are now fenced in," it is not only the wolf and the partridge that begin to be displaced by the professors of an ecology that, as Winthrop himself had reasoned the matter, discovers legitimacy in its very power to subdue wilderness and call the result "garden."[12] The Indians may still "come into the settlement, bringing the skins of beaver and otter, bear and elk, which they sell to Endicott for the wares of England," but these "red men have become aware, that the street is no longer free to them, save by the sufferance and permission of the settlers" who now "have dominion" and who make it a point to awe them, from time to time, with the "stately march" of their "mail-clad" train-bands. Such a display of "English power," as if they were preparing to assist Cromwell in "beat[ing] down the strength of a kingdom" (1032). Let the red men testify: a Revolution has taken place here as well. And then politely disappear.

As now they begin to do, about half-way through a performance that has promised to extend its notice down to the very nineteenth-century present but which in fact breaks off with the Great Snow of 1717. Retaining his loyalty to the symbolic, the self-effacing Showman turns now to matters more familiar to those acquainted with the earlier works of his self-concealing creator; and, having missed the import of the show's explicit point of political departure, its critics keep up their obtuse and reductive objections. The Great Migration introduces a cast of famous characters the Showman's instinct for Romantic History cannot resist assembling along the main street of his historical narrative—the

---

11. Q. D. Leavis long ago noticed that the image of the iron cage owes to Hawthorne's memory of *Pilgrim's Progress* where, "in the Interpreter's House Christian is shown a Man in an Iron Cage as an awful warning of what a true Christian should never be"; see Hawthorne as Poet," rpt. in A. N. Kaul, ed., *Hawthorne* (Hoboken, NJ: Prentice Hall, 1966), p. 35. But as Bunyan is not much at issue in "Main-street," one imagines that John Winthrop's "Little Speech" of 1645 may be the provoking cause of Hawthorne's judgment; see Richard S. Dunn, ed., *The Journal of John Winthrop* (Cambridge, MA: Harvard University Press, 1996), pp. 584–89. .
12. John Winthrop's famous "Reasons" for supporting the planting and settling of New England contain—perhaps even feature—the assertion that the New England natives "enclose no land, neither have any settled habitation, nor tame any cattle to improve the land by, and so have no other but a natural right [and not a civil] right" to their territories; see *Winthrop Papers*, Vol. 2 (rpt. New York: Russell and Russell, 1968), p. 141. For a discussion of this "ecology," see Cecelia Tichi, *New World, New Earth* (New Haven, CT: Yale University Press, 1979), esp. pp. 1–36.

"fiery" Hugh Peters, the "gentler, [...] kinder" Roger Williams, the incomparable John Winthrop; from quite another list, Thomas Morton of Merry Mount; and even the sainted Ann Hutchinson (1033–34). Just now the genealogist in the audience—the sort of historian Hawthorne once referred to as a "professor of biographical exactness"[13]— cries out against the evident "anachronism" for, though visitors to our old town from time to time, "these historical personages could not possibly have met together in the Main-street." And then, before anyone can say "Sir Walter Scott," the critique turns again to the question of mimetic illusion: "a wretchedly bedaubed sheet of canvas" for a background and "pasteboard slips that hitch and jerk along the front." Nor will the critic assist the illusion by sitting "further back," next to the "young lady" whose face has shown such signs of interest. Entirely proof against the imagination as a source of knowledge, he insists on remaining "precisely where I am" (1035). Balked but not entirely chastened, the Showman can only bow—to the reality of an audience with a somewhat more simplistic epistemology. And then proceed, hoping no doubt that someone can yet learn by subtle hint and by instruction.

For the critical interruptions appear to stand in the place of several very main-street episodes in the history of Salem, which old-time historians like Winthrop himself would recognize as important intimations of problems the very reverse of local. One of these we well remember as "Endicott and the Red Cross": there the vocal representative of Salem's separatism-in-fact cannot repress the question: "What have we to do with England?" The other, closely related, we might fairly entitle "Williams and the Massachusetts Charter," in which the only man in New England capable of imagining that Saints themselves might do well to learn Algonkian, is publicly heard to propose that Massachusetts return the King's Charter, rebuke his blasphemous self-characterization as a Christian Monarch, and buy their occupied lands from the Natives. Who surely owned it, he thought, if anyone did. These matters being complex and debatable to the point of ambiguity, perhaps the interruptions were strategic. Some questions may in fact be un-decidable. As, in recounting the causes of the war to neutralize the Pequots, no one is quite sure exactly how much weight to assign to the punitive and rather brutal expedition led by John Endecott and his band of volunteers in August of 1636. Art has its limits.

Time passes, in any event, and life becomes "sluggish," distinguished if at all by the peculiar Puritan gift to discipline and punish. "Happy are we," the Showman opines, not to live in those second- and third-generation times, when "one generation had bequeathed its religious gloom, and the counterfeit of its religious ardor" (1038). The Faith of the Founders—that original greatest generation—could no way reproduce itself; we suffer the declension still. Accused just now of perpetrating "a sermon," the Showman duly apologizes; but his determined revisionism goes right on to notice the harsh treatment of the Quakers, who are said to "trample upon our wise and well-established laws" (1039). The well-worn word appears to trigger a memory: "impious varlets," these dis-respecters of authority are "worse than the heathen Indians" (1040). As if the native population, supplanted in reality, lived on principally in the realm of rhetorical transference.

---

13. See "Sir William Phips" (1830), in *Tales*, p. 12.

Adults remember the Indian path, but children can scarcely credit a time when Main Street was not a "street indeed"—when the Red Man held sway and the Forest seemed the principal fact of life. "Vain legend" (1041) of wolves prowling here and of the "Squaw Sachem, and the Sagamore her son," ruling over the entire region and treating "as sovereign Potentates with the English settlers, then so few and storm-beaten, now so powerful." Just observe the present case:

> There stand some school-boys [...] in a little group around a drunken Indian, himself a prince of the Squaw Sachem's lineage. He brought hither some Beaver-skins for sale, and has already swallowed the larger portion of their price, in the deadly drafts of their fire-water.

Much moved, the sentimental Showman turns to his audience in direct address: does this pitiful picture not tell almost the

> whole story of the vast growth and prosperity of one race, and the fated decay of another— the children of the stranger making game of the great Squaw Sachem's grandson? (1041)

But the intelligence that has arranged the pictures—and written the story of progress under the sign of "trampling"—might fairly hope to arouse something more than "pathos." And the Showman himself, having noticed how the new-world children so easily eternalize the recent and factitious, may well expect some audience to question that sort of history in which the painfully factual becomes the comfortably fated. Always, it appears, in the eyes of those who win the day and tell the tale. Even when a Chosen People grow up to be not so much a biblical generation as an historic race.

Those less favored of fate may strike back, as they do in the very next paragraph: a march of soldiers along the main street "betokens the breaking out of King Philip's war." Retreated and retrenched, the Indian warriors will take a terrible toll on these young marchers, "the flower of Essex," sent out to defend the frontier villages on the Connecticut" (1042), but the Natives will not in the end prevail; and when men with names likes Hubbard and Mather—and not at all like Massasoit—come to reason on the slaughter, neither will think to ask if American might ever make a wrong.[14] And so, with present assurance of the past and its meaning, more is gained than lost in saying that the "brave Captain Gardener," "reigning in his mettled steed so gallantly," and seeming "the very soul and emblem of martial achievement," was himself "destined [...] to meet a warrior's fate." A really tough-minded critic might well insist on something a little less heroic—like "he died." Or inquire perhaps about the Pequots earlier: were there not any Salemites in Endecott's retaliatory expedition? The only objection, instead: "The mettled steed looks like a pig" (1043).

---

14. For opposing views of the meaning of King Philip's War—neither of which quite penetrates to the root cause of native displacement, see Increase Mather, *A Brief History of the War with the Indians in New-England* (1676) and William Hubbard, *A Narrative of the Trouble with the Indians in New-England* (1677); for commentary, see Jill Lepore, *The Name of War* (New York: Vintage Books, 1999).

But "Turn your crank" and "grind it out," the Critic now commands the Showman. And that Ironic Personage, having done his self-constricted best to move "the matter of the Indians" from the discourse of destiny to the arena of cultural clash and national responsibility, marches on the best he can. Oh, yes, the Salem Witchcraft, another a chance to denounce the antique superstition of Cotton Mather.[15] But also, perhaps, to remind the audience that, focused as it was on the psychodrama of an individual Puritan, "Young Goodman Brown" had scarcely told the entire tale. For, with friend looking "askance at friend, and the husband at his wife, and the wife at him, even the mother at her little child"—everyone suspecting a witch or dreading an accuser—there was indeed a "Universal Madness [run] riot in the Main Street" (1047). And then, after a few more quotidian observations, the machine breaks down. What a shame, for the audience was to have beheld its very own features in the faithful re-presentation of all that has passed along the main street of Salem in New England. And, fate for fate, what could hold more interest for this particular Showman than the brilliancy of that street "on the night of the grand illumination for General Taylor's triumph?" (1050).

Yet perhaps we have seen enough: a contemporaneous young lady has seemed rapt at even this pedestrian rehearsal of truth near home—atoning, perhaps, for the laughter of two of her fair townswomen, when a certain "Story-Teller" tried to localize the burial sight of Leonard Doane's Salem wizard; or for the churlishness of his portrayal of their giddy refusal of historic insight.[16] And a very current gentlemen, less gifted with the capacity for instructive illusion, has protested a certain strategic liberty taken with names and dates while sitting quite still for a remarkably inflated and tendentious reading of the symbolic significance of their funny little town. Choking on the well-defended practice of history as romantic art, they have swallowed once again the self-serving premise of the politically providential. Along the way, they have allowed themselves to be reminded of the well-publicized crimes against certain outmoded enthusiasts and other troublesome deviants; but the aboriginal crime, unnoticed in Felt—the supplantation of the native population—they have permitted to be covered over with a pathos they relish and with a meta-history they no longer recognize as such. Sad it was, they may think, but the red man had to disappear. Replaced, in the name of a destiny whose secularity refused to shed the garment of the sacred, by a higher civilization and a more adaptable race. Were it not obtuse to miss the tendency of history? Were it not sinful, somehow, to lament too much the operation of its sovereign logic?

To maintain their comfortable belief that Quakers and Witches no longer matter, the inhabitants of Salem will have to withstand the relentless moral logic of *The House of the Seven Gables*: we walk upon their graves as well; some of us even live in their houses.[17]

---

15. Very respectful of Cotton Mather in *Grandfather's Chair*, Hawthorne appears to delivers the verdict of "bloodthirsty" in "Alice Doane's Appeal" (*Tales*, p. 216)—raising the possibility, as I have argued elsewhere, that the Story-Teller is not an entirely trustworthy spokesman; see *Province*, pp. 83–98.
16. See *Tales*, pp. 214–15.
17. Allan Emery has convincingly argued that, in *The House of the Seven Gables*, the ouster of Maule by Pyncheon is a version of the originary conflict between Conant and Endecott—which Felt suppresses but which is well noticed in Thomas Hutchinson's *History of Massachusetts*; see

But for the literary imputation of that historic guilt the earlier works of Hawthorne the Salemite are already well known and highly regarded. Here, significantly, the verdict on "Puritan Origins" is pretty much a throw-away, almost a cliché:

> Let us thank God for having given us such ancestors; and let each successive generation thank him, not less fervently, for being one step further from them in the march of ages. (1039)

Fair enough, if historical literature be expected to teach its lesson in a single sentence. But here, in this rather rare invocation of "the matter of the Indians," the emphasis ought to fall not on the familiar ambivalence of ancestry but on the hard-won irony of destiny as a well-ordered "march": history moves along in an admirable straight line, getting somewhere always, only if we say it does; and even those who believe this in the name of God would do well to mark the trampling tread of their heavy shoes.

3

Perhaps it is significant that Hawthorne turns to the fate of the New England Indians at the very time he thinks, in anticipation of *The Scarlet Letter*, to defend his practice as a writer of historical fiction at greatest length. The effect is not to tip the balance of his cultural criticism away from the matter of the Puritans or of the Revolution but, in partially redressing a crucial omission, to remind his audience that certain issues may matter out of all proportion to the power of fiction satisfactorily to represent them. Art has indeed its limits. Among them is the need to deal with the things about which we can know or responsibly imagine. Heirs of a profoundly important Revolution we undeniably are; of one with unmistakable Puritan Origins. A redundancy of Forefathers both these complex events have given us, in heroism or in irony. But what was it like to be Algonkian? And to lose one's place in a world immemorially present and presumed? Not "owned," precisely, but not subject to alien standards of possession and propriety. Irving, Cooper, Sedgwick and others did what they could; knowing less than historical art might fairly require, they tried to portray the affect of cultural displacement. And of disappearance—though their somber lament often carried with it a sense of acquiescence in the inevitable.[18]

Hawthorne's contemporaneous distinction is that he well knew what he did not know. The literature of Puritanism—from the vestarian protest of a bishop named Aylmer to an assortment of diatribes against latter-day forms of Infidelity—he knew as few men have ever known it. The redundancy of once urgent texts that discover the ideological origins of the American Revolution he knew at least as well. But how could a man with his scrupulous—one might almost say obsessive—reliance on literary pretext learn

---

"Salem History and *The House of the Seven Gables*," in Bernard Rosenthal, ed., *Critical Essays on Hawthorne's House of the Seven Gables* (Boston, MA: G. K. Hall, 1996), pp. 129–49.

18. For a sobering view of what early nineteenth-century American fiction could and could not accomplish in the matter of justice to the Native Americans, see Eric J. Sundquist, "The Frontier and American Indians," in Sacvan Bercovitch, Gen. ed., *The Cambridge History of American Literature*, Vol. 2 (Cambridge: Cambridge University Press, 1995), pp. 175–238.

what it had meant, at the moment of contact, to be a Native American? Occasions he could arrange and speeches invent for characters like John Endicott and Roger Williams, General Howe, and Governor Hutchinson: confidently, for he knew the entire text of their world of many words. But how could a Romantic Historian with his sort of literary conscience make an Indian say a single word?

From Thoreau, perhaps, Hawthorne seems to have learned that the operative concept was not aboriginal or primitive but "wild"—which one might somehow learn to love "not less than the good." Not wild like Hester Prynne, in her best moments of unrepression; more like Pearl, perhaps, who wished to run free beyond the pace of daughter Una; or like his own summer self in the wilds of Maine. Yet, tauntingly, something else as well. Something which might seem, without essentialism on either side, genuinely other.

Theory may propose that Hawthorne never developed an appropriate "heterology," but the opposite may be nearer the truth: the man who thought of Southern Blacks as almost a separate species was not going to presume to put words in the mouth of the American Natives. What Hawthorne lacked, in fact, was an archive—which it had not been the gift of American wildness reassuringly to produce. Absent the necessary sources, the best he could do was to note, here and in a series of strategic reminders elsewhere, the displacement of the Natives, with whom, had they survived in their numbers, the Strangers might have had to negotiate the use and meaning of the land that for a short time they shared: pristine to the invaders but familiar and well-enough worn to the local population. This principal reminder he carried out with an art that explicitly defended itself against the belief that history must never invent incident or construct symbol. With an art that—identifying in irony the trope of retrospective prolepsis—would never avail itself of an over-belief that inevitablized the curious fact of historic rise and fall. And that would manage to imply, to an appropriate audience, that what our history does not yet know about the cultural other may be as important as all that puritanic conscience may discover about ourselves. To get that message, however, one would have to sit further back indeed.

Chapter Ten

"SUCH ANCESTORS": THE SPIRIT OF HISTORY IN *THE SCARLET LETTER*

By the time Hawthorne began composing *The Scarlet Letter*—at or near the time of his enforced departure from the Salem Custom House in 1849—he was already a very accomplished writer of subtly moralized fiction. But he was not in any sense a "novelist." True, this once obscure, now well-recognized writer of "twice-told tales" had begun his career with the publication of a novella called *Fanshawe* (1828); and, close to the moment in question, "Ethan Brand" (1849) may have been originally planned as a much longer work. But in the first case it appears that Hawthorne tried to dissociate himself from a piece of juvenilia almost as soon as it was issued; and the most the fifteen pages of "Ethan Brand" can claim is that they are "A Chapter from an Abortive Romance." So that, whatever his evolving intentions, the writer of *The Scarlet Letter* still would have to teach himself how to write what elementary theory calls a "specific continuous fiction"; and indeed the formal interest of this first of Hawthorne's three "American Romances" may well concern the question of how to make a luminous moral tale take 200 pages.

It is easy to imagine that, with the publication of his *Mosses from an Old Manse* in 1846, Hawthorne felt he had pretty well exhausted his short fiction method—of positing a moral premise, often inherited from history, and then watching it consume both itself and some unhappily credulous host, in a reading time brief enough to satisfy the minimalist demands of Edgar Poe. Clearly a tale like "Rappaccini's Daughter" (1844), the masterpiece of the *Mosses*, was pressing at the limits, both of length and of manageable allusion. And the sketch that introduces the *Mosses* concedes that it is "the last collection of this nature" the writer intends ever to publish. It may be a recognizable sort of false modesty for him to say "unless I could do better, I have done enough in this kind," but the note of completion sounds authentic; and though there is some ambiguity about the exact form in which the elongated tale of Hester and Dimmesdale was first planned to appear, it seems clear enough that the writer of *The Scarlet Letter* had prepared himself for a literary change of pace.

The method of the tales may have not been quite full-formed by the moment in 1825 when he came away from Bowdoin College well supplied with the contents of his first failed-collection, the "Seven Tales of My Native Land"; but by 1829, when he was trying and (again) failing to publish his "Provincial Tales," the mastery of short-form fiction—in tales like "My Kinsman, Major Molineux" and "Roger Malvin's Burial"—was simply perfect. Exemplary, one might say, except that no one since has had the nerve to follow the example. And the only thing that spoils our sense of the perfection of later tales like "Young Goodman Brown," "The Minister's Black Veil," and "The May-Pole of Merry-Mount" is the disturbing fact that we have lost the knowledge of their place in a complex network of "frame stories" to have been called "The Story-Teller." No doubt that work—broken up in 1834, but known to have begun with a striking piece of New England local color which all but hides an allegory of David Hume's skeptical epistemology—represents Hawthorne's first attempt to master a longer form. But the rule—both there and in the four brilliant tales called "Legends of the Province House" (1838)—was thematic interrelation, not continuous emplotment. And clearly the *Twice-Told Tales* (1837) was simply a miscellany.

From this earliest "Salem Period," perhaps the only work that got too long for itself is "The Gentle Boy," published in 1832 along with "Molineux" and "Malvin," but conceived on a different scale and executed according to a different plan. Where those two accomplished masterworks brutally punish their unsuspecting protagonists, according to the inflexible laws of conspiracy in the one case and false heroism in the other, "The Gentle Boy" takes its time to wonder whether any of its several centers of psychological interest quite deserves the pain which fate or karma is pleased to inflict. And as in *The Scarlet Letter*, there are—in addition to a hostile Puritan community—four individuals vying for central attention: a problematic child and three possible parents; except in this case there are two mothers and only one father. Perhaps part of the secret to extending a Hawthorne fiction will involve a look at matters of family, even if one that is well broken. Otherwise, we have only the tormented solipsist, brilliantly reduced by one resisting critic to the status of the "gloomy oddfellow."

Relative to the moment of *The Scarlet Letter*, however, all that was long ago. In between came a first custom house job, in Boston, 1839–40; then the better (or worse) part of 1841 at the educational/agricultural commune known as Brook Farm; then the marriage to Sophia Peabody, which a remarkable series of love letters strongly suggests had been too long delayed; then the move into the Old Manse in what was easily recognized as Emerson's Concord. Much shorter than his long residence in Salem, Hawthorne's three-year sojourn in Concord was sufficiently prolific to be recognized as a period in its own right; about two dozen new publications eventually went into the two editions of the *Mosses* (1846, 1854). Besides "Rappaccini's Daughter," "The Birthmark," "The Artist of the Beautiful" and a diptych made up of "Egotism" and "The Christmas Banquet" added themselves to the list of Hawthorne's distinctive fictional productions; and, together with a number of dramatic sketches, they indicate that Hawthorne was reinventing himself as something like an historian of his own times. A head-note to "Rappaccini" actually proposes that an assortment of persons loosely called "Transcendentalists" have clearly left their mark on "all the current literature of the world"; and if most of the Concord fiction does not come up to the high-water mark of the Salem Period, it clearly establishes that Hawthorne was more than willing to engage with the ruling assumptions of his own time and place. So that, when her moment came, Hester Prynne would be said to recall the heresy of Ann Hutchinson; but she would also predict, just as clearly, the morale of self-reliance and the mood of women's liberation.

Eventually, then, and ready or not, Hester's moment came to him in 1849. Hawthorne had been happy enough to land, in 1847, his second stint in a custom house; and clearly he was far from pleased to be summarily released from a position he felt he held as literary recognition and not as partisan reward. But he is also honest enough to admit that his one recognized world-class novel would not have been written if the political spoilers had found no cause to cover his dismissal. He may have been stirring himself, in 1849, to shake off the lethargy of tenured government service. But it is hard to imagine that what has been called his "Major Phase"—three "American Romances" in three years—could have been launched by any shock less severe than the discovery that he would again have to make his living by his pen, and the memory of his having bid farewell to his old reliance on the series of tales that grew up in time to be a collection. A novel must be had. But where?

2

Not, apparently, from the Dark Romantic premises of "Ethan Brand." Evidently it required far less than a novel to imagine and dispose the career of the Heroic Negative: scorning the paltry sins of ordinary men and women, the maker of a mighty Quarrel with God could declare himself beyond all ordinary influences, human and divine, and still end up as a bushel of lime, well fit for the fertilizing of fields or the cementing of houses. But if not this Puritanized Faust—the sort of "Brand" who, Cotton Mather to the contrary, solemnly vowed he could *not* be "Plucked from the Burning"—then what about those old-time Puritans themselves, in something nearer their own historical key? Ethan Brand would certainly count as what Hawthorne would call a "miserable distortion of the moral nature," but were there not other sad cases, less melodramatic, perhaps, but no less instructive, inscribed or implied in the annals of ancestral New England? Well removed in time, no doubt, but not perhaps in memory or implication. What might it have been like to be an ordinary sinner among those antique Puritans? Or else, at all events, what was it like to have had "such ancestors"?

And so the title of this essay—taken, as some readers may recognize, from a sketch called "Main-street," which Hawthorne managed to write and publish about the same time as "Ethan Brand." Therein, a self-effacing and much-embarrassed "Showman" is, with the aid of his show-box of historical prints, conducting an audience, pointedly specified here and there, on a fictional tour of the Main Street, in Salem, in Massachusetts, in the United States of America, in what we have no reason to doubt is approximately the middle of the nineteenth century. He keeps trying to represent their past symbolically, and to draw out, thereby, certain more-than-literal truths, but he keeps being interrupted.

Well into his performance, and already under attack both for the amateurish nature of his pictorial representation and for the improbability of some of his scenic arrangements, the Showman finds himself trying to average out the favorable and unfavorable influences the "Puritans" must have had on his own generation of Salemites, now far enough (even if just barely) from the founding ancestors to recognize their own difference and thus raise the question at all. "Let us thank God" for them, he proposes, as he comes to the end of a complex meditation about what might have been "sinister" to both the head and the heart of New England—particularly when, as he thinks, "one generation had bequeathed its religious gloom, and the counterfeit of its religious ardor to the next."

Let us thank God for having given us such ancestors; and let each successive generation thank him, not less fervently, for being one step further from them in the march of ages.

The idea of a "march," here, will bear some looking into, but the immediate reaction to this carefully formulated counter-piety, emphasizing Puritanism's "miserable distortions of the moral nature," is not historical or (as we used to say) material, but formal, indeed generic: "What is all this," demands a resisting voice from the audience, "A Sermon? If so, it is not in the bill."

Never able to answer any of his carping critics very successfully, the Showman here can but agree: not on the bill; "I ask pardon of the audience." Yet just as everywhere else, the ironic tone and the structure of this extraordinarily self-conscious sketch suggests some cogent answers that might well be made, by somebody less relentlessly committed than Hawthorne to the old (new-critical) idea that the teller has to pretty much let the tale itself do all the talking. To the aesthetic critic who complains that the showman's horse looks more like a pig, the Showman might have said done somewhat more than concede, humorously, that "Art has its limits," or even that this looker and listener needed to change his angle of inspection, so as to get the proper effect of the (Romantic) mix of "light and shadow." To the objection that, as Mrs. Endicott had no children, she can hardly function as a type of female beauty in New England, he might have offered something like this: the larger point of this sketch is concerned with the largely unhappy legacy of *Mr.* Endicott which—given the latitude offered by a Scott-inspired "History as Romantic Art"—might be thought very considerable, even if the connections are cultural and symbolic rather than personal and literal. So here: does anyone really suspect that serious history will lack a moral dimension? And if there is indeed a moral point, what harm if fiction, knowing itself everywhere as such, avail itself of "methods interdicted to professors of biographical exactness." The learned will smile to notice the strategy; others will simply get the point.

Published in 1849, and originally planned to be part of the same volume as *The Scarlet Letter*, "Main-street" is by no means the first time Hawthorne has tried to open a dialogue with his audience on the subject of "moral history." The phrase about "interdicted" methods is from a very early sketch called "Sir William Phips" (1831), the first of the Royal Governors of Massachusetts, who arrived in time to oversee the local inquisitions into the Salem Witchcraft. An interesting effort it remains, proposing first of all an entire theory of "Romantic History" and then, after outlining the principal events in Phips' remarkable rise from a ragged frontier life to both knighthood and the King's own deputed power, it offers to compress the political, social, and even the religious meaning of Phips' function as the unlikeliest sort of Christian Magistrate in a single brief look at "a day in the life." Nor can we possibly take the sketch in any other spirit. Nineteenth-century New Englanders felt obliged to know rather more about Phips than we do, no doubt, but also rather less than did, say, Cotton Mather, who wrote the "official biography" of Phips, to which Hawthorne is clearly responding. But this fact may indicate that significant historical interest is almost never a given: everywhere, it seems, readers have to be courted and coaxed to get over the notion that all literature happens right there in their own readerly present.

Equally pointed, and more fully developed still, is the dialogue which "Alice Doane's Appeal" (1835) carries on with its audience—characterized first as "not a people of legend or tradition" and then dramatized as naively unable to notice when fiction is telling them their own moral history. Evidently they can transpire at the suggestion of incest, tremble at the depiction of murder, and hang on the words of a wizard; but they shed tears only when presented with a manifestly reductive account of what happened in 1692. The narrator ends by proposing the erection of a "commemorative" monument to the "errors of an earlier race"; but this Story-Teller understands, as clearly as the Showman of "Main-street," that, past or present, the same race is involved; and he expects some reader to understand that his story is already a sort of negative monument.

And so, just less elaborately, with a number of other stories and sketches. Famously, of course, "Molineux" and "Malvin" have brief head-notes that appear to forgive the innocent of the burden of remembering (or learning) a little history but actually put in play certain ironies indicating that, not only in the obscure and perhaps limit case of "Lovell's Fight" but even in the central and most familiar case of the Revolution itself, the process of historical remembering, forgetting, and then happily misremembering is already well under way; so that the reader can prove his competence only by making sure he has at least as much knowledge as he is being forgiven. Much the same is true of "The May-Pole of Merry Mount" (1836), whose head-note not only implies a reasonable familiarity with certain "New England Annalists," but actually turns on a rare historical pun—namely that there are, crucial to the construction of the story, not one but two texts known as the "Book of Sports." And of course there is a footnote as well, which dares anyone paying attention to ask herself what the respectable if "eccentric" Mr. Blackstone is doing in the tale at all. It's not exactly rocket science, but neither is it common sense or common knowledge; or theory either. If the desire to know about these things can seem to some readers "pedantic," the conscious decision to avoid them can properly be called bad faith.

"Goodman Brown" advertises its relation to the problem of witchcraft in Salem not with a head-note, but by invoking names that come from nowhere but Cotton Mather's *Wonders if the Invisible World* where, as clearly as in the Spenserian pretext, the odd premise of "specter evidence" is raised from the status of superstition to the more-than-respectable position of epistemology. No head-note in "The Minister's Black Veil" either, but anyone now not wishing to repress altogether the question of what sort of things might get said in a "sermon before Governor Belcher" is, at the same time, whistling in the dark and dancing through the minefield. Even so slight a performance as "The Man of Adamant" cannot conclude its embarrassing display of natural imitation of the shameful parts of men and women without adding a sort of historical coda: religious separatism and sexual solipsism, however interrelated, have been, at all events, deeply buried and well concealed, thereby, from the everyday notice of those who come after. What the case requires, evidently, is what theorists have come to call "archeology."

A New Historicism—as anxious about our own now as the writer's (or character's) then—will prove no substitute for specific historical knowledge, of exactly the sort Foucault himself exerted so much labor to acquire, whether of sexual or medical or any other sort of "practice." Categorical precision is essential, of course, but sooner or later the durable interpretation of a literary text is going to require us to know many of the same things our author knew. Obviously, in the case of explicit allusion. If we discover that Melville's Pierre has been reading *Hamlet* or *The Divine Comedy*, nothing will serve except to review those texts in our own minds to see how the one text might bear upon the other. Nor has anyone thought otherwise. On the other hand, however, many accomplished readers of the brightest literary accomplishments of British high culture have appeared to balk when, in the attempt to read Hawthorne, the pretext, clearly advertised, turned out to be Mather's *Wonders* or Winthrop's *Journal*: criticism appears to be even longer than art, itself notoriously longer that a scholar's effective life. One simply cannot know everything. Even in a world where anything at all might be relevant or useful, teachers of literature all know what it is like, most days, to face a class with only part of the contextual information they would like to command. And will it be telling tales out of school to remark that, for the most part, students seldom notice what the professor does not know?

Yet there is always a risk. And never greater, perhaps, than in the case of Hawthorne's acknowledged masterpiece of world literature. For seldom has an author—though aspiring to a world-class reputation as fervently as the law of literary creation allows— taken more pains to distance his fictional world from the actual one with which audience had its own daily experience. Some, seizing on a hint of Hawthorne's own, have called this world the "neutral territory" of "romance" and have gone on to assume that dissociation from "realist" conventions or the willing suspension of our ordinary sense of plausibility will be tools enough; that writers have to take their readers pretty much as they find them and have no real right to make demands that ordinary good faith and a supple imagination cannot meet. Yet, fair or not, Hawthorne calls the world of *The Scarlet Letter* "Boston," and it has taken only a little ingenuity to figure out that the moral fall and social rehabilitation of Hester Prynne goes on between the years 1642 and 1649. He might have called her world "Salem," where his own ancestors rose, reigned, and were ruined; where he was just this minute working in a custom house; and where, accordingly, many half-attentive students suppose that he actually has. Or he might have said or implied, more generally, "New England," in days "back then," when almost everybody believed in superstition, when man's (and especially woman's) sexual nature had not yet been justified, and when all sorts of curious and harmful things went on, many of them in the name of religion. It is often hard to tell otherwise from student papers. But not from the novel itself.

It might be too much to suggest that Hawthorne demands that his readers repeat his own preliminary and contextual reading in the "Godly Letters" of seventeenth-century Puritanism, before re-reading the book they most likely disliked in high school. But they will do well to remember that Hawthorne's nineteenth-century audience knew more about those literal ancestors of theirs, who can be ours only by metaphorical extension or moral imagination. And it would not be wise to assume in advance that we have nothing to learn about—or through the use of—an odd pre-provincial world now gratefully lapsed. Books know only what they know. But where is it written that they must not teach us some of that?

3

If *The Scarlet Letter* is indeed to be read as an historical novel, then it may be that the somewhat obscure sketch called "Main-street" provides as useful an introduction as the famous and much-discussed "Custom-House"; or else, at very least, it may point us to what is most enduringly important about the prefatory gesture that got itself officially inscribed at the head of Hawthorne's masterpiece. Written after the novel was substantially complete, "The Custom-House" contains an unedited sentence which advertises the fact that the earlier, serio-comic dialogue-with-audience was originally scheduled to appear in the same volume with the sad affair of Hester and Dimmesdale; and probably we need to imagine that it was the way in which Hawthorne, years away from his all-but-original subject, wrote himself back into his once-familiar world of the seventeenth-century Puritans.

Conceived in some analogy to the quasi-biographical sketch of "The Old Manse," which had introduced the 1846 *Mosses*, "The Custom-House" came along only after the moral world of Winthrop's Boston had been powerfully re-invoked—to fill up a volume long enough to look like a novel and, significantly, to explain how the author came to free himself from the uncongenial conditions of a precarious political appointment. If "Main-street" dramatizes the writer's conscious wish to interest his audience in a mature consideration of their Puritan legacy, "The Custom-House" fictionalizes the strength of Hawthorne's own historical interest, his virtual inability to resist the summons of the past. And this psycho-literary question may be of more enduring interest than Hawthorne's personal estimate of his custom-house associates or of government service in general. Some part of a developing esthetic may have convinced Hawthorne that "a better book" than he would ever write lay waiting in the quotidian materials right there in the custom-house life itself; but what matters more is the account he gives of how the book he really wrote got written.

The restrained brilliance of the satirical prose in which Hawthorne defines and demoralizes the work-world of the customs service all but disguises the fact that, after many months of fair enough government service, he has begun to fear for his writerly life. He makes a nice little joke about the sane-making effect of seeing his signature in a whole new context—on "cigar boxes" rather than on pieces of fiction—but anyone who recalls the ten-plus years that elapsed before he actually saw his own name attached to any published writing can imagine the pain beneath the self-mocking comedy. He was not exaggerating much when, in an 1851 Preface, he remembered himself as "the obscurest man of letters in America." True enough, he could here propose, a little real-world experience might be good for the man who had lived among the Transcendentalists, conversed too much with Alcott the Platonist, but evidently a person can stand to be in under their head only so long. And just so with Hawthorne until, as if by magic, he finds his way back—to literature and to his most competent early subject, "The Matter of the Puritans." How it really happened, day by day, source by source, may well remain a mystery; but the fictionalized account is so richly suggestive of purpose and method as to require at least as much attention as the fascinating sub-textual question of just why and with what fairness Hawthorne got himself fired from the custom house and restored, thereby, to his more customary routine of reflection and writing.

That is to say, the extended episode of discovering a bundle of old manuscripts has a literary interest at least as great as the satiric portraits that surround it. The pen is rarely mightier than the political appointment; at best Hawthorne probably got even. But however that may be, he created, at the center of his after-the-fact introduction, one of the most memorable images of the operation of the historical imagination in all of world fiction. He also managed to deepen—confessionally and without much imaginary dialogue—the discussion he was having with his audience, now as well as then, about why the conscientious writer of fiction might eschew the novel's more or less literal mimesis of present actuality in favor of evoking those realms of human experience which, surviving only in some trans-personal memory, can only be imagined and can be imitated better in the convention of metaphoric types than in that of literal human singulars. The Preface to *The House of the Seven Gables* will remember, however briefly, to address these formal matters the next year. But the issue of history and the epistemology of romance is already there at the center of "The Custom-House."

Imaginatively, at least, it required a rainy day to prove that "the past was not dead." Earlier, at the Old Manse, a series of such inhospitable days had sent this first-time self-confessing writer inside, out of a natural world he found he could enjoy almost as much as Emerson and Thoreau, and up to the attic, where the ponderous libraries of the previous (clerical) occupants had all been religiously preserved. Accustomed to regard books from the past as sacred objects, he yet rejects all these as irrelevant—failing, by and large, to "touch upon their ostensible subject." The newer books, products of the Liberal and then the Unitarian persuasion, seem stillborn and particularly useless; but even the older works, "earnestly written" and once possessed of real "warmth," utterly fail to engage the moral historian's eager and susceptible imagination. The figure of this failure is striking indeed. As elsewhere in New England, a spiritual presence is widely believed to linger about the upper regions of this old clergymen's residence and, standing before the portrait of one such ministerial predecessor, Hawthorne confesses to have "met face to face with the ghost, by whom, as there was reason to apprehend, the Manse was haunted." Local color, we might think, if this were all. But in fact Hawthorne goes on to imagine a point of practical contact between this ghostly past and his own literary present: "Not improbably," he infers, this clerical spirit had "wished me to edit and publish a selection from a chest full of manuscript discourses that stood in the garret." Well might one heed such a call.

But no. Competent professional editor Hawthorne had long since proved himself to be. And—though the writer of "The Celestial Rail-road" might not say so for himself—surely no one in New England had a better ear for the change over time in the tone of New England religion. Yet evidently this is not his task, literal or symbolic: Hawthorne's gift was cautiously to estimate and not at all piously to extend the regimen of Calvinistic Puritanism. And so, after a few more observations on what one of his important predecessors had called "The Mutability of Literature," back out into the world of Transcendental Nature and off on a "fishing-excursion" with Ellery Channing.

And yet, as all ghosts are not the same ghost, when a comparable opportunity presents itself in a second attic, that of the Custom House, the outcome will be entirely different. Actually this will be the third upper room of Hawthorne's imagination, if we agree to count that "dismal chamber" on Herbert Street where, all implausibly, "fame was won." More fame, here, in all conscience, and a fair portion duly assigned to the mysterious influence of a certain Mr. Surveyor Pue, a sad but conscientious old custom-house antiquarian who appears to have haunted the upper regions of this ultimate attic years before Hawthorne ever dreamed of entering, in the world below, the employ of his worldly Uncle Sam. From his carefully preserved manuscripts we learn the basic facts of the story that has come to stand as the epitome of the Puritan will to discipline and punish—the woman made to wear the sign of her scarlet sin sewn into the clothing that covered her sexual body, if not into her heart. A tale needing to be embellished, to be sure, but given there in firm outline: an imaginative invention, to be sure, but also a donnee if there ever was one. "Given" as well, and from the same grateful hand, is the scarlet letter itself, faded but fascinating and sure to invite symbolic interpretation: who had been trying to say what to whom? Could the finder of the letter imagine the word which the letter ambiguated by abbreviating? And if he could, somehow, imagine what had been meant, could he confidently transmit the message from a fervent but unenlightened past to an alarmingly insouciant future?

Only by accident, it seems, does the finder of the letter happen to hold it up against his own bosom. And yet the gesture seems somehow necessary, for it suggests a kind of knowledge that could hardly come from mere research. Startled at the effect—yet daring the reader to disbelieve—he claims to have experienced a sensation

> not altogether physical, but almost so, as of burning heat; as if the letter were not of red cloth, but red-hot iron. I shuddered, and involuntarily let it drop to the floor.

Evidently one has to do more than read the documents: historical imagination requires as well that one actually "try on" the assumptions of the past. Unless its burning issues continued to generate heat for somebody, the entire enterprise of history became an exercise in curious weirdness, whatever the medium of transmission.

Hyperbolically expressed as magic, what this rare invention also emphasizes is the feeling of being not entirely free to find or make a fictional subject, as if the tale were choosing the teller and he, once chosen, could do no more than follow a lead given somehow from beyond. Or else, more pointedly, to obey a command. For, as this remarkable little fiction of discovery and authorization continues to unfold, the ghostly presence of Mr. Surveyor Pue actually issues the command in person. And the moment is anything but under-written:

> With his own ghostly hand, the obscurely seen, but majestic, figure had imparted to me the scarlet symbol, and the little roll of explanatory manuscript. With his own ghostly voice, he had exhorted me, on the sacred consideration of my filial duty and reverence towards him—who might reasonably regard himself as my official ancestor—to bring his moldy and moth-eaten lucubrations before the public. "Do this," said the ghost of Mr. Surveyor

Pue…"do this, and the profit shall be all thy own…" And I said to the ghost of Mr. Surveyor Pue—"I will."

True enough, the historical sobriety and somberness of this is more than a little relieved by mention of the motive of "profit," especially as the tenured ghost reminds his expendable descendent that he "will shortly need it; for it is not in your days as it was in mine, when a man's office was a life-time lease." And yet this trans-generational understanding survives less as an economic bargain than as a sacred trust: evidently there are some tasks of historic preservation one simply cannot refuse. Oneself or no one. For who but Hawthorne, in all the American nineteenth century, could have created the subtle moral shadings of *The Scarlet Letter*? And who in all the world could have represented his calling with so vibrant a mixture of spiritual mystery and human comedy?

Still, the trust could not be fulfilled at once. The time might be right—and the historical host might be inevitable—but the place was wrong. Much meditation would be required and, beyond that, an entire renewal of "fancy and sensibility," impossible in the present purposive space. Formalist criticism has made much of the image which follows—of "Moonlight in a familiar room," enchanting ordinary objects—and of the esthetic concept that accompanies it—the "neutral territory, somewhere between the real world and fairy-land"—but it has regularly neglected to notice that these minor-romantic musings are actually associated with an imaginative failure. Too much time in the Custom-House has left Hawthorne's imagination a "tarnished mirror": so that, arranging these conditions of light and shadow proved nothing to the purpose. He had to get out. And, more significantly perhaps, when the truly creative writing began again, it is the ghost of Mr. Surveyor Pue that enables the esthetic new departure. In point of strict psychological fact, the mood of moonlight on a child's shoe has absolutely nothing to do with the bitterly adult affect of the book Hawthorne was eventually able to write.

We have it on the considerable authority of D. H. Lawrence that Romance is when no one's shoes get muddy. And it must be confessed that Hester and Pearl, who walk about a bit, are never seen to wade through fens and bogs. As well they might have been imagined to do. But when Hester first appears on the scaffold, to the steady stare of a disciplinary populace, it is the unblinking sun and not the forgiving moon that lights the village square. When Dimmesdale holds his midnight vigil of insane but ineffective self-punishment, the scene is lit by a blazing comet, but the mellow moon is nowhere in sight. And when the well-born but ill-bred children of the Puritans torment the oddly dressed issue of an unlikely sexual union—was it really the "nauseous amour of a Puritan pastor"?—they probably throw something more like mud than moonlight.

However that may be, the overall effect of "The Custom-House" is to prepare us for a tale that required an unembarrassed imagination to invent and will demand at least as much from the reader. Just not an imagination of escapism or of softening. Quite like the sketch of "Main-street," "The Custom-House" exists to assert that the past, though inexorably connected to the present, is in many respects a foreign territory. To get beyond the comforting clichés of outworn superstition on the one hand and universal sameness on the other, one might have to go and live there for some fair period of time. Even try on, perhaps, some of their curious assumptions—about love and social unity, for example—which surely count for more than their funny costumes.

4

The very first page of *The Scarlet Letter* makes knowing reference to the world we are entering as somebody's idea of a "Utopia of human virtue and happiness"; but utopian notions are always hatched somewhere, and the overdeterminations we instantly encounter make it clear that this is a most specific "nowhere." Men in "sad-colored garments and gray, steeple crowned hats" may seem like stage Puritans, but a "first prison-house," lost to recorded history, but readily assumed to be on a plot of land once belonging to a certain "Isaac Johnson" gives substance to the easy evocation of human frailty and may even suggest that not all universals are false. Ugly weeds seem to have found a metaphorical home in "the soil that had so early borne the black flower of society," but the ones mentioned are in fact native to New England. A certain rosebush may be a survival (and a sign) of vivid original nature, but "the sainted Ann Hutchinson"—from whose footsteps it is said in legend to have sprung—is, in the annals of the Puritan determination to discipline and punish, as famous as it was possible for a seventeenth-century woman to become. Boston had no corner on outspoken dissent, to be sure, but no other woman of "ready wit and bold spirit" is known to have provoked an official account of the "Rise, Reign, and Ruin" of herself and her sectarian supporters. The reference could be casual of course, but even then it is extremely significant; for it assumes a reader who knows a thing or two about the American seventeenth century. The language of roses might almost pass without remark, but the mention of a notorious "Antinomian" raises the bar of interpretation more than just a little. Hester Prynne may be like Ann Hutchinson in theory or in practice, quite a lot or just a little, but ignorance of the facts is a poor basis on which to decide.

But while we are hesitating between the universal need of a prison and the specific case of the heretical woman who once was here detained—awaiting first banishment and then a retributive death by Indian attack—a Narrator who is proud (but not jealous) of all he knows reminds us that, as crimes change with the times, so does the public response: heterodox religion, native vagrancy, and the really awful offense of witchcraft are all taken with the utmost seriousness of judgment and "demeanor," for here we have "a people amongst whom religion and law were almost identical." This could be a simple slander: the Puritans were harsh, rigid, legalistic, altogether unlovely. Or, it could be the reason why, within an explicitly covenanted community, the problem of "antinomianism" arose at all. But before deciding we would have to know something about how and why, historically, the Magistrates of this special community had been urging the principal ministers to draw up a stable body of positive laws out of Scripture teaching and Jewish precedent: what crimes, including sexual transgressions, merited what punishments? Did not Leviticus make adultery a capital offense? Why then this strange lenience in the case of Hester Prynne? Some historical plot must be unfolding in the literary background.

Meanwhile, however, we are invited to expect no deep sympathy for the criminal this day to be exposed, and warned not to be too shocked if the women of this ancient age act more like rough Elizabethans than the gentler New England ladies of the present day. Ours is now a world of refined sentiment, he more than implies, but that was then. It may come as a surprise when—struck, it may be, by the singular beauty of the female prisoner when she finally does appear—a man gently reproves the lack of "mercy" in the vindictive speech of the assembled goodwives, but the narrative prediction is more than made good when only a single female voice is raised, twice, in protest against the consensus that the magistrates have been too lenient with the criminal and that she herself is, in her flagrant needlework, positively flaunting her lack of proper contrition. What they notice, correctly, is that the scarlet letter is not *yet* doing its office. On the other hand, we are explicitly admonished not to flatter ourselves too much with the pride of an evolved moral sense. But even this complicating caution emphasizes the essential point: even in 1850, this story is not happening "now."

And so the tale unfolds—with an historical overdetermination it takes a really urgent will-to-ignorance to resist. Students like to turn the interview between Hester and Chillingworth into the scene of a no-fault divorce, but actually they both end up admitting something like old-fashioned guilt. His quasi-scientific desire to identify her partner in adultery may seem more properly gothic than historical, but it certainly represents a powerful affront to any plausible presentist reading: this is strange stuff; it must be happening somewhere else. Then too, Hester's willingness to keep his identity a secret speaks to more than a general sense of fairness—keep one secret, keep another. For in the world in which her lawful husband has suddenly re-appeared, Hester will of course be expected to return to his proper home and fireside; and clearly she has something else in mind. Or so the Narrator deeply suspects. In answer to his own self-vexed question about why Hester does not simply move on, to any one of a number of places where no one has ever heard of scarlet letters, he answers that, though Hester may tell herself that this is where she somehow fatally belongs, the real reason is that she wants to be near Dimmesdale. And before anyone can sing a single note of "Stand By Your Man," he ascribes to her a love that would prefer to be in hell with this lover than in heaven alone. Or with Chillingworth. For what else can he mean by her looking forward to "a futurity of endless retribution"? And since it is, after all, his interpretative fantasy, whom else is there to believe?

The effect of this extravagant loyalty is fairly complex. In awe, the reader may well wish to echo Dimmesdale's earlier tribute to the "Wondrous strength and generosity of a woman's heart," but only with the proviso that strength and generosity may not always be the same as moral sanity. Elsewhere, Huckleberry Finn may decide he'd rather go to hell than betray his friend Jim, but this does not mean he has figured out that all his "conscience" has been taught to think about slavery is flat wrong. And just so here: at the outset, at least, Hester's moral sense is part of an episteme the modern reader can try to imagine but can hardly share. The fact that it may have endured long enough to sinew the irony of Twain (and Emily Dickinson as well) does not mean that we are not supposed to recognize it as such. We are accustomed to speak of "the triangle" as "eternal," but evidently the flexible form of the novel leaves as much room for specific historical insight as for the residue of common sense.

Puritan-specific too is her peculiar attitude toward Pearl. Named to recall the Scripture's "Pearl of Great Price," when a less spiritual system of notice might have suggested "Ruby rather—or Coral—or Red Rose," Pearl appears to Hester less as a full-fledged and well-formed natural child than as her "scarlet letter in another form." The elemental literary point is so clear as to be almost comic: on the scaffold Hester has tried to hide her scarlet letter from the prying eyes of the prurient public by covering it up with her agitated infant; but of course that were merely to hide the symbol with the fact. Still, Pearl is much more than a symbol—so much so as to remind us always to ask "symbol for whom?" And for what purpose? Fatherless, in social fact, born of a mother in extremis, and doomed, it appears, to a world given to allegory and finger-pointing, she is a natural child in need of all the loving nurture a single mother can manage. So it would be hardly proper child rearing to dress her to appear as but "the scarlet letter in another form." The gesture might serve to focus her own sense of ambivalent remorse, and perhaps to heighten the sense of her obedient defiance of official punishment, but what she principally accomplished is to turn little Pearl into the same sort of symbol the Puritan community has made of Hester herself. Whoever you deeply and variably are, to us you will be a Guilty Reminder.

Wondrous strong and generous Hester may everywhere appear, but not in every sense admirable. Certainly not saintly, except perhaps in the same ironic sense in which the Narrator honors the "footsteps of Ann Hutchinson." Perhaps not even quite sane. Betrayed by her sexual nature, we suppose, she is also the victim of assumptions that miserably distort the moral nature. Some of these she will live to outgrow, but in a way that is more predictive than transcendent. And for the moment she seems dangerously confused, for her odd outfitting of Pearl is in fact the less deleterious part of her hysterical behavior. Taught to believe that vows are binding, she refuses for a long while to believe that her liaison with Dimmesdale "had a consecration of its own"; and utterly unable to keep the moral order separate from the genetic, she daily peers at Pearl in the tortured expectation that some horrible deformity will soon appear. Her volatile Narrator can almost believe that "God, as a direct consequence of [her] sin [...] had given her a lovely child," but Hester cannot persuade herself of the felix culpa:

> She knew that her deed had been evil; she could have no faith, therefore, that its result would be for good. Day after day, she looked fearfully into the child's expanding nature, ever dreading to detect some dark and wild peculiarity, that should correspond with the guiltiness to which she owed her being.

And, as "no physical defect" appears in this infant "worthy to have been brought forth in Eden," Hester can only look to her uncontrollable exuberance—about like that of Una of Hawthorne's Notebooks—as the confirming sign.

Cautiously enlightened, the Narrator finds the entire process of requiring the physical to symbolize the moral to be "morbid," but somewhere he knows it is, under the aspect of Puritan history, far from unique. For unless we wish to dissociate him entirely from the man who wrote, years before, an historical sketch of "Mrs. Hutchinson" (1831), he will be remembering the moral satisfaction John Winthrop took in witnessing the dangerous ideas symbolically discredited in her "monster birth." And the glee with which his redactors ground out the punning story of her "misconceptions." Modern students—particularly sensitive young women most sympathetic with the plight and developing cause of Hester, and most resistant to the Narrator's right to have Hester's story his own way—tend to resist the comparison, but clearly Hester is expecting Pearl to exhibit analogous symptoms of monstrosity. The best one can say, perhaps, with studied sympathy, is that was then.

Eventually, of course, the reader will have to historicize the pitiable male weakness of Arthur Dimmesdale, whom no less an observer than Henry James took to be at the heart of the psychological drama: what must he be thinking all the years it takes for Pearl to outlive her mother's suspicion and come to the verge of her womanly confidence? Hypocrite he must surely be, but does that hard word name a moral essence or cover a variety of historic possibilities? For the moment, however, the place to center the novel's now intense, now casual evocation of the intense but distorted morale of the seventeenth century is on the scene in which Hester appears at a hearing before an official named Richard Bellingham. Governor of Massachusetts for one year only, nearly removed for a cause not entirely unlike Hester's own, but still elected to the list of those several "Assistants" to the General Court who also acted, regionally, as "Magistrates," Bellingham is asked to decide if the outcast and as yet un-reincorporated Hester is a fit mother for a child coming closer, year by year, to the age of moral reason. There is, of course, a wonderful Catch-22: if Pearl were in fact a demon-child, then surely the cause of her mother's soul required her removal; but if human, and capable therefore of "moral and religious growth," then she no doubt required a better nurture her sinful mother could provide. Oddly, only the intervention of Dimmesdale can prevent the otherwise inevitable separation of mother and child, and he, only when Hester appears to issue a threat: "Look thou to it! I will not lose the child! Look to it!"

Powerful as is the broken-family drama here, more fascinating still is the Narrator's editorial comment on the historical likelihood of the entire proceeding. Earlier he has permitted himself to skim over that fact that, in the real-life background of Hester's original public examination, the theocracy evolving around her is carrying on an intense debate about crime and punishment, including the possibility of capital crimes for sexual offenses. Now, however, and as if to make up for an historical failure, he all but dares the reader to learn a little more of the curious, indeed salacious Puritan backstory.

The reader might think the writer is taking liberties: could there really be so much official fuss about one woman's right to rear her illegitimate child? No such thing, he insists, for this was exactly the same period at which "a dispute concerning the right of property in a pig not only caused a fierce and bitter contest in the legislative body of the colony, but resulted in an important modification of the framework itself of the legislature." Ah yes, the famous dispute about the rightful ownership of Goody Sherman's pig, the resolution of which involved the vindication, finally, of the Magistrates' power to veto the actions of Deputies, giving us—voilà!—a properly bicameral legislature, as any sophomore major in American History is required to know. Piously repeated in history books everywhere, the story comes to us originally and authoritatively from the masterful

Journal of John Winthrop, well developed in a narrative cohesion of its own, but often intertwined with other stories only incidentally related or thematically parallel.

One such is the unlovely tale of Richard Bellingham, whom we first encounter in the novel's opening scene as the Governor who, along with "an assemblage of magistrates" and appropriate clergymen, stands on a balcony overlooking Hester's scaffold, encouraging her to solve the mystery of Pearl's paternity. Close students of then novel's implied chronology have wondered why it is Bellingham who stands there and not John Winthrop who, if the date is indeed June, 1642, would have just succeeded Bellingham as the chief executive officer of the Massachusetts theocracy. Why indeed—when, as we have long since been asked to believe, the writer of *The Scarlet Letter* appears to have had Snow's *History of Boston* open on the table before him? Why this one "error" in a text otherwise so pedantically correct? To avoid the distraction of implicating, in a fiction, a real life character about whom very much was in fact known? To protect the reputation of a Founder often held exempt from the smallest of Puritan peculiarities? Or, perhaps, for reasons—like the ones that motivate the importation of Blackstone into festivities at Merry Mount—that are both intensely thematic and devastatingly historical.

The first we hear of Bellingham in Winthrop's *Journal* is that he is, now and again, one of the Magistrates more sympathetic to the demands of those Freemen who insist on asking Winthrop where, in their Royal Charter, he gets the power to do this or that new thing. No story here. Then we learn that, while Governor, from May 1841 to May 1842, it fell to him to write to all the churches in the Massachusetts and Plymouth asking, in the wake of several sad cases of sexual misdemeanor in both colonies, what penalties were, in their reading of the Jewish Scriptures, exactly prescribed for what sexual crimes. Closer to the mark, clearly, for this is but a part of the uncertain legal background that permitted Hester's unusual punishment. And further, to read the bizarre and Latinate distinctions made in the responses to Bellingham's little questionnaire is to understand at once why the Narrator of Hester's crime and punishment might risk his harshest verdict against the old-time Puritans who press the case against Hester:

> They were, doubtless, good men, just, and sage. But, out of the whole human family, it would not have been easy to select the same number of wise and virtuous persons, who should be less capable of sitting in judgment of an erring woman's heart, and disentangling its mesh of good and evil than the sages of rigid aspect towards whom Hester Prynne now turned her face.

Dimmesdale might well be an exception, we think, being approximately equi-guilty of the same something or other. And maybe Bellingham too, if his truth were known.

But then of course it is: elected over Winthrop in May of 1641 as the more "democratic" candidate, he is voted out in May of 1642 for reasons of grave sexual misconduct, which Winthrop has been detailing all along. Within the course of his brief tenure as chief magistrate, Bellingham has, without bothering to publish the traditional and well warranted "banns," declared himself married, by his own magisterial authority, to a young woman already formally promised to another man, a grave matter in a society where many couples took their personal betrothal at least as seriously as the civil ceremony that made their union public. Some norms might be unclear, but nowhere in this evolving Protestant society did one simply marry oneself: if this last-minute change of partners were to be licit at all, Bellingham and his intended had needed to stand before some *other* magistrate, where they would, no doubt, have had some explaining to do. The thing was simply a scandal. The General Court kept calling on Bellingham to come in and explain himself, even if this would mean stepping down from his position of high authority; and when he would not, it remained for the popular vote to turn him out. We may have to invent our own bottom line, but we can easily invent one from which Winthrop and the Puritan majority would not dissent: marriage may no longer be the sacrament held forth by the Roman Catholics, but no one is yet allowed to say "What we did had a consecration of its own. We felt it so." Nor is it enough that "We said so to each other." For the covenant involved reaches to the interest of the entire community and stands, indeed, as the metaphorical model of all the others—as many as a Perry Miller might count.

And so, in fictional time 1645, when Hester and Pearl stand before Bellingham, we recognize the magistrate whom "the chances of a popular election had caused [...] to descend a step or two from the highest rank." And we remember the irony of those "chances": Governor taken in (something like) adultery. And then, as we reprise the novel's opening scene—in June, 1642—we get at once the point of Hawthorne's original metonym: Bellingham for Winthrop. Famous for his moving letters to Margaret, Winthrop remains a model of faithful puritanic love; but there, except for the grace of his maleness and his social position, goes? Bellingham. Right down there on the scaffold of sexual shame. Right along with the loving and lying Dimmesdale. Call that "The Third Secret of *The Scarlet Letter*."

And while we are debating the necessity of insisting on the geographic and demographic details provided by Snow's *History of Boston*—open before Hawthorne as he wrote—we might also, at a different level of figure and theme, consider another important pre-textual question as well: would not the serious reader would do well to keep the matter of Winthrop's *Journal* alive in his mind while reading? Overburdened undergraduates will surely object, with conviction and some cogency, that this makes Art *way* longer than Life on the Quarter System. But the same protest in the voice of the accomplished Professor of American Literature will, sooner or later, come to seem a little lame. Sooner or later, what went in will insist on being read out.

5

But to claim that *The Scarlet Letter* is a serious historical novel—authentically interested in trying to understand the complex moral climate of the seventeenth century—is not to suggest that Hawthorne was dissociated from his own political present. Once it was easy to regard this author as an isolated man whose solitary brooding carried him far away from the social questions of the late Republican and then the Antebellum Period—into a region of escape called simply "The Past." This "neutral territory" often looked something like Puritan Massachusetts, to be sure, but the idea that Hawthorne had strong reasons for engaging the issues of that time and place took a long time to develop; and so did a proper grasp of the contemporaneous questions that found their source or analog in that particular epoch.

By now the case seems clear: not only does *The Scarlet Letter* grow out of a deep and determined reading of some important texts from the Puritan past but, like most serious study of the past, it has powerful "presentist" reasons for pursuing its historical interest. The liberal theory of dissenting (or deviant) rights had to develop against the background of a "social covenant" whose rules, once assented to, were binding without personal exception. A conservative view of the moral nature and social place of women, a staple of early-modern societies, had encountered an exemplary challenge in a controversy that racked John Winthrop's "City set upon a Hill" at the outset. And the general habit of learning to live with difference, hoping for future agreement—politics, American style—may have its roots in the way a Puritan Commonwealth preserved itself through certain rituals of consensus. All this we now take as a given.

What may call for comment are the reasons why Hawthorne went back, in 1849, to the material that had been a regular subject of his writing in the 1820s and 30s, when it was widely assumed that "the matter of the Puritans" was an essential subject for an emergent American Literature; for, after his brief stint at Brook Farm, Hawthorne appeared to have moved definitively on, as the tales and sketches written in the 1840s bear all the marks of the man who had been living in Emerson's Concord and wanted to comment on "Idealism as it appears in 1842." Why not simply go on with that or some other purely contemporary interest? The shape of his career would be about as plausible if *The Blithedale Romance* had been the first of his full-dress American Romances. And would not many modern readers like him a good deal better if he had noticed, just then in 1850, that the 800 pound gorilla in the room was slavery? What then made the Puritan "ancestors" such a compelling topic? Was it just that, in moving from the tale to the novel, Hawthorne gravitated to the materials with which he felt most comfortable? Or did some other insistent issue of the 1840s remind the developing social critic of something the moral historian already knew?

By the time Hawthorne's friend, Herman Melville, wrote "Benito Cereno" (in 1855), no one could doubt that the Abolition had become the political question that threatened to crowd out all others. But the matter had not always been so clear. The authors of the Missouri Compromise (1820) might have predicted the long-term effect of their temporizing enactment; and certainly William Lloyd Garrison seemed to know what was coming when he began to publish *Liberator* in 1831, the same year as the slave revolt of Nat Turner. But other problems plagued the Jacksonian Era as well—the relocation of Native Americans, the extension of the franchise, the class-based issues of currency and banking. Americans may have been repressing race, but they were not yet obsessing slavery. Theodore Parker seemed prescient when, in 1840, he moved his post-Unitarian preaching into Boston's Music Hall, there to hammer home the need for abolition; but George Ripley, the other great reformer-contemporary of Emerson, clearly felt called otherwise when, the next year, he and a few fellow visionaries went out to Brook Farm, hoping to practice cooperation rather than competition and to provide all willing participants an equal access to culture. Hawthorne may not have agreed that this was "Christ's idea of society," but evidently he thought well enough of the experiment to join it at the outset; and though he left in less than a year, his memory of this gesture at social revolution remained strong enough to motivate, a decade later, a full-length "Romance."

The plot of *The Blithedale Romance* (1852) hinges on the return of a waif-like subheroine into something like white slavery, a significant fact in the wake of the Fugitive Slave Law enacted in 1850; but its moral premise is the possibility of a less artificial interaction—intercourse, as an earlier century would not blush to call it—between liberated persons. And between the sexes. Predictably so, perhaps, as George Ripley and his wife Sophia were both feminists as well as socialists. They may not have read Freud on "Civilization and its Discontents," but they had heard from other sources, including a French social engineer named Fourier, that monogamous marriage and the nuclear family, with a highly gendered theory of sexual need and social role, were not going to satisfy the liberated modern individual. Hawthorne's Preface renounces any wish to teach with authority on the issue of "socialism," but it does not at all disclaim an interest in the foundational question of sex and gender. *The Scarlet Letter* leaves us even more free to discover the author's historical interest in the conventions of sex and society. And we need to bear in mind that the pressing social context of this novel includes the emphatic separation, in 1841, of the women's rights movements from the abolition crusade; the publication, in 1845, of Margaret Fuller's epoch-making *Woman in the Nineteenth Century*, which reminded Emerson and others that "the soul" honors the distinction of gender as little as it does that of "persons"; the convening in 1848 of the first significant convention of the women's movement, at Seneca Falls, N.Y.; the founding, that same year, of a free-love (or, more properly, a complex-marriage) community in Oneida, N.Y.; and the determined continuation of a women's movement in the American novel, which seemed bound to call for women's political rights while dramatizing her domestic wrongs. Hawthorne could hardly fail to notice.

It would, in this context, be easy enough to read him as anti-feminist. The dominant male character in *Blithedale* certainly is such: Woman, in the view of reformer Hollingsworth, is the most admirable handiwork of God, in her true place and character.

> Her place is at man's side. Her office is that of Sympathizer; the unreserved, unquestioning Believer. [...] All the separate action of Woman is, and ever has been and always shall be, false, foolish, vain, [and] destructive of her own best and holiest qualities.

And Coverdale, the recessive counterpart, an inept and perhaps deceitful narrator, seems to endorse the idea of women's liberation chiefly for effect. Worse, perhaps, the strong female figure in the book, explicitly a feminist, falls so helplessly in love with the chauvinist male that she recants her interest in gender equality, consigning the cause to little girls and old ladies; also, significantly, she ends up rejected, desperate, and dead, possibly a suicide.

Hester Prynne comes out better, of course, but her resistance to puritanic authority cannot be called an entire success: the art of her needlework defiantly elaborates the punitive letter the Puritan Elders have sentenced her to wear, but wear it she does, and it forces her into an ostracism that endures until her departure from New England, seven years later, after the death of her adulterous partner; public scorn may lessen over the years, but the outcast is never entirely re-assimilated. She gets over her fantasy of an erotic hell, to be sure, as (eventually) she speculates her way out of most of the folk-beliefs which her contemporaries (including Dimmesdale) hold so firmly but, never openly proclaiming her "antinomian" departures from Puritan faith, she continues in the ignominious role of the guilty penitent. She wastes her life, it would seem, on a desperate minister one critic has called "a small man gone wrong." And, in a highly strategic epilogue, she comes back to the scene of her never-so-called adultery—to perform in good faith, as her Narrator wishes to think, the rest of her atonement: "Here had been her sin; here, her sorrow; and here was yet to be her penitence." An icon of conservative theology, perhaps, but not a powerful model of Woman in the Nineteenth Century.

And yet the steadiest of Hawthorne's feminist critics has continued to insist that Hawthorne is a sensitive and not entirely unfriendly observer of the women's movement. Everyone now knows that he hated having to compete with a cadre of female novelists he would refer to in a letter as a "damned mob of scribbling women," but not everyone has noticed that in a following letter he expresses great admiration for one particular woman writer and something like awe at the frank self-exposure of an entire group: "they come before the public naked, as it were." By extreme contrast, Hawthorne knew himself as a writer who always kept his "inmost me" behind a veil, who would never dream of serving up his heart "delicately fried, with brain sauce." He knew as well that his mode of "romance" implied indirection and symbolic substitution rather than literal imitation. And of course he was not a woman. Yet the question of female nature appeared to fascinate him, and something of his own admiration is expressed in the moment when Dimmesdale discovers that Hester "will not speak" (176). The irony, of course, is that contemporary women were indeed speaking, of the wrongs that betrayed their rights; and some part of Hawthorne may have preferred female strength in the mode of silence. But the strength was there, in either case.

And he had written about it before: in the moral superiority of the fated Beatrice Rappaccini, who ventures to assert that there has been, all along, less poison in her nature than in that of her distracted lover; and in the submissive death of Georgiana, a woman who allows herself to be destroyed by her husband's fastidious perfectionism. Earlier, he had recorded the love that binds a patient Elizabeth to the tormented minister who seeks his perfect consummation only "hereafter"; and in the baffled fidelity of two wives forced to endure their husbands' Shaker rejection of ordinary sexual life. In the most complex case, his early story called "The Gentle Boy" had split the strong and generous female in two, giving to one the task of nurturing, against opposition, the child of alien religion, and to the other the duty of following, with affection imperfectly weaned from maternal need, the Spirit's call to testify against oppression of conscience. And of course he had, at the outset of his career, offered his own version of the much-told tale of the arch-protester whose "sainted footsteps" are invoked on *The Scarlet Letter*'s first page. Revealingly, the very early sketch of "Mrs. Hutchinson" (1831) convicts this alleged Antinomian of an unruly pride, but it is far more critical of the men who sit in judgment of her destabilizing philosophy; and it reveals these archetypal patriarchs in the grip of a fearful admiration. Not quite a "feminist," this well received and then well suppressed public teacher might stand for the problem we have come to call "Private Woman, Public

Stage." Nor can the earliest Hawthorne refrain from associating her with the female writers who already control the scene of "cis-atlantic literature": predicting the caution of a Narrator horrified when Hester persuades Dimmesdale to desert his post in Boston, he solemnly warns us that "woman's intellect should never give the tone to that of man"; but he himself stands in awe of the resisting figure he names "The Woman."

But perhaps "the woman problem" in *The Scarlet Letter* is best approached not from the originary allusion to Ann Hutchinson but from the final image of Hester Prynne—ministering to women in troubles of a domestic nature, hearing their complaints with sympathy, and assuring them that some day the world will receive a "new truth," which will "establish the whole relation between men and women on a surer ground of mutual happiness." When this may happen is not at all clear: soon, it may be hoped, but not in any event now; and not through the agency of herself, a fallen woman. The substance of her vision is not hard to imagine: some day, women may vote and even hold place in some Great and General Court; certainly they will no longer be treated as their husbands' property; perhaps there will be no more marrying and giving in marriage: perhaps the much-libeled "Familists" foresaw some new way of living and loving. Not of "using women in common," to be sure; not of "using" them at all. Or using men either. Perhaps the world would yet think of a way to separate the passionate attachment from the reproductive function and, when reproduction is indeed the end, perhaps it does take a whole village to raise a child like Pearl. Not a purified "congregation," but some community where the interest of each and all really can be got to coincide. Hester has not encountered the theories of Oneida's John Humphrey Noyes, of course, but Hawthorne almost certainly has; and no matter, as the time for his "complex marriage" is not yet. Yet be assured: all such things will change. And who knows what may be revealed "in Heaven's own time"?

One daring critic has thought of Hester as anticipating nothing less than the appearance of Christ in the female form, but a more sober observer has noticed the fact that this radical change is being indefinitely deferred, that the women Hester counsels and consoles are being told not to rise up and demand their equal right but to wait; not to rebel but to endure. And so, read in the context of 1848—a year of world-wide revolution as well as local protest—the ending of *The Scarlet Letter* can seem quite conservative: it calls not for political action but for patience, similar to that which Emerson invoked, whenever "Experience" informed him that "the world I converse with [...] is not the world I *think*"; or which once caused him to prefer the sure administration of the "overgod" to the trial and error of the abolitionists. And there is no concealing the fact that, when Hawthorne came to write explicitly about that intractable issue, he too invoked providence and recommended patience. So here: as an intervention in the politics of feminism, *The Scarlet Letter* is fairly called a "Red Badge of Compromise." Far away from her violation of a deeply honored social norm, the offended community has all but forgotten the original transgression. Hester returns to serve to a society with which she has a profound and painful tie, and the society accepts the service; unaware of their own gradual change, perhaps, they yet accept the fact that her patient efforts predict, perhaps even enable, a further, gradual change. Ugly confrontation having subsided, both sides are living it out. Scarcely a program of activist reform. Evidently a theory of history.

But to blame *The Scarlet Letter* for not intervening more forcefully in "the whole relation between man and woman" may be to begin forgetting that it is indeed an historical novel: in that context, what more could we wish? A woman taken in adultery, in Boston, in 1642—who might have been stoned and, alternatively, who might have left—might well return to the scene of her sin; strong enough not to have died of guilt or of punishment, she might well have counseled women in the private way even John Winthrop would have permitted to the talented but unruly Anne Hutchinson. Hester foresees a wonderful future, but radical feminism is not yet and, in any case, Hawthorne had set out to write a tale of love and sex and sin and sorrow, not a feminist tract. No one has ever thought that *The Blithedale Romance* meant to become "everybody's protest novel," and it would seem an even greater mistake to convict *The Scarlet Letter* on this score. Hester and Dimmesdale must make their (separate) ways with the understanding their age has given them; their paths indeed diverge, wide enough, but neither leads directly to Enlightenment or Romanticism. Certain old-time confusions may be overcome, but we cannot expect some perfect new light to dawn—even if we no longer take sex in a puritanic way. Hester reasons on her case and does but what she can.

Furthermore, taken historically, *The Scarlet Letter* appears to make as much of Dimmesdale as of his female counterpart. Respecting the instinct of Henry James, the formalist reader can easily argue that the simple but powerful structure of the novel depends on Dimmesdale: secure on the balcony in the beginning, when Hester is in pain on the scaffold; on the scaffold, with Hester and Pearl in the very middle, but at midnight when no one can observe and inquire; and with them on the scaffold again, at the end, when all eyes will see, well, whatever it is they will see. Structurally, he is indeed the problem: why does this "subtle but remorseful hypocrite" refuse to get up on the scaffold, where his truth-loving heart knows he belongs? What will it take, finally, to get him up there? Will he need to speak as well as to appear? How will he speak? In the Calvinistic code of depravity in the abstract, as so often in his pulpit? Or with a directness no one can possibly mistake? Does he in fact do this? Or is he still trying to relieve the guilt without quite confessing the sin?

Nor is this the only ambiguity in the character whose Calvinism is trumped only by his weakness. What are we to make of his quasi-Protestant rationalizations about the need for confession? We readily suspect that his self-flagellation is merely an attempt to beat sin out of his flesh, as if it never touched his will—as if he were not living in fear that he loves Hester more than Christ, the Bridegroom of his (female) soul. And we are suitably instructed, by his revelations in the forest, that he has "for all these past seven years" been trying, more or less unsuccessfully, to believe himself a saint in spite of his sin. Yet the evidence has come to seem clear: "Of penance I have had enough! Of penitence there has been none!" So now, since he finds himself "irrevocably doomed," this low-road antinomian may as well seize the day—boldly "snatch," that is to say, "the solace allowed to the culprit before his execution." As the students are wont to say, "Predestination? Let's party."

Borrowing Hester's strength, he decides to run away. Yet he does not. But when does he change his mind? And why? Pitiably, as the Narrator observes, his proposed flight will not occur until after his election sermon: "No public duty unperformed, or ill performed!" Does he change his mind while writing the sermon? Or earlier, as a result of the lurid temptations on his way home through the forest? Or later, in the procession, as he walks in triumph, refusing to look aside at Hester and Pearl? Or in the very giving of that sermon?—a treatise of covenant blessing without being quite a proper Jeremiad. Or only after, when nothing but the Spirit could supply the breath expressed in his final prophecy? And, in the end, how spiritual is the breath of his confession—which may indeed "show forth" but which says "he" where the authentic Puritan subject had better say "I"? All this represents an intensely historical treatment of sexual guilt. Better than Foucault. For some readers it might well sustain a novel that did not at all interrogate the old status of the new woman. Indeed, one critic has boldly declared that, given his puritanic need to choose the Bridegroom Christ over the fleshly lover, Dimmesdale is himself the woman of the piece.

But if the intellectual structure is Dimmesdale, the literary texture is clearly Hester. From D. H. Lawrence on down, modern criticism repeatedly suggests that the deepest interest of the novel is the struggle of the Narrator to keep her from running away with his book; and that his attempt to discipline and punish his own wayward invention does not entirely succeed. He well remembers, from "Mrs. Hutchinson," that woman's morality is "not exactly the material for masculine virtue," but his admiration for Hester remains undiminished. A single mother, his Hester toughs it out: in a town that means to reduce her to a sermon against sin, she never entirely concedes that guilt is her only true self. Nor is her proleptic self-reliance without appropriate expression: a nineteenth-century woman might take to writing novels, but Hester can earn her way only through the artistry of her needle, which she turns to political subversion as well as to economic advantage. The Narrator-Historian, who has discovered her story in some old manuscripts, is shocked by his suspicion that she wants to get back together with her lover, even in hell, but he clearly permits us to admire her for admitting to herself—Emily-Dickinson-fashion—that she loves him more than God. And, though this might not satisfy all feminists, he dramatizes the fact that she loves her child more than her sexual freedom. Unable to repress the gothic suspicion that Pearl may have inherited some special share of original sin, she will yet not allow her be taken away. In her threat to Dimmesdale we may detect the suggestion that the woman may love her love child even more than her lover.

But though the novel's love affair with Hester tilts the affective emphasis toward the nineteenth (or the twenty-first) century, it would be a serious mistake to forget that she walks "in the footsteps of" Ann Hutchinson who is, after all, not implausibly taken as a sort of foremother of American feminism. In a second explicit reference to that deeply disturbing and destabilizing personage, the Narrator imagines that, except for her tie to Pearl, Hester "might have come down to us in history, hand in hand" with Hutchinson as "the foundress of a religious sect" and not just a smoldering private visionary. To be sure, what Hutchinson had wished originally to teach was strict theology and not reformed social practice, but when the push of the Spirit came to the shove of the Governor, she did insist upon her right to teach. And though the court that banished her in 1637 was "satisfied" that her weekly religious meetings were intolerably disruptive, modern readers are not so easy to convince. No doubt she was a little too blunt in implying that most pastors and teachers in New England were not able ministers of the gospel and, sadly, she made the confession of her personal troubles too pregnant with prophetic significance. But she had a point: Christians are constantly tempted to speak too much of sin and of law. And Hester Prynne might well be her prime exemplum. Or, over in the arena of private hysteria, Dimmesdale: trying in vain to believe that he is *simul peccator, simul sanctus*.

Such matters had to be left to Hutchinson's trial before the Church of Boston; and there the attention turned to her eccentric belief that, though the Spirit is indeed immortal, the soul of man dies with his body, to be revived (or not) by God himself on the last day. Her motive seems to have been something like "God Glorified in Man's Dependence," but her judges were afraid she meant to license her mortal followers to eat, drink, and be merry. John Cotton, her sometime mentor, had the nerve to predict that, if she persisted in her views, she would almost certainly prove unfaithful to her husband.

Dirty Old Man, we are tempted to think. Yet the hint of sex, as well as of gender, would never be very far from the center of Puritan response to Ann Hutchinson. Winthrop's *Journal* for 1637 guardedly characterizes her as "a woman of ready wit and bold spirit," but in the account offered in his *Short Story of the Rise, Reign, and Ruin of the Antinomians, Familists, and Libertines* (1644) all semblance of gender neutrality drops away: a "seducer" of the unwary, she is also a woman whose boldness had caused her to act more like a preacher than a hearer of the Word; and, in a figure that threatens to become standard, "more like a husband than a wife." By the time Edward Johnson handled the matter in his *Wonder-working Providence* (1654), she has become "a master-piece of woman's wit" whose followers had set her up "as a priest of their own profession and sex," and who promised "Revelations, full of such ravishing joy that [they] should never [again] have cause to be sorry for sin." In the pages of Cotton Mather's *Magnalia* (1702), she proves that "subtle women" are the "the most remarkable of seducers" and that social "poison" spreads fastest when "women's milk is the vehicle." And it is Mather who seals the "witty" connection between the spirit of the woman's "false conceptions" and the "monstrous births" brought forth from her menopausal body. Thus gendered and even sexualized, the Hutchinson story appears to come agonizingly literal in the career of Hester Prynne.

And of course her Narrator as much as calls her an Antinomian. Though deeply troubled by what he proposes in "Another View of Hester"—her radical speculations, her self-doubting need to harbor them in private, and above all her turn from feeling to the supposedly masculine province of thought—he nevertheless forces us to recognize that this fallen woman turned single mother is far from the resigned and value-conserving woman so much honored by the sentiment of the nineteenth century. Where else are we to look for social change? Not to settled authoritarians like Governor Winthrop or Pastor Wilson. Hardly to the flirtatious Bellingham, who can do no more than bend the rules to his own advantage. Certainly not to Dimmesdale, who cannot even tell the sex of his own soul. Only to "The Woman": silent now, in the latter days of her prideful penance, and modest later, in her return to the "office" of the scarlet letter, but potent in her power to recognize as convention what others take to be nature. And to refuse it as such. Dangerous it may be to cast it all away as "the fragments of a broken chain," and frightening to hear a woman declare—if only in the indirect discourse of a self-baffled Narrator—that "the world's law was *no law* for her mind." But the truth of history appeared to require it.

So powerful was Hutchinson's challenge to convention, sexual and otherwise, that it almost certainly helps to explain one of the most startling changes of metaphoric perception in all of Puritan literature. Aboriginally, John Winthrop's theory of holy love in a holy commonwealth—fairly called "utopian"—depended for its credibility on the figure of the affective, perhaps even the erotic feminine. It is, as I have argued elsewhere, hard to tell whether Winthrop's reference is to Eve or to Adam's own virgin soul, un-fallen and gendered female in any case. But the point is clear in either case: Man or Woman, the New England Saints love one another the way an aroused woman loves those nearest her heart: "She must have it one with herself. His is flesh of my flesh [...] and bone." Utopia, however, is not forever, and when the prime theorist of New England's love-in came to rework, in his 1645 "Little Speech on Liberty," his founding figure, the man who had helped his court conclude that Ann Hutchinson had acted too much like a husband, now made it clear that the true model of the loving female was in fact an obedient wife: saintly citizens are like the woman whose "own choice makes such a man to be her husband," just as the redeemed soul chooses Christ; but after that "she"—the woman or the soul, it hardly matters—finds her only freedom in subjection to the husband so chosen. Love, to be sure, but nothing unruly; love within and above the law of nature's own admirable hierarchies.

Of course we break the law: even in saintly New England there will need to be a prison and a scaffold. But when we sin, from time to time, we will remember our typic identity with the dutiful wife: "if through frowardness or wantonness" she should "shake off" the easy yoke of the her love's own law, she finds "no rest until she take it up again." Like Hester in the forest, perhaps, at several ironic inversions, putting her hair back up and re-attaching her letter at the non-negotiable demand of the lawless Pearl. And then, as if to predict Hester's repeated demand that lover-but-not husband Dimmesdale not for any reason "frown upon her," this final instruction:

> And whether her Lord smiles upon her and embraceth her in his arms, or whether he frowns, or rebukes, or smites her, she apprehends the sweetness of his love in all and is refreshed, supported and instructed by every such dispensation of his authority over her.

Theology, political theory, and sexual sociology all run bafflingly, memorably together: disimbricate and apply as needed; with particular application to *The Scarlet Letter*.

No doubt it was Winthrop's inspired city-on-a-hill sermon—the "Model of Christian Charity"—which emboldened Hawthorne to use a hard word like "Utopia" on his very first page. And quite likely it was his long speech on "Liberty and Authority" which prompted the Showman of "Main-street" to suggest that what his ancestors "called liberty" was somewhat more "like an iron cage." Specification might well abound: what is this, a sermon? But what matters here is simple enough: evidently those same Patriarchs who came to regard marriage a civil affair and were willing enough to permit divorce had nevertheless tried to make sex and marriage into a master metaphor: saintly citizens obey duly constituted authority exactly as wives obey husbands; and both, with no qualm of gender, as souls obey the Bridegroom Christ. Perhaps some new truth was indeed to be revealed.

What *The Scarlet Letter* suggests, then, beyond all agitated Correctness or Academic Marxism, is not only that the nineteenth-century women's movement may have, like so much else, deep roots in the religious history of New England, but that men may have more to hope than to fear from its gradual, compromised success. Men in the present may have reason to fear the woman's power to nullify the standing order, but they have reason in the future to be grateful. The best Hawthorne's men can do is to break the laws they make but never can quite keep and, breaking them, fall hopelessly into doubt. Woman—ever what D. H. Lawrence calls "the nemesis"—is also the hope of moral revolution. No doubt awakened women will continue to help men break the law, even when (in the House and in the Senate) they help to make it; but they will still be there to assure them that it was, after all, only a law to someone's mind. The flesh will surely keep its own account. So may the spirit.

Or, if that account seems tendentious, a more properly professional conclusion is possible as well. The "history" of *The Scarlet Letter* is not a question of either/or: its motive is double and so is its power of historical insight. It tells us quite a bit about the morale of the American seventeenth century where, in the inadequate language of undergraduate criticism, the story of Hester and Dimmesdale is "set." And it never lets us forget that its remarkable female protagonist, based at least in part on the "sainted" Ann Hutchinson—is herself a strong prediction of feminist protest at its own moment of first appearance. Neither antiquarian curiosity nor ill-disguised ideology, *The Scarlet Letter* does exactly what we always require of history in the best sense: knowing well the definitive differences between then and now, it nevertheless permits us to see both analogy and connection.

Clearly interested in the question of what nineteenth-century America owed to its "Puritan Origins," an artfully constructed Hawthorne surrogate had soberly concluded—in a work originally intended to appear in the same volume with *The Scarlet Letter*—that New Englanders at least ought well to consider their complex fate: thank god for "such ancestors" but thank Him as well for the possibility of moral revolution. Provoking the generalization is the reflection that the heroic days of original Puritanism had not lasted very long, and that one generation had "bequeathed to the next," not only its "gloom" but the "counterfeit of its religious ardor." And indeed, Hawthorne's "Main-street" seems largely a registry of Puritanism's "distortions of the moral nature." These find their way into *The Scarlet Letter*, notwithstanding its evocation of the decade before the Declension: Hester's original judges have almost no humane understanding of her errant woman's heart; a suffering Dimmesdale never can get God and sex into the same sane sentence; and Hester herself can just barely get over the notion that she and her lover belong in hell together. But something else is there as well: the sense that the natural heart of the greater community can find a way to get past their covenantal hysteria; and the inspired intuition that a woman's heart might have to lead the way.

And to what? Not to any "Utopia of human virtue and happiness," to be sure; and not even to the Nineteenth Amendment. But to a moment when, painfully perhaps, but rightly and necessarily, matters such as individual and society, man and woman, love and sex, freedom and restraint, might be opened to discussion and literary revision. *The Scarlet Letter* clearly anticipates that outcome, not only in its ill-repressed admiration of Hester's self-reliance, but in its evocation of the feminist moment, when "the whole relation between man and woman" would be openly debated, if not quite revised. That is to say: *The Scarlet Letter* rigorously and faithfully subjects its characters to the limits of seventeenth-century possibility, but its conclusion opens out into the world of Margaret Fuller and Fanny Fern, of Charles Fourier and John Humphrey Noyes, and of the socio-sexual world implied by *The Blithedale Romance*. The precise inspiration of this double act—of recovery and of derivation—is yet to be discovered; its epistemology yet to be theorized. But its complex effect, rare in the canon of historical fiction, is scarcely to be denied.

Chapter Eleven

INHERITANCE, REPETITION, COMPLICITY, REDEMPTION: SIN AND SALVATION IN *THE HOUSE OF THE SEVEN GABLES*

Do we really need Hawthorne's word to tell us?—*The House of the Seven Gables* was intended to be a "sunnier" book than *The Scarlet Letter*. That remarkable work, which buried Hester next to Dimmesdale, but not close enough for their ashes to mingle, and which had sent Sophia Hawthorne to bed with an "esthetic headache," had most certainly failed to discover any "sweet moral blossom" which might "relieve the darkening tale of human frailty and sorrow." But was not the affect of that tale much gloomier than Hawthorne knew his own to be? Would not his audience form the wrong impression of the happily married man who produced it?[1] So this next novel, begun within a few months of *The Scarlet Letter*'s publication, was written with something like a will to happiness: plausibly mated or not, Holgrave and Phoebe will discover one another within the glow of that romance that makes the world ever new; and such old-time curses as refuse to vanish even when called out by the name of superstition will have to be content with the half-life of remission, memory, and romance.

Nor is it only the plot that appears to have a will of its own. For all that the book's protagonist incorporates—spouts, in places—the secular ideology of Thomas Jefferson,[2] its lurking theology comes pretty close to being a gloss on the lingering question of "something, somehow like original sin": could that sort of thing really be inherited, genetically, in the same way as certain physical and mental traits, of the Pyncheons and their chickens?[3] The romantic plot may seem to imply that the white magic of a little country-girl

---

1. As Arlin Turner aptly observes, "By the time Hawthorne began writing HSG, he had grown self-conscious about the gloom in his writing"; see *Hawthorne* (New York: Oxford University Press, 1980), p. 224. And in the wake of its publication, he confided to Evert Duyckinck that, compared to *The Scarlet Letter*, the new book seemed "a more natural and healthy product of my mind"; see *Hawthorne: The Letters* (Columbus: Ohio State University Press, 1985), XVI, p. 421.
2. Jefferson's core belief—that "the earth belongs always to the living generation"—inspired not only his radical wish to have all laws (and even constitutions) re-written with each new generation but also his opposition to the theory and practice of primogeniture in the state of Virginia; see C. Ray Heim, "Primogeniture and Entail in Colonial Virginia," *William and Mary Quarterly*, 25.4 (1968), pp. 545–86. Thus the early (pre-conversion) credo of Holgrave, extended and parodied in Clifford's manic effusion on the train.
3. On my reading, the poisoned shrub at the center of RD recalls Augustine's biological—"rotten root, rotten branch"—theory of original sin. So that, whether Dr. Rappaccini figures as God

goodness can effectively counteract the force of an inbred and self-repeating evil that has had the world its own way for several centuries. But there is room for doubt. And anyone who, like Austin Warren, has ever worried that Hawthorne was the sort of more-than-Puritan thinker who believed in sin but not in grace should consider the aptness of Hyatt Waggoner's opposing conclusion, that *The House of the Seven Gables* contains Hawthorne's "Pelagian Heresy."[4] Not only is Phoebe herself rather too good to be true, but her naïve little self sometimes seems to defeat evil by simply not believing in it. Holgrave's art tries, repeatedly, to provide the elements of a graphic initiation but, as any seventeenth-century minister could point out, looking at a picture is not the same as being there.[5] Evidently Hawthorne means to protect as well as to instruct her magical innocence.

Yet none of the book's programmatic optimism can quite outweigh the sense of a gloom—and quite properly of a doom—which overhangs a house which, metaphorically at least, was built on the grave of the witches. Furnished under theoretical duress, the "moral" conditionally provided by a Preface which manages to unsay much of what it presses itself to say, can be read to mean that "the wrong-doing of one generation lives into the successive ones, and, divesting itself of every temporary advantage, becomes a pure and uncontrollable mischief" (4)[6]—unless somehow it does not. Some sin in the Pyncheon past was real, whether the popular response to it was appropriate or not. Nor was it the sort of private misdemeanor which might come before a panel of social arbiters one day and slip the next into the record of that sort of immoral behavior the law never would have the power to control. In fact, somebody accused somebody else of witchcraft and, when the charge was made to stick, he found himself in possession of a very desirable piece of property, on which he reared a handsome and very durable house and within which he raised up a dynasty. Someone, that is to say, in a world on its

---

or as Adam, sex itself is sinful and original sin is a sort of venereal disease. For the theories of original sin most common in Hawthorne's day, see H. Shelton Smith, *Changing Conceptions of Original Sin* (New York: Scribner, 1955), esp. pp. 1–55.

4. Not repeated in his latter treatments of HSG, Hyatt Waggoner once suggested that gentle Phoebe is "Hawthorne's tribute to his wife, his gesture of rapprochement to the optimistic humanism of his time, his Pelagian heresy"; see *The House of the Seven Gables* (Hyatt H. Waggoner, in Harold Bloom, ed., *Bloom's Modern Critical Interpretations: "The House of the Seven Gables"* (New York: Infobase Learning, 2013). The judgment was briefly echoed by Edward M. Holmes: "Hawthorne occasionally drifted into his own Pelagian heresies, but the rest of the time [...] he was a classicist" (485); see "Hawthorne and Romanticism," *New England Quarterly*, 33.4 (1960), pp. 476–88. For the more-than-Melvillean view of Hawthorne's sense of evil, see Austin Warren, "Introduction" to *Hawthorne* (New York: Appleton Century, 1934), pp. xix–xl. Warren softens this view in *The New England Conscience* (Ann Arbor: University of Michigan Press, 1966), pp. 132–42. And of course Waggoner's foundational study of Hawthorne stresses his "classic Christianity"; see *Hawthorne* (Cambridge, MA: Harvard University Press, 1955), p. 14.

5. On the justly famous account of sin theorist Thomas Hooker, "There is great odds betwixt the knowledge of a Traveler" who has seen the "barrenness and meanness" of an actual country and someone who "views the proportion of these in a Map"; see Perry Miller, ed., *The Puritans* (rpt. New York: Harper, 1963), p. 292. Phoebe, one might say, has just moved into the country of sin.

6. All citations of the text of *The House of the Seven Gables* are to the Norton Critical Edition of Robert S. Levine (New York, 2006).

way to finding great pride in its democracy, had got the moral drop on someone else and, in the name of God, had found a way to make the transaction pay big bucks. "Pretty good business" (225).[7] And, as both the property and the prestige persisted, so did the injustice. Until someone should give the property back—which someone thought of but no one ever did. Perhaps the sin itself could not be inherited, but the worldly advantage certainly could. The sin came, again, whenever anyone proved willing to profit from unjust arrangements he merely inherited. Complicity—as when people bought cotton at a lower price because there were slaves in the system.

All this is to argue that, for reasons that may require deeper analysis than literary criticism can practice on the dead, the conclusion of *The House of the Seven Gables* does not quite live up to the promise of its premises. After prophesying the end of the real estate industry, Clifford asks Hepzibah to take charge; she leads him home to the Seven Gables. Phoebe and Holgrave leave the Pyncheon-Maule feud on the marriage altar; and Holgrave amends Jeffersonian tearing radicalism to read that all houses should be, not torn down, but *redecorated* with every new generation. Was it Hawthorne himself who wanted it this way? Or merely his own "Phoebe," the healthy-minded but headache-prone Sophia? She whose fictional version earlier planned to cure egotism with love. No matter: we know whose name is on the title page. What must not be overlooked, however, is how very far *The House of the Seven Gables* had tried to shift its focus to Hawthorne's own generation: you know it's "romance" when some grim past bears heavily on the otherwise free and inventive spirit of the present; or when there's a ghost in the attic. You suspect it may be a novel as well when the aged suspects use the rail-road to try and run away from it all, or when somebody sells gingerbread men to little boys in a cent shop. And—Lionel Trilling's famous "hum and buzz" to the contrary notwithstanding—you find the balance tipped when, without benefit of Marx, you realize you are in a story about the curious formation and plausible maintenance of class distinction.[8]

The problem, then, is this: a sense of sin broods palpably over The House That Maule Built, but no one in the novel is remotely capable of entertaining the old-time notion of "imputation"—the venerable theory in which God treats Adam and his posterity as a moral unit; and, as chickens are not understood to be moral agents, the genealogy of dominant and recessive is not much closer to the mark.[9] The problem is less unavoidable inheritance than biased repetition: something in the structure of the world—or is it only in civilization, or in capitalism?—invites the same bad thing to keep happening. How, without a clear retreat to superstition, are we to understand that dynamic? And more

---

7. So comments the street-smart Dixey, when Hepzibah "rides off in her carriage, with a couple of hundred thousand," in Pyncheon family inheritance.
8. On the famous theory of Lionel Trilling, American's well-known resistance to the idea of class made it hard for the novel proper (as opposed to the romance) to establish itself in nineteenth-century America; see "Manners, Morals, and the Novel," in *The Liberal Imagination* (rpt. New York: Doubleday, 1957), pp. 199–215.
9. Hawthorne appears not to have required the later (1866) lectures of Gregor Mendel to have imagined Jaffrey and Clifford as the "dominant" and "recessive" versions of the Pyncheon genetic heritage.

seriously, perhaps, how can that dynamic be thought to structure a novel that ends in a marriage that seems predictable on every ground but that of palpable desire? Evidently Hawthorne has a moral case he wishes to make. Is the sobriety of that case sufficient to outweigh the novel's otherwise annoying will to happiness?

2

Romance-wise, Hawthorne's deceptively simple Preface openly confesses, the problem begins in the past—Puritan, but not aboriginally so, and maybe not so distinctively Puritan as to offer us the familiar excuse of pseudo-historicism: that was then; things like that happened. Somebody cried witch on somebody else and ended up with his property. Bad business. But what if, begun earlier, witch-hunting did not end in 1692? Or else, even if it did, what if the damage had not been entirely undone? Not much earlier, the notoriously a-political Hawthorne had observed, quietly but with a certain emphasis, that the "Main Street" of Salem had been laid across "the Red Man's Grave";[10] now, it appears, *The House of the Seven Gables* is on the verge of suggesting that the aristocracy of New England is founded upon the legalized murder of the witches. Not everywhere in the literal, one supposes, but in some figure of dis-creditation and displacement that needs to be explored. It is as if, in a society of Saints and others, charging a person with witchcraft were in fact that epitome of "pulling spiritual rank."

What is perfectly clear from the outset, of course, is that the replacement of the Maules by the Pyncheons is offered as a general and representative rather than a unique and singular occurrence; and that an entire community is called to witness—and also, one fears, to sanction—that definitive event. What else can be the import of the principal scene in the novel's very first, most historical chapter, the Pyncheon's grand housewarming party? Someone might well think to stay away in protest, but we do not hear that anyone does; and if any of the attendees are thinking "usurpation," they all nevertheless accept the blessing of official Puritanism, and all appear to confer, thereby, their sense of acceptance and legitimacy. It really is one of the most telling representations of political co-optation from anywhere in the nineteenth century; and Jefferson, elsewhere a major presence in the novel, can nowhere be found to imagine a more revealing example of how the merely historical—in this case the criminal—comes to appear inevitable. Perhaps the Hawthorne who has much more to tell us about gender than about race, has also quite a bit to suggest about the etiology and indeed the definition of class. We need to look quite closely and be prepared to object and intervene when the rhetoric of the scene—call it the Romance of Community—passes over from familiar if impossible social ideal to its meretricious and cynical co-optation.

Blessed by the notorious Quaker-hunter, John Higginson, the scene *might* be the confirmation or latter-day realization of tightly knit covenant identity proposed and valorized by Bradford and his quondam minister Robinson, or inscribed into a metaregional posterity by Winthrop's famous "Model"; but it is not. Bradford and Winthrop

---

10. See my "Red Man's Grave," in *Nathaniel Hawthorne Review*, 36 (2010), pp. 134–42.

believed in a hierarchy ordained by God, and maintained in good order by exceptional men like themselves, but they never could quite be got to endorse usurpation. Just as, much later, "a person of imaginative temperament" might be tempted to make an Edwardsian allegory of the "many peaks" of the new house "*consenting* together in the clustered chimney" (201, my italics)[11]—misreading the scene of morbidity and ugly death as "the residence of the stubborn old Puritan, Integrity" (201), so here the holy appearance only emphasizes the sense of shameful reality of what we are invited to see and hear:

> The Puritan magistrate bade all the town to be his guests. A ceremony of consecration, festive as well as religious, was now to be performed. A prayer and discourse from the Reverend Mr. Higginson, and the outpouring of a psalm from the general throat. (9)

A small irony attaches to the observation that all this was "to be made acceptable to the grosser sense by ale, cider, wine, and brandy" (9); but where is it written that "the general throat" is not to be soothed by a drop or two of the good creature? Yet it is that "general throat" that most attracts our attention—as if Rousseau were being called in to testify that Puritan people were surely one people if ever any people were.[12] The swell of invited population has the air of "a congregation on its way to church," and the myth of perfect unity seems embodied in the fact that, pointing sharply to the sky, "the seven gables "presented the aspect of a whole sisterhood of edifices breathing through the spiracles of one great chimney" (11).

But of course the property has been stolen, and the Pyncheon who cried "witch" on Maule, a Quaker, has built his house "over an unquiet grave" (9). Another man—like Samuel Sewall, for example—might express remorse and seek forgiveness, but what the Pyncheon of the moment wants is validation—tacit but recognizable acceptance by the whole community and a kind of sacralization by the church. Exactly as the dramatic scene makes clear: entering at a portal "which had almost the width of a church-door" (10), all social ranks attend the carefully arranged and scripted ceremony; class differences are carefully noted, and yet—communion indeed—all partake of the generous offerings of food and drink; and all signify, thereby, that the self-consciously aristocratic House of Pyncheon has every right to be. And to endure in the superiority its imposing presence was designed to announce.

---

11. Technically—but also famously—"consent" is the word Edwards uses not only for the notion of true virtue—"consent to Being in General"—but also to the metaphorical significance of gravity, as it figured to him as a natural "type" of human harmony; see *The Nature of True Virtue* (rpt. Ann Arbor: University of Michigan Press, 1960), pp. 1–13; and cp. "The whole material universe is preserved by gravity or attraction, or the mutual tendency of all bodies to each other. […] This is a type of love or charity in the spiritual world"; see Perry Miller, ed., *Images or Shadows of Divine Things* (New Haven, CT: Yale University Press, 1948), p. 79.
12. For Rousseau's less-than-empirical concept of a "general will" that accepts the limitation of liberty by authority, see his 1762 work entitled *The Social Contract*, trans. Charles Frankel (New York: Hafner, 1947), esp. pp. 18–19, 23–27, 55–57.

Elsewhere Hawthorne appears to imply that people usually get the government they deserve,[13] but how are we to understand the evident complacency of this population in the moment of their own de-classification? The suggestion seems to be that, quite like priestcraft, "classcraft" needs to appear, at its inception, as entirely innocent. Of course there is a better sort, and if most of them happen to be connected with the dominant religion, so much the better. Puritans in, Quakers out—which latter group of pacifists could not even hang on to power in Pennsylvania. But there is an irony lurking here. A powerful part of the Puritan establishment, where, though church and state were by no means identical, still they lovingly cooperated, like Moses and Aaron, Pyncheon could have had no trouble getting the local (Quaker-hating) minister to bless his house-warming. But what about "the people"? Is it enough to think that they can be bought off with cakes and ale? Like slaves soothed to service by a Christmas feast? Or is it that a little pomp and ceremony carry their own conviction? And that an established religion, which New England Congregationalism had been since that day in 1631 when Governor Winthrop's General Court decided that the Saints would also be the voters, had already come to seem not wildly factitious but divinely inevitable? However it is, the leaders say it's just fine and people say Amen. All we lack is a band to play a "sacred air," from the indomitable ship of Captain Vere.[14]

But something else is going on in this richly suggestive first chapter. Granted the existence of some sort of religion-based aristocracy in the unfolding socio-religio-politics of early New England, making it possible for somebody to pull religious rank on somebody else, why did Puritan Pyncheon want the land of Quaker Maule in the first place? Somewhere—off in the Connecticut Valley, in fact—somebody named Pyncheon (William Pynchon) had established himself as a sort of neo-feudal landlord;[15] but nothing such is being suggested back here in Salem. It's just *this land* he has wanted. Turns out, "A natural spring of soft and pleasant water—a rare treasure on the sea-girt peninsula where the Puritan settlement was made—had early induced Matthew Maule to build a hut" (6) in just this place. Motive indeed, and subject of a long dispute. Lucky thing Maule could be executed as a witch, as the heirs of such could no way inherit. And here the Narrator's ironic indirection can scarcely control itself.

---

13. In the beginning of "The Gray Champion," for example, the New England populace seems only too willing to respond to portentous but awkward colonialism with something like paranoia.
14. Those who approve the politics of Captain Vere should re-read then re-re-read the paragraph in which, in spite of a whole assortment of variances from ordinary usage, everything *else* goes on just as usual: all go to their assigned places "when not at the guns." As if the Narrator were Jonathan Swift.
15. As the researches of William Cronon have shown, the Pynchon family and the Native Americans had widely varying ideas of what their land "purchase" actually entailed, the Natives imagining they were merely conferring the same sort of non-possessive usage they themselves enjoyed; see *Changes in the Land* (New York: Hill and Wang, 1983), pp. 66–68. See also Stephen Innes, *Labor in a New Land* (Princeton, NJ: Princeton University Press, 1983), pp. 3–16, in which Innes emphasizes the nature of Pynchon's Springfield as "a company town"—exactly as if everything in town had the Pynchon name on it.

But if this story of legalized murder and usurpation is too obvious to require an author's cold prose, other, older, more nearly originary stories quietly suggest themselves—not only the rather questionable replacement of the competent Roger Conant by more aggressive John Endicott,[16] but also, down the road apiece, the removal of the Rev. Mr. Blackstone from the garden a great migrating group of Puritans found him tending on Beacon Hill. A separate tale, of course. We know it only if we pursue the implications of that odd, self-cancelling note in "The May-Pole of Merry Mount": he got there first; he took possession of "the only spring of fresh water on the peninsula"; and, formerly an Anglican priest, he wore the flagrant surplice as he tilled the soil; then he disappeared, turning up again in an orchard in Rhode Island.[17] I wonder how that happened. Was it the surplice in Boston every bit as objectionable as, down the road, a maypole? Or was it the water? Answer: yes. Evidently the Pyncheon Sin is not in every sense original. For Puritanism read Displacement, Supplantation. Evidently the Natives were not the only ones dislodged by a Migration Great enough to invent its own legitimacy. Quaker? Failed Anglican? Ordinary Guy? The Land-lords work in strange ways.

Or is this all too literal?—founding a self-advertised Romance on facts not readily in evidence. The author of *The Scarlet Letter* appears to have been well read in Snow's *History of Boston*—and Winthrop's *Journal* too.[18] And sooner or later a scholar with the instincts of an Allan Emery was bound to discover the rich, more than allegorical influence of Felt's *Annals of Salem* on the details of the *Seven Gables*.[19] But it's fiction and not history, right? Full of metaphors of art as photography, to be sure, but with a ghost in the attic to prove its gothic credentials. Don't over-read. Don't reduce. On the author's own authority.

In the wake of the publication of *The House of the Seven Gables*, Hawthorne received a couple of letters objecting to the negative portrait of one or another Pyncheon. The first reply—professing ignorance of the fact that there had been an actual Pyncheon family residing in Salem—can seem a little disingenuous, protesting further that the name seemed to him "as much the property of a romance-writer as Smith."[20] But it must have been in anticipation of some such response that, in the name of Romance,

---

16. For the significance of the replacement (ouster?) of Conant by Endicott—as narrated in Joseph Felt's *Annals of Salem*, see Allan Emery, "Salem History and *The House of the Seven Gables*," in Bernard Rosenthal, ed., *Critical Essays on Hawthorne's HSG* (New York: Cengage Gale, 1995), pp. 129–49.
17. For the problem of Blackstone's puzzling (footnoted) presence in "The May-Pole of Merry Mount," see my *Province of Piety* (Cambridge, MA: Harvard University Press, 1984), pp. 268–72.
18. Well before I insisted on *The Scarlet Letter*'s two allusions to Anne Hutchinson, historical criticism had established Hawthorne's detailed reliance on Caleb Snow's (1825) *History of Boston*; see Charles Ryskanp, "The New England Sources of *The Scarlet Letter*," *AL*, 31 (1959), pp. 257–72.
19. In a letter to Oliver (see note #21), Hawthorne protests that, living in the Berkshires, he did not have his Salem source(s) with him at the time of writing. So he may indeed have forgot the Pynchons of Salem, but on the close account of Allan Emery, he appears to have remembered quite enough.
20. For the letter in question, from Peter Oliver (lawyer and author of *The Puritan Commonwealth*), see Vol. XVI of the Hawthorne Centenary Edition, *The Letters, 1843–1853* (Columbus: Ohio State University Press, 1985), pp. 427–29; for a follow-up letter, from Hawthorne to Fields, see pp. 435–37.

an otherwise useful Preface instructs us—or else, at all events, a certain kind of reader, satirically evoked in "Main-street," perhaps—to refer the events and personages of the story more to "the clouds overhead" rather than to "any portion of the actual soil of Essex County."[21] One gets and almost accepts the point: the work in question is not to be read as *roman a clef*; imaginative literature involves the introduction of personages who are "really of the Author's own making, or at all events, his own mixing." He is "laying out a street that infringes on nobody's private rights, and appropriating a lot of land which had no visible owner, and building a house, of materials long used for the construction of castles in the air" (4). So: don't write him any letters.

But all this is hyperbole, of course, expressing impatience with an audience understood to be, epistemologically speaking, a little unsophisticated. It seems equal and opposite to the credulity of people eager to believe everything they hear from the tour guides of Salem. And well signaled by the reference to "Essex County," which political entity may do the land surveying but is not the name of anyone's home address; for had he said "the town of Salem," Allan Emery had been there to give him the lie. Fiction must be allowed to have a life of its own. On the premise of Hawthorne's Preface, the Romance more so than the novel. And it may not have a "moral" more evident "at the last page than at the first" (4). Still, names may matter, and one doubts that the choice of "Pyncheon" was accidental. Maule was not. Neither was Higginson. And inserting names like Edward Johnson or Samuel Sewall would be like beginning *The Scarlet Letter* with a reference to Anne Bradstreet.

Then too, when Hawthorne received a second letter of protest—this one from one T. R. Pyncheon of Stockbridge—he conceded that "The name was suggested to me by that of the Massachusetts Patentee [William Pynchon, 1590–1662] who, as you state, returned to England."[22] Indeed: Pyncheon the landlord, as already been mentioned. But the odd allusion-plot thickens when we recall (discover?) that the same William Pynchon wrote the first book ever to be banned in the territory that would become the United States. Printed in England in 1650, *The Meritorious Price of our Redemption* made bold to dispute a well-established and widely-accepted (Anselmian) doctrine of the Atonement. To some commentators the doctrinal divergence has seemed rather slight; and no doubt the official condemnation owed something to the fact that Pynchon had already associated himself with those who were, not so quietly, seeking a more generous policy of church membership and hence full voting citizenship. Then too, the position Pynchon advocated—the price of man's redemption lay in "Mediatorial Obedience" of Christ, rather than in His "suffering of God's wrath for us"—could be associated with the major heresy of Socinianism, which held that an atonement by obedience did not

---

21. From one point of view, Hawthorne's "Main-street" is principally concerned with an audience unprepared to read historical fiction with anything approaching a proper sophistication; see my "Red Man's Grave," pp. 1–18.
22. See *Letters*, XVI, p. 446. As Stephen Innes suggests, "William Pynchon's return to England did not sever his ties with Springfield," as "His son John remained in Massachusetts" and—in a chapter called "Dominance"—quickly stepped into his father's entrepreneurial shoes; see *Labor*, pp. 16–43.

imply the divinity of the atoner. Exit thereby the necessity of a Trinity. And perhaps the Establishment resented the intrusion by a theological amateur, especially as his book was cast in the form of a dialogue between a "Tradesman" and a "Divine." But whatever the dynamics of the contest then, the reader now, who knows that the historical Pynchon is the remote ancestor of a canonical novelist, is also supposed to know that the name, repeated mercilessly in Hawthorne's first chapter, evokes not only problematic land policy but also a debatable, arguable a more "liberal" soteriology. And so it makes some sense to ask, who saves who(m)—and how—in Hawthorne's House of Puritan Inheritance.

3

Obviously, and without much power to elicit praise for originality or profound insight— the marriage of country-girl Phoebe Pyncheon and No-First-Name Holgrave (nee Maule) is supposed to redeem something or other. Way back when, a Pyncheon stole a Maule's property and, even though a Maule did vital carpenter did work on the neighborhood edifice of iniquity, the workman's family and the aristocrat's lineage have been at personal and classist odds ever since. Along the way, one Pyncheon, who somehow got the point, thought to right the wrong by giving the property back to the family of the original owner who, in decent Lockean terms, had "hewn out of the primeval forest, to be his garden-ground and homestead" (6).[23] But no: given the unspeakable tumult which the old gentleman's project awakened among his Pyncheon relatives," his purpose was suspended. Nor did he, as had been feared, "perform after death, by the operation of his last will, what he had so hardly prevented from doing, in his proper lifetime"—because, as the Narrator reasons, almost nothing can cause men "to bequeath patrimonial property away from their own blood" (19).

On the other hand, a modern Maule, with some wizardly hypnotic power which "modern psychology, it may be, will endeavor to reduce [...] within a system" (21), manages to come across class lines long enough to enslave and ruin the mind and person of the lovely Alice Pyncheon, whose ravaged spirit continues to haunt the Evil Mansion. But as revenge is not the same as atonement, the gothic tale of sin and bad results continues into the novel's (novelistic) present. Where Holgrave, who seems to have some of the same hypnotic (or merely literary?) power, finds himself, after a dramatic reading of his story about Alice Pyncheon, in the tempting position to draw the innocent

---

23. Lurking—given the logic of "Main Street"—is the question of the state of the "property" before Mathew Maule baptized it with his labor. Native Americans did not imagine that they "owned" any land, but were they hunting and gathering in the area? Deeper still is the root question raised by French philosopher, P. J. Proudhon, "What Is Property?" Famously, Theft! (or "robbery" in some translations). George Ripley seemed sure he owned the Brook Farm property, sure enough to sell Hawthorne a $500 share; but not everyone associated with the social revolution would have agreed. For the relevance of Proudhon's refutation of both the civil right of property (based on occupation) and the natural right (based on labor), see R. Clark Stern, "Hawthorne's Politics and *The House of the Seven Gables*," *Canadian Review of American Studies*, 6.1 (1975), pp. 74–83.

Phoebe entirely under his spell. (No, not again, please!—the dentist's assistant was going to mesmerize Sophia; don't let them do it!).[24] Happily, and with measurable thematic significance, Holgrave resists the temptation, and some degree of resolution is hereby accomplished: someone in the present specifically refuses to repeat an evil act entailed in the circumstances of a plot long ago begun. Equable marriage, not psychic invasion.

But the reader is bound to feel that this blissful union of warring factions is not quite enough to "right the uneven balance" of accumulated guilt and suffering: North and South might well marry after the Civil War, as in *Miss Ravenel's Conversion from Secession to Loyalty*, but everyone was still dead and the "color line" remained uneffaced. Of course it helps that the Pyncheon of the present day dies horribly in the scene just before the representative couple discover the love that (somewhere) conquers all. And the old-time question of "Who Killed Judge Pyncheon" has life in it yet. Chillingworth may indeed have poisoned the Dimmesdale he lived to torment: who knew what dose of atropine might be fatal to a minister losing weight every day? The case against Coverdale is cold but still wide open.[25] More plainly, there is no plot in *The Marble Faun* unless somebody kills somebody. And though it is hard to imagine the long-enfeebled Clifford suddenly rising up to strangle Hawthorne's determined epitome of the hypocrite, one can easily imagine that the very sight of this embodiment of the family's recessive love of the beautiful might one day cause the dominant figure of sleazy politics to choke on his own meretricious blood. Consummation devoutly to be wished. In any event, the active purveyor of guilty past into puzzled present is well out of the way. The very opposite of a Christic death, no doubt, but evidently somebody has to die: Tom Paine thought God should have hung Satan on the cross, so there is some theoretical precedent.

The marriage between Phoebe and Holgrave may seem more the result of authorial will than of raging hormones, still the death of the Monster Hypocrite leaves the unific couple free to move into another Pyncheon property—less specifically guilty, perhaps, but not without some generalized taint of ill-gotten wealth, making Phoebe herself complicit. But as the entire Pyncheon establishment was built on the grave of a Maule, perhaps the whole thing presents itself as a sort of moral equivalency. And since nobody *except* Thomas Jefferson believes in tearing things down every thirty years, no, every nineteen and one half—eek, no, there's one born every minute![26]—the reader probably forgives

---

24. Famous in the history of Hawthorne's developing relation to Sophia Peabody is his quasi-hysterical response to the idea that mesmerism—as practiced by Dr. Joseph E. Fiske, Nathaniel Peabody's new dental assistant in Salem and then, later and, to Hawthorne's imagination, more dangerously, by Connie Park—might be the cure for her chronic headaches; see T. Walter Herbert, *Dearest Beloved* (Berkeley: University of California, 1993), pp. 136–37.
25. See Alfred Marks, "Who Killed Judge Pyncheon?" *PMLA*, 71 (1956), pp. 355–69. For the much-disputed case against Chillingworth see Dr. Jemshed A. Kahn, "Atropine Poisoning in SL," *New England Journal of Medicine*, 311.6 (1984), pp. 1438–41; see also Wanda Faye Jones, "Scopolamine Poisoning and the Death of Dimmesdale," *Nathaniel Hawthorne Review*, 32.1 (2006), pp. 52–62. For that against Coverdale, see John Harmon McElroy and Edward L. McDonald, "The Coverdale Romance," *Studies in the Novel*, 14.1 (1982), pp. 1–16; and cp. my "Nobody's Protest Novel," *Nathaniel Hawthorne Review*, 34 (2008), pp. 1–39.
26. For Jefferson's problem with the mathematics (and stubborn biology) of defining a human generation, see Daniel J. Boorstin, *The Lost World of Thomas Jefferson* (rpt. Boston: Beacon, 1964), pp. 204–13.

"Holgrave's Curious Conversion": already a Jack of all New England trades, let him try his hand at interior decoration. Tear down those grim old family portraits, Holgrave, as Sophia did the ones at the Manse in Concord; replace them not with Madonnas but with daguerreotypes of the sunshiny present. Just as the world appeared after the morbid death of Ethan Brand.[27]

So far, then, a familiar Hawthorne problem: a pretty convincing evocation of past guilt extending its gloomy influence into the present, but only a half-hearted—novelistic—way of imagining the redemption. Rosina imagines she has cured the quasi-puritanic Egotism of Roderick Ellison but, given his response in "The Christmas Banquet"—Joy to the world, creation sucks—the reader is not convinced. More generally, "Main-street" offers only the consolation of being, one day at a time, further from the "miserable distortions"[28] of the New England past. *The Scarlet Letter* finds no sweet moral at the end—only Hester's prediction of NOW and ME TOO, which, in *The Blithedale Romance*—do not turn out so very well. Evidently the will to happiness is not all it takes to write a sunny book. Or, should we say, the redemptive influence of Sophia-Rosina has not yet done its office.

Now comes Phoebe: sharing one of Hawthorne's pet names for Sophia, and clearly recalling the ill-disguised Rosina, she enters the present world of sinful inheritance as if from some other dimension. A boarder in house, Holgrave-Maule is watching the debut into cent-shop business of aging Hepzibah Pyncheon, forced by the exigencies of modern depression economics to forego her station as a Lady and sully her aristocratic hands with the lucre of trade. With satire—and yet some real feeling—the Narrator treats the event hyperbolically, as if this Fall were of epic proportion; and Holgrave, there to observe the comic last act of a story tragic enough, offers not so much help as the ironic assurance that work does a person good. Evil may lurk, but not so that a person like Phoebe could notice. Clifford will soon appear, released for unjust incarceration but blighted in mind and spirit; and the Judge himself will come along, reeking with hypocritical good will and asking for a little kiss. This plot could thicken.

But not at first: this innocent relative from the country, can be, with her plebeian virtues, of very good use in the cent shop and may even serve to cheer up poor old Hepzibah, whose gloomy smile is worse than many a grimace. She is, first of all, so different—hardly a Pyncheon at all, as the text goes out of its way repeatedly to emphasize. With no sense of the family history, she must be led from room to room, with Hepzibah identifying the subjects of some darkened old portraits and naming the original owner of inherited silver and flatware. This of course is not the only education she will need to

---

27. According to the account offered in Hawthorne's preface to *Mosses from an Old Manse*, the "grim prints of Puritan ministers that hung around" were quickly replaced by "the sweet and lovely head of one of Raphael's Madonnas, and two pleasant little pictures of the Lake of Como; see "The Old Manse," in *Hawthorne: Tales and Sketches* (New York: Library of America, 1996), pp. 1124–25. For Melville's (repented) misreading of the "sunny" ending of "Ethan Brand," see my "Artificial Fire," in *Nathaniel Hawthorne Review*, 33 (2007), pp. 1–22.
28. Grateful enough to have had "such ancestors," the Showman of Hawthorne's "Main-street" yet suggests that Puritanism, especially after the first generation, produced "miserable distortions of the moral nature"; see *Tales and Sketches*, pp. 1039, 1038.

receive: more darkly, what was cousin Clifford doing in jail? and who was that oleaginous gentleman who wanted a peck on the cheek? With somewhat different motives, Holgrave will be assisting in this historical education as well, showing Phoebe daguerreotypes of mysterious personages. But nothing of this at first. And Phoebe, whose name feminizes that of Phoebus Apollo, seems like a ray of sunshine let into a place darker than ever darkened her innocent imagination. And—once again—in all her country simplicity and sunny good nature, she hardly seems a Pyncheon at all.

Hepzibah notices it at once. "A cheerful little body" (55), by her own admission, and, more surprisingly, "a nice little housewife" who had been, last summer, a "schoolmistress for the little children," Phoebe seems a capital exception: "these things must have come from your mother's blood. I never knew a Pyncheon who had any turn for them" (57). And a page or so later, Hepzibah observes, "What a nice little body she is!" Everything but a lady; but no, "that's impossible." Phoebe is no Pyncheon. "She takes everything from her mother!" (59). For verification—and also, of course, for emphasis—she appeals her genealogical judgment to wise old Uncle Venner: "Can you tell me if there ever was a Pyncheon whom she takes after?" His reply: "I don't believe there ever was." And then, raising the ante somewhat, "I never knew a human creature do her work so much like one of God's angels" (60). It turns out that Phoebe will in fact exercise some quasi-magical function of protection; yet as angels do more to announce than to effect salvation, angelhood may not be Phoebe's most important symbolic identity.

Of course Phoebe is every bit a human being. And in fact she is a Pyncheon right enough—"one little offshoot of the Pyncheon race," from somewhere off in "a rural part of New England" (52). As this good little body in feeding the (inbred and somehow mysteriously entailed) Pyncheon chickens, the ever-observant Holgrave, noticing the ease of both the feeder and chickens, proposes a certain proper familiarity and inquires, more for confirmation than instruction, "For you are a Pyncheon?" The answer, as simple as one could imagine, yet strikes the reader who has noticed the marked contrast between the freshness of the new visitor with the dismal ruin of the house, with the force of an oxymoron: "My name is Phoebe Pyncheon" (66)—as if she had said, I am Sunlit Darkness, or Sprightly Decrepitude, or Innocent Evil. And it is from this point that Holgrave, who may well know all there is to know about the dynasty whose decline and fall he is making it his business to observe, takes over the business of educating Phoebe Pyncheon in some of the things a simple country girl may not have ever heard or imagined. For openers, a daguerreotype of the living Judge Jaffrey Pyncheon, which Phoebe brilliantly misidentifies as her "Puritan ancestor, who hangs yonder in the parlor"; somehow, she imagines, this new art of making "pictures out of sunshine" (66) has changed the clothing of the old colonel without altering the person. No, Phoebe, the Past is palpably present, but not in that way. Stay tuned.

More apparent than the slow and probably imperfect education of this innocent, however, is the detailing, in a series of character-pairing chapters, of her beneficent influence on (almost) all those around her. Her effect on the house itself is noticed from the beginning—a ray of sunlight let in, on a sudden, to a world where darkness seems to sustain and nourish itself; a smile that almost effaces the scowl of her gloom-enveloped aunt. Then too, more actively but also without much consciousness, there is the magical way she has of arranging flowers—which grew outside all along. What may seem a gratuitous tribute to the gendered genius of the feminine, is in fact an early indication of Phoebe's redemptive capacity: having "gathered some of the most perfect of the roses," she proceeds to arrange them with the kind of "natural magic, that enables [certain] favored ones to bring out the hidden capabilities." And not just the flowers. With the same "homely witchcraft," but without "preliminary design," she

> gave a touch here, and another there; brought some articles of furniture to light, and dragged others into the shadow; looped up or let down a window-curtain; and, in the course of half an hour, had fully succeeded in throwing a kindly and hospitable smile over the apartment. (53)

And though she cannot quite turn Hepzibah's established scowl into a smile, our clear sense is that her entrance into the scene not only guarantees a modest success for the cent shop but offers a pleasing new sight to that antique maiden's sore eyes.

Even more noticeable, perhaps, is Phoebe's effect on Clifford, a born "Sybarite" (79), as the Narrator admits, but doomed to suffer not only within the four gray walls of a prison but also, as we are asked to infer, within the walls of New England's puritanic culture, gray enough in its own pleasure-fearing way. He should have been a pair of ragged claws; well, no, that's another story. But almost immediately upon his arrival in The House, he requests the removal of the "odious portrait" of his "evil genius" (80); then, assured that Hepzibah and Phoebe will do wonders in covering it with a "crimson curtain in a trunk above-stairs," he cries out in desperation:

> Why should we live in this dismal house at all? Why not go to the South of France?—to Italy?—Paris, Naples, Venice, Rome? Hepzibah will say, we have not the means. A droll idea that. (81)

Wondering at the exact economic meaning of the "glance of fine sarcastic meaning" he throws at Hepzibah—what exactly is the state of the family fortune and who controls it?—the reader may miss the contextual effect of "droll": which of Hawthorne's New England characters could use that word? And what do we imagine as Hawthorne's own interest in the capitals of European art and pleasure? He's walked some, in summers, up to Maine, no doubt, and, with the aid of the Erie Canal, he's got himself as far West as Detroit, but he's not yet written his way to Liverpool; or saved his way to France and Italy. One almost imagines that Clifford—so much admired by Melville[29]—is an exaggerated version of Hawthorne's own affective imprisonment in New England.

However that may be, Clifford's response to Phoebe is instantaneous and vital, more simply redemptive than anything Hawthorne might ascribe to Sophia. Crediting her with a "spiritual force" (98) likely to be underestimated, the Narrator notes that Phoebe's

---

29. In a letter of April 1851—the one which appears to confuse Hawthorne's "power of blackness" with that of Ahab—Melville praises the remarkably original characterization of Clifford; see *Correspondence*, which is Vol. XIV of the Northwestern/Newberry *Writings of Herman Melville* (Evanston, IL: Northwestern University Press, 1993), pp. 685–86.

presence, and the contiguity of her fresh life, was usually all that "the blighted one" required. But they also talk; and she sings, often choosing "a strain of pathos [rather] than gaiety." In any case, as he becomes "habituated to her companionship," Clifford soon shows himself capable of imbibing pleasant tints, and gleams of cheerful light from all quarters" (99). Youth and beauty restoring something of the same to a lover of beauty grown old in prison. But there is more:

> Phoebe's presence made a home about her, that very sphere which the outcast, the prisoner, the potentate, the wretch beneath mankind, the wretch aside from it, the wretch above it, instinctively pines after—a home! (101)

And more even than this: beyond the domestic sentiment—there in Hawthorne since the touching phrases of "The Gentle Boy"—the sentiment of sex, perfectly chaste, of course, yet recognizable as such. "Endowed with the liveliest sensibility to feminine influence," yet never having "quaffed the cup of passionate love," Clifford recognizes the girlish Phoebe "as a woman." She is, in fact, "his only representative of womankind." So that, quite like song, we are asked to regard Phoebe's sex as a natural grace.

Less dramatic, but noticeable nevertheless, is Phoebe's influence on Holgrave who, in the chapter called "Maule's Well," and again, more briefly in "The Daguerreotypist," gets a rather full exposure to the curious charm of Phoebe's innocence. She appears to resist the implication of his portrait of Judge Pyncheon, namely, that there is a sort of moral identity between his and the progenerating Colonel of the seventeenth century, and she cannot see his point about our slavery to the past. Indeed they disagree about almost every topic they discuss; yet something else appears to be going on. She cannot avoid the discovery that things may be other, darker, than they seem; and he may well be learning that innocence is not altogether unlike integrity. Hepzibah believes that this homeless and altogether unconventional man may yet have "a law of his own" (63); but he sounds very dangerous when, envious of Phoebe's access to the soul of Clifford, he professes that, given her privileged access, "no scruple would prevent me from fathoming Clifford to the full extent of my plummet-line" (127). Unpardonable sin, by one authoritative account.[30]

Phoebe's natural poetry has described Clifford's damaged but reviving spirit as "holy ground where the shadow falls." Holgrave notices "How prettily [she] expresses the sentiment" and professes to "understand the feeling, without possessing it" (127). Yet when the time comes, in the very next chapter, to drop that plummet-line into the soul of Phoebe herself, all but hypnotized by the tale of Alice Pyncheon, he waves the opportunity quite away. And Hawthorne—obsessed with, studied in, though not quite on the subject of mesmerism, cannot let the opportunity pass:

---

30. According to a famous passage from Hawthorne's *American Notebooks*, "The Unpardonable Sin might consist in a want of reverence for the Human Soul" (Columbus: Ohio State University Press, 1972), p. 251. Witness the (aborted) question of Ethan Brand and "the Esther of our tale" and the paradigmatic tale of Goethe's Faust and Gretchen behind it.

> To a disposition like Holgrave's, at once speculative and active, there is no temptation as great as the opportunity of acquiring empire over the human spirit; nor any idea more seductive to a young man, than to become arbiter of a young girl's destiny. (154)

Not quite a rape fantasy, one supposes, yet temptation indeed. Temptation resisted. Credit Holgrave's "integrity," no doubt, but also the natural grace of Phoebe herself. Irresistibly in operation—as if she had already said to him, "I wish ... you would feel more like a Christian and a human being" (154).

No one of course can save "The Pyncheon of Today," whose image recalls the unctuous Man of God who got Hawthorne fired from the Salem Custom House,[31] and whose well-managed hypocrite smile makes Hepzibah's endemic scowl appear positively benign. The best we can say is that, whoever killed Judge Pyncheon, it was certainly not Phoebe, who had not yet re-entered the house when the body was being discovered; and that the heavy-handed dancing-on-the-grave-of-a-sonofabitch rhetoric pronounced over his unresponsive corpse, though it pleased the nineteenth-century public, would have puzzled her simple sensibility.[32] Her influence, though evidently powerful, is also somewhat delicate. The Author himself has to do the heavy lifting.

The final evidence of Phoebe's capacity to redeem the lost is the evidence of what, tragically, almost cataclysmically, happens when her preternatural influence is withdrawn. Somewhat like Coverdale later, Holgrave has been just waiting to witness a catastrophe many years in the making; and he is certain enough to intimate the imminent possibility to the unsuspecting Phoebe. But what? And when, exactly? Well evidently when she happens to leave. Uncle Venner predicts the worst, when her angelic presence is removed. Quite properly, Phoebe denies that she is an angel: nobody's soteriology works that way. But she has also heard Holgrave observe that "Whatever health, comfort, and natural life exists in the house, is embodied in your person. These blessings came alone with you, and will vanish when you leave the threshold" (153). And though she is uncertain whether Holgrave may wish Hepzibah and Clifford "well or ill," he might almost have said that her simple caring has already begun to redeem the heartless curiosity she painfully detects.

---

31. For the part played by the Reverend Charles Upham in Hawthorne's dismissal from the Salem Custom House, see Arlin Turner, *Nathaniel Hawthorne* (New York: Oxford University Press, 1980), pp. 180–85; and for a full account of Upham as the proximate source for the unctuous hypocrisy of Judge Jaffrey Pyncheon, see Jonathan A. Cook, "The Most Satisfactory Villain That Ever Was," *New England Quarterly*, 88.2 (2015), pp. 252–85. Yet as this identification remains a subtext, it may not quite fulfill Hawthorne's express desire to "kill and scalp [Pyncheon} in the public prints" (*Letters*, 16:270).
32. Though modern criticism largely disagrees, the anthology of Stedman and Hutchinson includes it as a prime example of Hawthorne's matchless prose; see "A Night with Judge Pyncheon," in E. C. Stedman and Ellen Mackay Hutchinson, comps., *A Library of American Literature: An Anthology in 11 Volumes*, Vols. VI–VII, *Literature of the Republic*, Pt. III, 1835–1860 (New York: Charles L. Webster, 1892), pp. 200–210. In the judgment of accomplished biographer Edwin Haviland Miller, "It is not Clifford but Hawthorne who, in a chapter entitled with obvious irony, 'Governor Pyncheon,' dances over the corpse in a virtuoso display of sadism unequaled in his writings"; see *Salem Is My Dwelling Place* (Iowa City: University of Iowa Press, 1991), pp. 331–32.

In any event, she leaves—and all hell breaks loose. And after that, all madness. Convinced that poor Cousin Clifford possess the secret to some fabulous family wealth, Judge Pyncheon, to the increasing distress of Hepzibah, demands to interview him: he *will* talk, or the Judge, who has set the neighbors to observe Clifford's odd behaviors, will have him committed to "a public asylum, for persons in his unfortunate state of mind" (167). Pyncheon pretends good will, but Hepzibah knows better: he is Evil. So does the reader, who might well have been spared the ironic details of Pyncheon's reputation for civic virtue. Rhetoric flourishes and psychic disaster looms. But wait!—Clifford is not in his room. Where has he gone? Has he perhaps committed suicide? The Judge himself must help her find him. But just then, Clifford, deadly pale and pointing to the parlor where the hysterical Hepzibah has left her villainous relative. They must flee—"leave the old house to our Cousin Jaffrey" (176). They do flee. By train, on which Clifford's mania outdoes anything Holgrave (or Jefferson) could imagine: not just inheritance must perish, but "real estate" itself—"the solid ground to build a house on [...] is the broad foundation on which nearly all the guilt of this world rests" (185). And then those "rapping spirits"—what spiritual revelations do they not portend? And "electricity"! And in this wildly advancing modern age, what not?

Until the mania quietly subsides and "The Flight of Two Owls" ends in sight of an old church, somehow split in half, and an old farm, uninhabited and fallen into ruin, even in a country where peasants were not flocking to the city. The world as it was. No electricity, but still the possibility of prayer: "Oh, God—our Father—are we not thy children. Have mercy on us!" (188). Hepzibah's words, but Hawthorne's own—conservative Christian--recognition—that not everything can change at once. And that conscientious endurance cannot be all bad. Maybe the words "roof and hearth-stone" (185) are soon to pass away. But maybe not yet. The New Fortune of Brook Farm may have been worth the Hazard, but it had not worked out very well. Neither, long ago, had the Pilgrim experiment of permitting the economic proper to encroach upon the spiritual common. Evidently the jury was still out.

5

By the time Phoebe returns to the house, it's all over. All except the Narrator's invention of Some Sensitive Person's misreading of the harmoniously consenting gables. And Holgrave's final holographic instruction and sentimental revelation. Don't you go in, Phoebe; "There's something wicked there" (210)—such the advice of young Ned Higgins, who buys little racist cakes and otherwise makes street-smart remarks. Yet in the end he is the innocent one. Phoebe, whose smile was noticeably less innocent when she leaves than when she first entered the Gables, and who has confessed that she has "been happier than I am now—at least, much gayer," is now ready for the completion of her conversion, from childish good nature to moral adulthood. In she goes, through the garden, fallen into disarray since her departure, and then "across the threshold" (211) of the House of the Seven Gables. And more. Ready now to face the problem of evil, she stares straight at Holgrave's picture of the repetitious, evil, but still dead Judge Pyncheon. "This is death" (213), she simply says; but the reader may hear somewhat more: here is the fatal conclusion of an age-long mystery I now sadly feel without quite understanding.

All this is to say that Phoebe's centrality to the story is a little more complicated than might first appear. She saves them all, to be sure, all whose will has not been fixed in Evil; but she herself has her own redemptive process to undergo. Whoever Hawthorne is instructing—the young magazine readers who could not get the presentist application of the tale of "Alice Doane"; the complacent Rosina, sure that "the Idea of another" could put to rest all those old snaky fantasies; his own sweet wife, whose liberal upbringing prepared her to declare Emerson "pure tone"; or some wider New England audience, offered the liberal opportunity of salvation without atonement. The antique Anselmian theory of a human being who needed also to be God might be part of the transient rather than the permanent in Christianity; but, as we learn from "The Celestial Railroad," it brought with it a truly sobering sight of sin. To which Hawthorne's happiest novel brings its female protagonist to the verge.

But no further: the reality of evil in the world, the opportunity of every human being to fall, the lasting effects of un-repented injustice. Yet "the true sight of sin" is not quite of her own soul. In the classic terms of Thomas Hooker, Phoebe is still looking at, if not a map, then clearly a daguerreotype.[33] Probably this is what Hyatt Waggoner had meant in promulgating the idea of some liberal heresy at the root of *The House of the Seven Gables*. At some level Young Phoebe Pyncheon is a female version of Young Goodman Brown: virginal and more innocent in other ways but, like him, about to learn many dark things of which the parents and grandparents did not speak. Of course we now know how the premise of "specter evidence" relieves Hawthorne of the personal belief that all mankind is totally—and irredeemably—depraved, given over to the devil; but there is nothing in this novel to compare with the Narrator's reference there to "the instinct that leads mortal man to evil."[34] That, no doubt, were somewhat too much for someone in *this* audience to bear.

Then too, a little more precariously, there is the question of whether Phoebe's redemption of the Pyncheons has any more subtle religious overtones important enough to be examined. First of all, the salvation of the foredoomed Pyncheons appears to be entirely a "vicarious" matter: none of the principals—neither Hepzibah nor Clifford (nor Holgrave for that matter)—seems capable of doing anything to lift the curse they all seem to be under; indeed, their best efforts only seem to be making things worse. Some outside influence seems to be required. It would not be quite true to say that Phoebe, whose lightness suffers perceptibly from their heavy darkness, endures this suffering on their behalf. She saves by offering the happy qualities she has to those able to profit by them and finds herself made a little more sober into the bargain. Still, it is her entry from beyond

---

33. Cf. note #5. Hooker rejects the sight from a book as well as a map.
34. Just here did Henry James, without benefit of Cotton Mather, decide that the dark tale of Goodman Brown "evidently means nothing as regards Hawthorne's [...] conviction of universal depravity [...] for the simple reason that, if it meant anything, it would mean too much"; see *Hawthorne* (rpt. Ithaca, NY: Cornell University Press, 1956),
81. And see my analysis in *Province*, pp. 6–8.

that demands attention. To my (overdeveloped) professional sensitivities, the emphatic insistence that Phoebe is and is not a Pyncheon sounds alarmingly like the definitive Anselmian teaching that Jesus, in order to function in fact as The Christ, must be and at the same time not entirely be a human being. No tough talk here about two natures in one person, to be sure, yet it appears that Phoebe must be an authentic member of the community of offense and yet be separate enough to do some real good. A liberal enough atonement, this, but then that may be part of Hawthorne's heresy of happiness.

And oddly enough, this noticeable liberality might actually be connected, long since, with the name of Pyncheon—or Pynchon, as the name was then spelled. Turns out the Hawthornes were not the only Salemites to practice familial metonomy. As we earlier observed, William Pynchon was not just a preemptive landlord in the territory in and around Springfield, Massachusetts, which he controlled almost absolutely; he also wrote a remarkable but rejected book about the atonement which, contrary to the not-yet-seriously-challenged program of Anselm, claimed that it was not Christ's sacrificial death that did the atoning work but rather his "performing unto his Father that invaluable precious thing of his Mediatorial obedience"—which of course entailed an obedience unto death.[35] Exemplified here is an atonement that does not absolutely require the sacrificial death of the atoner; nor need the magical outsider be a card-carrying member of the One, no Many, no really One God. Nearer to hand one might look to William Ellery Channing or Andrews Norton for some such resistance to the (barbarous?) notion that God had to die so that Man might live.[36] But Pynch(e)on is the name we are given. Unless we think Hawthorne pulled it out of a hat.

A precarious association, no doubt. One that will probably never get *The Meritorious Price of Our Redemption* excerpted in any future casebook or critical edition. Maule's *Truth Held Forth* will stay in, no doubt, as the Maule of history is something quite like the one evoked in Hawthorne's first chapter. Identity always; allegorical implication much of the time. Multiple and complex allusion, not so much. Cautious, positivist historicism is like that. But the fact remains: at the center of *The House of the Seven Gables* we are asked to witness "something, somehow like" a vicarious atonement—and that by admirable virtue and not by sacrificial death.

The premise is, not proven, of course, but rendered not implausible by the more obvious fact that the "original sin" of the Pyncheons is not so much inherited as it is repeated. The Pyncheon chickens are hopelessly inbred, and anticipations of Mendel may tell us much about the Dominant Jaffrey and the Recessive Clifford: oh, dear, why

---

35. Quoted from Philip Gura, *A Glimpse of Sion's Glory* (Middletown, CT: Wesleyan University Press, 1984), pp. 304–22.
36. In his epoch-making sermon/essay "Unitarian Christianity," William Ellery Channing, while uncertain of exactly what meaning to assign to the death of Jesus, is clear and forceful in his rejection of the Anselmian atonement; see Sydney E. Ahlstrom and Jonathan S. Carey, ed., *An American Reformation* (Middleton, CT: Wesleyan University Press, 1985), pp. 208–12. Indeed American Unitarians are such precisely because they reject the premise that Jesus had to be God to perform the atoning function. See also Andrews Norton, "Statement of Reasons for Not Believing the Doctrines of the Trinitarians" (Boston: Wells and Lilly, 1819), also excerpted in Ahlstrom and Carey, ed., *Reformation*, 67–75.

does one of those strong but ugly people keep appearing in every generation.[37] But there is nothing here—as there well may be in "Rappaccini's Daughter"—anything like the Augustine's (plainly Manichean) "rotten root, rotten branch."[38] The bad people have their chance, and though their genes may create a powerful bias, as does their property inheritance, not one of the evil ones is guilty until he actually sins. Melville may imagine Hawthorne as Calvinist *malgre lui*, and not without the evidence of "Young Goodman Brown" and "Egotism; or the Bosom Serpent."[39] But not in this book. Hawthorne may concede a little too much to the Liberal who led him down from his "dismal and squalid" upper chamber, but he has set his heart here on somewhat more that happiness. Jaffrey sins and Clifford does not. Hepzibah, not unlike a character in Faulkner, suffers but endures. Holgrave has a perfect chance to capture the will of Phoebe, but he will not. Doubtless Hawthorne is nowhere up to the level of Edwards' semantic analysis of freedom to act but not to will. But the buck has to stop somewhere. Whatever we inherit, it is not sin as such. That, we commit. *Why*, may well remain a Melvillean "Mystery of Iniquity."[40] But in fact, if Hawthorne is ever to be found to err on the side of Liberal Theology, *Seven Gables* is that place. Evidently repeated sin is sin enough. And salvation? Well, who knows? It might come from anywhere.

Still, the strong thing about *Seven Gables* is not the wispy rumor of salvation by the appropriation of somebody's slender grace. Stronger, more insistent, is the need for that gracious person to learn the sort of guilt-ridden world into which we all are born: a world we never made but one which implicates our conscience in its a priori arrangements nevertheless. Strongest of all, in that regard—and significant enough to save the book from its own happy self—is the undeluded view of the question of ownership and inheritance. Somebody squatted on and worked a property, and Somebody Else, closer to the power structure, found a way to dislocate that apparently rightful owner—unless of course we ask, with Hawthorne's "Main-street," who might have been there, well, aboriginally.

---

37. Clearly Hawthorne possessed a near-medical interest in the biology of inheritances, but prior to the revolutionary theory of Gregor Mendel the state of the art was so disparate and confused that Hawthorne's proleptic suggestions—like some of his anticipations of Freud—might well be considered inspired.
38. By most accounts, St. Augustine got over his early dalliance with the Manichean heresy; see, for example, Scott Macdonald, "The Divine Nature," in Eleonore Stump and Norman Kretzman, eds., *The Cambridge Companion to Augustine* (Cambridge: Cambridge University Press, 2001), esp. pp. 73–75, 79–80. But not by my account: his theory of "seminal transmission" makes original sin a sort of venereal disease, makes procreation itself an actual sin, and makes model Christians of the Shakers—as Hawthorne and Emerson probably agreed on one of their long walks. Austin Warren would assure us that Hawthorne was "not a Pelagian, but an Augustinian"; see "Introduction," p. xiv. Semi-Pelagian Hawthorne may have been in *Seven Gables*; but what he was not, was Manichean. Melville, maybe. Hawthorne, not hardly.
39. Significantly, Melville's first and most detailed response to Hawthorne's "something, somehow like" Puritanic Calvinism is offered in response not to "Young Goodman Brown" but to "Egotism: or The Bosom Serpent"; see my "Life within the Life," *Nathaniel Hawthorne Review*, 30 (2004), pp. 1–31.
40. The phrase from *Billy Budd* becomes the title of an enduringly useful study of Melville's poetry; see William R. Shurr, *The Mystery of Iniquity* (Lexington: University of Kentucky Press, 1972).

Property *itself* might or might not be "theft," but perhaps only Adam had it straight from God. And the problem could be everywhere. Except perhaps for chasing ambulances, nothing keeps lawyers busier than fighting to establish "clear title."

Perhaps Phoebe and Holgrave should have gone off to live at Brook Farm. Or Fruitlands. Or, fed up with New England, at New Harmony, Indiana. Except that all those high-minded experiments had already failed. Way too early to rent a suite in Salem's Hawthorne Hotel. But wait a month or so and then beg a room in The Wayside. Yet even houses duly purchased from Social Idealists might not be completely innocent. There might still be iniquity somewhere. As Emerson suggests, one can always push one's "criticism on the state of things [...] to that extravagant mark, that shall compel [one] to suicide."[41] What else? Well, one is required to notice that existing arrangements, though compelling, are mostly factitious and quite often dishonest. And in a world where, from the outset, everything, including the local elm tree, is named Pyncheon, it can be hard to see where the common leaves off and the proper begins. Jefferson helped to abolish primogeniture in Virginia, but maintained a household full of slaves. Where was the Revolution to start? Roused from his Sybaritic Slumber, Clifford seemed about to discover the way, but then he ran out of breath.

Christian conservative that he repeatedly reveals himself to be, Hawthorne tried it out at Brook Farm but he never really joined The Movement. Like Emerson, he was a Writer and not properly a Reformer. Writers have to write. Then too, sadly enough, he is on the record as pitying certain poor whites more than the slaves, men and women who never owned even themselves.[42] Yet Hawthorne in the distracted 1850s was very far from being A-political, as Sacvan Bercovitch was scarcely the first to notice. Besides evoking the morale of love and law in the first decade of American Puritanism, *The Scarlet Letter* keeps "The Woman Question" steadily in view. And, allowing the aging Hester Prynne to predict a proper sexual revolution, he wrote *The Blithedale Romance*—to suggest, however obliquely, that a thing like sex might not be all that easy to reform.[43] And in between, *The House of the Seven Gables*: not much sex here, but a question that may lie just as deep: what does it mean to *own* something?

Not quite prepared to proclaim that "Property is theft"—or profess, with the saintly Thoreau, running wildly away from the squatter ambitions of Baker Farm, to "Enjoy the land, but own it not—"[44] Hawthorne seemed and happy enough to borrow the money he

---

41. See Ralph Waldo Emerson, "Man the Reformer," in *Emerson: Essays and Lectures* (New York: Library of America, 1983), p. 145.
42. In a letter to Zachariah Burchmore—and well in advance of the outbreak of war—Hawthorne wrote that he had "not half so much [sympathy for the slaves] as for the laboring whites, who, I believe [...] are ten time worse off than the Southern negroes"; see *Letters*, XVI, p. 496.
43. All credit to Sacvan Bercovitch for insisting, against widespread opinion otherwise, that the issues of *The Scarlet Letter* were deeply related to contemporary political questions. Yet I stand by the view that SL is also a deeply historical novel; see my "Introduction" to the Harvard Library Edition (Cambridge, MA: Harvard University Press, 2009), pp. ix–xlvi. Nor—in a rush to convict all American writers of some theological Americanism—will it do to ignore the searingly ironic politics of the early tales, particularly, "Roger Malvin's Burial," "My Kinsman, Major Molineux," and the four "Legends of the Province House." See my, well, you know.
44. Cf. *Walden* (New York: Norton Critical, 2008), p. 142.

needed to purchase, at long last, a home at The Wayside. Nor, with Emerson—another prime property holder in Concord—did he ever come round to suspect that the notion "'*This is mine*'" is one of prime "delusions of the mother of the world."[45] Yet he dared to raise the question of inheritance (and the entailed question of ownership) to the level of a religious problem: how do we come to own something in the first place? And what then? What are the political and moral implications of inheriting something that was the product of somebody else's labor? Or—much worse—his covetous envy and his legal lies?

Others might remain more deeply involved in the tangled (and in the end unsolvable) question of Adam as a human representative and/or the seminal transmission of moral turpitude. Evidently Hawthorne found the question of ownership more pressing, and the sin of supplantation more than sufficiently original. Adam had his own problems, no doubt. But one of them was not who owned the Garden before him. And—Abel being dead—if he had to decide how to divide the territory East of Eden between Cain and Seth, the fact has gone unrecorded. In any event, what we inherit is not sin but, likely as not, a structure of injustice. In which case, mere ownership may well imply complicity. Close enough to count as "something, somehow like."

---

45. See Emerson, "Illusions," in *Essays and Lectures*, p. 1123.

Chapter Twelve

"INEXTRICABLE KNOT OF POLYGAMY": TRANSCENDENTAL HUSBANDRY IN HAWTHORNE'S *BLITHEDALE*

Of course it's only an accident that Hawthorne's most suggestively political novel was published the same year as *Uncle Tom's Cabin* (1852). Yet it seems significant that, though *Blithedale* made Melville even more envious of Hawthorne's popular success, it was the Stowe novel that became the runaway "best seller." Significant, too, that her work has found its way into the modern canon for reasons that have much to do with questions of race and gender. Within certain limits, sharply outlined in a famous essay by James Baldwin, *Uncle Tom's Cabin* knows very well what it is about: chattel slavery is an unmitigated evil which must be ended; this will happen only when men become more like women—more Christian and, in the sense we now more readily accept, more "sentimental." Baldwin may well be right in asserting that Mrs. Stowe does not really understand and indeed is fundamentally afraid of black people, but she knows her occasion and her audience. She could hardly have written a more popular work if she had set out to do no more than sell books. And it remains "Everybody's Protest Novel."[1]

By contrast, and from precisely the same political moment, *The Blithedale Romance* (1852) seems not entirely clear about what it is for. It certainly entertains the urgent question of "woman in the nineteenth century," and it may refract the Compromise of 1850 even more pointedly than does *The Scarlet Letter*; but it makes no very overt reference to the increasingly volatile question of race slavery; and indeed its drama, set in a theater at some remove from ordinary life, seems so painfully interpersonal as to be, in some fundamental sense, pre-political. It may easily be thought to recoup or to repent Hawthorne's nine-month stay at Brook Farm in 1841; and no doubt the novel could not have been written without that rare personal stimulus. But the cast of fictional characters is so different from that of the life experience that even the most ingenious attempts at reading *roman a clef* have fallen flat, just as Hawthorne predicted they would.[2]

---

1. First appearing in *Notes of a Native Son* (1955), Baldwin's essay may be conveniently consulted in Elizabeth Ammons, ed., *Uncle Tom's Cabin: A Casebook* (New York: Oxford University Press, 2007), pp. 49–55. With the familiar ethic of Adam Smith in mind, the curious ethical opposition of *Blithedale* and *Uncle Tom's Cabin* is noticed by Robert S. Levine, "Sympathy and Reform in *The Blithedale Romance*," in Richard H. Millington, ed., *The Cambridge Companion to Nathaniel Hawthorne* (New York: Cambridge University Press, 2004), esp. pp. 207–29.
2. Of all the proposed "keys," the most cogent suggest that Hollingsworth's attendance upon Coverdale may recall a loving approach of Melville to Hawthorne in the Berkshires, and that

Nor does *Blithedale* appear to attack the communitarian movement as such: Coverdale sounds—for him—convincingly thematic when in retrospect he muses that his odd little cohort "had struck upon what ought to be a truth," one which "Posterity" might "dig up, and profit by" (3:245–46).³ We may well wonder why the Hawthorne who pondered, all his shy and private life, the limit-question of lonely self-enclosure, did not somewhere imagine a practical alternative. Yet the book reads nothing like a utopian tract; and indeed its Preface is never more convincing than when it disavows, most generally, "the slightest pretensions to illustrate a theory, or elicit a conclusion [...] in respect to Socialism" (3:1). The capitalization emphasizes a scorn of political discourse perfectly Jamesian. Swarming agents of correctness care little enough for such questions of taste, of course, but the problem of genre remains: an art-novel if there ever was one, *The Blithedale Romance* presents a morale nothing like that of *Uncle Tom's Cabin*.

The problem is, above all, the narration. Mrs. Stowe—or whatever we decide to call the voice that tells the tale that turned the tide of Northern sentiment—speaks to us directly, more directly than Whitman, even, in a poem that insists we let his "dark patches" fall on us as well. Hers is not a literary strategy disguised as natural speech and designed to assure us of the identity of reader and writer in the Unity of the Soul. It is a plea from person to person. What Stowe wants to say is something like this: you, cautious and comfortable reader, whoever you are, are complicit in the worst crime against humanity the American Republic has so far to show; take the sufferings and death of Uncle Tom as a fair example. Let the fictional representation, drawn from sternest reality, change your mind and heart; then do whatever else you can to change the world in this regard. So help you God. But what does Hawthorne want to say? Or ask us to do? About what exactly? And, in point of sorest contention, how is he saying it? We know he hides his "inmost me" behind some veil or other. Nor ever serves his own heart up, "delicately fried, with brain sauce": all negative capability, he sympathizes with us, not we with him.⁴ But here the familiar reserve may strike us as excessive. In *Blithedale*, bad things are happening between and among people sworn to act out of the very noblest of humane principles. The character who stands by to watch these events appears not entirely to understand what is going on and, considering himself a sort of "Chorus" (3:97), does nothing to intervene when he does understand; and as that crippled character is also the

---

the un-feminist marriage and drowning of Margaret Fuller may be reflected in the life and death of Zenobia; but then none of this bears on the membership of Brook Farm; and, in point of fiction, Zenobia is beautiful.

3. Citations of *Blithedale* refer to vol. 3 of the Centenary Edition of the *Works of Nathaniel Hawthorne*, ed. William Charvat et al., 23 vols. (Columbus: Ohio State University Press, 1962–93). Further quotations from Hawthorne's works will be cited to this edition and noted parenthetically by volume and page number.

4. For the "brain sauce" denial, see "The Old Manse" (10:33). Just less famously, an 1842 letter to Sophia suggests that a certain negative capability informs all his writings: people "might think that I am pouring myself out in a tale or essay," but in reality "I sympathize with them—not they with me"; see the *Letters 1813–1843* (15:612–13).

narrator—a "point of view" as fiercely formal as any James could imagine—there is no one else to tell us what to think.

Early interpreters, keenly interested in the novel's Brook Farm foundation, and aware that much of what the Narrator is given to reflect or opine comes pretty much unchanged from Hawthorne's own letters and notebooks, quite confidently assumed that "Coverdale" is a transparent pseudonym for Hawthorne himself. Against this biographical dogma, the critical claim of "unreliable narration" had to work its way upstream.[5] The literalist logic seemed so clear: Coverdale comes to express without embarrassment the ingrained conservatism that led Hawthorne to puzzle over and then to reject the premises of that "ferment" of reform that seemed to him to identify the American 1840s as an age of Universal Reform; Hawthorne distrusts Reformers and discredits The Protest. Retiring from Blithedale to seek the company of "the writers of the North American Review, the merchants, the politicians, the Cambridge men," and all those old "conservatives" who keep a "death-grip on one or two ideas which had not come into vogue since yesterday-morning" (3:141), Coverdale seems but a fuller and more explicit version of the author figure who, a decade earlier, wished to withdraw from a theatre of ideal speculation and reformist vision called "the Hall of Fantasy": let us quit this place at once, he begs his companion, "or I shall be tempted to make a theory—after which, there is little hope of any man" (10:181). And there is no denying that the man who held that large-scale reform efforts never achieve their stated goal—and who here has cast the failed feminist reformer Zenobia in the mold of Spenser's Nature-opposing figure of Mutability—has some deep loyalty to the way some things inevitably are. Somehow or other, Hawthorne seems to predict the conservative conclusion of James's Basil Ransom: "The human race has got to learn to bear its troubles."[6]

---

5. For a good example of the conservative sense of Coverdale as "equated with Hawthorne in many conspicuous ways," see Arlin Turner's Introduction to *Blithedale* (New York: Norton, 1958), pp. 5–23. For the beginnings of the newer, less autobiographical readings, see William Van O'Connor, "Conscious Naivete in *The Blithedale Romance*," *Revue des Langues Vivantes*, 220 (1954), pp. 37–45; Frederick C. Crews, " A New Reading of *The Blithedale Romance*," *American Literature*, 29 (1957), pp. 147–70; William L. Hedges, "Hawthorne's *Blithedale*: The Function of the Narrator," *Nineteenth-Century Fiction*, 14 (1960), 303–16; John W. Schroeder, "Miles Coverdale as Actaeon, as Faunus, and as October," *Papers on Language and Literature*, 2 (1966), pp. 126–39; and Louis Auchincloss, "*The Blithedale Romance*: A Study of Form and Point of View," *Nathaniel Hawthorne Journal*, 10 (1972), pp. 53–58. As Crews later observes, "No narrator ever had worse luck than Coverdale in learning the most essential facts about the figures whose story we are supposed to enjoy"; see *Sins of the Fathers: Hawthorne's Psychological Themes* (New York: Oxford University Press, 1966), p. 196. More recently still, as if to prove the point well taken, Richard Brodhead asks: "Did ever a book miss so much of the story it purports to tell?" See *Cultures of Letters: Scenes of Reading and Writing in Nineteenth-Century America* (Chicago: University of Chicago Press, 1993), p. 58.
6. See Henry James, *The Bostonians* (New York: Modern Library, 1956), p. 24. The apposite article on Hawthorne and the "Mutability Cantos" is that of Buford Jones, "Hawthorne's Coverdale and Spenser's Allegory of Mutability," *American Literature*, 39 (1967), pp. 215–19. For a more contemporanous account of the sources of Hawthorne's political conservatism, see Larry J. Reynolds, "'Strangely Ajar with the Human Race': Hawthorne, Slavery, and the

And yet, once adverted to, the internal evidence of Coverdale's formal unreliability seems overwhelming; indeed the surprising thing is that professional criticism could have missed the signs for so long.[7] From the very first, our curious but self-protecting point-of-view character misses his chance to get up close to the motives that control the unhappy unfolding of events at Blithedale. And from this initial failure of relation he never quite recovers. The result appears to be a novel about a man writing a novel about things he does not sufficiently understand. Unless—worst case scenario—he should prove an accomplished liar from the outset. That case may well be un-decidable; and while we are a long time un-deciding, what happens to the politics?

2

When Moodie arrives at Coverdale's bachelor quarters, on the eve of the latter's well-publicized departure for Blithedale, to ask a "great favor," he meets a fairly chilly response. Though a great mystery to first-time readers, Moodie's request can only be for Coverdale to take his daughter Priscilla with him to Blithedale—and to watch over her, perhaps, if the new community should fail in this matter of common concern; or if Zenobia, ignorant of her half-sisterly relation to Priscilla, should refuse the task. It takes a little while for the reader to make these necessary inferences, of course, but then that is precisely the point: failing to let himself become involved in some primary relation to the principal persons at Blithedale, Coverdale merely wanders, as it seems, in search of clues from the outside, finding some and missing many others, leaving us to make things out, little by little, the best we can.

We could say, of course, that Coverdale lost touch with the central action he is now trying at a distance to remember and reconstruct because he became seriously ill at the outset, lying in bed recovering and feverishly analyzing his social partners, while they themselves are discovering less clinical possibilities of relationship. And this we might ascribe to character or karma: not Prince Hamlet and not meant to be, he falls hopelessly behind the events of a curious season in which "any individual, of either sex, [might] fall in love with any other, regardless of what would elsewhere be judged suitable and prudent" (3:72). Coverdale may be contracting a fatal attraction for Hollingsworth, but gay sex, though clearly a possibility, seems far from the primary interest of that single-minded theorist; and though Coverdale clearly appreciates

---

Question of Moral Responsibility," in Millicent Bell, ed., *Hawthorne and the Real: Bicentennial Essays* (Columbus: Ohio State University Press, 2005), pp. 40–69.

7. It is hard to reconcile the latter-day observation that *Blithedale* "remains the least admired of Hawthorne's longer narratives" with at least *some* contemporary responses: no less a figure than George Eliot judged the work "unmistakably the finest production of genius in either hemisphere, for this quarter at least": and, closer home, E. P. Whipple—almost recognizing the originality of its narrative method—pronounced it "an entirely new product of the human mind"; See Crews, *Sins of the Fathers*, p. 194; and cp. Arlin Turner, *Nathaniel Hawthorne: A Biography* (New York: Oxford University Press, 1980), p. 240.

the tender ministrations of this rough yet priestly and somehow womanly attendant, he seems more interested in the body and soul of Zenobia. But the simpler point is more cogent: it is already too late. Received with what Coverdale's rhetoric absurdly calls "but little alacrity of beneficence," Old Moody immediately goes elsewhere—"to some older gentleman" (3:7)—with his request. To Hollingsworth, it soon appears: he shows up at Blithedale the very same evening with the frail and fragile Priscilla in tow. Coverdale is not very interested in Priscilla's identity or in her story. He notices that Priscilla fixes her "large, brown, melancholy eyes on Zenobia," and he imagines that she may be one of Hollingsworth's "guilty patients," brought to Blithedale in search of "spiritual health" (3:27); but he makes no further connection. Hollingsworth confesses that "an old man brought [Priscilla] to my lodgings" (3:30), but Coverdale does not seem to realize that he himself had been the old man's first choice to escort Priscilla. His second response to Moodie had been one of awakened "interest," but it was too little and too late.

A readily available sexism might suggest that Priscilla is the kind of girl who will fall for the first man who is nice to her, and that Coverdale's insufficient "alacrity of beneficence" has cost him (and us) a proper love interest; but the more sober point is that his cool self-possession—his selfishness—has ruined at the outset his relation to his fictional material. Given a little generosity and a little trust, Priscilla might have told him quite a lot of her story. He will, at one point, blurt out the hypothesis that Zenobia is "the sister of the Veiled Lady" (3:45), but he does not appear to know what he is talking about. Only much later does he learn that Zenobia and Priscilla are—quite apart from the implications of Zenobia's explicit feminism—literal half sisters; and he never appropriately registers the fact that the young woman Old Moody wanted *somebody* to take to Blithedale is the very subject of the mesmeric experiments he has just been to witness, and that she desperately needs to escape the power of the side-show spiritualist Westervelt. Some degree of real friendship might have allowed him to learn whether this pale inner-city woman has indeed been working, as Zenobia proposes, as a "seamstress"; and, with a little more delicacy, he might even have discovered whether that innocent-looking word carried, in her own sad case, the established nineteenth-century connotation of "prostitute."[8] Perhaps Westervelt has been her pimp as well as her psychic handler.

Coverdale expresses concern that Priscilla might fare badly in a love triangle with Zenobia and Hollingsworth—it would "be no child's play" (3:72)—but he is not above taunting her about the same possibility: "observe how pleasantly and happily Zenobia and Hollingsworth are walking together" (3:126). But somewhere between the "malice" he here confesses and the seemingly benign egotism he everywhere exhibits, he continues to miss his chances to learn something of Priscilla's real history and, from that, to gain some sense of what may really be going on among the characters in whom he takes such

---

8. For the traditional connection between the sewing trades and the career of prostitution, see Barbara F. and Alan B. Lefcowitz, "Some Rents in the Veil: New Light on Priscilla and Zenobia," *Nineteenth-Century Fiction*, 21 (1966), pp. 263–75.

an intense but ineffectual interest. Earlier, watching her blossom in the new environment, and observing with an odd sadness "her simple, careless, childish flow of spirits," he asks her "What is the use or sense of being so very gay?" And more soberly still, "What kind of a world [do] you imagine this to be, which you are so merry in?" Refusing the answer that "I never think about it at all," he presses her less philosophically: "Have you nothing dismal to remember?" (3:74–75). Evidently this is an important moment, for clearly Old Moodie had been anxious to help his daughter escape something seriously unpleasant. And Coverdale, who has somehow managed to ask the right question, ought to pay close attention to the answer.

"Ah!" says Priscilla very slowly, as if remembering something dismal indeed. "And then came that unintelligible gesture, when she seemed to be listening to a distant voice." The voice of Westervelt, we readily infer, at the infernal bidding of whose mesmeric power Priscilla has been induced to behold worlds or perform acts we can only imagine. Wait a moment, Coverdale, and see what she will say next: your career as a novelist may depend on it. But no: "For my part," he selfishly interrupts, "beneficently seeking to overshadow her with my own somber humor, 'my past life has been a tiresome one enough; yet I would rather look backward ten times, than forward once'" (3:74–75). The inhibitory effect is easy to imagine: enough about me; let's talk about me. And so the moment passes, without significant revelation. Beneficence, indeed.

One major irony of the novel is that, though it is Zenobia who comes to a tragic end, it is Priscilla for whom Coverdale expresses continuing concern. And whom he seems unable or unwilling to aid. From his leafy retreat high up in a tree, he imagines sending a bird to warn her that "her fragile thread of life has inextricably knotted itself with other and tougher threads, and most likely it will be broken" (3:100). And more to the same romantic/pathetic effect. As if in the old-time ballad, that other Miles—Standish—had thought to court his own Priscilla—Mullins—by carrier pigeon. But this quaint, literary disinterestedness is only part of the problem. From the same leafy retreat, Coverdale overhears part of the conversation between Westervelt and Zenobia: evidently Westervelt is trying to pressure or to bribe Zenobia into returning Priscilla to his vulgar, perhaps sexual power; and from his hotel room Coverdale appears to witness the transaction by which she is in fact returned. Only later does he appear to grasp the significance of what he has witnessed: Zenobia has indeed delivered Priscilla back into some sort of (at least) spiritual slavery; and, for some sickening reason, Hollingsworth seems to have aided her in this vile traduction—though this too we learn only later.

Well may the reader wonder whether Coverdale's ignorance is not significantly culpable—whether he is not complicit in the central event in the tragedy he cannot seem clearly to discern or to write as such. The first-time reader may know much less about all this than Coverdale, but the critical analyst has got to learn much more. And to wonder, perhaps, why he has been put in the position of having to probe for the motives and to assemble the narrative of this tale of betrayal pretty much on his own. As if it had been Hawthorne's intention merely to invent the self-deconstructing postmodern novel.

Evidently Zenobia has herself been involved with Westervelt before the action of the present story, and no doubt he has some sort of hold on her still: he appears to be threatening to expose something which will damage her personal and literary reputation;

perhaps she too has been one of his prostitutes.[9] Beyond that, however, evidences of sexual tension, competition, and jealousy have been all around the newly recovered Coverdale, and we easily imagine that Zenobia returns Priscilla to Westervelt to rid herself of a rival: as they say in the song, "Lord help the sister."[10] Hollingsworth's participation in this betrayal might be a little harder to understand, for he has apparently been "recklessly tender towards Priscilla" (3:78). And yet, when Coverdale confronts Hollingsworth much later in the novel—"What have you done with Priscilla?" (3:200)—the question stabs him like a knife. And so we consult our deepest suspicion: perhaps money is involved in the transaction, money which Hollingsworth will need to establish his institution for the reforming of criminals, after the failure of the Blithedale experiment, which he takes entirely for granted and is biding his time to await. What might NOT this most avid and single-minded reformer be willing to do in pursuit of the one Master Reform? Coverdale came early to suspect that Hollingsworth's tender care had all been for the "ulterior purpose" of making him a "proselyte" (3:57). And he has seen powerful (almost psychiatric) evidence that, in the heart of this committed ideologue, private affection is no match for his public commitment. Indeed his dull-witted witness of this terrible fact may constitute the clearest proof of his utter unreliability.

The very moment before expressing his "horrible suspicion" about the ulterior motive of Hollingsworth's loving kindness, at the end of chapter VII, Coverdale has been rehearsing his view that "at this period of his life, Hollingsworth was fast going mad" (3:56). The provocation is his discovery that this single-minded reformer is utterly unable to consider the social plans of other theorists with anything approaching objectivity. Reading rather widely, during his convalescence, in the ambient literature of protest and project, Coverdale tries to sound out his reformer friend on the subject of "Fourier," surely a name to conjure with in the context of "freedom's ferment."[11] The talk is rather general, politely skirting the fact that the un-illuded social engineering of Fourier's 1600-person "Phalanx" takes full account of the human being's more-than-monogamous sexual need; but no doubt both men understand this greater sexual freedom as one of the "beautiful peculiarities" of his system.[12] Nor, in any event, could Hollingsworth's response

---

9. The Lefcowitcz's recognition of the similarity between Zenobia's strangely luxurious city quarters and the look of a high-class bordello is also cogent. An adept of the trade herself, Zenobia would be handing Priscilla back into some quite literal prostitution—a public performance-profession not mentioned in Brodhead's otherwise exhaustive study of "Veiled Ladies"; see *Cultures*, 48–68.

10. For the moral ambiguities of literal and political sisterhood in *Blithedale*, see the excellent article by Angela Mills: "'The Sweet Word,' Sister: The Transformative Threat of Sisterhood and *The Blithedale Romance*," *American Transcendental Quarterly*, 17 (2003), pp. 97–121.

11. No less an authority than F. O. Matthiessen assigned the age to the twin figures of Immanuel Swedenborg and Charles Fourier; see *American Renaissance: Art and Expression in the Age of Emerson and Whitman* (New York: Oxford University Press, 1941), pp. viii–ix.

12. For an informed summary of what New England intellectuals might well know about the sexual side of Fourier's social engineering, see Robert D. Richardson, *Emerson: The Mind on Fire* (Berkeley: University of California Press, 1995), pp. 365–69; and cp. Carl J. Guarneri, *The Utopian Alternative: Fourierism in Nineteenth-Century America* (Ithaca, NY: Cornell University Press, 1991), pp. 94–98, 197–203, 353–63.

be more puritanical: the very idea of choosing "the selfish principle, the very principle of all human wrong" as the basis of social re-organization! Call *that* the "Unpardonable Sin" (3:53).

And yet, in the view of Coverdale's amateur analysis, single-hearted devotion to a more high-minded project takes another, more disturbing form as well: Hollingsworth's dedication to his own idea seems as obsessive as it is intolerant; he simply cannot stop making models of the new, ideal-form prison he will build—one day, not far off; just as soon as he gets possession of the Blithedale property and a little seed-money to begin the construction. This, Coverdale proposes, is "Hollingsworth's one castle in the air," which he "caught hold of [...] the more strongly" and clutched "the more pertinaciously, by rendering it visible to the bodily eye." Thus "I have seen him, a hundred times, with a pencil and sheet of paper, sketching the façade, the side-view, or the rear of the structure, or planning the internal arrangements, as lovingly as another man might plan those of the projected home, where he meant to be happy with his wife and children" (3:56). Coverdale is, of course, a bachelor—"frosty" at the time of his writing—and very far, in his own view, from being a domestic sentimentalist; but he seems to know how ordinary (straight) life is supposed to work: young men focus their hopes (or blame their ambition) on wife and family and, if they plan for some rosy future, they imagine, and even sketch out, from time to time, the cottage or the mansion which will house their bliss (or embody their success). But not Hollingsworth: the measure of his obsession is that he relentlessly fashions a model of a prison in the exact space where sanity imagines domestic bliss. Coverdale's analysis may be partial, or even false, but it certainly is clear and emphatic; and no one else in or about the region of Blithedale is in a position to make this precise observation. So it will seem surprising when he fails to see the practical significance of his own special insight. As very shortly he does.

Chapter IX—"Hollingsworth, Zenobia, Priscilla"—finds Coverdale worrying whether he is not in danger of over-analyzing the three principal characters in his unfolding mental drama. The reader may wonder how he can interest himself so much and yet uncover so little; or suspect that he is negotiating, for Hawthorne himself, the difference between effective observation and the unwarrantable prying. But Coverdale himself proposes, sanely enough, that it is not "a healthy kind of mental occupation, to devote oneself too exclusively to the study of individual men and women." Undue self-analysis, he thinks, is sure produce a "diseased action of the heart": someone here seems to have read about a "Bosom Serpent." More to the present issue, however, is his observation that "if we take the freedom to put a friend under our microscope, we thereby insulate him from many of his true relations, magnify his peculiarities inevitably tear him into parts, and, of course, patch him very clumsily together again. What wonder, then, should we be frightened by the aspect of a monster—a construct based on real deformities, to be sure, but created mainly by ourselves" (3:69). Yet he seems unable to help himself: having surrendered to "an over-ruling purpose," reformers like Hollingsworth have "no heart, no sympathy, no reason, no conscience" (3:70); they might be capable of anything. And the definitional over-statement is allowed to stand, even though, on meeting its human subject once again, Coverdale is moved to remind himself "He is a man, after all!" (3:71).

What follows this self-dramatized example of the danger of over-analysis is the scene in which Coverdale conspicuously fails to learn anything about Priscilla's "dismal" past and then, more generally, tries to make sense out of what is going on within the triangle of characters from which he is excluded. Zenobia is proposing, humorously enough, to "fill the place of a maiden-aunt" for Priscilla, who may or may not require instruction in the very "morals, manners, and proprieties of social life" (3:77–78) which we imagine Zenobia's explicit feminism has been busy denying; and nothing obscene may shadow her command, at the end of a discussion of her possible anger, for Priscilla to "come to my room, this moment, and let me beat you." But she cannot help noticing how "recklessly tender" (78) Hollingsworth can be to Priscilla. Nor can Coverdale, who constantly assumes that, if this theory-mad reformer has any ordinary love at all, it must be centered on the darker, more exotically sexual Zenobia. He can imagine that she may well be "merely at play with Hollingsworth"; and if so she may be "sporting with a power which she [does] not fully estimate" (3:79), but it never occurs to him that Hollingsworth's interest in her might be in every way ulterior to the question of matching and mating.

And so he seems satisfied enough with "the gossip of the Community," which "set[s] them down as a pair of lovers. They took long walks together, and were not seldom encountered in the wood-paths; Hollingsworth deeply discoursing, in tones solemn and sternly pathetic. Zenobia, with a rich glow on her cheeks, and her eyes softened from their ordinary brightness, looked so beautiful, that, had her companion been ten times a philanthropist, it seemed impossible but that one glance should melt him back into a man" (3:79). Certainly he ought to love her. Probably he does, Coverdale appears to think, so far as a lover of the genus man can love as well a specific woman. Surely they belong together, under conditions he feels competent to recommend:

> Oftener than anywhere else, they went to a certain point on the slope of a pasture, commanding nearly the whole of our own domain, besides a view of the river and an airy prospect of many distant hills. The bond of our Community was such, that the members had the privilege of building cottages for their own residence, within our precincts, thus laying a hearthstone and fencing in a home, private and peculiar, to all desirable extent; while the inhabitants should continue to share the advantages of an associated life.

No Fourierist dogma here, the well-instructed reader will suitably infer; and no very explicit desire to destabilize the monogamous marriage and the nuclear family. A cottage at a commune: what a nice little compromise (like having Bartleby close by but behind a screen). And small wonder if all suppose that these intense young persons "intended to rear their dwelling on this favorite spot" (3:79–80).

But while the too-well-instructed reader is wondering whether he can be hearing distant echoes of the private and peculiar logic that undid the little commonwealth at William Bradford's Plymouth,[13] many social paradigms ago, Coverdale proceeds to

---

13. The *Blithedale* text invokes the Pilgrim example more than once, and the connection was well recognized, long ago, in A. N. Kaul, *The American Vision: Actual and Ideal Society in Nineteenth-Century Fiction* (New Haven, CT: Yale University Press, 1963), pp. 196–213. Read seriously as

offer his advice about the exact placement of the love nest in question. Appropriately consulted, he should have recommended "a site further to the left, just a little withdrawn into the wood, with two or three peeps at the prospect, among the trees. You will be in the shady vale of years, long before you can raise any better kind of shade around your cottage, if you build it on this bare slope" (3:80). It would be very hard to miss the cover-dale-ism of this point: pull back a little, shade yourself just a bit, peep out at others while avoiding, yourself, what they will come to call "the gaze." But no such thought occurs to Hollingsworth—who, in spite of the diction of domesticity—assumes Coverdale is talking not about the old-time cottage of some bachelor's private fantasy but the new-style prison of the reformer's dream. And so his answer is to us altogether predictable: "But I offer my edifice as a spectacle to the world, [...] that it may take example and build many another like it. Therefore I mean to set it on the open hill-side" (3:80). And we readily imagine the appropriate response: Oh, dear, excuse me; now I see; we were not talking about the same thing, at all: I about the ideal dwelling of the matched and mated human couple; you about, well, your Reformer's "City on a Hill." I—we all—thought you and Zenobia were making love, talking about where to settle down. Silly me: you were only trying to recruit her, right? Just the way I more than half suspect you were with me, earlier on. Except that she is thought to have more money than I. Oh, dear, how could I be so wrong?

How indeed. The misprision here is so evident that, were this not such an early and well-formed instance of unreliable narration, one would almost accuse the hint of being too obvious. Or else, at some other, almost un-supposable extreme of artifice, that Coverdale is only pretending to be monumentally imperceipient. Let's see: Hollingsworth wants his cottage to be not shady and secluded but open and exemplary—"an idea in the mind, and the sun shining?" Well:

> Twist these words how I might, they offered no very satisfactory import. It seemed hardly probable that Hollingsworth should care about educating the public taste in the department of cottage-architecture, desirable as such improvement certainly was. (3:80)

The answer to this reflection, if said out loud to Hollingsworth, would be a baffled, almost speechless surprise: what the hell did you think? What am I *always* talking about?

What indeed. Given its tolerance of various lifestyles—and given the usual appearances of love and courtship—the Community can easily be forgiven their mistake. But not Coverdale. For he is the one who has already suspected Hollingsworth of offering love in exchange for political support and who has premised, if only under a sort of scrupulous erasure, that reformers can have strange consciences, capable of excusing anything. And of course he is the one who has just told us, quite explicitly, that the distinguishing

---

a report on the fate of an authentic Puritan commune, Bradford notices that the failure of his project owes to the painfully arrived at decision to allow families to "set corn every man for his own particular" (3:120); but he also gives us reason to suspect that the problem may have begun earlier, with the Pilgrims' insistence on maintaining private interest in separate houses; see William Bradford, *Of Plymouth Plantation* (New York: Modern Library, 1967), pp. 36–41.

mark of Hollingworth's monomaniac reformism is that his project has altogether obliterated his sense of a domestic sphere;[14] that he designs and builds prisons exactly where sane men project their home. The point is more than formal. No doubt it is unkind of Hawthorne to have imagined that a committed feminist might fall head-over-heels in love with a man lacking both the domestic sensibility and the ordinary conscience. And so the responsibility for Zenobia's fate must rest in a certain sense upon him. But within the world of his fiction, only Coverdale is in a position to realize her very deep danger. And he cannot seem to get it.

3

And so we wander through the early chapters, never entirely sure what is really going on and not well guided about what thematic sense to make of our accumulating suspicions: Priscilla has a past, as Westervelt's "Veiled Lady," but then Zenobia has been mixed up with that unpleasant, probably degenerate character as well. Priscilla knows that she is Zenobia's half-sister and Zenobia does not, but perhaps this is not supposed to matter in a world where feminist "sisterhood" is often thought to trump the merely biological sort. And how exactly are they relating to one another? Westervelt shows up, asking for her back, just after Old Moodie shows up, asking if anyone has been asking for her. Evidently Zenobia complies with his request, even threatening Priscilla, beforehand, with the otherwise melodramatic conclusion of her buy-before-you-try "Legend" of Theodore and the Veiled Lady: throwing the veil over Priscilla looks exactly like a way of saying, I know your story, little sister; so watch your step with Hollingsworth or I'll send you back to you-know-where.

But before that, what? Priscilla appears to live for the smiles of her older companion, but what about Zenobia's inviting her to a private beating? Or, if that seems a little rough, what are we to make of Coverdale's observation that, upon a sudden Blithedale spring, the two "had been a-maying together"; and that "Zenobia—who showed no conscience in such matters—had rifled a cherry-tree of one of its blossomed boughs" (3:58). Perhaps

---

14. Some accounts insist that not all communitarian efforts tried actively to destabilize the nuclear family; see, for example, Sterling F. Delano, *Brook Farm: The Dark Side of Utopia* (Cambridge, MA: Harvard University Press, 2004), esp. pp. 39–107. Yet it seems clear that, in vocalizing Fourier's utter dedication to the phalanx alternative, Albert Brisbane speaks for the consensus: "The system of isolated households, or system which assigns a separate dwelling with a separate interest, is the fundamental defect of our societies" (185); for, within this system, "Each family seeks to forward its own interests, separate from, or at the expense of all the other families around it" (186): see "Association and a Social Reform," *Boston Quarterly Review* (April 1842). For the generality of this verdict, see Raymond Lee Muncy, *Sex and Marriage in Utopian Communities* (Bloomington: University of Indiana Press, 1973), esp. pp. 51–57; and cp. the foundational study of Alice Felt Tyler, *Freedom's Ferment: Phases of American Social History from the Colonial Period to the Outbreak of the Civil War* (1944; rpt. New York: Harper Torch, 1962). What Muncy makes clear is that even the most conservative communities had to face—and never could quite solve—the problem of what to do with the threat that small-unit love posed to the greater good.

it is all quite innocent but (moving beyond the present text for one literary moment) Henry James did not appear to think so when he created the Boston Marriage of Olive Chancellor and Verena Tarrant in the (deformed) image of Zenobia and Priscilla. This could be Coverdale's fantasy, overheated still from his sickbed imagination of Zenobia in the garb of Eden; or her leaning over his bed, inviting (or merely daring) his bachelor imagination to probe her inmost being. But then what exactly are his own sexual proclivities? From the first, his attraction to Zenobia seems more convincing than his last-page confession of love for Priscilla. And his interest in Hollingsworth seems to compete with both these heterosexual possibilities: at very least he is grieved that Hollingsworth wants him as a convert and not what Hawthorne's notebooks call a "friend of friends." And in this context many serious readers cannot rid themselves of the memory of Hawthorne's recent, oddly blighted relationship with Herman Melville.[15] If it was indeed a time and a place where anyone could fall in love with anyone else, "regardless," perhaps we are being invited to consider all sorts of possibilities not otherwise suitable and prudent.

But with what thematic motive and to what political end? It is easy enough to hear Hawthorne's own dismay behind Coverdale's "startled" response to the "hardihood" of Zenobia's (largely unexpressed) sexual philosophy (3:44). The author who had required Hester Prynne to postpone, a century or two, her expectation of a "new truth" about "the whole relation between man and woman" (1:263) was now writing in the midst of the deferred prediction; and soon enough he would find himself shocked (as well as fascinated) at the "naked" self-presentation of the frustrated loves of certain female novelists with whom his own more veiled productions had to compete.[16] Alarmingly, Zenobia

> made no scruple of oversetting all human institutions, and scattering them as with a breeze from her fan. A female reformer, in her attacks upon society, has an instinctive sense of where the life lies, and is inclined to aim directly at that spot. Especially, the relation between the sexes is naturally among the earliest to attract her notice. (3:44)

Without being at all specific, these observations are extremely suggestive. Evidently Zenobia has said (or written) somewhat more than Coverdale is telling us, and quite possibly Hawthorne himself has some writers or issues particularly in mind. Margaret Fuller, emphatic about the consequences of gender differences, is conventional enough on the subject of human sexuality; but George Sand is not, and Coverdale confesses to have been reading her romances "interminably" (3:52); neither is Harriet Martineau

---

15. For a recent review of the "friendship with Melville" question, see Andrew Rosenblum, "The Idea of Another: Hawthorne's 'Friend of Friends,' Dissociation, and *The Blithedale Romance*," *Nathaniel Hawthorne Review*, 30.1 (2005), pp. 1–28. For the lurking possibility of a Coverdale-Hollingsworth romance, see Lauren Berlant, "Fantasies of Utopia in *The Blithedale Romance*," *American Literary History*, 1 (1989), esp. pp. 36–38.
16. For Hester Prynne's "compromising" prediction of the sexual order to come, see my "Woman's Heart, Woman's Choice," *Poe Studies*, 39 and 40 (2006–7), pp. 104–14. Something of the same curious ambivalence may be read in Hawthorne's astonished response to the sexual frankness of his "damned mob of scribbling women," who are not unwilling to "come before the public stark naked, as it were"; see *The Letters 1853–1856* (17:304–8).

or Mary Gove or Frances Wright, whose flagrant theories seemed to have troubled the young life of Salemite Jones Very.[17] More generally, Brook Farm was not known as a "free love" experiment, but the Oneida Community certainly was, and many of the women there seem to have been as enthusiastic about its liberated sexuality as its men. Founded the same year as the Seneca Falls Convention (1848), its liberating premise of the "complex marriage" was widely publicized and discussed; and probably, if the truth were told, nearly all the various "brotherhood" experiments of the 1840s meant to discredit and destabilize the foundational reality of the monogamous nuclear family.[18]

But while we meditate these unsettling contextual questions, Coverdale himself moves swiftly from Zenobia's ideas to her person: a "magnificent woman," meant for "the stage" or, better, to be the subject of "painters and sculptors"—preferably the latter because (as Coverdale's imagination turns semi-pornographic) "the cold decorum of the marble would consist with the utmost scantiness of drapery," so that, "chastely," he insists, "the eye might be gladdened with her material perfection, in its entireness" (3:44). The diction is of course absurd, but the sexual subtext survives the comedy: he wants to see her nude; no, the word is naked. Again, just as earlier, at the moment of their first introduction, he had willingly pursued the invitation to imagine her in "Eve's earliest garment" (3:17). Nor does he picture marble as he dwells on "the flesh-warmth over her round arms, and what was visible of her full bust" (3:44). And then, again, a fit of decorum: he has to close his eyes. Yet on he goes, with something hard to distinguish from prurience, to imagine the course and quality of her sex life: "a woman to whom wedlock had thrown wide the gates of mystery" (3:47). So, she's not a virgin: get over it. Maybe she was married (or mistress) to Westervelt: what might that mean to the story you have been trying to remember and recount? But no. He stares, at the full figure bending over the bed of his convalescence. She challenges the nature of his prurient interest. Perhaps she means to arouse it. Either way, he once again finds the need to close his eyes.

What happens here, early on, will happen again and again in the novel: brought intriguingly to the brink of some urgent life-question about the power and the regulation of love and, inevitably, the consequent arrangement of society, we find ourselves drawn, irresistibly, back into the art-question of Coverdale's curiosities as a character and function as a narrator. As if, having committed itself utterly to the modern premise of one invariable point of view, the novel were trying but not quite succeeding at the task

---

17. Very's single mother was much influenced by the radicalism of "Fanny" Wright, and young Jones may have had her in mind when he resolved to swear off "Beauty" as his "bosom idol"; see Edwin Gittleman, *Jones Very: The Effective Years, 1833-1840* (New York: Columbia University Press, 1967), pp. 152–55.
18. After Fourier and Brisbane, the most outspoken critic of the nuclear family was probably Charles Lane who, at Fruitlands, almost persuaded Bronson Alcott to stop living on ordinary marital terms with the mother of many children; see Muncy, *Sex and Marriage*, pp. 89–91. In his view, expressed in *The Dial* for 1844, the "grand problem" faced by any reformed "Community" was "whether the existence of the marital family is compatible with that of the universal family" (quoted from Muncy, p. 82).

of overcoming its own ineluctable subjectivity. Character trumps plot. And politics seems relegated to an entirely different sort of discourse.

A more complex instance suggests the same sort of difficulty. Chapter XII ("Coverdale's Hermitage") begins with as astonishingly suggestive a figure as one may hope to find outside of an explicit allegory; but it comes to us as but a whim of Coverdale's own vagrant imagination, and there is no one around to insist on its explication. The "hermitage" is of course Coverdale's little "leafy cave, high upward into the air, among the midmost branches of a white-pine tree" (3:98). From here Coverdale will send Priscilla his feckless little message by bird; and from here he will *almost* overhear what motives or blackmail threats Westervelt has employed to corrupt Zenobia. And no one can blame the readers who emphasize those facts in their ongoing attempt to characterize the character who is characterizing his characters. Yet the figure appears to insist on itself:

> A wild grape-vine, of unusual size and luxuriance, had twined and twisted itself up into the tree, and, after wreathing the entanglement of its tendrils around almost every bough, had caught hold of three or four neighboring trees, and married the whole clump with a perfectly inextricable knot of polygamy. (98)

Perfect image of the novel itself, the greedy reader is tempted to exclaim: twistings that seem to defy disentanglement; and more than that, a powerful bond that holds Zenobia, Priscilla, Hollingsworth (and probably Westervelt as well) in a complex sexual interconnection that might as well be called polygamy. And this in a world where one signal form of sexual revolution holds that redeemed men and women might come to regard one another not as brother and sister but as husband and wife.

But as the figure is no more than the momentary product of Coverdale's poetic fancy—invoking a congenial setting for his inconclusive meditations rather than defining his sense of a problem to be solved—there is not much pressure to unravel its implications any further; little, that is to say, to force our attention outside Coverdale's self-enclosing text. One perspicacious reader has ventured to suggest that the figure implies not the general theory of Oneida so much as one specific moment in the sexual evolution imagined by Fourier: the "erotic quadrille," as he calls the frustrated social dance of two couples, caught in a web of "amorous desire and deceit," and needing to work their way up "from monogamy, to plurigamy to cryptogamy to delphigamy to omnigamy."[19] Nor,

---

19. Quoted from an inspired but unpublished (1984) essay by Robert D. Richardson: "Regeneration through Exile: Brook Farm, Hawthorne, and Fourier." As Richardson notes, Sophia's letters testify that she and Hawthorne were "reading Fourier extensively in the original French in 1845"; and that, by 1851, Hawthorne had read the whole of the crucial Volume Four of Fourier's *Complete Works* (Paris, 1841)—where, under the heading of "*Quadrille du conflit erotique,*" Fourier examines "modern love." The same biographical details are publicly recorded in T. Walter Herbert, *Dearest Beloved: The Hawthornes and the Making of the Middle-Class Family* (Berkeley: University of California Press, 1993), p. 114. "Attractive labor" might be Fourier's widely advertised subject, but closer home lay the question of the family and, beneath it, the need for "la verite en regime d'amour" (61). To these basic insights may be the provocative arguments of Lauren Berlant, "Fantasies," esp. pp. 38–42; Andrew Loman in "*Somewhat on the*

given the depth of our difficulties with the plot, is there more than a momentary desire to decide what un-translated passage of Fourier a convalescent Coverdale decided to read to an attending Hollingsworth, so to arouse his moral sense and competitive social instinct. How can we be expected to ask what is provoking this story while we are so caught up in the question of what it fundamentally is?

But of all the instances of this enforced internalism, none is more compelling than the last thought we are likely to have of Coverdale: he confesses at the end that he himself had been in love all along with Priscilla, that he lost her to Hollingsworth as bitterly as Zenobia lost him to Priscilla; but only the most innocent of readers will find this confession quite credible. There is, for one thing, the stuttering suspense of the melodramatic punctuation: "I—I myself—was in love—with—PRISCILLA" (3:247). More plausible would be the claim that, like both the women, he too was in love with Hollingsworth. But what if we resist this fashionable possibility and suspect that the interest he has shown in Zenobia is less theoretical than he has tried to make it seem—that it is in fact as sexual as it is obsessive. His lust may be incompetent; indeed it may be refusing to confess itself as such. But then this would hardly be the first time when a character in Hawthorne did not quite know his own motive. On this hypothesis, his buried story would be that Zenobia has rejected him, as painfully as she herself has been rejected by Hollingsworth. Why, apart from some such obsession, would he insist in the end on taking (and keeping) Zenobia's shoe, which the conventional wisdom of Silas Foster has offered to Hollingsworth. And it is in this mood—of suspecting that Coverdale has something *else* to confess—that one begins to notice certain alarming features of Coverdale's behavior in the last chapters of his oddly self-revealing, self-concealing tale.

No reader can fail to notice that Coverdale takes the lead in discovering Zenobia's body. One may easily be distracted by the fact of this sudden, active and primary involvement of a character who has preferred to think of himself as playing the part of a "Chorus" in a play whose mode seems more and more tragic: he himself takes note of the "strange tone" (3:229, 230)—of purposeful action—in which he summons first Hollingsworth, then Silas Foster to the task of finding out what has become of the woman he was last seen trying to comfort in the moment of her rejection. One may even be tempted to relish, in the moment just prior to this outburst of activity, a final instance of Coverdale's emotional incompetence. Zenobia has charged Coverdale not only to write up the tale she suspects he has been rehearsing with all the pathos it deserves, with all the passion he says he feels, but also to take a message to Hollingsworth. Solemnly accepting the task, he never does perform it—not even a message by bird. Instead, he says, he falls asleep, "worn-out," as he protests, with "emotion [...] and sympathy" (3:228). As if the Poet had written: "I fall upon the thorns of Life/ I sleep." Zenobia's message is ambiguous, even self-contradictory: first, "Tell him he has murdered me" (3:226), and then, "I intend to

---

Community-System": Fourierism in the Works of Nathaniel Hawthorne (New York: Routledge, 2005), esp. pp. 1–31, 89–95; and (online) Kathryn Tomasek and Adam Tuchinsky, "'Spirits Bound to the Same Haven': American Fourierists, Marriage, and the Political Economy of Love" (www.iisg.hl/nwomhist/tomasek.doc).

become a Catholic, for the sake of going into a nunnery" (3:227). But the implication seems quite serious in either case: Zenobia is in extremis; so that Coverdale, on his very own account, must seem complicit in her death. Yet the careful reader must wonder if this narrated but un-confessed—and in fact unrecognized—guilt is all there is to suspect.

Coverdale's story is that he has dreamed Zenobia's final catastrophe. If so, it must have been a graphic dream indeed; for, without the aid of any veiled-lady clairvoyance, he leads the group of searchers to the exact spot where the body is to be found. He even tells them he is familiar with the river's depth from having fished there in the past: odd, as we had not thought of this wine-bibbing, cigar-smoking friend of citified bankers and editors as much of an outdoorsman; odder still, since he has earlier denied knowing the river at all. Then too—as one brave article some time ago pointed out—the forensic evidence is not entirely consistent with the premise of death by suicidal drowning.[20] No one thinks to wonder whether the wound in her breast was indeed made by the rake used to probe for the body; or whether it could have been made earlier, but by some other sharp implement. Nor to ask, as would a modern coroner, whether there was in fact water in the lungs. They all notice the attitude of terrible rigidity into which Zenobia's body has arranged itself and, resisting the quarrel-with-God implications, they wonder that so young, so vital, so gifted a woman could commit the last-last crime of self-murder. Women have died from time to time, but is it pure cynicism that leads Westervelt, scorning the claims about that "troublesome organ" called "her heart," to observe that if "Love had failed her," it was not for the first time: "She survived it, and loved again—possibly, not once alone, nor twice either" (3:240). Well might Coverdale wish to hear more of this, but nothing else is forthcoming, and so we are left with our own troubled knowledge that persons who die by drowning do not suffer quite so dramatic a form of rigor mortis.

And with it, perhaps, the question of whether Zenobia has indeed been murdered—not by Hollingsworth, as in her poetic prediction, but by Coverdale, in a moment well concealed from the attention of the reader and perhaps hidden better still from his own conscious mind. One striking instance seems worth our careful consideration. Coverdale reports that Zenobia leaves him, after charging him to tell Hollingsworth something or other; yet Coverdale reports a strange sense that she is not really gone, that she "was still hovering about the spot, and haunting it." This "haunting" suggests, if only ambiguously, that she may already be dead; and his seeming to "feel her eyes" upon him suggests guilt as clearly as anything else. And then one most arresting detail: "It was as if the vivid coloring of her character had left a brilliant stain upon the air" (3:228). This striking image may be pure poetry, but it seems a little too good for a man of Coverdale's insisted-upon limitations. Surely it reads better as a pathological memory—a concealing revelation of the blood that flowed from a literal wound made in what Westervelt scorned as Zenobia's heart.

The question may well be un-decidable, but sooner or later it was bound to arise; and students alerted to Coverdale's unreliability now raise it without ever reading the article

---

20. See John H. McElroy and Edward L. McDonald, "The Coverdale Romance," *Studies in the Novel*, 14 (1982), pp. 1–16.

that first suggested the dire possibility. Coverdale's story does not quite hang together: and what looks like incompetence may well be elaborate deception, a devious attempt to (almost) confess without running the risk of the consequences; or else—Reuben Bourne-like—a compulsive return not only to the scene but also to the actual memory of a crime that may well have astonished and then distorted his own civilized mind.[21] Surely the question is worth discussing. But—and this is the point that seems beyond debate—while we are wondering if the story is meant to recall Edgar Poe or to inaugurate some other, yet more subtle form of detective fiction, the issue of the book's politics, sexual and otherwise, recede into the background. Again and again, it seems, questions essential to the nature of this work as a fictional construct postpone, deflect, or subsume questions about the world out of which it was so evidently constructed. As if, for this one time only, the new critical doctrine of narrative succeeded in preventing the new historical premise of discourse. The effect might well satisfy the high formalism of the 1950s, but it can only baffle or irritate the criticism of a more worldly and political generation. Unless we can discover—and narrate to ourselves—some story in which Coverdale is not a controlling and entrapping center of literary intelligence, but only one more worldly instance. The artfulness of this truly revolutionary novel can hardly be made to disappear, but its protest might come to seem all the more subtle for that reason.

4

So: where *do* we find ourselves? In need, it seems, of a criticism that will prevent us from becoming permanently caught up in the necessary—and endlessly fascinating—question of how—and how artfully—Hawthorne implies the action of his most deeply emplotted novel; one that will show us how to talk about *Blithedale* in a non-reductive political way from the outset.

Psychologically speaking, we seem always to have known that the Hawthorne who refers the judgment of Zenobia to Spenser's definitive trial of Mutability by Nature harbors a deep and abiding skepticism about the likely success of radical reform;[22] and just here, quite likely, is where James's hero has learned his conservative moral about learning to bear our troubles. But as we learn about this much from dramatic sketches like "Earth's Holocaust" and "The Hall of Fantasy"—or the shocking critique of Holgrave in *The House of the Seven Gables*—it will not quite do to keep repeating that simple conservative, atavistically Christian message in a novel where the stakes of human hope seem so genuine and so high and the disposition of critique so complex.[23]

---

21. See Frederick C. Crews, "The Logic of Compulsion," *PMLA*, 79 (1964), pp. 457–65.
22. Again, that formidable biographical positivist Arlin Turner may speak for the antique consensus; see "Hawthorne and Reform," *New England Quarterly*, 15 (1942), pp. 705–11. For a more or less complete review of the old-time "Hawthorne and Reform" problem, see Gorman Beauchamp, "Hawthorne and the Universal Reformers," *Utopian Studies*, 13 (2002), pp. 38–52.
23. More shocking, almost, than the 1853 defense of the compromising policies of Franklin Pierce is the explicit intrusion by which the author of *The House of the Seven Gables*—no blaming a Narrator, here!—thinks to correct the political enthusiasm of his youthful protagonist: wrong, he was, to think that "his age, more than any other," was to accomplish the needful re-ordering

Nor, as we have seen, will it advance the case of an appropriate political criticism to go on noticing how remarkably original—and potentially ambiguous—is this most definitively modern of Hawthorne's fictional constructs, rivaling any point-of-view novel James himself could ever produce; teaching him, no doubt, how to do it, though he seems never properly to have realized that fact. "Exit Author,"[24] with a vengeance: Hawthorne himself entirely disappears; or rather, he morphs into the problematic figure of an author who does not quite understand the story he is supposed to be telling; or else, subconsciously represses many of its essential details. The lesson may have been painful to learn: the 1982 reviewer in *American Literary Scholarship* found the Coverdale-as-murderer hypothesis not intriguing but "bizarre";[25] just so, as I recall the 1950s, did a certain well-intentioned

---

to the world; and also, more painfully to our activist sensibilities, "that it mattered anything to the great end in view, whether he himself should contend for it or against it" (2:180). Troubled by the bewildering variety of reform activities, and put off by the reformers' often arrogant tone, Emerson suggests we learn to trust "the Overgod." In Hawthorne's more traditional vocabulary—and with the assistance of Sophia's diamond—"God is the only worker of realities." For a timely review of the problem in question, see Michael T. Gilmore, "Hawthorne and Politics (Again): Words and Deeds in the 1850s," in Bell, ed., *Hawthorne and the Real: Bicentennial Essays* (Columbus: Ohio State University Press, 2005), pp. 22–39.

24. The classic response to the modern practice of authorial retreat makes much of Henry James but has to do its theoretical work without the signal example of Hawthorne; see Wayne Booth, *The Rhetoric of Fiction* (Chicago: University of Chicago Press, 1961), esp. pp. 3–86.

25. Rita K. Gollin, "Hawthorne," in *American Literary Scholarship* (Durham, NC: Duke University Press, 1984), p. 33. The murder hypothesis was taken up by Beverly Hume in "Restructuring the Case against Hawthorne's Coverdale," *Nineteenth-Century Fiction*, 41 (1986), pp. 387–99; but, turning aside to some ever-present meta-themes, she reaches the more cautious (metaphorical) conclusion that Coverdale is guilty of "a murderous betrayal both of the human heart and the artistic process" (p. 388). Beyond that, the murder hypothesis—indictable if not provable—is rarely mentioned in the criticism; and then only to be summarily rejected: see Laura E. Tanner, "Speaking with 'Hands at Our Throats': The Struggle for Artistic Voice in *The Blithedale Romance*," *Studies in American Fiction*, 21 (1993), pp. 1–19; and Kenneth Kupsch, "The Modern Tragedy of Blithedale," *Studies in the Novel*, 36 (2004), pp. 1–20. Yet men did kill Georgiana and Beatrice, not entirely by accident. And related rumors persist: How exactly DID Judge Pyncheon die?—see Alfred H. Marks, "Who Killed Judge Pyncheon?" *PMLA*, 71 (1956), pp. 355–69. And are we SO sure that Chillingworth did not—by accidental overdose, more likely than on purpose—cause the (un-)timely death of the man he was treating with drugs designed to torture? See Jemshed A. Khan, "Atropine Poisoning in Hawthorne's *Scarlet Letter*," *New England Journal of Medicine*, 311 (1984), pp. 414–16. Men have died from time to time, but rarely from adultery; so that, according to my own verdict—wasted, years ago, on the interviewer from PBS—There once was a Lady from Boston, Who grieved that her virtue was lost on A Minister thin, who thought it was sin, But actually he died of surreptitious atropine poisoning. So, while criticism has been busy turning desire into guilt and homicide into artistic betrayal, our "blue-eyed Nathaniel" seems all along to have been preparing for the blatant and graphic murder in *The Marble Faun*. Just where, in *Blithedale*, do we imagine Hawthorne to have put that extra dose of "the devil"? Is it just that Professor Westervelt carries "a stick with a wooden head, carved in vivid imitation of that of a serpent" (3:92)? Perhaps we need to rethink the gothic back into the shifting paradigms of Hawthorne criticism—well identified by Gordon Hutner, "Whose Hawthorne?" Millington, ed., *The Cambridge Companion to Nathaniel Hawthorne* (New York: Cambridge University Press, 2004), pp. 251–65.

Professor of English at a second-rate Jesuit college respond to the Catholic nun whose Saturday-morning seminar report wanted to argue, against all the known biographical facts, that Coverdale is not quite the same as Hawthorne. The dramatic modernity of Hawthorne's narrative is now beyond dispute. And the murder-hypothesis begs to be raised and, once raised, it remains a live and non-disconfirmable possibility. But murder or suicide, the problem of love and friendship, affection and passion, sex, marriage, and other possible forms of social organization remains unresolved and largely unattended to: intractable in reality, perhaps, but in glaring need of critical attention nevertheless.

What we need, it seems, is a criticism that will translate the antique prediction of Hester Prynne into a working vocabulary; for, plainly, love and sex are far more than a discursive background of this original and highly provocative novel. Where an older analysis found in the post-coital romance of *The Scarlet Letter* the puritanic theme of "guilt," a newer, more archeological critique uncovers an important site of enduring sexual metaphor.[26] And here, it seems, the problem is a good bit less figurative. The question is not only who may be having what sex with whom, and where, and how frequently, though these questions will continue to fascinate fiction as fatally as other less artful forms of social gossip; but also the more scientific, even Freudian question of whether human being is not so essentially sexual that any ideal of orderly regulation—traditional or liberated—is little more than a fantasy. Mighty repression, on the one hand, can come to seem a catastrophic mistake, as even the quintessentially pre-Freudian William Bradford had come to suspect.[27] But on the other hand, perhaps enlightened plans to re-route the streams in which human desire has been found to flow amount to a dangerous tempting of fate, even a blasphemous insult to the great god Eros. We are accustomed to say—or politely omit to say—that we do, now and again, have sex. But perhaps it is sex that, every moment, has us.

In the end Coverdale sadly confesses that the Blithedale Reformers have nothing new to say about death. Apparently his novel wants to say, with or without his consent, that sexuality too is beyond their power not only to reform but even satisfactorily to articulate. And ours. Desire being essentially irregulable—and necessarily so, for the survival of the race over centuries of famine, war, and plague—the idea of devising, testing out, and promulgating some new sexual rules seems a little like preaching a fast-day sermon to the sharks. Perhaps the bad old ways, perfectly easy to cognize as the sign and root of civilized discontent, are, though bad, about as good as social planning can hope to arrange.

---

26. See my "'Woman's Own Choice': Sex, Metaphor, and the Puritan 'Sources' of *The Scarlet Letter*," in *Doctrine and Difference: Essays in the Literature of New England* (New York: Routledge, 1997), esp. pp. 217–27. In my view, further work on *Blithedale* might well pursue a subtle abolitionist subtext: not only prostitution but the plight of women in general was regularly thought of as a kind of slavery; and the return of Priscilla to Westervelt looks very suspicious in the context of the Fugitive Slave Law of 1850.
27. Of his many, semi-baffled attempts to explain the outbreak, in 1641, of various sorts of sexual "wickedness," Bradford appears to hit upon a modern truth: "it may be in this case as with waters when their streams are stopped or damned up. When they get passage they flow with more violence"; see *Plymouth*, p. 316.

The signal victim of this conservative discovery is, of course, Zenobia. If the compromising logic of his *Life of Franklin Pierce* cost Hawthorne the friendship of many persons of the abolitionist persuasion, his decision to push his would-be emancipated women hard enough to fall hopelessly in love with an unrepentant male chauvinist cannot have pleased any observant member of the feminist community. Coverdale may propose, however hypothetically, a generous feminism as against Hollingsworth's fiercely conventional definition of woman's "place" and "office" and "sphere" (3:122–23), but Zenobia herself will come almost immediately to forswear it all: "Women possess no rights [...]; or, at all events, only little girls and grandmothers would have the force to exercise them" (141). "Curious conversion," indeed.[28] From one point of view, therefore, the best thing that could possibly happen to Zenobia is in fact to be murdered by Coverdale; for otherwise she would inevitably figure as one more victim of some profound form of female self-betrayal. Men have died from time to time, and worms have eaten them but, in literature at least, it is women who seem cursed with the rare gift to die for love.

Whether she kills herself, or whether she has been murdered by the submerged passion of the unusually aroused and terminally frustrated Coverdale, Zenobia stands for the belief that neither stipulated good will nor the revocation of ordinary taboos will be able to remove or even soften the effect of sexual jealousy. If Coverdale kills her, it is because her fatal attraction to Hollingsworth has insulted his own less aggressive manhood. If she kills herself, it is because Hollingsworth is incorrigibly attached to the pliant Priscilla. But *why*, in either case? Why don't the four of them all just marry one another, in the manner of John Humphrey Noyes? Or simply admit they are caught up in that intermediate state of sexual evolution Fourier had called the "erotic quadrille"?[29] And maybe invite Westervelt to the dance as well: he clearly belongs; and surely he, if anyone, is well past the old sexual drama of ideals, curiosity, arousal, passion, and guilt. Let him

---

28. Surely Zenobia's flat foreswearing of the politics of feminism is no less "curious" than is, in *The House of the Seven Gables*, Holgrave's amazing swerve from the revolutionary politics of Jefferson; see Rudolph Von Abele, "Holgrave's Curious Conversion," in *The Death of the Artist: A Study of Hawthorne's Disintegration* (The Hague: Nijhoff, 1955), pp. 58–69. For the feminist problems connected with Coverdale's vision of Zenobia as Ophelia, see Joel Pfister, *The Production of Personal Life: Class, Gender, & the Psychological in Hawthorne's Fiction* (Stanford, CA: Stanford University Press, 1991), pp. 80–91. And for the view that, given his own anxiety about the "erotic female," Hawthorne must have Coverdale "'kill' Zenobia to 'save' Priscilla," see Jennifer Fleischner, "Female Eroticism, Confession, and Interpretation in Nathaniel Hawthorne," *Nineteenth-Century Literature*, 44 (1990), pp. 514–33. These two among very many "new readings" which undertake the "urgent" work of "reconstructing Hawthorne's representations of the relations between men and women"; see Hutner, p. 264.
29. The full daring of Fourier's utterly uninhibited, service-oriented view of human sexuality may not have been evident until the relatively recent publication of *Le Nouveau Monde Amoureux* (Paris: Editions Anthropos, 1967); but its basic premise—no natural instinct left unfulfilled—was on the record in Volume Four of the *Complete Works*, which Hawthorne read and reread in French. Moreover, it was pretty well known to Charles Lane, who had been to France to work with Fourier, and to Brisbane as well; they might be cautious, but they could not be entirely silent; see Guarneri, esp. pp. 93–98.

substitute for Coverdale whenever the delights of poetry (or a good cigar) overcome all other temptations.

But in fact no one at Blithedale is free from the power of what Melville would call "Amor Threatening."[30] Not Westervelt, obviously, as his "spiritualist" need to peer behind the veil of his pliant female accomplice seems as virulent a perversion of ordinary desire as Hawthorne could imagine—a kind of soul rape, as Hawthorne's letters to Sophia prefigure his odious position.[31] And, whatever we should think to call his lurid reversal of Coverdale's customary sublimation, his leering, near-Satanic presence broods over every other gesture of love and friendship. Not the passive Priscilla, whose final escape from the base usages of Westervelt—and perhaps from the possibility of a "Boston Marriage" with Zenobia—appears to depend on a magical rescue by a man whose once-reckless approach to Zenobia seems a guiltier form of prostitution than that of any inner-city "seamstress." Not Hollingsworth, ever, as only the incurably innocent will fail to recognize his zeal for criminal reform efforts as a particularly nefarious form of sexual displacement: self-declaring prisons where there ought to be quiet cottages. And certainly not Coverdale himself. He ends by confessing, in a sentence with rather too many dashes, that he was, himself, in love with Priscilla all along. Perhaps in some strange sense he was: to no other Fair Priscilla did this un-soldierly Miles think to send a love-message by bird. But most readers would be less surprised if he had confessed a smoldering, submerged, frustrated and ineffectual passion for Zenobia. And/or for the strangely womanlike Hollingsworth, who courted his devotion every bit as assiduously as he did that of Zenobia. And with—shall we confess it?—even more Melvillean zeal.

Suppose, then, it was a time and place—earnestly anticipated and vaguely predicted by Hester Prynne at the end of *The Scarlet Letter*—in which, in innocence or under the aegis of social reform, anyone could indeed pursue an amative attachment to anyone else. The organizers of Brook Farm were, in its first incarnation, cautious to express their respect for the ordinary family; nor would very many of the American communities publicly advertise a full-scale program of sexual reform. Yet soon enough the Transcendental idealism of Brook Farm lapsed to the social engineering of a Phalanx; and virtually all the new "Social Plans" shared the same quarrel with the isolationist, therefore competitive nature of the nuclear family. And—epitome or reductio ad absurdum—the new order of free sex within the complex marriage of all concerned seemed to flourish, for a time at least, in the almost-real world of Oneida: the New England conscience had

---

30. In a surprisingly modern poem called "After the Pleasure Party," Melville warns women—but also, it seems, human beings in general—that "soon or late [...] One's sex asserts itself"; see *Collected Poems of Herman Melville* (New York: Hendricks House, 1947), p. 217.
31. For Hawthorne's philosophical—and nearly hysterical—response to soul-violation he felt at risk in Sophia's plan to have her headaches treated by the mesmerism (hypnotism) in use in her father's dental practice, see his letter of October 18, 1841 (15:588–90). The violence of this response might, by itself, render the search for new-female examples like Jenny Lind somewhat de trop; see Brodhead, *Cultures*, p. 52. So too, a fortiori, would the swelling question of "psychological slavery": see Russ Castronovo, "The Antislavery Unconscious," *Mississippi Quarterly*, 53 (1999), pp. 41–57.

long ago been taught, at the church trial of Anne Hutchinson, to hate and fear the idea of "using of women in common"; but the women in the exemplary community of John Humphrey Noyes appeared to enjoy their passional liberation about as keenly as the men; perhaps there was no question of "use" at all. As this perfectionist prophet of sexual liberation soberly argued, as far as alternatives to the old order of sexuality and its discontents were concerned, it was complex marriage or celibacy: Oneida or the Shakers.[32] And who knows but it might yet take a whole community of husbands and wives to raise a child to a suitable social stature?

At the fictional Blithedale, however, the results are altogether tragic. Why is this so? Why do the new views of love and sex—hidden barely if at all beneath the attempt to reform the competitive exclusiveness of the nuclear family—seem doomed in Hawthorne's imagination from the start? What besides heterosexual hysteria might dictate that, in a world so conceived, passion and its deceitful simulation might flourish while faithful commitment based on honest caring is hauntingly absent? Probably not Hawthorne's own marriage, unless the painful problems of that less-than-ideal union have been somewhat over-drawn.[33] Possibly only the conservative's preference for things long established, along with the settled conviction that the human race is indeed predestined to "live with its problems." Among them, sexual dis-ease as the premier "discontent" of what Freud was pleased to call "Civilization."[34]

Or perhaps Hawthorne had seemed to see, in the theorists of the new order, an old wish for selfish un-restraint disguising itself as liberation and enlightenment. Such is exactly the puritanic view of Hollingsworth, when Coverdale taunts him with the famous name and, implicitly, the shocking ideas of the era's most radical sexual engineer. Hawthorne left Brook Farm, of course, well before it became a Phalanx on the model of Fourier, but we can hardly imagine him as feeling at home among the statistical 1600. With or without the blessed Sophia. And what do we imagine he, or the two of those idealized literary lovers, would make of an arrangement in which a single member of two associated couples might find available three partners? The more liberated and eccentric of Fourier's proposals for complete sexual freedom were not well publicized by his American followers; evidently one had to wade through some rather long books, in French, to learn of them in any detail. But surely the Ripleys knew about them. And Hawthorne too, who could read French about as well as anybody in New England, and

---

32. For the specter of the sixteenth-century "Familism" of Munster haunting the moral imagination of New England, see my account of the church trial of Anne Hutchinson, in *Godly Letters: The Literature of American Puritans* (Notre Dame, IN: Notre Dame University Press, 2006), pp. 398–400. For Noyes's (retrospective) challenge for sex-and-the-family reformers to find any middle-ground between his complex marriage and the celibacy of the Shakers, see his *History of American Socialisms* (1870; rpt. New York: Dover, 1966), pp. 595–657. And for the women's response to the new sexual order at Oneida, see Lawrence Foster, *Women, Family, and Utopia* (Syracuse, NY: Syracuse University Press, 1991), pp. 75–102.
33. For a bracing account of the local stresses and generalized un-satisfactions of what was once taken to be *the* ideal middle-class marriage, see Herbert, *Dearest Beloved*, esp. pp. 107–211.
34. For Fourier as a precursor of Freud, see Richardson, *Mind on Fire*, pp. 366–67.

who assures us that such works were a major part of Coverdale's sick-bed reading at Blithedale. And surely Hawthorne knew, as well, of the famous four-partner marriage into which John Humphrey Noyes had entered just before establishing the institution of the "complex marriage" at Oneida. Either of these eccentric arrangements could have provoked Coverdale's arresting description of vines binding three or four trees into a "veritable knot of polygamy": three in *The Scarlet Letter*'s old, innocent model of adultery; four with Noyes or Fourier in mind. The text of *Blithedale* may be studiously chaste, but its urgent subtext—like the social pretext of this most daringly suggestive novel—is unblushingly sexual. "A Knot of Dreamers" (3:14) barely disguising a knot of polygamy. And that old-time marriage knot—"The Curious Knot God made in Paradise"—kept well out of sight.[35]

Nor should we fail to emphasize the fact that nearly all the communes founded in the 1830s and 1840s had, at least implicitly, some quarrel with the trans-personal implications of the nuclear family: tight-knit it certainly was and, centered on an angelic (or at least a morally superior) woman, it was certainly easy to valorize as a refuge in a rough and often even brutal public world; but could it not also serve, as often as not, as both a basis and a rationale for the very competition that made the public world so unhappy in the first place? The husband might or might not think he owned the wife; the parents the same with the children; but was it not this precious little group in whose name the husband was motivated to compete? He had to do the best for his family, didn't he? So it is not at all surprising that, in most of the new communities, one called one's new associates brother and sister when they were no such thing in blood. Society at large simply had to find a way to extend the sense of familiar love beyond the limits of natural propagation and instinctive protection. Wife and child might keep at bay the haunting dread of solipsism, but evidently something else seemed required to teach the lesson of large-scale cooperation.

But what if it turned out that the virtues required to sustain the quasi-natural group of the precious few were radically different from those needed to sustain a life of peace and harmony within a group whose members were connected by ideals rather than by nature? Family values might well be, as Jonathan Edwards had patiently explained, an example of virtues that are merely natural rather than "true," but what if it required nothing less than "benevolence to being in general"[36] to sustain a group whose bond was not blood or exclusive possession or instinctive protection but only some curious interest in expanding the limits of family feeling. Could trans-natural families be in fact sustained

---

35. See "Upon Wedlock, and the Death of Children," in Donald E. Stanford, ed., *The Poems of Edward Taylor* (New Haven, CT: Yale University Press, 1960), p. 468. A reader of Milton on divorce—and not of Taylor on indissolubility—Hawthorne may well have disagreed that "Weddens Knot [...] ne're can be unti'de." On the one hand, marriage was never more mystified than in Hawthorne's letters to Sophia (see Herbert, *Dearest Beloved*, pp. 113–16); on the other, *The Scarlet Letter* surely questions John Winthrop's metaphorical elaboration of the woman's marital choice. Between these literary extremes, Hawthorne evidently did not wish to see the ordinary bond of marriage entirely undone.
36. As it is against the lingering Puritan fear of familiar idolatry that the morale of domestic sentimentality must be thought to have evolved, so it is the tough analysis of Edwards that this soft

by anything less than "true virtue"? Projector and historian of the first American love-in, John Winthrop clearly thought not. So indeed did John Humphrey Noyes: the starting point of his theory of complex marriage is, as he emphatically tells us, nothing less than Christian perfectionism. Saints may well love one another—more literally and technically than Winthrop had probably imagined—for the image of God or Christ they recognize therein.[37] But would that not mean that only the truly converted could make love at large? And was it not everywhere evident that natural desire is somewhat more prevalent than sexual grace?

From this point of view, *The Blithedale Romance* is a disturbingly negative book, with even more of the predicted "devil" than we have been prepared to notice. It may even be, in the terms used by certain original reviewers of *The Scarlet Letter*, something like a dirty book:[38] sex is nowhere allowed to appear as a sacrament of creation, a source of creative energy, or even, as in a simple "apologue" like "The Man of Adamant," the available antidote for solipsistic self-enclosure; it does not even figure as a "cure for the present distress." Instead, though all the characters are in the grip of sexual desire, most of them are using it as a way to manipulate other people. Sublimation, as we might think, in its very worst form. And this at a community dedicated to the happy premise that love can teach us to cooperate. Hollingsworth seems sure that Fourier's basest idea is to have made expanded sexual service the basis of social reform. And Hawthorne himself seems to know that this engineered selfishness is no way to make things better; but then his own sexual cynicism seems to imply that there is *no* better way. Perhaps a novel that wished to suggest this much had needed to have, in the nineteenth century at least, a certain indirection, even obtuseness of narration. Otherwise constructed, it might have read like a scandal report from some renegade Shaker; or just less far down "Beneath the American Renaissance," like a George Lippard exposé of "The 'Mysteries' of New England."[39]

But perhaps the last word should be not sex but its most common consequence: not intercourse but family—as glaring in its simple absence from the action of *Blithedale* as is sexual desire in its quenchless insistence. First of all, on the fringes of the reforming project, one can scarcely imagine Westervelt in the role of *pater familias*: women may well

---

ethic must face; see *The Nature of True Virtue* (Ann Arbor: University of Michigan Press, 1960), esp. pp. 75–97.

37. Widely anthologized in partial form, Winthrop's famous "Modell of Christian Charity," appears complete in *Collections of the Massachusetts Historical Society*, 3rd series (Boston, 1838), 7:31–38. For my commentary, see *Godly Letters*, pp. 416–18.

38. Thinking that his audience might judge him too gloomy, Hawthorne consciously decided to make *Seven Gables* a "sunnier" book. Then, fearing on the other hand that his readers might not accept from him two happier books in a row, he promised his friend Bridge that *Blithedale* would contain "an extra touch of the devil" (16:462). For early reviews of *Scarlet Letter*—including the Arthur Cleveland Coxe's famous evocation of its subject as "the nauseous amour of a Puritan pastor"—see John L. Idol Jr. and Buford Jones, eds., *Nathaniel Hawthorne and the Contemporary Reviews* (New York: Cambridge University Press, 1994).

39. For the seamy underside of the Hawthorne's literary world, see David S. Reynolds, *Beneath the American Renaissance: The Subversive Imagination in the Age of Emerson and Melville* (New York: Knopf, 1988), esp. pp. 167–278.

be on his copious agenda, but soul science and sexual cynicism are a poor seedbed for commitment and nurture. Similarly situated, Old Moodie has fathered two daughters, but they are only half-sisters, and nothing like an ordinary family can be thought to bind him to the four women of his life. Indeed, Priscilla is being sent to Blithedale precisely because, having fallen into bad hands, there is no other refuge to which she can repair. As the poet almost said, family is where, when you have to go there, they have to take you in. But of course the enlarged or extended Blithedale family proves to be as dysfunctional as any we might imagine. Reassuringly, Farmer Foster has brought along the wife of his youth, but there is no evidence that they have had any children, and his chief contribution to the idealized community seems to be his inside knowledge of the pig market. Voluminously overflowing elsewhere, domesticity seems a little scarce in this corner of the literary world.

As rare at the center as on the outskirts. Coverdale's inveterate bachelorhood might almost go without saying: definitively asserted at the outset, it remains firmly in place for all the years between his rare experience and his curious confession; his narrative may be trying to recall the warming influence of that first-night fire at the yet unnamed "Blithedale," but nothing he felt there has persuaded him to exchange his cherished independence for the normative pleasures of home and hearth. In this his career contrasts most sharply with that of his inspired creator: Hawthorne went to Brook Farm, arguably, to see if the practice of communal living were any defense against the specter of solipsism which, as "The Christmas Banquet" seems to suggest, haunted him almost as much as it did Emerson.[40] Long enough engaged to Sophia Peabody, of course, and barely able to support himself with his fiction, he also needed to know if, at a commune like Brook Farm, two could live as cheap as one. And if he left for reasons that leave the theory of socialism largely untouched—he simply could not write and shovel cow dung at the same time—his next move was into the traditional state of marriage and the family: whatever the financial consequences. Imagine that domestic arrangement to have been as complex and painfully troubled as the modern critic of domestic mythology can possibly paint it, still the status of husband and parent is one he never came to regret. Doubtless he did not experience it as the salvific cure a certain Sophia-like Rosina offers a certain Nathaniel-like Roderick, but he seems to have accepted it, with all its discontents, as the best solution to the familiar human situation of congenital loneliness troubled by urgent desire.

Zenobia lives just long enough to recant her feminist theories—open marriage, free love, women without men, whatever we imagine them to have been—but the novel does little or nothing to lament the failure of their implementation in the present. Nor does her recantation come with any (Hester-like) prediction of a more perfect arrangement in yet another sexual future. Unlike the social protagonist of *The Scarlet Letter*, whose sexual victimage has been far more simple and traditional, Zenobia appears to have had her full swing in the world of liberated sexual desire: Westervelt clearly implies that he has not been her only lover; he may be wrong in thinking she could have gone on, from her

---

40. See my essay, "'Life within the Life': Sin and Self in Hawthorne's New England," *Nathaniel Hawthorne Review*, 30.1 and 2 (2004), pp. 1–31.

disastrous encounter with Hollingsworth, to love again (and again?), but the logic of the novel at large implies that she would have been quite content to marry that passionate but misguided man in quite the old-fashioned way. Perhaps she dies to keep Hawthorne from having to face, in fiction as in his own life, the story of a man who married a woman somewhat more than his sexual equal.

However that may be, it is the frail (even if experienced) Priscilla who ends up married to Hollingsworth; and there is scarcely enough evidence to judge the psycho-sexual success of that penitential union. Perhaps their marriage amounted to a prison less reformed than the ones Hollingsworth had once theorized. Yet clearly both are better off than either had been before—she rescued, finally, from some form of prostitution, and he liberated by love from the fantasy of criminal meliorism. Significantly, however, they appear to remain childless: neither has seemed very promising parent material, and possibly Hollingsworth's project of life-long self-punishment, a form of egotism still, precludes the possibility of "washing dishes and baby clothes." Or maybe that outcome too is a matter of authorial fiat, as if it were to be the law of this relentlessly committed novel that, in pursuing the possibility of sexual reform, no figure of the old-time domesticity should be in any form permitted to appear. Elsewhere, Mrs. Stowe's most dehumanized villains were busy destroying, for their own nefarious purposes, the possibility of family life for the Africans they have imported and enslaved. Here, it seems, Hawthorne's idealistic reformers have done the same thing for themselves. Why, we might wonder, has the one case been so much more noticeable?[41]

Perhaps it may be useful to remember that, in the years of Brook Farm's first foundation, and before the enactment of the hated Compromise of 1850, Negro slavery was not the only cause commanding the attention of reformers. Of Hawthorne's committed contemporaries, Theodore Parker turned one way, toward abolitionism, but George Ripley turned quite another. Not knowing any more than Emerson, for example, what exactly to say about slavery—let alone what to *do* about it—a conscientious-enough Hawthorne followed in the direction he knew best, concerned (no doubt) to see if the Family of Man might admit of a larger-than-nuclear model. Unhappily, perhaps, but unambiguously in any case, he soon became convinced that it did not. Perhaps he would have agreed with John Humphrey Noyes, that there were only two possible alternatives to the present distress, the celibacy of the Shakers or the regenerate free love of Oneida. Not wishing to end, even in theory, the cycles of generation we call the world, and unwilling to share the intimacy of his "Dearest Beloved," he evidently went back to the established way: his first significant act after leaving Brook Farm was not to write but to marry; and to begin at once to raise not only the squashes set out by Henry Thoreau but the family of his own seed-planting. And the tale he tells, in 1846, of his idealized new birth at "The

---

41. As my patient and ever-percipient Editor has suggested, "The absence of the family in *Blithedale* is as glaring and important a detail as the fact that Hester Prynne sprang from the rose bush of Anne Hutchinson or that Dimmesdale is from Oxford." Thanks, Fred. And thanks to Hannah Nahm, who questioned some unguarded assertions (and reviewed the footnotes).

Old Manse," may stand for the conservative security out of which the bold critique that is *Blithedale* was resistantly written.

It may well be vain to imagine the advanced and thrilling topics Hawthorne says he discussed with minor Transcendentalist poet Ellery Channing, but clearly Hawthorne would have us remember their spirit: rowing effortlessly along the mild stream of the Concord, the two men talked their way into a "freedom [...] from all custom and conventionalism," became in fact "so free to-day, that it was impossible to be slaves again tomorrow" (10:25). "Slaves, indeed," the Conscience of Correctness will more than whisper, but the point of Hawthorne's own protest-alternative is worth following to the end. Men on a rowboat outing—men without women—might say one thing, might indeed say *anything*; but men more fully associated appear to know better:

> And yet how sweet—as we floated homeward adown the golden river, at sunset—how sweet it was to return within the system of human society, not as to a dungeon and a chain, but as to a stately edifice, whence we could go forth at will into a statelier simplicity.

The little boat trip, that is to say, had been like a moment in "The Hall of Fanatsy": wonderful to visit, as often as required, but no place to build a home. "Be free! Be free!" the "leaves of the trees that overhung the Assabeth" had whispered to Hawthorne and his minor-transcendentalist companion (10:25); and no doubt the brief excursion into Nature, in the boat purchased from no less a liberation theologian than Henry David Thoreau, was enough to prove the Rousseauvian point that what is called civilization can easily exact too high a price in our biological naturalness. Still, the return is to a stately home and not at all to a prison.

Sophia Hawthorne's response to the brief absence of the man they both agreed she should idolize is not recorded. And we can well suppose that Ellery Channing, who had already drifted away from a brief and unsuccessful marriage to Ellen Fuller, and who may have helped to inspire Emerson's observation that "We are not much to blame for our bad marriages,"[42] might dissent from some of this recovered piety. But the voice of the happily married man—the reformed solipsist—goes right on:

> How gently, too, did the sight of the Old Manse—best seen from the river [...]—how gently did its gray, homely aspect rebuke the speculative extravagances of the day! It had grown sacred, in connection with the artificial life against which we inveighed; it had been a home, for many years, in spite of all; it was my home, too;—and, with these thoughts, it seemed to me that all the artifice and conventionalism of life was but an impalpable thinness upon its surface, and that the depth below was none the worse for it. (10:25)

And so much for what Emerson had called "The Protest."[43] Except that, when written out at the length of a novel, a protest against the protest is noticeably a protest.

---

42. See Emerson, "Illusions," in *The Conduct of Life* (New York: Library of America, 1983), p. 1118.
43. Privately declining Ripley's invitation to Brook Farm, then publicly rebuking the urgent abolitionist entreaties of William Henry Channing, Emerson could nevertheless hardly come to the

The moment is a little like that in *The House of the Seven Gables* when, after a dizzying trip on a train—and an even dizzier speech on the cyclical return of human life to the higher nomadism—two characters entrapped by the institutions of the past come to rest before a dilapidated church and an abandoned farm house. Faced with this composite image of an ineluctable reality, they fall to their knees in prayer. The difference is that here, in "The Old Manse," where the Narrator is as close as that needful figment ever comes to being Hawthorne himself, the speaking voice not only prays but goes so far as to risk a somewhat unlikely symbol expressly for the purpose:

> Once, as we turned the boat to the bank, there was a cloud in the shape of an immensely gigantic figure of a hound, couched above the house, as if keeping guard over it. Gazing at this symbol, I prayed that the upper influences might long protect the institutions that had grown out of the heart of mankind. (10:25–26)

There may be, of course, no final (recoverable) truth about the origin and historical function of the monogamous nuclear family. But this small piece of domestic piety may come about as close to the heart of Hawthorne's social conservatism as we are likely to get. And certainly, given a different narrative strategy, it might have served as a partial, evolving, and self-disputed moral for *The Blithedale Romance*.

We have it from Hawthorne's own prefatory pen, of course, that his Romances do not wish to be reduced to any simple moral maxim. Yet in spite of his "new critical" sense that the meaning of a work of imaginative literature is "seldom any more evident on the last page than on the first," this thankless task of self-reduction is seldom left undone: in the *Seven Gables*, the need to recognize that "the wrong-doing of one generation lives into the successive ones," becoming at last "a pure and uncontrollable mischief" (2:52). And, in *The Scarlet Letter*, more concisely still: the obligation to "Be true"—by showing "freely to the world, if not your worst, yet some trait whereby the worst may be inferred" (1:260). And, taken with a grain of salt, these perfunctory moral translations will surely do no harm. In *Blithedale*, by contrast, the Narrator's best approximation of the apposite moral learning seems a little too general: not altogether misguided, those reformers who had dreamed of a "noble and unselfish life" might well have "struck upon what ought to be a truth"; so that "Posterity" might well "dig it up, and profit by it" (3:246). The exact nature of that truth—its relation to "socialism," its difference from the rumors of "free love"—he declines to specify. But then this Narrator is a man who either cannot or will not tell the truth. So what more could we expect?

---

end of his need to assess the meaning of the reform passion sweeping through New England in the 1840s. Beginning with "The Protest," delivered as part of a lecture series for 1837–38, Emerson expresses increasing reluctance simply to praise the motive or morale of radical reform; see also "Reforms," in the lectures for 1838–39, "Man the Reformer" (1841), the first three lectures in the 1841–42 series on "The Times," "The New England Reformers," in *Essays, Second Series*, and (most confidently but most disturbingly) in the "Ode" inscribed to W. H. Channing of 1845.

Somewhere, however, in the dustbin of sayings that proper literary form has rendered unsayable, it may well be written that, naïve inflation of family values notwithstanding, it is not altogether foolish to believe that marriage and the family lie somewhat closer to an evolved human nature than certain inspired social planners may like to recognize; that there is in fact no civilized or gracious cure for sexual jealousy; so that the world has still not "grown ripe for" an entirely new sexual dispensation. Or, to risk the privilege of a reduction usually left to the novelist himself: "Be true" is everywhere a safer mantra than "Be free." Such mumbled verses of thematic doggerel may seem to us less vital than those which loudly propound that the iniquity of race slavery is altogether odious, but in a world where sexual reformers appeared to promise, by enlarging the circle of intimate love, a cure for civilization's prime discontent, even a convoluted denial must count as theory. Call the fictional experiment, A Year without Families. Name its genre, Domesticity without Sentiment. And in the flagrant world of Fourier and Noyes, the oblique but determined protest of *The Blithedale Romance* is recognizable as one that probably needed to be made.

Chapter Thirteen

INNOCENCE ABROAD: HERE AND THERE IN HAWTHORNE'S "LAST PHASE"

Calling the period in which he wrote "Ethan Brand," "Main-street," *The Scarlet Letter*, *The House of the Seven Gables*, and *The Blithedale Romance* Hawthorne's "major phase" may have the effect of the slighting the period from 1825 to 1838 in which, not counting the works he may have destroyed, he wrote more than sixty separate tales and sketches, some of them among the best and most durable in the language.[1] "Roger Malvin's Burial," "My Kinsman, Major Molineux," "The Gentle Boy" at the outset, "Young Goodman Brown" and "The Minister's Black Veil" just after that; and at the end the four "Legends of the Province House" all defy critical comparison and, supported by a redundancy of other thoughtful and skillfully short works, would make Hawthorne a major American writer if he had died in 1838. Or gone into the stagecoach business with his uncles. But the period is unquestionably major in terms of its high-energy output, and in comparison to the scattering of works that came later. Even though some of the later works have significant merit.

Biographers love the *Notebooks*, from England and then from France and Italy, and indeed they are more revealing than those written earlier in America, which consist mostly of un-philosophized observations and ideas for stories. These got published in the later 1860s, under the watchful eye of his wife, and they created something of a stir at the time; but no one has ever made the claim, familiar enough in the case of Emerson and Thoreau, that these "Journals" are the prime literary product.[2] Hawthorne's métier is reflection, then dramatization—and not what his one-time Concord neighbor called "consciousness"; nor did he ever imagine himself as offering, anywhere, what Thoreau

---

1. Beginning with "The Hollow of the Three Hills" and ending with "John Inglefield's Thanksgiving," and counting the three parts of "Old News" as a single work," The Library of America edition of the T*ales and Sketches* offers some sixty-seven short works from the Salem Period. For the question of works destroyed—as from the aboriginal and ill-starred "Seven Tales of My Native Land," see Nelson F. Adkins, "Hawthorne's Early Projected Works," *PBSA*, 39 (1945), pp. 119–54; and Arlin Turner, *Nathaniel Hawthorne: A Biography* (New York: Oxford University Press, 1980), pp. 50–58. And for informed speculation about the likelihood of other (unsigned) tales, see Thomas Woodson and L. Neal Smith, "Historical and Textual Commentary," in the Centenary Edition of *Hawthorne's Miscellaneous Prose and Verse* (Columbus: Ohio State University Press, 1994).
2. In *Writing Nature* (Oxford University Press, 1985), for example, Sharon Cameron argues that the Journal is Thoreau's primary work, taking precedence over the books Thoreau during his lifetime.

famously demanded in the opening of *Walden*, "a simple and sincere account of his own life."[3] *Quod scripsi, scripsi*, the public works all seem to declare: read them all and then you'll know the real me, as much as any such thing is indeed possible. As if he were to say, when I go looking for myself, I find always some fictive premise.

Yet *Our Old Home* is indeed a significant work of close cultural observation. And when one goes looking for the background of his history of moral awareness in America, it is well to start here—with the sense that this, rather than any novel or romance, is the prime result of Hawthorne's lengthy, attentive stay in England; and that it stands as an important work in a genre more popular in its own proto-scientific time than in ours. Noticeably less than the book produced a few years earlier by Emerson—which, after two chapters of biographical introduction, offers us general considerations such as "Race," "Ability," "Manners," "Truth," and "Character," and, later on, "Aristocracy," "Religion," and "Literature"—still it does not suffer much by comparison;[4] indeed many readers will find it not only more genial but also more sincerely appreciative. Most of Hawthorne's chapters are place names—"Leamington Spa," "About Warwick," "Lichfield and Uttoxeter," "A Pilgrimage to Old Boston," identifying trips the Hawthorne family took, setting out from their base in Liverpool. Working in the well-established Romantic and Victorian tradition of the literary "Excursion," Hawthorne allows memory and association to suggest matters for social definition and moral critique. And where Emerson works hard to prove England's declension from a former, truly impressive age, Hawthorne, though his criticism can be tart, is everywhere capable of a simpler love of the past, and so takes significant delight in much that richly remains.

The Preface, roundly criticized by the professional Abolitionists, elaborately recognizes Hawthorne's lifelong friendship with Franklin Pierce, college friend grown up to be the president who, in reward for a campaign biography that put the best face on a "patient" approach to the question of southern slavery, had appointed Hawthorne to the noticeable position of American Consul to Liverpool.[5] The job may have shut down the pace of Hawthorne's literary production, but it gained him financial security for the first time

---

3. Thus the conscientious but possibly naïve disclaimer in the very first page of *Walden*. For Hawthorne, the issue is less "consciousness" that "reflection."
4. See *English Traits* (Cambridge, MA: Harvard University Press, 1956), Chapters 4–8 and 13, 14, 15.
5. Published in 1852, *The Life of Franklin Pierce* (1852) infamously suggests that the intractable problem of slavery as "one of those evils which divine Providence does not leave to be remedied by human contrivances." The question, evidently, was not whether slavery was a great evil, but how, preserving the Union, was it to be abolished. Unwilling to let it go at that, however, Hawthorne goes on, infamously to suggest that "in its own good time, by some means impossible to be anticipated, but of the simplest and easiest operation, when all of its uses have been fulfilled, it causes to vanish like a dream" (p. 417). Emerson too would rely on Time, but at least he would make no mention of the "uses" the Over-god might be making of slavery; and though Martin Luther King would agree with his belief that the long ark of history bends towards the right, he also noticed, famously, that time is when people do or do not the good they would. Pierce's appointment of Hawthorne as Consul to Liverpool was made 1853 and Hawthorne continued in the post until 1857.

in his life. And it gave him the opportunity to live outside of America for—again—the first time in his life. And to write a book about continuity and rupture in the case of an emergent and still unstable American identity. A "strange fate," Henry James would call it. Not quite the double selfhood of Emerson or, later and more famously, of DuBois, and yet puzzling enough on its own account. A new thing under the sun in many ways, yet anything but a creation *ex nihilo*. Where in fact do we come from? Well worth a book or two.

Yet not quite the book he had wished, or so the Preface confesses. There should have been a proper novel: that was what all the notations and reflections in the *English Notebooks* had been for. But no. No time or place for the play of the fictional imagination: "The Present, the Immediate, the Actual" proved, as he says, "too potent".[6] Out of the *Italian Notebooks* would come the puzzling but deeply reflective work first titled "The Romance of Monte Beni"; and a passing remark about the "American appetite for English soil" (20) well predicts the later, un-completed work known as "The American Claimant"; but for the moment, a series of personal reminiscences, rich with local observations which often enough provoke reflections on the history, culture, and even the collective personality of England and its people.

Thirteen chapters in all, beginning, naturally enough, with a lengthy account of the author's "Consular Experiences" and formally concluding with a jocular and not entirely favorable account of "Civic Banquets." At the outset we learn—from the man who had already made much of a certain upper room in the Custom House at Salem, and before that the rainy day, book-storing attic of the Old Manse in Concord, and before that, the "dismal and squalid chamber" of his mother's house where, yes, indeed, "fame was won"—about the "dusky and stifled chamber" in which he spent "a considerable portion of more than four good years of [his] miserable existence" (9). That he had not sought and did not thoroughly relish the tedious life of a minor public servant might have gone without saying: the born writer became only half-willingly the hack politician. More interesting is the repeated effort to specify the locus of his writing. Like Descartes at the beginning of his famous *Meditations*, but with opposite philosophical intention, Hawthorne seems intent on assuring himself that it's not *all* imagination: a real person in a real place (with a real day-job) is about to offer a sample of his fancies, for the possible edification of real readers. Ah yes, I write, therefore I am; and yet I was really real before I penned a single thought. Me. My desk. My chamber, my curious visitors. Interesting. Better even than seeing one's name imprinted on a pepper bag or box of cigars. Especially the visitors—making the American Consul "better acquainted with many of our national characteristics, during those four years, than in all [his] preceding life" (10).

First of all, he learns that Americans are great travelers: "no people on earth have such vagabond habits as ourselves." Nor is it uncommon for a young American "deliberately

---

6. Citations of *Our Old Home* are from the Centenary Edition of *The Works of Nathaniel Hawthorne*, vol. V (Columbus: Ohio State University Press, 1970).

to spend all his resources in an aesthetic peregrination about Europe, returning with pockets nearly empty," having reserved just enough money "to bring them to the door of my consulate." After a few experiments in nationalistic charity, the consul in question manages to grow "reasonably hard-hearted"—"though it never was quite possible to leave a country-man with no shelter save an English poor-house." Otherwise, he cautiously concludes, "American ingenuity may be pretty safely left to itself" (12–13).

Then the more interesting cases: first off, a man trying to get home after "wandering [...] precisely twenty-seven years," who reminded this cultural observer of Melville's Israel Potter (13), and whose "story seemed to me almost as worthy of being chanted in immortal song as that of Odysseus or Evangeline" (14–15). Other cases concern Americans convinced they are the rightful heirs of some rich English estate, enough in fact to provoke his reflection:

> The cause of this insanity lies deep In the Anglo-American heart. After all these bloody wars and vindictive animosities, we still have an unspeakable yearning towards England. When our forefathers left the old home, they pulled up many of their roots, but trailed along with them others, which never snapt asunder. (18)

Even so late as these days, he continues, England remains "entangled with our heart-strings." And then this pointed, quite caustic, political observation:

> It has required nothing less than the boorishness, the stolidity, the self-sufficiency, the contemptuous jealousy, the half-sagacity, invariably blind of one eye and often distorted of the other, that characterize this strange people, to compel us to be a great nation in our own right, instead of continuing virtually, if not in name, a province of their small island. (19)

Patriotism without politeness.

On their side, the English tried their best to "shake us off"; and, folly or fate or Providence, it were well that they did. Or else "the massive materiality of the English character would have been too ponderous a dead-weight upon our progress." And worse:

> If England had been wise enough to twine our new vigor round about her ancient strength, her power would have been too firmly established to ever yield, in its due season, to the otherwise immutable law of imperial vicissitude. The earth might then have beheld the intolerable spectacle of a sovereignty and institutions, imperfect but indestructible. (19)

No chance now of that "inauspicious [...] amalgamation"; only that the individual American may feel "deep-rooted sympathies that belong more fitly to time gone by" and "a blind, pathetic tendency to wander back." Rather like the author himself, absent the "wild dreams [...] about English inheritances." These, which "might fill many pages" (20), are well-explored in the "Claimant Manuscripts," and, there as here, seem to Hawthorne to express somewhat more than a lust for wealth or pride of place. Endicott's jingoism to the contrary, Hawthorne is still asking, "What have we to do with England?"[7]

---

7. Thus, in "Endicott and the Red Cross" (*Tales*, 548) does this arch-Puritan address his train band, as he learns of the possibility of an Archbishop-Laud directed invasion, aimed at recalling the Massachusetts Charter.

Several other episodes of American Claimants—"Two ladies, bearing a letter of emphatic introduction from his Excellency the Governor of their native state" (20); then, at greater length, a "gentleman of refined manners" (21) who had nevertheless been something of an adventurer and, with *elan* comparable to Gulliver's, filled the Consul's hours with his fantastic reports. Then, in his position of "general adviser and helper," an "Elderly Irishman," a naturalized citizen, who entreated him "to be a 'father to him'" (24); then, again at greater length, the tale of "a certain Doctor of Divinity" who, like a character out of Melville's *Pierre*, appeared to "exemplify the natural accordance between Christianity and good-breeding" (25). Gone missing for "precisely a week" (26), he reappears, unrecognizable at first, in a "blue military surtout" (27). Unable to understand the change—and finding challenged the "boyhood faith" that had regarded a "good old, silver-headed clergyman" as a "Saint [...] on earth" (28)—he sternly admonishes the sadly fallen man, remembering too late that this "desecrated wretch," "laboring under the shape of delirium tremens," quite probably "bore a hell within the compass of his own breast" (29). A moral seems required: a consulate proves all too "congenial" a place "for a man with a tendency to meddle with other people's business." No more of such from this man:

> For myself I have never been in the habit of feeling that I could sufficiently comprehend any particular conjunction of circumstances with human character, to justify me in thrusting in my awkward agency among the intricate and unintelligible machinery of Providence.

He has even hated to "give advice" (30). Man's accidents may be the novel's purposes, but Sin and Salvation keep another road entirely.

Finally, and as if these novelistic experiences were all "incidental" to this Custom-House Part Two, a sort of apology for his well-meaning but inexpert handling of "the real business of the office": where the decapitated Surveyor had done his best to annihilate his duplicitous political enemies, the retiring Consul essays to wrap it all up in a perfectly businesslike way.

Lots of issues between "the seamen and officers of American ships," and though "newspapers all over England contained paragraphs, inveighing against the cruelties of American shipmasters," the Consul in question concluded that "there appeared to be no right side to the matter, nor any right side possible in so thoroughly vicious a system as the American merchant marine" (32). He once "thought of writing a pamphlet on the subject," but—Melville, thou shouldst be living at this hour—he "quitted the Consulate before finding time to effect my purpose" (33).[8] Instead, a few paragraphs here on the character of the seamen, "the off-scourings and refuse of all the seaports of the world," and the captains, who developed themselves into men of "iron energies, dauntless courage, and inexhaustible resource, at the expense [...] of some higher and

---

8. Severely critical of the practice of flogging in the American navy, Melville's *White Jacket* (1850) has been credited with the ending of that practice in the American Navy; see Laurie Robertson-Lorant, *Melville: A Biography* (New York: Clarkson Potter, 1996), p. 235.

gentler traits." Lesser men, no doubt, than "that excellent body of respectably educated New England seamen" who used to grace the profession (like the one who died of a fever in Surinam?), but on the whole agreeable to talk to, though they much "disliked the interference of a Consul with their management on shipboard" (34).

Other, more technical matters, are well entrusted to "faithful, upright, and competent subordinates, both Englishmen, as ever a man was fortunate enough to meet with, in a line of life altogether new and strange to him." Instructed to replace them with Americans, this novice Consul but sadly experienced public servant knows enough of his "own interest and the public's," he "kept hold of them; being little inclined to open the consular doors to a spy of the State Department or an intriguer for my own office" (35). Waxing wise, the Consul suggests that "an appointment in the Diplomatic or Consular service of America is too often what the English call a 'job,'" protesting the practice of "removals for no just cause, just when the incumbent might be beginning to ripen into usefulness" (36), even suggesting that lengthy tenures would assure the city of his residence that "it has a permanent inhabitant and a hearty well-wisher in him." Just not this particular Consul:

> For myself, as the gentle reader would spare me the trouble of saying, I was not at all the kind of man to grow into such an ideal Consul. [...] I never in my life desired to be burdened with public influence. I disliked my office from the first, and never came into any good accordance with it. (37)

He hated public speaking, found the banquets and public celebrations a "bore" (38), the official business "irksome." But what was a poor patron of a not-yet-thriving American literature to do? Never *very* well paid, he protested the mid-course adjustment made in his salary structure and—so he declares—was only too happy to greet his successor, "a Southern Fire-Eater" appointed by President Buchanan.

After this familiar enough disavowal of interest in federal employment—or was it just in any old day job?—the even more familiar protest of dissociation:

> For myself, [—that's twice in the same paragraph—] as soon as I was out of office, the retrospect began to look unreal. I scarcely could believe that it was I, that figure whom they called a Consul, but a sort of Double Ganger, who had been permitted to assume my aspect, under which he went through his shadowy duties with a tolerable show of efficiency, while my real self had lain [...] in a state of suspended animation. (38)

As in the Salem Custom House? Or even at Brook Farm? I do not write, therefore I do not exist? And, come to think of it, the "Doctor of Divinity," the "Oriental adventurer," the "poor old wanderer, seeking his naïve country through English highways and by-ways for almost thirty years"—were they "more than shadows"? (39). Any more than, say, the figures a certain Gervayse Hastings saw, years ago, dancing on the wall before him?[9] Did

---

9. Repeated several times in "The Christmas Banquet" (1844), the phrase seems to describe a figure suffering something like Platonic (or merely Castesian) schizophrenia; see my "Life within the Life," earlier in this volume, pp. 77–98.

you need Emerson or even Plato to write that? Could you have imagined the problem of specter evidence if Cotton Mather had never lived? You write, therefore they are.

Stop. No more of this. What was I thinking? About to offer my brain "delicately fried," with heart sauce. Here's a version less intense. Liverpool proved "a most delightful and admirable point to get away from"—to London, Chester, North Wales, Cumberland and Westmorland, even Edinburgh, Glasgow, and Loch Lomond. Wonderful escapes from "the imprisonment of my consular servitude" (39). And no, you do not "compromise [your] American patriotism" by acknowledging that, from time to time, you were "conscious of an hereditary attachment to the native soil of our forefathers, and felt it to be our own Old Home" (40). If only we knew which of you was saying that.

Thus introduced, this memoir—which subsumes an instructed amateur's adventure in socio-political critique—proceeds as an (interrupted) sequence of reminiscences about excursions to sites of historic interest, which provoke, as the genre demands, reflections on the residual meaning of places an American literary ancestor had called "storied."[10] "Leamington Spa," a busy well-attended English vacation spot, is less so, and though the Hawthornes visit it fairly often, the writer finds himself given to "rural walks about the neighborhood," on a footpath probably older than "Roman ways." "An American farmer," he observes,

> would plough across such a path [...]; but here it is protected by law, and still more by the sacredness that inevitably springs up, in this soil, along with well-defined footprints of centuries. Old associations are sure to be fragrant herbs in English nostrils; we pull them up as weeds. (51)

And just so, when writing "About Warwick," he suggests that "an American cannot but admire the picturesque effect produced by the cropping up of an apparently dead and buried state of society into the actual present, of which he himself is a part" (70); and, per contra, the sudden sound of the railroad unsettling, interrupting a "pleasant kind of dream for an American" who has found "a piece of the sixteenth century set into our prosaic times" (84). Everywhere such nostalgic observations tend to offset the book's sharp political and social criticisms.[11]

The succession of curious if not quite passionate "pilgrimages"—yes, somewhere between Washington Irving and Henry James—is complicated when the chapter which "hardly dare[s] to add [...] to the innumerable descriptions of Stratford-on-Avon" devotes itself to certain "Recollections of a Gifted Woman," namely Delia Bacon, early and eager sponsor of the theory that all those famous plays were written in fact by her

---

10. In "The Author's Account of Himself," Washington Irving grants the sublimity of American scenery, but imagines he will much prefer the "storied" scenes of Europe; see *The Sketchbook of Geoffrey Crayon, Gent.*, in *Irving: History, Tales and Sketches* (New York: Library of America, 1983), p. 744.
11. Oddly, British reviewers tended to focus as much on matters like "the fat English dowager (in 'Leamington Spa')" as on questions of morality and class; see Claude M. Simpson, "Introduction" to Our Old Home (Columbus: Ohio State, 1970), p. xxiii.

own illustrious ancestor. Hawthorne finds Miss Bacon rather more presentable than he had imagined, suggesting that she must have been "exceedingly attractive once"; but though he listens most politely to the voluble presentation of her theory, he regards it as essentially "monomaniac" (106) and can just barely refrain from telling her, in terms that recall Melville's famous review of the Shakespeare in Hawthorne himself, how it really works. Good thing, or this woman with "as princely a spirit as Queen Elizabeth herself […] would at once have motioned me from the room" (107). And so this remarkable recollection continues, balancing an utter disbelief in the Baconian theory with a genuine appreciation of the sort of passion that drove its missionary proponent to research and publication. Earlier, such an obsession might have landed her a place in his "Hall of Fantasy," but here it moves to the poignant report of her feeling a "strange sort of weariness,' a sort of "regret that so stupendous a mission had been imposed on the fragility of a woman" (113). Have Zenobia say this.[12] Of course he could be lying; but maybe Delia Bacon really felt this way.

After this oblique meeting with the great Shakespeare, the next chapter takes us into the space and the moral world of Dr. Samuel Johnson, whose classical conservatism may well have served to temper Hawthorne's romantic tendencies. The pilgrimage takes Hawthorne through Lichfield, where a Gothic Cathedral inspires a momentary meditation on the sense of earthiness rendered so well in "The Hall of Fantasy," struggling with a "half smothered yearning to soar beyond" and attend to something that "whispered deeply of immortality" (125); but the mood passes quickly, and the Hawthorne who was content to let Melville worry that question turns instead to the "intricate and multitudinous adornment that was lavished on the exterior wall" of the cathedral and, significantly, perhaps, to "the empty niches whence statues had been thrown down" (126). Reverence returns, however, as Hawthorne approaches Johnson's birthplace and, after noticing some of the statuary devoted to the man he remembered as weighed down not only with a "weary bulk of flesh, together with [a] ponderous melancholy," he sets out (the next day) "for Uttoxeter, on one of the few purely sentimental pilgrimages that I ever undertook," to stand on the very spot where Johnson had stood, "doing penance for an act of disobedience to his father, committed fifty years before" (132–33). And this memorable homage ends with Hawthorne's discovery that a little boy standing by had never heard that story. Rather like the Salemites who, in "Alice Doane's Appeal," could not "tell, within half a century, so much as the date of the witchcraft delusion."[13] As always, Hawthorne's piety points toward the past.

Moving from a deep psychic instance to something more like a literary subject, a "Pilgrimage to Old Boston" takes us to the church, and to the spot where had stood the vicarage of the man "these English people consider as the founder of our American

---

12. In Chapter XVI of *The Blithedale Romance*, the would-be radical Zenobia suggests that "women possess no rights, […] or, at all events, only little girls and grandmothers would have the force to exercise them."

13. Thus—in a lengthy historical headnote to the redacted tale called "Alice Doane's Appeal"— does Hawthorne's somewhat aggressive Narrator (possibly his recently relinquished "Story-Teller"—lament the historical ignorance of his imagined audience.

Boston" (161); problem is, it takes rather a long, uneventful time to get there; and once arrived we learn little enough about John Cotton, teacher at the New Boston church of John Wilson, the one specifically mentioned in *The Scarlet Letter*, the other an absence powerfully implied. On the way, a palsied old lady whose head shakes as if she were "making a stern and solemn protest" against something or other and causing this imaginative observer to "fancy that it might have had its origin in some unspeakable wrong, perpetrated half a lifetime ago" (141)—Hester Prynne, perhaps, failing to return to the New Boston and lacking the feminist foresight. Another Cathedral, reminding us that we are still reading a journal; a row of houses old enough to have been seen by Mr. Cotton's "own bodily eyes" (157); a look in on the shop of the local bookseller; a brief appreciation of "the interior of St. Botolph's—"very fine and satisfactory, as stately, almost, as a Cathedral" (162); a climb "up, up, up" to the church's tower, then down again, noticing "a bird, which appeared to be at home there, and responded with its cheerful notes to the swell of the organ" and, more to the Puritan point, the places where once had stood two statues, some of Mr. Cotton's parishioners [being] probably responsible for the disappearance of these stone saints" (164). So thinks Larzer Ziff: evidently Hawthorne the moral historian knows more than Hawthorne the tourist is willing to share.[14]

Ecclesiology behind, this pilgrimage ends, far more energetically, with a mixture of deep personal recollection and curious sociological suggestions. Across a river,

> The crooked streets and narrow lanes reminded me much of Hanover-Street, Ann-street, and other portions of the North End of our American Boston, as I remember that picturesque region in my boyish days. It is not unreasonable to suppose that the local habits and recollections of the first settlers may have had some influence on the character of the streets and houses, in the New England metropolis. (164)

Deeper still is the sense of some unbroken connection, marking one important difference between Hawthorne's psychological search for "Home" and Emerson's more sociological investigation of "Traits":

> It is singular what a home-feeling, and a sense of kindred, I derive from this hereditary connection and fancied physiognomical resemblance between the old town and the well-grown daughter, and how reluctant I was, after chill years of banishment, to leave this hospitable place, on that account. (165)

Evidently Hawthorne felt the attraction of real-life England in a way the more ideological Emerson never did.

Even more surprising is the transition from the connection between the two Bostons to the memory of the place to which Hawthorne, like the bad penny, had often found himself returning, and to which he had seemed to bid a full and final farewell in 1850:

---

14. On the question of John Cotton's political naivete, see Larzer Ziff, *The Career of John Cotton* (Princeton, NJ: Princeton University Press, 1962), pp. 51–52.

Moreover, it recalled some of the features of another American town, my own dear native place, when I saw the seafaring people leaning against posts, and sitting on planks, under the lee of ware-houses, or lolling on long-boats, drawn up high and dry, as sailors and old wharf-rats are accustomed to do, in sea-ports of little business. (165)

Had that famous second preface to *The Scarlet Letter* protested too much? Or was it simply that Hawthorne's deep domestic feeling—never merely sentimental, and never fully embodied in a novel—was getting a chance to find expression. As if to say, our hearts were made for something older and more substantial than a mother's dismal attic, or a rented manse, or a fantastical commune. Or indeed a country made up from scratch the day before yesterday. The question comes up again in "A London Suburb," where the Hawthorne family spent their homey and comfortable summers. On this view, the deep subject of the now-reverent, now-caustic *Our Old Home* is the problematic of home as such. England may or may not be "the best of existing nations," but it's been around long enough to feel comfortable.

For an ending—as if embarrassed by the degree of personal exposure—Hawthorne calls up a rather unpleasant street scene of lowing and bleating and pushing and shoving on Old Boston's market-day. But then he balances the real-life scene with the fantasy that the tower of St. Botolph's was looking "benignantly down," bidding him farewell, "as it did to Mr. Cotton, two or three hundred years ago" and urging him, like the ghost in some attic, to remind "the people of the American city" that they are kin "if not to the living inhabitants of Old Boston, yet to some of the dust that lies in the churchyard." And then, finally, as if further to question Americans' foundational belief that they are something entirely new under the sun, the discovery that "they have a Bunker Hill in the vicinity of their town" and that, remarkably, the people there "seem proud to think that their neighborhood has given name to our first, most widely celebrated, and best remembered, battle-field" (166). As some later American in England would yet say, "a complex fate to be an American."

The first thing to say about "Near Oxford" is that we never get that near. The pilgrimage is instead to the famous museum at the Blenheim Palace, passing through a gate, into a garden, and coming at last to "a battlement tower and adjoining house," provoking the suggestion that "If such good fortune ever befell a bookish man, I should choose this lodge for my own residence, with the topmost room of the tower for a study" (170), as if by 1863 this tour guide to Rome and now, with less intensity of literary purpose, to the less dense attractions of England had not already established himself in the absurd tower he added to the Alcott house in Concord.[15] The collection of pictures is judged to be "exceedingly valuable" (173), but more attention is paid to the chapel "where we saw a splendid monument to the first Duke and Duchess, sculptured by Rysback, at the cost,

---

15. Returning to Concord from his extended stay in Europe, Hawthorne "wasted no time in arranging for the expansion of the Wayside"; the new wing included an Italian-style a third-story tower "which Hawthorne planned to use as his study," but which never proved very serviceable; see James R. Mellow, *Nathaniel Hawthorne in His Times* (Boston: Houghton Mifflin, 1980), p. 532.

it is said, of forty thousand pounds" (175). England, it appears, suggests economic considerations more than had Rome; or, perhaps, the wish to be an art critic, along with the will to fiction, had lately lapsed. The fantasy that "a good and happy life might have been spent in a Paradise" like the palace and grounds of Blenheim is ascribed to the mentality of a "Republican" who can yet "love to think that noblemen lead noble lives"; and then the American walking in the footsteps of anglophile Washington Irving confesses that he too is missing some of the big stuff: "all that I have written is pitifully meagre, as a description of Blenheim" (177).

Further peregrinations take the party to some "other places of interest, in the neighborhood of Oxford" (178): I'll be the judge of that, the reader is likely to propose; and the interest picks up only momentarily when the displaced author hears "a gentleman ask a friend of mine whether he was the author of "The Red Letter A'" (181). Only at length, and after a boat ride "upon the Thames, or some other stream" (187) do we find ourselves in the vicinity of Oxford where, in the kitchen of the old family of Harcourt, Hawthorne remembers the vivid description years before by Alexander Pope. Then the obligatory church, then a boat ride "upon the Thames, or some other stream; for I am ashamed to confess my ignorance of the precise geographical whereabout" (187), only that the party was evidently "some miles above Oxford"—past which, on yet another boat, they drift past Christ Church meadows, where "troops of naked boys bathing," as if this were "Arcadia, in the simplicity of the Golden Age." Finally, after a pretty full account of the "table [that] had been laid in the interior of our barge" (190), a formal farewell to Oxford, left undescribed, as "there being no literary faculty, attainable or conceivable by me, which can avail to put it adequately, or even tolerably, upon paper" (181). There used to be a name for the fallacy which says "it must remain its own sole expression," but not, apparently, if you're a very famous writer with a very friendly editor.

But if the wonders of Oxford are left undescribed, the next chapter—"Some of the aunts of Burns"—reminds us that the Romancer obsessed with the geography of guilt narrowing down to the landscape of anxiety is nevertheless pretty good at describing the merely real. Indeed, from the very first, the Notebooks are full of detailed observations that might well have served the Novelist as such; so that the wish to write like Trollope was more than a mid-life fantasy. Off the boat now, and into the streets where walked the second most famous Scot author in Hawthorne's literary background, the details, not always attractive, are all but overwhelming. An example or two will serve.

On the way to the Burns farm, the driver offers Hawthorne the opportunity "devoutly" to pluck a branch from a "hawthorne, growing by the wayside," said to be "Burns' 'Louisa Thorne.'" Then, after the fantasy, the place itself. We then turned into a rude gateway, and almost immediately came to the farm-house of Moss Giel, standing some fifty yards removed from the high-road,

> behind a tall hedge of hawthorne, and considerably overshadowed by trees. The house is a white-washed stone cottage, like thousands of others in England and Scotland, with a thatched roof, on which grass and weeds have intruded a picturesque, though alien growth. There is a door and one window in front, besides another little window that peeps out among the thatch. (201)

As the details pile up, we begin to be aware that, more than any castle or cathedral, this is the sort of shrine that inspires Hawthorne's literary devotion. One remembers Geoffrey Crayon's fear that he might "miss the great objects studied by every regular traveler" and find he had sketched only the "nooks and corners and bye-places." More than that, however, we get a sense of literary devotion and, along with it, a sense that here a literary man had been at home. And so the long paragraph goes right on, bravely sketching "two other buildings of the same size, shape, and general appearance as the house," all three of them looking equally "fit for human habitation" and still "more suitable for donkey-stables." But such is the reality. Nor can a barking dog turn the party away from this "threshold of Robert Burns" (201).

Inside, first, a kitchen: squalor, one gathers, registered by the polite formula of "a deplorable lack of housewifely neatness." Upstairs, even worse: "the wretchedest little sleeping-chamber in the world," probably that of Burns himself. Overall, a "frowzy smell, and also a dunghill odor," making it hard to understand "how the atmosphere of such a dwelling can be any more agreeable or salubrious morally than it appeared to be physically". Indeed, "such a habitation is calculated to make beasts of men and women." And yet not, somehow, of Burns.

> It is sad to think of anybody—not to say a poet, but any human being—sleeping, eating, thinking, praying, and spending his home-life in this miserable hovel; but, methinks, I never in the least knew how to estimate the miracle of Burns' genius nor his heroic merit for being no worse a man, until I thus learned the squalid hindrances amid which he developed himself. (202)

Okay, there's the word: "squalid," the one Sophia felt she needed to remove from her husband's American Notebooks. Did it reflect badly on his mother's housewifely neatness? Or, as Hyatt Waggoner supposed, had it a moral meaning?[16] No need to make the distinction here, as Hawthorne's purified new world imagination has already concluded that "No virgin, surely, could keep a holy awe about her while stowed higgledy-piggledy with coarse-natured rustics into this narrowness and filth" (202). Cleanliness, that is to say, is right next to Puritanism.

No such moralism informs the account of the discovery of Burns' actual birthplace, but the formal registration of literary admiration continues. Currently "a public house," it is kept in good repair, with tables varnished over to erase the scribbled names of visitors, as "a portrait of Burns, copied from the original picture by Nasmyth" (207). One other room, a kitchen, with a new window, "opened through the wall, towards the road,"

> but on the opposite side is the little original window, of only four small panes, through which came the first daylight that shone upon the Scottish poet. At the side of the room, opposite

---

16. See Hyatt H. Waggoner, on moral meaning of "squalid"; see *Hawthorne's Lost Notebook* (State College: Penn. State University Press, 1978), p. 25.

the fire-place, is a recess, containing a bed, which can be hidden by curtains. In that humble nook, of all places in the world, Providence was pleased to deposit the germ of the richest human life which mankind then had within its circumference. (208)

To be sure, there will be no novel incorporating any of this, but who knew?—that the author of "The Holy Fair" (199) and the lover of "Bonny Jean" (205) had made so deep an impression on an American writer who gave up on poetry very early. What if there really was such a thing as "honest poverty"? What if a man really is "a man for a' that and a' that"? Here, at any rate, as at Uttoxeter, the details express the morale of pilgrimage. And—as they're not all buried in the "Poet's Corner"—this one has been an entire success: "We shall appreciate him better as a poet, hereafter. We shall know him in a kind of personal way, as if we had shaken hands with him, and felt the thrill of his actual voice" (212).

Details abound as well in "A London Suburb," but the mood could hardly be more different: the subject is the estate lent to the Hawthorne family in the summers, while their owner spent the season on the continent. Though the author refers to himself and his family as "pilgrims and dusty wayfarers" (214), and though the freeloading Consul himself must at this season make the occasional commute up to London, this highly personal essay is really about home—away from home, perhaps, but evidently the "home feeling" (215) is where you find it. Here, "a particularly delightful abode in the neighborhood of London," a place that was "not only rich in all the material properties of a home, but had also the homelike atmosphere, the household element, which is of too intangible a character to be let even with the most thoroughly furnished lodging-houses" (213). And then the details:

> A friend had given us his suburban residence, with all its convenient elegancies, And snuggeries—its drawing rooms and library, still warm and bright with the recollection of the genial presences that we had known there—its closets, chambers. kitchen, and even its wine-cellar, if we could have availed ourselves of so dear and delicate a trust—its lawn and cosey garden-nooks, and whatever else makes up the multitudinous idea of an English home—

all transferred to the "dusty wayfarers" in question. Refuge indeed from the life of "shivering by hearths which, heap the bituminous coal upon them as we might, no blaze could render cheerful" (213–14). Refuge too, the reader is bound to notice, from the squalor that haunted the poor man Burns; so that, every now and then at least, we are reminded of literary structure as well as of moral texture.

It might be too much to suspect that the sybarite buried (but not too deep) in Hawthorne's nature might well have enjoyed life as a British aristocrat, but it would be too little merely to notice that this once oddly-rooted, then footloose man never did, in his maturity, find himself perfectly at home in the world. But here, almost so:

> Now, at last, we were in a genuine British home, where refined people had just been living their daily life, and had left us a summer's inheritance of slowly ripened days such as a stranger's hasty opportunities so seldom permit him to enjoy. (214)

Borrowed time, of course, like property on loan, but somehow the feeling was there. And somehow we begin to forgive Hawthorne for allowing the vagrant Holgrave to settle down so easily in yet another Pyncheon property; and for renaming (and adding a dumb tower to) a house in Concord. Or else, as a conscientious correctness revives, shall we not observe that Hawthorne's moralistic hatred of poverty did not in every mood lead him on to a suspicion of its relation to the capitalist counterpart?

In any event, the homely mood goes on, insistently—to the point of self-indulgence, one might almost say, as it is hard to imagine an audience for this highly personal reminiscence. Close by to the "vast London whirlpool," Hawthorne imagines himself as having "drifted into a still eddy" where he found "the quiet of my temporary haven more attractive than anything that the great town could offer" (214). Earlier, he confesses, his "unweariable and indiscriminating curiosity" he had immersed himself in "the dream city of my youth"; and, finding it better than the dream, he had come to discover a "home-feeling there, as nowhere else in the world," although, he thinks to add, he "afterwards [...] came to have a somewhat similar sentiment in regard to Rome." He even dares a generalized conclusion: "As long as these two great cities shall exist, the cities of the Past and of the Present, a man's native soil may crumble beneath his feet without leaving him altogether homeless on earth." (215) A bit sententious, perhaps, and not everyone's definition of Citizen of the World, but not bad for the Kid from Salem trying to make a buck in the Business of Literature.

But now he is free of the city, "free to spend a whole summery day in our garden" (217). (What you mean "our," Dusty Wayfarer?) But ah, as the best things in life are free, "Our chief enjoyment was the weather," nothing like it in Italy or America. But also to wander, abroad, but only in the near vicinity of their oasis, "grown up [...] on the wide waste of Blackheath, offering "a vast extent of unoccupied ground in singular proximity to the metropolis" (219–20). There one could wander, as "afterwards [...] on the Campagna of Rome." Here, a proper miscellany: the reassuring sound of police patrols, a sight of "immense London, four or five miles off" (221), cricket matches, enjoyable only to the English and, in the neighborhood, many "other amusements" (222). On to Greenwich Park, not the loveliest in the land, but beautiful enough—"a spot where the art of man has conspired with Nature, as if he and the great mother had taken counsel together how to make a pleasant scene," with the added appeal that "it is a people's property and play-ground in a much more genuine way than the aristocratic resorts in closer vicinity to the metropolis" (223–24). There you find "the people—not the populace," whose Sunday clothes are a distinct kind of garb from their week-day ones. If only one could know them, their households, "their politics, their religion, their tastes, and whether they were as narrow-minded as their betters." But no: amateur sociology can go only so far. Nevertheless,

"An Englishman is English, in whatever rank of life, though no more intensely so, I should imagine, as an artisan or petty shopkeeper than as a member of Parliament" (224)—funky syntax competing with platitudinous redundancy, but it comes with the generic territory.

So too the Emerson-like observation that "The English character [...] is by no means a lofty one," appearing to have "a great deal of earth and grimy dust clinging about them" (224). Witness:

> They adhere closer to the original simplicity in which mankind was created, than we ourselves do; they love, quarrel, laugh, cry, and turn their actual selves inside out, with greater freedom than any class of American would consider decorous. (224–25)

And there they are, in the park, on Sunday, offering "very satisfactory glimpses of Arcadian life among the cockneys [...] picnicking in the grass." One even sees "pairs of love-making youths and maidens, along the sun-streaked avenues." And "herds of deer" that would "nibble a bit of bread out of your hand" (225). Ah yes: simple: natural pleasure, and not the enforced gaiety of Morton's Merry Mount or whatever the hell was being expressed in the hysterical celebration of fiesta in Rome.

Yet Rome comes immediately to mind: "The aspect of Greenwich Park, with all those festal people in it, resembled that of the Borghese gardens under the walls of Rome, or a Sunday or Saint's day." No doubt. No strict Puritan Sabbatarianism in either old country. But then this:

> I am not ashamed to say, it a little disturbed whatever grimy ghost of Puritanic strictness might be lingering in the somber depths of a New England heart, among severe and sunless remembrances of the Sabbaths of childhood, and the pangs of remorse for ill-gotten lessons in the catechism, and for the erratic fantasies or hardly suppressed laughter in the middle of long sermons. (225)

Who knew? The comic regularity of the "Sunday sickness" at Bowdoin argues a certain detachment from the rigors of Christian nurture, as does the knowledge that the parents were something like proto-Unitarian; but evidently it was not all summers running free in Maine.

Not like Holmes comparing latter-day notes with Stowe; or even little Emily Dickinson forbidden to climb for berries; but not nothing, either. Not quite a heart "delicately fried, with brain sauce," but more than we were prepared to expect.[17]

But then, as he reports an occasional attempt "to take the long-hoarded sting out of these compunctious smarts by attending divine service in the open air," the diction indicates that the remorse is less than what a Puritan expert might call conviction; or even compunction. So, occasional attendance at the service in Greenwich Park (225); and we are further assured when, combined with the hot sabbath sun, the "inward flame" of the Methodist minister threatens him with a meltdown. And as if to prove that criticism is not the same as faith, the frank acknowledgment that elsewhere, in cathedrals, he had "never found it possible to give five minutes attention to any other English preaching" (226).

---

17. Introducing his *Mosses from an Old Manse*, Hawthorne promises that this collection will be the last of its sort:

After the Park, Greenwich Hospital, home for men disabled in pursuit or in defense of British empire, with a Painted Hall, filled with portraits of old Admirals who, "if their faces tell truth, must needs have been blockheads" (231)—exception granted to Nelson, "a man of genius" (232)—only superficially rendered in Southey's biography. Here at any rate is "the English capacity for hero-worship full to the brim." Yet even a man "belonging to another parish" is brought to acknowledge "that Nelson expressed his life in a kind of poetry which I had as much right to understand as these burly islanders" (233)—bristling up with the rest when some visitor (not an American, thankfully) offers some disrespect to the portrait.

And then, at large and in conclusion to a long chapter begun in the privacy of home, the memory of a loud and somewhat boisterous fair in the town nearby the park, where the sentient American learned why "Shakespeare, in speaking of a crowd, so often alludes to its attribute of evil odor" (235); where he forgave a petty thief taking only his "pocket-handkerchief," sparing him his "purse" (235–36); and where, on the whole, the man not easily amused admits he is only moderately amused. Least of all by the ever-present "sharp, angry sort of rattle" (236) produced by a small contraption everyone rubs on everyone else's back; not that funny. An elaborate kissing game elicits the prejudicial preference for the "trim little damsels of my native land" to England's "country-lasses, of sturdy and wholesome aspect, with coarse-grained, cabbage-rosy cheeks" (240): Puritanism is next to Anorexia, just ask Emily Dickinson.[18] And then to the conclusion that, so far as sexual mores are concerned, "the England of today is the unscrupulous old England of Tom Jones and Joseph Andrews, Humphrey Clinker and Roderick Random" (241). Are the Americans better? Well they had better be, "because, making higher pretension, or, at all events more carefully hiding what may be amiss, we are either better than they, or necessarily a good deal worse" (242).

Finally, as if to prove that Romancers can somewhere still be moralists, a sober meditation of that old scarlet problem of sex and privacy:

> It impressed me that their open avowal and recognition of immoralities served to throw the disease to the surface, where it might be more effectually dealt with, and leave the sacred interior not utterly profaned, instead of turning its poison back among the inner vitalities of the character at the imminent risk of corrupting them all. (242)

What? No matter—as "these English are certainly a franker and simpler people than ourselves, from peer to peasant" and—more on this later—"they owe those manly qualities to a coarser grain in their nature, and, with a finer one in ours, we shall ultimately acquire a marble-polish of which they are unsusceptible" (242). Prejudicial, puritanical,

---

18. For samples of Dickinson's problematic relation to food, see "I had been Hungry" Johnson (240/579), "It would have starved a Gnat" (254/612), and "God gave a Loaf" (323/719); see Thomas H. Johnson, *Final Harvest* (Boston: Little, Brown, 1964). One often suspects even Emerson, who faithfully reports in "Experience" that, unlike himself, the Children of Nature do not "weigh their food"; see Joel Porte, ed., *Emerson: Essays and Lectures* (New York: Library of America, 1983), p. 481.

a little prim—and a strange enough ending for a chapter that began with domestic satisfaction of a blissful suburban precinct. Has Hawthorne stayed too long at the fair? Or would the increasingly conservative author of *The Blithedale Romance* be suggesting that, in the home or in the village square, human sexuality turns out to be simply irregular, but that sublimation is nevertheless the basis of culture?

Now where to? Starting out from "the upper portion of Greenwich," where the last article had left the author "loitering," the inland voyage called "Up the Thames" quickly leaves the "cheerful, comely, old-fashioned town" (243) and introduces us to some pretty disagreeable sights and sounds; so that if we know that what comes next are some "Outside Glimpses of English Poverty," we may well sense some sort of a "turn"—not unlike the one in Emerson's *English Traits*, where the studious spiritual sympathizer turns abruptly into the harshest social critic. No more Mr. Nice Guy, as the steamers which "offer much the most agreeable mode of getting up to London [...] might be exceedingly agreeable, except for the myriad floating particles of soot from the stove-pipe," and…well, a very long list of inconveniences, including the crowds that barely allow you "standing room" and the constant "possibility of getting your pocket picked" (243–44). Still, "The panorama along the shores of the memorable river [...] render the trip far preferable to the brief, yet tiresome shoot along the railway-track" (244). Memorable, perhaps, but not entirely edifying.

Unprepared for an eventual and very respectful account of Westminster Abbey, a place Hawthorne says he "had dreamed about more reverentially, from [his] childhood, than any other in the world" (264)—or for the more than dutiful homage offered to some of the writers buried there—the first-time reader will be struck by the extremely negative tone with which the sketch begins: so much hostility compressed into so short a voyage. First of all, ugliness—"as if the heart of London had been cleft open for the mere purpose of showing how rotten it had become." Indeed, one knowing "nothing more of the world's metropolis" might well have a sense of the "downfall [...] commercial and financial prophets predict." The river itself, no better:

> And the muddy tide of the Thames. Reflecting nothing, and hiding a million of unclean secrets within its breast—a sort of guilty conscience, as it were, unwholesome with the rivulets of sin that constantly flow into it—it is just the dismal stream to glide by such a city. (245)

And after ugliness, incompetence—five pages on the grotesque financial failure of the brilliantly engineered tunnel under the river. The Yankee instinct for "trying to endow the unfortunate result with some kind of usefulness" (248) might repurpose the thing as a dungeon, but in fact "this mighty piece of work" appears to provide nothing but "new sites for a few old women to sell cakes and ginger-beer" (247).

Then a sudden shift of perspective, geographic as well as moral, reminding us that in the year of publication America is also a disaster. More bitter than anything in "Chiefly about War Matters," it is worth quoting at length.

> Could I have looked forward a few years, I might have regretted that American Enterprise had not provided a similar Tunnel, under the Hudson or the Potomac, for

the convenience of our National Government in times hardly yet gone by. It would have been delightful to clap up all the enemies of our peace and union in the dark together, and there let them abide, listening to the monotonous roll of the river above their heads, or perhaps in a state of miraculous suspended animation, until [...] when the turmoil shall be all over, the Wrong washed away in blood, [...] and the Right firmly rooted in the soil which that blood will have enriched, they might crawl forth again and catch a single glimpse at their redeemed country, and feel it to be a better land than they deserve and die. (250–51)

Still, in the interest of fairness and balance, the notice returns to England, to its fabled Tower, and to a complex meditation on England and America, also worth quoting at length.

Passing the Traitor's Gate many times, I never observed that anybody glanced at this shadowy and ominous trap-door, save myself. It is well that America exists, if it were only that her vagrant children may be impressed and affected by the historical monuments on England in a degree of which the native inhabitants are evidently incapable. These matters are too familiar, too real, and too hopelessly built in amongst and mixed up with the common objects and affairs of life, to be easily susceptible of imaginative coloring in their minds; and even their poets and romancers feel it a toil, and almost a delusion, to exact poetic material out of what seems embodied poetry itself to an American. (253)

Elsewhere, famously, Hawthorne will—almost seriously—regret that America has no long, storied monumental past. Here the problem seems a bit more complex: familiarity breeds, well, familiarity.

Arriving at London Bridge and boarding another steamer, we encounter a different mood entirely: "Whitefriars, the old rowdy Alsatia" and, adjoining it, "the avenues and brick squares of the Temple," "Somerset House, and further on, the two new Houses of Parliament" (254); Close by, a "glimpse of the roof and upper towers of the holy Abbey" and, on the opposite side of the river, Lambeth Palace. End of trip, Chelsea, with "some famous gardens" and "Chelsea Hospital" (255), where one of the "gray veterans [...] touched his three-cornered hat and asked if I wished to see the interior" (255–56). A chapel, with "trophies of battles," including flags, one American, "taken at [...] Washington" (256), suggesting that "a good method of teaching a man how imperfectly cosmopolitan he is, [is] to show him his country's flag occupying a position of dishonor in a foreign land." Still, "the whole system of a people crowing over its military triumphs" (257) is one this Peaceable Man takes pains to prophesy against. Then the famous Crystal Palace: redundantly described elsewhere, the Dusty Pilgrim's refrains, suggesting instead that "the chief delight" of this sort of travel literature is "not for any real information that it supplies to untraveled people, but for the recollections and reawakenings of emotions of persons already acquainted with the scenes described; cf. "Mr. Tuckerman's 'month in England'" (259).

But no such diffidence restrains the sixteen or so pages lavished on the site and on the associations of Westminster Abbey. Though coyly introduced by a passage "through a side-entrance in the time-blackened wall of a place of worship" (259), and featuring a "puny" voice preaching a puny sermon, the power of the place suddenly erupts: voice and thought seem "impertinent at such a time and place."

> The structure itself was the worship of the devout men of long ago, miraculously preserved in stone without losing an atom of its fragrance and fervor. It was a kind of anthem-strain that they had sung and poured out of an organ in centuries gone by, and being so grand and sweet, the Divine benevolence had willed it to be prolonged for the behoof of auditors unborn. (260)

Better, therefore, to look and not to listen to the "evidently uninspired mortal who was venturing—and felt it no venture at all—to speak here above his breath" (260).

A brief overall description ends with the suggestion that "it is the test of Gothic sublimity to overpower the Ridiculous without deigning to hide it" (261)—rather like the Romance, which trembles always "on the brink of an absurdity." Then a focus on "what was immediately about me in the transept," namely statues: Canning, nearest, others of various levels of distinction, most removed by art "as far from the aspect of ordinary life as possible." Exception: "Mr. Wilberforce, whose actual self, save for the lack of color, I seemed to behold, seated just across the aisle" (263). Ah yes, how do you get marble to represent a person of color? And then a timely mock-apology for having "lapsed into [a] mood of half-jocose criticism" the spot so long revered. Still, he reasons, the thought that the place is grand—one might almost say self-reliant enough—to permit a variety of moods: the "mild awfulness will take care of itself" (264). Divine service—remember that?—many worshipers "linger in the nave or wander away among the mysterious aisles," when the critic *malgre lui* finds his "foot upon a stone, inscribed with this familiar exclamation—O RARE BEN JOHNSON" (265–66). And that provokes the recollection of "many other days" when the passionate-enough pilgrim had sought out Poet's Corner" (266).

And there they were: Jonson, Spenser, Butler, Milton, Gray "and many other sculptured marbles"—and how very reminiscent:

> It seemed to me that I had always been familiar with the spot. Enjoying a humble intimacy—and how much of my life had else been a dreary solitude!—with many of its inhabitants, I could not feel myself a stranger there. It was delightful to be among them. (267)

So many of them there, together, duly recognized and as it were reconciled, "whatever personal hostility or other miserable impediment, had divided them far asunder while they lived." For Hawthorne, this is the only sort of really valuable memorial as "We neither remember nor care anything for the past, except as the poet has made it intelligibly noble and sublime to our comprehension." Upping the ante on Irving's sense of the "storied," and dismissing other sorts of fame, he emphatically continues:

> The shades of the mighty have no substance; they flit ineffectually about the darkened stage where they performed their momentary parts, save when the poet has thrown his own creative soul into them, and imparted a more vivid life than ever they were able to manifest to mankind, while they dwelt in the body. And therefore—though he cunningly disguises himself in their armor, their robes of state, or kingly purple—it is not the statesman, the warrior,

or the monarch that survives, but the despised poet whom they may have fed with their crumbs. (267)

Or their political appointments? To be sure, Hawthorne's reputation as an early Master of American literature will survive even if the Correctness Police tear down his statue in the village square in Salem; but will we not also remember his tendency to bite the hand that fed?

So we get a brief mock-apology for the outburst, and then, passing from Poet's Corner into the chapels, which contain the sepulchers of Kings and great people, a recognition that "this recondite portion of the abbey presents few memorials of personages who we care to remember" (267–68). Edward the Confessor might matter but otherwise "Rank has been the general passport to admission here," and Addison is there for that reason, "not on the plea of his literary fame" (268). Doing his best to appreciate what British culture has sought to memorialize in its past, this accomplished moral historian of early America, living to become a Citizen of Somewhere Else, finds himself most at home in the company of canonical writers in English.

Accordingly, back in Poet's Corner, he finds himself wondering if the crowded space of this spacious Abbey can find room for "poets of our own and the succeeding ages"—especially as "men of other pursuits have thought it decent to intrude themselves" into "this small nook of sanctity" (269). Brooking no toleration even for the idea of a holy war, this eager aspirant seems here quite comfortable with the idea of literary sainthood; and so he is willing to question some of the literary inclusions, for "to confess the very truth, their own little nook contains more than one poet whose memory is kept alive [solely] by his monument." As if the "divinest poets who consecrate the spot and throw a reflected glory over the humblest of their companions" had been in it for their "posthumous renown" (269). Still,

> We cannot easily rid ourselves of the notion that those, who have bequeathed us the inheritance of undying song, would fain be conscious of its endless reverberations in the hearts of mankind, and would delight, among sublime enjoyments, to see their names emblazoned in such a treasure-place of great memories as Westminster Abbey. (270)

For example, Leigh Hunt might "be pleased, even now, if he could learn that his bust had been reposited in the midst of the old poets whom he admired and loved" (270). And so, after a word of praise for the man's "unmeasured poetry"—literary theory giving place to personal memory—this almost religious chapter ends with a long account of Hawthorne's first interview with the "beautiful old man" Leigh Hunt (271).

And then, a turn most severe. Contrasting with the reverent account of Westminster Abbey, but well prepared for by the ugly boat trip up the Thames, the "Outside Glimpses of English Poverty" finds the well-established "inhabitant of a great English town" turning aside from the "prosperous thoroughfares" and wandering into places that remind him of "some of Dickens' grimiest pages." The first result, a Philosophy of Dirt: an unremovable mark of the fallen human condition, but English poverty abuses the privilege; and for the first of several times the unstrung American, used to the relative cleanliness of the well-regulated towns, prays for a new Deluge, as "nothing less than such a general washing-day could suffice to cleanse the slovenly old world of its moral and material dirt" (278). And after that, the most devastating attack on the underside of England's imperial wealth since a certain chapter in Melville's *Redburn*. Unforgiving and, in its length, unremitting, yet yielding to a surprising religious meditation.

Gin shops and pawn-brokers are bad enough, but the ambient population makes things worse. Creeping forth from "the foul misery of their interiors," they gather in the streets as if in a "common hall,"—women and children, mostly, the condition of these latter almost mak[ing] a man doubt the existence of his own soul, to observe how Nature has flung these little wretches into the street and left them there, so

> evidently regarding them as nothing worth, and how all mankind acquiesce in the great mother's estimate of her offspring. (282)

Without some "infinite faith," one as easily believes "a blessed futurity for [the] hideous bugs and many-footed worms" crawling about "as for these brethren of our humanity" (282). There may be dramatization here, allegory, even, but no hyperbole. Well removed from the reassuring cleanliness of the New England village, a faith that had survived even Melville's despair was fighting for its fragile life.

> Ah, what a mystery! Slowly, slowly, as after groping at the bottom of a deep, noisome, stagnant pool, my hope struggles upward to the surface, bearing the half-drowned body of a child along with it, and heaving it aloft for its life, and all our lives here. (282)

Immortality? How very unlikely. And yet

> Unless these slime-clogged nostrils can be made capable of inhaling celestial air,
> I know not how the purest and most intellectual of us can reasonably expect ever to taste a breath of it. The whole question of eternity is staked there. If a single one of those helpless little ones be lost, the world is lost. (282)

Elsewhere—in the Elixir of Life manuscripts—the issue might be just longer lives for those who have something to contribute; but here we encounter, unabashed, the man who once proposed that "Nothing, not God himself, can compensate us for being born for a single moment short of all eternity." No wonder Melville remembered Hawthorne as more doubtful and less composed than he often seemed.[19]

---

19. Though the editor of a recent edition of Melville's poetry disputes the received claim that Melville's "Monody" (1864) is necessarily about Hawthorne, the identification, in *Clarel*, of Vine with Hawthorne (as of Rolfe with Melville himself) seems well established; there, the character whom Clarel and Rolfe have observed as bored and generally superior, confident, and self-assured, is seen, alone, to be "quivering" and, in the word of Walter E. Bezanson, appears simply "scared"; see the Introduction to *Clarel: A Poem and a Pilgrimage* (New York: Hendricks House, 1960), p. xcvi; and more recently, cp. Herschel Parker, *Herman Melville: A Biography*,

But the moment does not last. The issue of the cleanliness that is right next to Puritanism returns with the observation of mothers on doorsteps "nursing their unwashed babies," and with it the equally puritanic need to glance aside from the nursing bosoms—for the sake of all womanhood, because "the fairest spectacle is here the foulest" (282–83). Then, in the man whose fallen Puritan woman reminded him of the Virgin Mother of Jesus, some natural faith revives: "Yet motherhood, in these dark abodes, is strangely identical with all we have known it to be in the happiest homes"; so that, though this privileged observer may smile to hear "a gaunt and ragged mother priding herself on the ways of her ragged and skinny infant," he is nevertheless constrained to admit that "no womanly characteristic seemed to have altogether perished out of these poor souls" (283). And the debate continues: on the one hand he wants to believe that "there were laws of intercourse which they never violated"; but on the other he remembers "how rude and rough these specimens of the feminine generally were," reminding him of "Molly Seagrim and other heroines in Fielding's novels" (283–84).

And on it goes, reminding us that Puritan Cleanliness is right next to what we used to call Purity. Some of the young women achieve, in their shabby garb, a grace entirely absent in women who court fashion. Or, one sees a woman

> knitting or sewing on her door-step, just as fifty other women were; but round about her skirts (though woefully patched) you would be sensible of a certain sphere of decency, which, it seemed to me, could not have been more impregnable in the cosiest little sitting-room. (286)

Then too—as a certain obsession with the quality of female sexuality continues to complicate this outward but curious, near-prurient glimpse of English poverty—

> Maidenhood had a similar power. The evil habit that grows upon us in this harsh world makes me faithless to my own better perceptions; and yet I have seen girls in these wretched streets, on whose virgin purity, judging merely from my instincts as they passed by, I should have deemed it safe, at the moment, to stake my life. The next moment, however, as the surrounding flood of moral uncleanness surged over their footsteps, I would not have staked a spike of thistle-down on the same wager. (286)

Too much of this clearly: where was the Sophia who red-penciled the notebooks' notice of women's upper arms?

And yet so much appears to depend on this undecidable question. Unable to embarrass itself, the outside glimpse of the sexual mores of young British girls of the lowest urban class presses on: "The miracle was within the scope of Providence." And:

> Unless your faith be deep-rooted and of the most vigorous growth, it is the safer way not to turn into this region so suggestive of miserable doubt. It was a place "with dreadful faces thronged," wrinkled and grim with vice and wretchedness (286)—

Volume 2 (Baltimore, MD: Johns Hopkins University Press, 2002), pp. 780–82; and Robert Milder, *Hawthorne's Habitations* (New York: Oxford University Press, 2013), pp. 233–34.

leaving this miserable doubter to imagine that those faces appearing to Adam and Eve were not "fiends from the pit" but the "more terrible foreshadowings of what so many of their descendants were to be." And yet, for all this outside observer can perceive, most pitiable of all was "the sort of patience with which they accepted their lot, as if they had been born into the world for that and nothing else" (287). Indeed, blue-eyed but aging Nathaniel, had better look elsewhere for supports to a failing faith in life eternal.

Much more remains of these glimpses, but the rest are somewhat less personally revealing—children, whose sense of duty promises well for their salvation; beggars, once again, whose unfamiliarity to Americans makes them rather easy prey; and then, in a section all to itself, a look into the sort of "home provided for the inhabitants at public expense." Fearing they must be utterly "comfortless," Hawthorne is surprised to see "what an orderly, full-fed, sufficiently reposeful life" seemed there to be led, he can conclude that it is "that very orderliness, and the cruel necessity of being neat and clean" that, compared to the houses, gave the streets their advantage of a certain "charm," like "the life of the forest or the prairie" (293). Then too, he supposes, there must be difficulties in getting oneself admitted. In any case, the women, though more quarrelsome than the men, and forbidden or without the means "to follow out their natural instinct of adorning themselves" (295) seemed well cared for, and their sleeping-chambers exhibited "the beauty of perfect neatness and orderliness." But the laundry, "vaporous with steam of wet garments and bedclothes," proves more than one had bargained for and offers more than one touch of nature.

> This atmosphere was the pauper-life of the past week or fortnight resolved into a gaseous state, and breathing it, however fastidiously, we were forced to inhale the strange element into our inmost being. Had the queen been there, I know not how she could have escaped the necessity. What an intimate brotherhood is this in which we dwell, do what we may to put an artificial remoteness between the high creature and the low one! (299)

Powerful to produce a democratic moral, it also prompts a complaint we have heard before: "How superficial are the niceties of such as pretend to keep aloof!" You mean, even Victoria poops? Then "let the whole world be cleansed, or not a man or woman of us all can be clean" (299). Not even a Puritan from Massachusetts.

Aware that Roman Catholicism and Roman Carnival taught this legitimate son of New England something he did not much want to know about the universality of love and sex and death, one is tempted to suggest that this immersion in nothing more than the outside of urban poverty taught him even more about the way of all flesh. How very pure had been his fictions. How allegorical, even when deconstructive. How utterly abstract. Yet the confession has its own redeeming honesty, as one is forced to conclude that, unlike a more famous evocation of "Life among the Lowly," the distressing revelations here know themselves as an "outside" view. Bobby Burns lived in a hovel. Almshouse laundry smells bad. But what can it have been like within the walls of the ragged women who nursed their ragged offspring in the street?

Redemption there may or may not be, but for the born writer there had to be at least the sense of an ending. Not the differently abled little boy whose pathetic insistence forced the institution's governor to take up the "loathsome child" and caressed it "as tenderly as if he had been its father's" (301). Not the sight of the woman "holding a baby, which, beyond all reach of comparison, was the most horrible object that ever afflicted [his] sight.

> It seemed to lie on the floor of my heart, polluting my moral being with the sense of something grievously amiss in the entire conditions of humanity. The holiest man could not be otherwise than full of wickedness, the chastest virgin seemed impure, in a world where such a babe was possible. (303)

Ah, yes, the lurking "something, somehow like original sin"—or something worse, only partlyrelieved by the information that it was the child of "unhealthy parents." Say it, then: "Diseased Sin was its father and Sinful Disease its mother." Yet no Allegory can blur the memory of eyes that, "seemed to stare at the bystanders out of their sunken sockets knowingly and appealingly, as is summoning us one and all to witness the deadly wrong of its existence" (303). A challenge to faith more deadly than anything faced by Goodman Brown or those quarreling with God at some blasphemous Christmas Banquet, but somehow he cannot simply look away from the face of temptation.

The "school-rooms" are slightly less depressing, but after discovering "only a single child that looked healthy," the utterly "depressed" observer can only repeat his wish for "a new Deluge." And then this well contrived blasphemy:

> So far as these children are concerned, [...] it would be a blessing to the human race, which they will contribute to enervate and corrupt—a greater blessing to themselves, who inherit no patrimony but disease and vice, and if there be a spark of God's life, this seems the only possible mode of keeping it a-glow—if every one of them could be drowned tonight, by their best friends, instead of being put tenderly to bed. (304)

Of course we have no right. But no solution in "Providence" (305) suggests itself. And nothing in a "bake-house" or the "brew-house," or a "tailor's shop," or a "shoe-maker's shop" can turn the tide of this mortal blackness.

What finally ends this descent into gloom is the memory of two weddings, both in the "black and grim old [...] Cathedral at Manchester" (306–7), the first of some "poor English people" (306–7), attended by "the mere rags and tatters of the human race" (307), the other "not very long afterwards," featuring

> a bridal party coming down the steps towards a carriage with four horsemen, with a portly coachman and two postillions, that waited at the gate. One parson and one service had amalgamated the wretchedness of a score of paupers; a Bishop and three or four clergymen had combined their spiritual might to forge the golden links of this other marriage bond. (308)

No mention of the prospects of the first couple: evidently the life of poverty already glimpsed. Of the other, this happy evocation:

> They were going to live on their abundance in one of those stately and delightful English homes, such as no other people ever created or inherited, a hall set far and safe within its own private grounds, and surrounded with venerable trees, shaven lawns, rich shrubbery, and trimmest pathways, the whole so artfully contrived and tended that summer rendered it a paradise, and even winter could hardly disrobe of its beauty. (309)

Not at all unlike, the reader may remember, the one some British Aristocrat had offered on summer loan to the Visiting Writer and Part-Time Democrat. But no guilty pang as yet.

And certainly none from the couple whose right to luxury seems almost as divine as that of the monarch to inherit the throne.

> All this fair property seemed more exclusively and inalienable their own, because of the descent through many forefathers, each of whom had added an improvement or a charm, and thus transmitted it with a stronger stamp of rightful possession to his heir. (309)

Then this, from the man who, finding out the flaw in the deed to "Pyncheon House," wondered aloud if property were not something like theft:[20]

> And is it possible, after all, that there may be a flaw in the title-deeds? Is, or is not, the system wrong that gives one married pair so immense a superfluity of luxurious home, and shuts out a million others from any home whatever? (309)

Welcome, Hawthorne—and better late than never—to this rude introduction to the way the other way-more-than-other-half lives.

Elsewhere, Emerson, who lived through the threat of some red revolutions on his visit to England in the 1840s, would do much to identify and discredit the "piratical" origins of the aristocracy in England. But Hawthorne, always the avowed if often ironic Democrat, sounds like the man who, born elsewhere, might have ended up a Marxist:

> On day or another, safe as they deem themselves, and safe as the hereditary temper of the people really tends to make them, the gentlemen of England will be compelled to face this question. (309)

Faith shaken, or faith surviving, the man who tried hard to detect the immortal soul in the filthy faces and tattered rags of some utterly unexpected sub-proletariat, ends with something like a threat to the "gentlemen of England." And now, thus prepared, a glimpse into their confident and well-fed world.

---

20. See Chapter Eleven in this volume, esp. pp. 193–214.

Assuming Hawthorne had read and nourished the magazine pieces Melville had dashed off, brilliantly, in the several years before his final, revealing interview with his mid-life mentor in Liverpool, it makes some sense to propose that the last two chapters of *Our Old Home* are imitating the order while revising the emphasis of "Poor Man Pudding" and "Rich Man's Crumbs." With a memory of "The Paradise of Bachelors" added in for good measure. In "Pudding," an observer slightly more sensitive than a friend who thinks the American poor do all right all by themselves—learning, for example, to turn the snow that would freeze them in a "Poor Man's Manure"—visits the cottage of a rural family certifiably poor. The scene is altogether more cleanly than that of a London Street, but to the reader at least the scene is hardly less edifying: the woman who serves what *they* do not call a "poor man's pudding" mourns the death of several children and, unaware of the algebraic logic of Thomas Robert Malthus, she has for comfort only the counterintuitive piety of Phillip Doddridge.[21] In "Crumbs," the same experimenter finds himself suitably instructed in the rare charity that permits, indeed encourages, the hand-to-mouth population of the London streets to feast on the left-overs from a banquet very like the ones Hawthorne is irreverently recalling. Having moved the scene of poverty from the compulsive neatness of the New England cottage to the compelled squalor of the London streets, Hawthorne takes us into the bloated and gourmandish world from which the crumbs are permitted to, well, "trickle down," as we might say. After Poverty at its most wretched, Wealth in its civil sacrament.

With this semi-blasphemous beginning: how can an Englishman "reconcile himself to any future state of existence, from which the earthly institution of Dinner shall be excluded"? Years ago, in "The Hall of Fantasy," one of Hawthorne's half-serious narrators has protested against a futurity from which all manner of earthiness has been eliminated. But this is quite different: the "fragrance of flowers," the "cheerful glow of the fireside," the "country frolics" are in no way linked to "Church and State"; the English Dinner is, by contrast, a civil and political rather than merely a natural event. Melville had made it seem a curious affair of gay bachelor-lawyers. Hawthorne shows it as a National Cultural Treasure, almost a sacrament: "Dinner has a kind of sanctity quite independent of the dishes [...] upon the table; so that if it be only a mutton-chop, they treat it with due reverence." And it makes them fat. Learning to distrust "appetite," Americans remain thin; but then, on their puritanic side of the water, "people never dine." Indeed, "the highest possible dinner has never yet been eaten in America" (311).

Not that all the English dine this way: the "unpolishable ruggedness of the national character is still an impediment to them." And actually, our *gourmet malgre lui* can remember "only a single dinner" he would judge "a perfect work of art." Sad, though, that the growth of all the ages, which appeared to have been ripening for this hour,

---

21. The "Doddridge" mentioned in "Poor Man's Pudding" (PMP) is the author of the very popular (and perhaps consoling) work entitled *The Rise and Progress of Religion in the Soul* (1744); for the significance of Thomas Robert Malthus in PMP, see Beryl Roland, "Sitting Up with a Corpse," *American Studies*, 6.1 (1972), pp. 69–83.

since man first began to eat and to moisten his foods with wine [...] must lavish its happiness upon so brief a moment, when other beautiful things can be made a joy forever.

Especially as "a dinner like this is no better than we can get, any day, at the rejuvenescent Cornhill Coffee-house" (312–13). As Keats appeared to know.

Wait!—that was a digression; the point was "to give a slight idea of those public, or partially public banquets, the custom of which so thoroughly prevails among the English people." Not "merely occasional, but of stated recurrence in all considerable municipalities and associated bodies" (313). They *dine*, therefore they are. In a civil and social sense. Accordingly, "The Mayor's dinner-parties occur as often as once a fortnight" (317). And the first of these attended by the rather fastidious American observer included "two Judges and a good many lawyers" (318): but some others as well, or the affair might have collapsed into the broad satire of Melville's "Paradise of Bachelors." No, the abstemious American is trying to be fair:

> what can be prettier than a snow-white table-cloth, a huge heap of flowers as a central decoration, bright silver, rich china, crystal glasses, decanters of Sherry at due intervals, a French roll and an artistically folded napkin at each plate[?]. (321)

Still, having eaten in moderation, he has "the great pleasure in seeing the Englishmen toil toward the end"; and drinking too, with a "taste in wines [...] not exquisite" but without the "foppery of an intimate acquaintance with rare vintages." And, also to their credit, they know enough "not to fill [their] glass too often" (322).

> Be that as it may, the dinner offered an opportunity of "conversation"—called "pleasant" but leaving one to wonder. On the one side, a lawyer "expatiated with great unction on the social standing of the Judges" (322). A vital topic to every American, clearly. On the other, a thick-set, middle-aged man, uncouth in manners, and ugly where none was handsome, with a dark, roughly hewn visage that looked grim in repose, and seemed to hold within itself the machinery of a very terrific frown. He ate with resolute appetite, and let slip few opportunities of imbibing whatever liquids happened to be passing by. (323)

Wonderful: like sitting next to a sweaty fat man on an airplane. And yet, surprisingly, the two diners appear to hit it off: all at once "this grisly featured table-fellow turned to me with a surly sort of kindness, and invited me to take a glass of wine." One touch of nature, and "We began a conversation that abounded, on his part, with sturdy sense, and, somehow [...] brought me closer to him than I had yet stood to an Englishman." Not appearing to be a "scholar of accurate training, yet he seemed to have all the resources of education and trained intellectual power at command" (323–24). Introducing himself as "Sergeant Wilkins," he turns out to be "one of the prominent men of the English bar, and a terribly strong champion in criminal cases," and he impresses his surprised admirer as "not rich in attractive qualities," yet possessed of "the most attractive one of all—Manhood" (324).

Cloth removed, more drinking follows, toasts to "Our gracious Sovereign," and, almost spontaneously, a heartfelt rendition of "God Save the Queen"—expressing a complex, capacious "sentiment of Loyalty" an American can scarcely imagine. This one responds with a "superior" smile, but suggests that we lose something by "caring no more about our President than for a man of straw, or a stuffed scarecrow straddling in a cornfield." On the other hand, however, it seemed "ludicrous"—

> to see this party of stout, middle-aged and elderly gentlemen, in the fullness of meat and drink, their ample and ruddy faces glistening with wine, perspiration, and enthusiasm, rumbling out those strange old stanzas from the very bottom of their hearts and stomachs, which two organs, in the English interior arrangement, lie closer than in ours. (325)

And somehow, "the rudest old ditty in the world" had found a way to express the national faith in the "Almighty's [...] respect for that redoubtable little island," including "His presumed readiness to strengthen its defense against the contumacious wickedness and knavery of all other principalities or republics." Not that America itself had no civil religion, just not the civic occasion. Nor yet so simple a song—the equal of which "Tennyson himself" (325) could not produce.

More toasts, to "the great institutions and interests of the country" (326), all fatuous enough, and then, surprisingly, an authoritative call for a public performance by the American guest. "It's a nothing," assures the Sergeant; "A mere acknowledgment," the less said, the better. Then perhaps they would like it best if he "said nothing at all": so much for American civic intelligence. But no, if the "gentle reader" desires it, here's the account, offered "quite as indifferently as if it concerned another person." As indeed it does, for "it was not I in my proper and natural self, that sat there at the table or subsequently rose to speak" (328). Once again, the familiar dissociation: I write (or I meditate a possible fiction), therefore I am; but someone else stands up to speak. So—after the Mayor waxes friendly and the band plays "Hail Columbia"—which could easily have been "'God Save the Queen' over again," and the fellow diners cry "Hear," he manages something or other. Or, rather, "Nothing," as the Sergeant had said. But then how explain "the sound of my own voice, which I had never before heard at such a declamatory pitch, and which impressed me as belonging to some other person." Yet somebody or other "sat down amid great applause" and to Sergeant Wilkins' assurance that it was all "handsomely done" (329).

Enough of this would have been quite enough, but prudence—and some awareness of the "the necessity of an office which I had voluntarily taken on my shoulders"— required some uneasy preparations for the future. And also, it appears, a home-made theory of oratory: any half-wit can learn it, and only a

> true man [...] can keep his own elevated conception of truth when the lower feeling of a multitude is assailing his natural sympathies, and he who can speak out frankly the best there is in him, when by adulterating it a little, or a good deal, he knows that he may make it ten times as acceptable to the audience. (330)

Ah, yes, hell is other people. And, as we have heard more recently, so much for the primacy of speech over writing. The writer, it appears, is freer to invent an audience, tell the truth, and hope for the best. So we like Nathaniel Hawthorne better than Daniel Webster.

The last part of Hawthorne's "slight article on the civic banquets of England" is given over to "an attempted description of a Lord Mayor's dinner at the Mansion House." Better might have been "the annual feast at the Guildhall" (331), but no such luck. A physical description is provided, but the primary interest here, for Hawthorne and probably for us, is "the presence of ladies"—principally, he assumes, "the wives and daughters of city-magnates" (333), who provide an opportunity for the American moralist to confess that he has been revising his sense of comparative female attraction. Once the "meagerness (Heaven forbid that [he] call it scrawniness!)" characteristic of the women of New England had seemed all but normative; call them angels. Recently, however, certain "English ladies, looked at from a lower point of view," have come to seem "perhaps a little finer animals than they"—something to do with "a few additional lumps of clay on their shoulders and other parts of their figures" (334). (Help, Sophia!—he's doing it again.)

Turtle soup—and a theory of the function of the "bill of fare" (335) in the practice of execution of British "gourmandism" interrupts this episode of belated gender education, but the inhibited connoisseur of feminine pulchritude cannot fail to notice, opposite him "a young lady in white" whose "supereminence in beauty" (336) he is tempted to describe; but no, she would be recognized. So too the ugly man by her side. Why, yes, "Any child would have recognized them at a glance [...], Bluebeard and a new wife." And a finer masculine intelligence can detect, already, "a mysterious gloom overshadowing her fair young brow." But then "dessert" and a "silver basin [...] of rose-water" interrupt the emerging melodrama. So too, understandably, does the notice of "a man in armor, with a helmet on his head, standing behind the Lord Mayor's chair, himself to be replaced by "another official personage" whose mission was to make "a solemn and sonorous proclamation" identifying the "principal guests" (337).

And then—what else?—the Lord Mayor drinks from and proceeds to pass around the "Loving Cup," which passage leaves the entire company "inextricably intertwisted and entangled in one complicated chain of love" (338). The American guest notices that the "antique and richly ornamented silver goblet" holds about a "quart of wine, of which no one drinks very deeply": was it "fastidious repugnance to so many compotators in one cup" (as Judas murmured to Philip before leaving the party) or merely a comment on the just quality of the wine? Quite possible the latter, as the visitor's "honest sip" reveals it to be "Claret of a poor quality, largely mingled with water, and spiced and sweetened" (338–39). Except for this rare display of lingual discrimination, the American bias is evident in the diction: Emerson knows the word "intwisted," but not "intertwisted"; and no one I know has ever said the word "compotator." Unless they were throwing potatoes on the compost heap. Ceremony is important, and love is more forgiving than social satire, but leave the cup in church already.

Still, lest what goes without saying go all unsaid, something a little more explicit: the toasts were just as boring as "the specimens of table-eloquence" aforesaid. Except for the "maiden oratory" of a "bashful young earl," the "weight and gravity of the speakers" was, in a word, "absurd" (339). Why follow dinner and Champagne with "speeches as heavy as an after-dinner nap"?—without the nap's refreshment. Nobody tried—and nobody expected them to try—to lighten it up. It was all "the sad sincerity, the too-earnest utilitarianism, of modern life."

> People used to come to [these banquets], a few hundred years ago, for the sake of being jolly; they come now with an odd notion of pouring sober wisdom into their wine, by way of wormwood-bitters, and thus make such a mess of it that the wine and wisdom reciprocally spoil one another. (340)

And this from the man who once accused Endicott-style Puritanism of killing the joy of modern life. Evidently Utilitarianism will spoil the sport about as well. And, for the record, Hawthorne probably knows the story better than anyone else at table.

Or, were the "foregoing sentiments" owing to the memory of what was to happen next?

So far, all had been "felicitous"—the brilliant scene and "three very pleasant English friends"—one a well-known lady and one "the man to whom I owed most in England." Francis Bennoch, one may learn, the man who led the American visitor "to many scenes of life, in town, camp, and country, which [he] could never have found out" for himself. So he "never felt safer or cosier at anybody's fireside, even my own, than at the dinner-table of the Lord Mayor" (341). Then, "Out of this serene sky [...] a thunderbolt": your turn to speak, "eminent gentleman," with this impossible introduction:

> His Lordship got up and proceeded to make some very eulogistic remarks upon "the literary and commercial"—I question whether those two adjectives were ever before married by a copulative conjunction, and they certainly would not live together in illicit intercourse, of their own accord—"the literary and commercial attainments of an eminent gentleman there present." (341)

What followed this astonishing solecism was an entirely upbeat account of "the relations of blood and interest between Great Britain and the aforesaid eminent gentleman's native country," more "intimate than [...] ever before," and promising a continuance devoutly to be wished. Another "wearisome old toast," and then, your turn to speak, "eminent gentleman" (341). "Treachery": "better if his Lordship had sent me an infusion of ratsbane in the Loving Cup" (342).

And then the backstory, politically obscure and rhetorically oblique, but tending toward the most severe critique of English political intelligence in the entire book. Hawthorne's attendance at the Lord Mayor's dinner occurred in the mid-1850s, but even then a civil war seemed looming on the horizon and, with it, the possibility that England might somehow be dragged in, on one side or another—the North, for moral values, the South, for the price of cotton. But the point of view here seems that of the 1860s, nearer to the date of publication. To be sure, "All England, just *then* (my italics), was in one of those singular fits of panic excitement" that stem from "their dependence [...] on other sources than their own examination and individual thought," making them, accordingly, "more sudden, pervasive, and unreasoning, than any similar mood of our own public." But what follows, astonishing in its own right, clearly refers to some *now*:

> In truth, I have never seen the American public in a state at all similar, and believe that we are incapable of it. Our excitements are not impulsive, like theirs, but, right or wrong, are moral and intellectual. For example, the grand rising of the North, at the commencement of this war, bore the aspect of impulse and passion only because it was so universal. […] We were cool then, and have been cool ever since, and shall remain cool to the end, which we shall take coolly, whatever it may be. (342)

So you say, but "cool" is hardly the word one would use to name the tone of the rhetoric we know as "Patriotic Gore."[22]

Still, the point concerns not so much the actual Americans as *their* astonishing and incorrigible image of us:

> They imagine us, in our collective capacity, a kind of wild beast, whose normal condition is savage fury, and are always looking for the moment when we shall break through the slender barriers of international law and comity, and compel the reasonable part of the world, with themselves at the head, to combine for the purpose of putting us into a stronger cage. (342)

And, to a man, they all think the same thing: "You have the whole country in each man" and, when questioned, none of them "can give a reasonable ground for his alarm." And, besides the United States, only France "can put England into this "singular state" (343).

Now what, the often cool but suddenly passionate pilgrim wants to know, can possibly explain a political hysteria this instantaneous, universal, and self-sustaining?

> It is the united sensitiveness of a people extremely well-to-do, careful of its country's honor, most anxious for the preservation of the cumbersome and moss-grown prosperity which they have been so long consolidating, and incompetent (owing to the national half-sightedness, and their habit of trusting to a few leading minds for their public opinion) to judge when their prosperity is really threatened. (343).

So let us here set them straight: there may indeed be some chance of war "now, when law and right are really controverted on sustainable or plausible grounds" but "there was very little danger of war at that particular crisis." *Then*—if he remembers correctly—it was "a mere diplomatic squabble" (343) about, well, who any longer cares? Nevertheless, the "Lord Mayor, like many other Englishmen, probably fancied the War was on the western gale" and was glad to have even some insignificant American "harp on the rusty old strings of national sympathies, identities of blood and interest, and community of language and literature, and whisper peace where there was no peace." Probably why he was invited. But as "his Lordship" no doubt "meant well by all parties" (344), the insignificant American forgives him.

Forgives him, personally, of ill intent, but not for his representative national stupidity. Better not to end a complex, often sympathetic essay on this sour note. Better, some

---

22. For the un-cool-ness of Northern political rhetoric, see Edmund Wilson, *Patriotic Gore* (New York: Oxford University Press, 1966).

ironic confession of personal incompetence. So, while the Lord Mayor was speaking the old familiar platitudes, the hapless political victim begs one of his three friends to help him think of something to say. Begin by flattering the Lord Mayor, express some sense of "hereditary reverence in which his office was held by the descendants of the Puritan forefathers," then, well, just wing it. OK, here goes:

> Seizing this handful of straw with a death-grip, and bidding my three friends to bury me honorably, I got on my legs to save both countries, or perish in the attempt. The tables thundered and roared at me, and suddenly were silent again. But, as I have never happened to stand in a position of greater dignity and peril, I deem it a stratagem of sage policy to close these Sketches, leaving myself still erect in so heroic an attitude. (345)

Unaccustomed as he is to public speaking. Shy as a young girl. Always a writer, never a politician. Author of outmoded allegories, conceived in too retired a shade. What more could we have possibly been expecting? Especially as the conclusion here is to "Sketches." And, come to think of it, even "Romances" may end without a moral.

Still, the reader might well have preferred some other sense of an ending to this variously composed, partially rewritten, and generically multiform literary product. On the one hand, the man who kept apologizing for producing snatches of autobiographical writing in which he revealed nothing very significant, has offered us, at intervals, a good deal of information about the shape his extra-American life has unexpectedly taken—helping hapless countrymen to get back to America, visiting historic sites and the shrines of literary heroes, living pleasurably in a wealthy man's suburban home. Further, the writer famous for his representation of and tolerance for moral ambiguity, has said some sharply dogmatic things about sex and, more generally, about the way a decent human life is supposed to be led. And then, the politics: subtly displaced but lurking allusively in the early tales, standing in the wings but singing an urgent undersong in the three American Romances, the democratic yet conservative propositions have here come bravely out of the closet. But then, these are only sketches. And remember, he's only an "insignificant American." The first American readers might be obsessed with Hawthorne's dedication to "that arch traitor Pierce," and British reviewers by Hawthorne's portrait of a certain "fat dowager," but in the long run other matters matter more.

Emerson found this book—destined in the long run to compete with his own—"pellucid but not deep"; and Hawthorne himself, instructing his publisher to send no more notices, called it "not a good or a weighty book."[23] Yet a certain depth and weight attaches. Where Emerson loved the history of an earlier England for its commitment to a spiritual philosophy, Hawthorne seemed to value it more simply for its sense of tradition, its regard for the past, its reverence for the importance of history as such. And while they both agreed that its political philosophy and social practice were, in the present, deeply flawed—both assigning the future to a more just and moral America—Hawthorne's book dares to dirty itself with details. And to immerse itself in the bizarre comedy of absurd

---

23. See Simpson's "Introduction," p. xxviii.

local dignitaries defending the survival of civilization. That is to say, where Emerson is more deeply conceptual, more nearly social-scientific, Hawthorne is more literary. Emerson explains exactly where England went terribly wrong, failing to maintain its antique moral dignity and dooming itself to irrelevance in the future. Hawthorne, for all the warmth of his conservative sympathy, lets you see why you might not really want to live there. And why—despite the ugly approach of a hateful civil war—you probably had to come back to your new old home.

II. CIVIL WAR AND THE PURSUITS OF PEACE

Though based on observations thoughtfully recorded in the mid-1850s, *Our Old Home* (1863) is in fact one of the principal achievements of the so-called "Last Phase" of a career that a series of politically sponsored day jobs breaks into four parts, this last extending from the publishing of *The Marble Faun*, in England in 1859, in America in 1860, till his death in 1864 at the age of 60. Longer lived than Poe, who died at 46, and Thoreau, at 55, but not than his oddly alienated friend Melville, who died at age 72, as did Whitman: and not than Emerson, who made it to all the way to 77, Hawthorne has come to seem relatively short-lived, so it has made some sense to wonder what else he might have achieved had he lived a decade longer, past the Civil War and into a dawning age of "Realism," well advertised by a novel like the sectional study John William Deforest called *Miss Ravenel's Conversion from Secession to Loyalty* (1867). The evidence is mixed: reams of remaining manuscript material indicate that, despite the painful distraction of the angry and bloody Civil War, and despite his already expressed sense that he knew of a highly different way of writing which he genuinely admired but could never hope to practice, he left behind various attempts at two major fictional projects, known to scholars as The Elixir of Life and the American Claimant manuscripts. Of the two, the former is often misrepresented as a return to the "earthly immortality" theme of "Dr. Heidegger's Experiment" (1837), even though that idea was pretty clearly discredited in "The Virtuoso's Collection" (1841); the idea, rather, is that if human beings did not have to die as early as they do, often when they were finally on to something important, the history of the race might look entirely different. Not earthly immortality, just a significantly longer life. But no: as an aging Hawthorne wrote in a study for his "Septimius" project, "God wants short lives."[24]

More intriguing, perhaps, the tale of an American seeking to validate a claim to an impressive English estate appears to be encoding the widespread idea that, England having had its day, the future of progressive civilization belonged to America. Then too, with so much material drawn from the *English Notebooks*, this ambitious but unfinished fiction not only extends the cultural work of *Our Old Home* but completes the investigation begun in *The House of the Seven Gables*: the Puritan past was powerfully alive in nineteenth-century New England, but what realities lay behind that? Very early in Hawthorne's

---

24. See the Centenary Edition of *The Works of Nathaniel Hawthorne*, Vol. XIII (Columbus: Ohio State University Press, 1977), pp. 529–30.

career as a moral historian, a narrow and chauvinistic John Endicott has demanded to know of his proto-revolutionary compatriots, "What have we to do with England"? Evidently Hawthorne took the question seriously enough to pursue it in an extended fiction as seriously as he had in his earlier, more sociological study.

Minimally, then, one can suggest that with a few more years of healthy life Hawthorne might well have added two more romances to an already impressive body of long fiction. He may never have managed to capture the qualities he admired in the Victorian novels of Anthony Trollope, in which it appeared that "some giant had hewn a great lump out of the earth, and put it under a glass case, with all its inhabitants going about their daily business, and not suspecting that they were being made a show of"; or ever produced the "better book" of quotidian reality imagined and lamented in "The Custom House." For in truth he never entirely outlived what he called his "inveterate love of allegory."[25] Yet he may well have given the post-bellum writers who have fairly been called "the school of Hawthorne" a bit more anxiety of literary influence. He might even have challenged the cultural pity of a condescending and, in this case at least, imperciptient Henry James, who otherwise failed to recognize the unreliable narrator of *The Blithedale Romance* or to give proper recognition to the generic originality of the international novel called *The Marble Faun*.[26]

On the other hand, however, there is no convincing evidence that, living beyond 1865, Hawthorne would ever have written the sort of work that would keep Daniel Aaron from referring to the bitter sectional conflict of the early 1860s as *The Unwritten War*. Or ever reversed our politically correct consensus that Hawthorne never outgrew a certain Christian Conservatism. Nothing like a card-carrying abolitionist, he never expressed the sort of sympathy for an enslaved population that even so restrained an observer as Emerson was provoked to express on his 1844 lecture on the anniversary of British abolition in the West Indies. Indeed Hawthorne's expressed sympathy is for some hapless Southern captives and for the white workers in the South.[27]

"Chiefly about War Matters," which appeared in the *Atlantic* for July, 1862, is ascribed to "A Peaceable Man" and it recounts the trip, taken with friend and publisher William Ticknor, through the towns and country between New England and the scene of civil warfare. Studded with footnotes testifying to editorial deletions and some of Hawthorne's own, appearing to take back some incorrect political opinions, it calls attention to its extreme literariness in other ways as well. Conceived as an "Excursion," it begins in "the

---

25. Thus the coy preface to the works of Aubepine; see also Hawthorne's preface to the 1851 edition of *Twice-told Tales* (Columbus: Ohio State University Press, 1974), pp. 3–7.
26. In his generalized discussion of Hawthorne's "Three American Novels," James "hardly know[s] what to say [...] save that it is very charming" (112) and that Coverdale, who is a lot like his creator, is "evidently an exceptional fellow" (113). And, in a chapter called "England and America," the closest he comes to critical intelligence is his observation that Hilda, whom he appears to adore, is a "pure and somewhat rigid New England Girl" (142); see *Hawthorne* (1879); quoted from the Doubleday Dolphin edition (n.d.).
27. Thus Hawthorne expressed himself in a letter on June 15, 1851, to Zachariah Burchmore; see the Centenary Edition of *The Letters*, 1843–53, Vol. XVI (Columbus: Ohio State University Press, 1985), p. 456.

long, dreary January of our Northern year" and works its way to "mild and balmy" at Philadelphia, thus meeting the spring "half-way, in her slow progress from the South," and half expecting to "get through the Rebel line" and discover "strawberries, and all such delights of early summer" (404).[28]

It notices in New York "a rather prominent display of military goods at the shop windows," but also a lack of the ordinary "bustle and movement" as "so large a proportion of its restless elements had been drawn towards the seat of the conflict" (405). A battle being expected, the peaceable wanderer wonders if America will ever see "half a score of years without seeing the likeness of a soldier, except it be in the festal march of a company on its summer tour" (406). And then, turning aside from anything like ordinary patriotism, the dismal prediction that soon enough "military notoriety [...] will be the measure of all claims to civil distinction" and then—possibly with the thought of citizen-soldier Pierce in mind—that "one bullet-headed general will succeed another in the Presidential chair." Next—moral irony trumping even anti-military politics—the reflection even this is not the worst, substituting as it may for "the many shams on which men have heretofore founded their claims to public regard" (407). Not quite a prayer for William James' "Moral Equivalent of War," but a thought shared by both Melville and Whitman: for once, perhaps, the talkers would leave off their talking.[29]

By now, any reader expecting boilerplate anti-slavery rhetoric or anything approaching "patriotic gore" will of course be completely disappointed. An editorial footnote relieves us of the obligation of reading "several paragraphs" about some prominent Members of Congress that seem "liable to misconstruction." Instead, several pages about "one man [...] at the Capitol [...] satisfactorily adequate to the business which brought him thither" (408), namely the painter Emanuel Gottlieb Leutz, famous to us for his "Washington Crossing the Delaware" but honored by Hawthorne as an artist earnestly working at his calling and producing works likely to outlast the present unpleasantness, however it might turn out. Less a judgment of esthetic merit, from the man who in *The Marble Faun* had written up the program of Italian art for culture-hungry American tourists, the passage is more an endorsement of the necessity of art as such. And this on the occasion of a proto-apocalyptic war of Good Versus Evil.

Most famous for its first broadly comic, then finally reverential portrait of Lincoln, the essay endures, chiefly, as a proof of Hawthorne's deep revulsion from Civil War politics and of the refusal of his moral imagination to make literature out of the horrors of war, closely observed elsewhere, as in the deluge of photographs just then becoming

---

28. All citations of "War Matters" refer to Volume XXIII of the Centenary Edition of *The Works of Nathaniel Hawthorne* (Columbus: Ohio State University Press, 1994). the old standard (Riverside) *Hawthorne's Works*, Vol. XII (Boston: Houghton Mifflin, 1883).
29. Near the opening of the sequence of the Civil War poems he entitled *Drum Taps*, a still enthusiastic Whitman remarks that there are "no bargainers' bargains by day"; a similar sentiment appears, briefly enough "Apathy and Enthusiasm," where, marching off to war, the enthusiastic young men think "how tame the Nation/ In the age that went before." For William James's call for a warlike integrity and courage in times of relaxation and peace, see "The Moral Equivalent of War" (1900).

available. Holgrave's brave new art of painting with the sunshine is up to the task of bringing out the grim reality behind the polite smile of the Pyncheon hypocrite of today, but Hawthorne never set him the task of daguerreotyping a pile of dismembered dead bodies. Indeed, it may be only a slight exaggeration to suggest that the American Civil War very nearly paralyzed Hawthorne's literary imagination—as it almost certainly energized that of Melville. Certain it is that "Chiefly about War Matters" is nearly negligible when compared to the masterpiece that is Melville's *Battle Pieces* (1866). Two visits to the front, one producing an essay of curious, barely political reflections; the other, completed after the war, includes an essay which appears to echo many of Hawthorne's "peaceable" sentiments, but offering fifty-odd poems that constitute a masterwork of narration and commentary, a major engagement with national ideology and its insistent theological subtext. Of course, Hawthorne was fifteen years older; nor had life experience ever taught him to imagine, revel in, and then discipline the esthetics of bravado. In any event, he simply hated and was demoralized by such news from the front as Melville turned into the bitter patriotism of grim, ironic verse.

Other excursions follow the Lincoln portrait—first to fortifications at Alexandria where a group of escaping slaves strike the creator of Count Donatello as "quite unlike the specimens of their race" to be seen in New England, and then, daring to "excite [...] wrath," as "not altogether human, but perhaps quite as good, and akin to the fauns and rustic deities" (420)—wishing them well but doubting that this "present generation of negroes" will fare very well in the near future. Then, after a sketch of the politically embattled General McClellan, an excursion to Harper's Ferry, occasioning a thorough repudiation of the reputed sainthood of John Brown—"Nobody was ever more justly hanged (427)—but also an approval of the use of the place as a prison for captured Rebels, who strike the incurable literariness of this garden-variety Northern racist as bumpkins and "peasants [...] people with whom our northern rural population has not a single trait in common" (429) Had it ever been, he seems to keep asking, had it *ever* been one nation, under God or history of some Providence whose rationale was making less sense every day. Forcing the unhappy observation, learned back in the heyday of The Protest, if not before, that "No human effort, on a grand scale, has ever yet resulted according to the purpose of its projectors" (431). To which we might respond that "Man's accidents" may or may not be "God's purposes"[30] but had either side known what the Civil War would cost them in what we now call blood and treasure, some other compromise or blunder would probably been attempted.

A visit to Fortress Monroe discovers a number of "ships of war and transports [all] wearing the Union flag—'Old Glory,' as I hear it called in these days" (433)—provokes a proto-Melvillean reflection that the "pomp and splendor" of naval warfare are gone

---

30. Originally scratched by Sophia Hawthorne in a window at the manse in Concord, Hawthorne deploys this famous mantra just here in "War Matters": "The advantages are always incidental. Man's accidents are God's purposes. We miss the good we sought, and do the good we little cared for" (332).

by: the *Monitor* looks like a "cheese-box" and predicts, for the navies of the world, "a race of enginemen and smoke-blackened cannoneers" (434), trapped in iron too thick for anything like heroism to be perceived.[31] And then, as if to prove that iron has not this grumpy old man's capacity for irony, this: the Millennium is certainly approaching, because human strife is to be transferred from the heart and personality of man into "cunning contrivances of machinery" (437). Would that the prediction had been realized: my battle-bot is just a toy and my drone can't even find its way to the local Safeway. But the point is clear: old men—even savvy old writers—do not much like the world they know they will soon be leaving.

The extended meditation on "war matters" ends with some forgiving remarks about the mind of the South—for which an editorial footnote hastens to apologize. The Peaceable Man begins by wondering "what proportion of all these people" gathered about Washington are, in their hearts, whole-hearted supporters of the Union cause, supposing that many of them "so far sided with the South as to desire nothing more or better that to see everything reestablished a little worse than its former basis." Many of them no doubt contrast the "genial courtesy, the warm and graceful freedom of that region" with what some—though not the speaker!—call "the frigidity of our Northern manners, and the uncouthness of Uncle Abe's" (441). Still, he supposes that the war must go terribly on, achieving, at the expense of "greater trouble [...] than any other people ever voluntarily suffered," eventual peace and "a truer union." Or not—and here is where the editor takes umbrage—for "heaven was heaven still, as Milton sings, after Lucifer and a third part of the angels had seceded from its golden palaces" (442).

Thus only at the very end—and incredibly in the light of what has gone before—do the devilish claws of radical Abolitionist rhetoric peep forth. And the final line suggests that dissolution of the Union might leave the Northern heaven "all the more heavenly, because so many gloomy brows, and soured, vindictive hearts, had gone to plot ineffectual schemes of mischief elsewhere," leaving the Editor to insist that it is really "Rebellion" (and that on behalf of slavery) that has "put reason herself into a rage" (442). So that if Hawthorne got his incorrigible Conservatism published, he also got it censured. And not since his biographical defense of Franklin Pierce had he so exposed himself to the hatred of Northern radicals. But there it was. On the one hand, he seems never to have felt outrage that human beings were being dehumanized. And on the other, he thought the war a very bad idea, likely enough to preserve a Union he did not in any sense sacralize, but probably not God's way of establishing freedom, and justice for all. The best we can say for his published position is that he knew it would be unpopular in the North and that, as the footnotes imply, he knew his bias and well understood that, on territory absolutely inimical to his genius, he might be simply be wrong. Maybe the Civil War was indeed an Accident of Providence.

---

31. Cp. the sentiments of Melville's poem, "A Utilitarian's View of the Monitor's Fight," in *Battle Pieces* (1866); see *Collected Poems* (New York: Hendricks House, 1947), pp. 39–40.

III. ROMAN HOLIDAY

When all this and much else has been said, however, the fact remains that after Hawthorne's third (and most remunerative) venture into the world of ordinary work, the significant and lasting achievement is the now brilliant, now truly puzzling work finally named *The Marble Faun* (1960), the fourth and last of his completed romances. Conceived and "sketched out" during Hawthorne's lengthy sojourn in Italy, "rewritten and prepared for the press in England,"[32] and separated by more than seven years since his last such fictional venture, the Preface to this longest and morally most complex of his novel spends most of its time worrying that the ideal reader for his own not-very-novelistic productions may have vanished in the long interval. As we have said, Hawthorne was always aware of his tendency to allegory, and he was becoming increasingly conscious of an important shift in literary epistemology: aware, no doubt, that the novel was born of a growing interest in the imitation of an "existent literary singular," Hawthorne is begging pardon for once again committing romance. Or else, at very least, pleading for a tolerant reception of one last performance in the older, less "realistic" fashion.

Significantly, therefore, Hawthorne's "fanciful story, evolving a thoughtful moral," excuses itself of any novelistic attempt at "a portraiture of Italian manners and character." And then, the familiar, hypersensitive hyperbole: "Italy […] was chiefly valuable […] as affording a sort of poetic or fairy precinct, where actualities would not be so terribly insisted upon" in the humming and buzzing thing the novel was teaching itself to be. Or, as he says, "as they are, and must be, in America"—where it may be centuries before his "dear native land" acquire the gloom and ivy necessary for a "proper Romance." Just so, *The House of the Seven Gables* protested that its fiction had "more to do with the clouds overhead, than with any portion of the actual soil of the County of Essex": don't write me any letters about the character of your Grandfather.[33] Then too, the venue of *The Blithedale Romance* was "a theatre, a little removed from the highway of ordinary travel, where" the fictions of the fancy would not suffer from "too close a comparison with the actual events of real lives": Zenobia is not Margaret Fuller, Idiot; put your *clef* back in your *poche* and move along. It has been well suggested that a sensitive Hawthorne was always trying get out ahead of the criticism he expected.[34] It is also true that he protested a little too much: his fictions are about things real and important and he knows it.

The Marble Faun may or may not know enough about Italian art to justify its old-time reputation as a veritable guidebook for culturally starved Americans; it certainly does not intend its "Faun," the artist Donatello, as an epitome of Italian character or imagination; or pretend to make Miriam's rumored Jewishness by itself a preeminent moral fact. But it

---

32. Published first in England in February 1860, as *The Transformation*, it appeared in America in March as *The Marble Faun*.
33. See *The House of the Seven Gables* (New York: Norton, 2006), p. 4. For discussion, see Chapter Eleven, p. xxxx.
34. For Hawthorne's tendency to anticipate and, with some irony, to accept the criticism he expects, see Adam Gordon, "The Critic on Main Street," in Carol M. Bensick, ed., *A Passion for Getting It Right* (Bern: Peter Lang, 2016), pp. 223–40.

knows that Rome is far older than London and Boston; that Roman Catholicism, though very far from being universal, is more nearly aboriginal that Anglicanism or its curious Congregational offshoot; and that a darkly experienced Miriam is hardly more properly American than is Donatello. As are, emphatically, parodically, Hilda and Kenyon. Attenuated children of the Puritans, painfully obvious in the case of the rewriting of a Phoebe-like innocence, and well enough revealed in the character of the sculptor too marble-like to be a painter or a poet, they find themselves well out of their depth in a world without an Enlightened beginning. Rome: Pagan, Catholic, Modern. Fairy Precinct, with a history that leads back and then disappears somewhere in the lost neighborhood of Origins. For all its languid luxuriating in Italian art, *The Marble Faun* is as much about America as a later work called *The American*, which it influenced more than its accomplished expatriate could afford to admit.

Like many other Hawthorne works, *The Marble Faun* is about guilt, the thing that killed Arthur Dimmesdale—with the assistance, no doubt, of some psychotropic drug from the stash of Dr. Roger Chillingworth. Not the guilt of original sin, in the classic Calvinist sense, universal, inevitable, and definitive. That august notion got a fair try-out in "Rappaccini's Daughter" (1845) and again, later and at length in *The House of the Seven Gables*,[35] but in *The Scarlet Letter* the thing is entirely *actual*, if not in every sense voluntary: adultery, unless the husband really were long dead. "What we did had a justification of its own!"—or so it must have seemed. But no. Big-time guilt. What to do? Pretend to confess from the pulpit, knowing full well—this "subtle but remorseful hypocrite"—how a worshipful congregation would interpret his coded remarks? What else? If only there were a Catholic priest closer to Boston than Quebec. The alternative, masochism and self-separation: whip the lustful body and pray that the sin was not also in the will. Lucky Hilda, so many confessionals, and all so handy-by. And she, self-confessed heretic, only *witnessed* the sin. Evidently the book is about innocence as well as guilt.

And yet there are, really, actually, guilty parties. What are we to make of Miriam, child of Abraham more nearly than of John Calvin or Thomas Hooker, who appears under a cloud of suspicion, and then, more currently, out of some mysterious relation with the monk who was her model, and who then disappears so mysteriously at the end? Where to? And into what remorse? She did not *do* the murder, but was she not also guilty by some sort of conscience, or "something in its stead"? After all, was not the murderer, with whatever motive of passionate jealousy, acting in her defense? And exactly what did her eyes tell him in the nanosecond of in-deliberation? Oh dear, can there be an *actual* sin that is not a fully human *act*? A question Hilda might well have thought to ask of the fearful Jesuit who did not quite know how to hear the confession of a confused innocent.

---

35. A tale which asks if its scene is "the Eden of the present world" has naturally suggested the question of Original Sin; see for example, Sheldon Liebman, "Hawthorne and Milton: The Second Fall in 'Rappaccini's Daughter'" *New England Quarterly*, 41.4 (1968), 521–35; Judith Fryer, *The Faces of Eve* (Minneapolis: Minnesota University Press, 1973); William H. Shurr, *Rappaccini's Children* (Lexington: University Press of Kentucky, 1981); Agnes McNeill Donahue, *Hawthorne: Calvin's Ironic Stepchild* (Kent: Kent State University Press, 1988). For my own brief suggestions, see Chapter Six, pp. 99–122. For that question in *Seven Gables*, see Chapter Eleven, pp. 193–214.

A sympathetic Melville knew Hawthorne was troubled by "something, somehow like" guilt.[36] Perhaps he barely knew the half.

And what of Donatello, that preternatural innocent turned passionate lover who "murders" a criminal stalker? No Puritan heritage in this innocent son-of-a-faun. Artistically gifted, this otherwise minimal man is, like some Budding Billy, about to perform his first moral action. And that one immoral.[37] Is that how it all started, Adam? It seemed like a good idea at the time? The right, the necessary thing. But there were consequences. Is it not that first Augustine and then Calvin did little more than muddy these relatively shallow waters? He loves her; she wishes her tormentor dead; understandably, perhaps righteously; and one little push gets the whole thing started. Confusion, remorse, prisons, convents; even Henry James will rue and recognize their place. Fly we from this even older old home. To America? To New England? Land of Hooker and Edwards? Might not work.

But, as with *The Scarlet Letter*, the story is also about sex. A different question yet annoyingly the same. And if the unavoidable yet unsolvable problem of guilt and innocence unites the atavistic Etruscan with both the Christian and the Jew, the question of sex reveals some deep cultural division. Donatello and Miriam love one another credibly, passionately; Hilda and Kenyon fall together *faute de mieux*. Like Phoebe and Holgrave earlier. Evidence indicates that Sophia enjoyed the pleasures of the bedroom at least as honestly as her long-single husband; but Hawthorne cannot seem to bring himself to say so in print.[38] Hilda marries Kenyon on the rebound—from the sight of a homicide perpetrated in the name of passion. And because there is nothing else to do. And Kenyon marries her because, well, you can't marry a statue. Ovid and Shaw to the contrary notwithstanding.

The scene which defines Kenyon's American dismay at the originality and inevitability of sex appears in one of the novel's (and the nineteenth century's) most revealing scenes. Not since Bradford's sore puzzlement at the libertine celebrations at Merry Mount had the Puritanical imagination operated in such frank undress. The difference being that Hawthorne well understood both sides of the story: yes, sex is to celebrate at least as much as—lots of luck—to regulate; and yes, a lot of Roman Catholicism is indeed paganism covered with a vestment. So? Deal with it. And we are privileged to watch—as Kenyon, trying anxiously to find Hilda, gets caught up in a parade of old-world horribles.

---

36. Apropos of Hawthorne's fascination with the portrait of Beatrice Cenci—in *The Marble Faun* and again in *Clarel*, Edwin Haviland Miller suggests that Melville suspected Hawthorne may have "shared Ethan Brand's secret and unpardonable sin"; see *Melville: A Biography* (New York: George Braziller, 1975), p. 339.
37. With all due respect to the "American Adam" of R. W. B. Lewis, one needs yet to explain how one gets from St. Augustine's Adam—with all those wonderful *dona superaddita*—to the sociological sport imagined here, and to the Pseudo-Darwinian experiment Melville named Billy Budd.
38. For Hawthorne's sense of his wife's somewhat aggressive sexuality, see T. Walter Herbert, *Dearest Beloved: The Hawthornes and the Making of the Middle-Class Family* (Berkeley: University of California Press, 1993), pp. 122–24.

In the streets tumultuous with Roman Carnival, where a "care stricken mortal has no business," but on an errand most sober and commanding, Kenyon finds his fine but not rich senses assaulted, first by "five strapping damsels (so, at least, their petticoats bespoke them, in spite of an awful freedom in the flourish of their legs") inviting him to dance; then "a gigantic female figure, seven feet high at least, and taking up a third of the street's breadth with the preposterously swelling sphere of her crinoline skirts" who—or should one say which?—assaults his heart first with "amorous glances," then with "a vast bouquet of sunflowers and nettles," expressing her pressing sexual need with "all sorts of pathetic and passionate dumb-show." Rejected, as she must indeed be rejected by anyone with a sense of reason and order, she then fires a pistol straight at his hardened heart, but covering him all over "with a cloud of lime-dust," into which the "revengeful damsel strode away." Allegory of Love and Death in the American novel? Not quite. More like a drugged and soporific William Bradford waking up beneath Morton's maypole at Merry Mount. With that poetic Master of the Revels teaching renegade servants and uninstructed native women to sing "Yo to Hymen."[39]

And the sensual assault continues as a "whole host of absurd figures [pretend] to sympathize in his mishap":

> Clowns and parti-colored harlequins; orang-outans; bear-headed, bull-headed and dog-headed individuals; faces that would have been human, but for their enormous noses; one terrific creature, with a visage right in the center of his breast; and all other imaginable kinds of monstrosity and exaggeration (446).

"Imaginable," perhaps, but not quite by Hawthorne himself, to whom something like this seems actually to have a-happened: Why me? I'm just a writer, here to get material. Nudes in museums may have been on my menu but nothing like this. Poetic license, to be sure, but not licentiousness enacted in public. Romance, I said: the irruption of the impossible probable. The carnivalesque, in a pinch. The phallic, not so much.

What Hawthorne had appeared to recognize in "The May-Pole" is that his sources had turned the pragmatic question of trading guns and rum to the native population into an allegory of national difference: having been endorsed, even encouraged by King Charles I, Mayday celebrations had come to stand for an Old World way. But as maypoles were atavistically a phallic symbol, with or without some lascivious verses attached, Bradford was perfectly willing to endorse the symbolic castration performed, not by Miles Standish on the day of Thomas Morton's arrest, but by a newly arrived John Endicott, whose action suggested that, whether idol or merely idle, maypoles had no place in the New England State of grace. And symbolically at least, the deed had resonance.[40]

---

39. For a steady-enough account of William Bradford's hysterical response to what Hawthorne would call the "jollity" of Pessonagesset turned Wollaston turned Merry Mount—about to turn Dagon—see chapter Two in my *Godly Letters* (Notre Dame, IN: Notre Dame University Press, 2007).

40. To me at least it appears that it was Endicott's belated, virtually allegorical hacking of the King-James-endorsed maypole which caused Bradford to change his emphasis from guns and rum to the less political question of "dancing, frisking and worse practices"; see *Godly Letters*, pp. 61–66.

The point is subtle enough to bear emphasis. Of course the Puritan Patriarchs wore out their wives in pregnancy and childbirth; and of course more than one male author from that age has left us his conscientious worry that he loved his wife more than God; but, though clichés on this subject abound, no one has ever suggested that the Puritans settled New England in order to liberate Eros. Or to free the soul from guilt. Cotton and Hutchinson may have tried that, in a fairly technical way, but Hooker and Shepard won out. Much changed over the years: guilty men eventually learned to flatter their wives with the ascription of innocence (and also, perhaps, of the absence of sexual desire). Surely sex is not the only question of which men—and perhaps women too—have learned to "make conscience," but it appears to be right up there. Hawthorne's Faun, the implausible fantasy of a young, benign and sensitive sociopath, may discover conscience in the act of something somehow like murder. But the motive is, in part at least, a newly aroused sense of sexual competition.

The obvious connection with "The May-Pole of Merry Mount" suggests that an important feature of Hawthorne's comparatist imagination had not, over the years, changed very much: there as here not only ritual but sexual attitude is seen to define a cardinal difference in transatlantic cultures. Once famous for the "ambivalence" of its handling of the contest between Puritan and Reveler,[41] Hawthorne's maypole story does its best to suggest that something of what his (entirely fictional) Lord and Lady of the May experienced at Merry Mount was not to be repented. Nor was it to be obliterated by the regimen of Endicott's Salem: mature love may make life more solemn, but it need not extinguish joy. Here, the Narrator, who may also be suffering some attenuation of affect, tries even harder to justify the sexual monstrosity that has so assaulted his sensibility. Can he understand if not actually love the public celebration of what the Aliens on *Star Trek* refer to as "the biological function"?

Convinced on the one hand that the Roman Carnival—"a few afternoons of early spring when [some] moldy gaiety strays into the sunshine"—is altogether "traditional, not actual," that it exists, "this present year, only because it has existed through centuries gone by," he nevertheless goes on to concede, echoing Melville, that

> there is a Wisdom that looks grave, and sneers at merriment; and again a deeper wisdom that, that stoops to be gay as often as occasion serves, and oftenest avails itself of shallow and trifling grounds of mirth; because, if we wait for more substantial ones, we seldom can be gay at all. (437)

Evidently, as "The May-Pole of Merry Mount" seemed almost to know, the undersong of life is sufficiently sad that even a forced gaiety must have its place; so that, had it been possible, Kenyon would have done well "to mask himself is some wild, hairy visage, and plunge into the throng of masquers." But then the residual puritanic self points out that, though one might at first think "the whole town gone mad," in fact this "apparently

---

41. Leaving ambiguity and ambivalence to other ("newer") critics, Q. D. Leavis emphasizes Hawthorne's sense of the "gain and loss" of America's nouvelle culture; see "Hawthorne as Poet," *Sewanee Review*, 59.2 (1951), pp. 179–205.

unbounded license is kept strictly in within a limit of its own" (441). And no doubt it is something of this reverence for restraint that keeps this, quasi-omniscient Narrator, even in a "Postscript" demanded by an unsatisfied audience, from revealing—from admitting, from even knowing?—in exactly what ominous and guilty way Miriam and her model had been connected.

Strangely unforthcoming at other moments, as when, just after the scene of Kenyon's "martyrdom," he declines to make the question of Hilda's long absence "a matter of formal explanation with the reader," offering instead the fantasy that this ardent copyist "had been snatched away to the land of Picture." And as when, in the testy Postscript grudgingly offered to readers who appear to have missed the point about the epistemology of the Romance, he suggests they might as well be asking "how Cuvier might have classified poor Donatello," this instance of reluctant, resistant, self-limiting omniscience is an important moment in the career of a writer who had almost always relied on the friendliness of narrators, but who, in *Our Old Home* and again in "War Matters," would find a more or less comfortable way to write at length *in propria persona*: how *can* a Narrator know more than any single human being? But it is something else as well. Less formally, it is an admission of a personal and also a cultural unwillingness to write about what Hawthorne once called "love in its technical sense." Sex, obviously, but also passion, something that makes sex somewhat more than what Henry James would later call a "sentiment."[42]

In the context of the *The Bostonians* (1891), the most American of his mature novels, James meant to notice that, among other things, no doubt, the woman's movement had taken away some of the respect in which, in fiction at least, the business of courtship and marriage had long been held. What he might also have said—as a professional critic of French fiction—that the passionate dimension of human sexuality was almost entirely absent from American fiction to that point, well made later by Leslie Fiedler.[43] A matter of an audience's expectation and therefore of publishers' restriction, the absence is yet significant by the way it calls attention to itself. Not so much the pre-textual mating of Hester and Dimmesdale, but in their passionate reunion in the forest, where the Narrator's tight-lipped declaration that "Then, all was spoken" is clearly a prediction of Old Hollywood's fade to black. To be sure, there is no such problem in *The House of the Seven Gables* where, to his political credit, Hawthorne is interested in more than who is sleeping with whom. But it comes back with a vengeance in the redundantly if surreptitiously sexual pages of *The Blithedale Romance*. Hollingsworth and Priscilla get together in the end: who cares; so did Holgrave and Phoebe. But who, all along, has been doing what to whom?—in a theatre more like Noyes' Oneida than Ripley's Brook Farm. And

---

42. Speaking of his distinctively American novel *The Bostonians*, Henry James's Journal for 1883 speaks of "the decline of the sentiment of sex"; see Leon Edel, *Henry James: The Middle Years, 1882–1885* (Philadelphia: Lippincott, 1962), p. 137.

43. Following Freud, and also D. H. Lawrence, Fiedler suggests, early on, that "the best [American] attempt at dealing with love is *The Scarlet Letter*, in which the physical consummation of adultery has occurred and all passion burned away before the novel begins"; see *Love and Death in the American Novel* (New York: Stein and Day, 1966), p. 25.

what is it, really, between Coverdale and Zenobia: Priscilla he sends a warning by bird, but Zenobia is the one he admits to have been mentally undressing. The problem is not really did he kill her—I did the autopsy elsewhere: there was no water in her lungs—but only if he has hysterically forgotten the fact; and also, whether the event was something of a *liebestod*, the only scene powerful enough to satisfy Coverdale's repeated wish for some truly cathartic climax; and also, perhaps, his prurient but otherwise repressed passion.[44]

Yes, no, maybe. Here the question is that the Narrator cannot quite face the question of Miriam's powerful sexuality, a literary fact more evident than the way an earlier one had tried to keep Hester from starting a precocious sexual revolution in the seventeenth century. On the one hand, the passion she feels for the newly awakened, newly aroused Donatello is posited but not really exhibited. One might almost say that the moment of the murder, the climax of their relationship, is also its orgasm. Like Zenobia and Coveredale, perhaps. And worse, much worse, is the way the grudging omniscience of this unstable Narrator tries to keep us from asking about Miriam's exact relation with her Model, the monk who stalks his way to his own death. What were they to one another? What is his strange hold over her? Using with her the deep-thematic word "innocence" (97), he says he does not believe her guilty of the reputed crimes that drove her abroad in the first place. But in this more proximate—and more fatal—situation he can manage to be only vague, hypothetic, hopeful, probably naïve.

Waxing philosophic, he imagines that the "solitude [that] had suddenly spread around" the artist and her model owes to the law that "misfortune" or "some great crime [...] makes the actor in the one, or the sufferer of the other, an alien in the world" (92) OK, I guess, but don't sell your sociology books just yet, as this dutiful but cautious Narrator blames this fact for not knowing all that the reader might be expecting. Well, sort of: "Owing, it may be, to this moral estrangement," he has heard only "a few vague whisperings of what passed in Miriam's interview, that afternoon, with the sinister personage who had dogged her footsteps ever since the visit to the catacomb." Poor Narrator: he must weave "these mystic utterance into a continuous scene"; why, it's just like gathering up and piecing together the fragments of a letter, which has been torn and scattered to the winds.

> Many words of deep significance—many entire sentences, and those possibly the most important ones—have flown too far, on the winged breeze, to be recovered. (92–93)

Poor Narrator: what if "we insert our own conjectural amendments" and in doing so "we perhaps give a purport utterly at variance with the true one" (93)? First of all, what you mean, "we," White Man? Oh, yes, I forgot the royal-authorial-stupidass plural.

But in any case, who talks this way? Coverdale, perhaps, but he was either incompetent or dishonest or both. And like they said, rhetoric is a meretricious art. Yet evidently "we" have to practice it, for

---

44. See Chapter Twelve in this volume, esp. pp. 215–244.

unless we attempt something in this way, there must remain an unsightly gap, a lack of continuousness and dependence in our narrative; so that it would arrive at certain inevitable catastrophes without due warning of their imminence. (93)

Hate them unsightly gaps. But no more than this meta-literary posturing. You either want to write this book or you don't: this latter possibility has not gone unnoticed.[45] Or maybe it's just that the personage who loves to begin and end a book by assembling together "Miriam, Hilda, Kenyon, Donatello" deserves to be thought of as a character in his own right. Poor Guy, he had to write a book that could not quite be written: things happen, witnesses disappear, motives are private, in the end inexpressible, nobody can know everything, no, not even enough; what's a writer to do? Well, let's see how he fills the gap.

For sure, "there seemed to be a sadly mysterious fascination in the influence of this ill-omened person over Miriam"—such as "beasts and reptiles" have over their victim. Or, it was as if there were an

> iron chain [...] round her feminine waist [...] which perhaps bound the pair together by a bond equally torturing to each [that] must have been forged in some such unhallowed furnace as is only kindled by evil passions and fed by evil deeds. (93)

Right. One of those. Is it really enough to propose that the writer of "Romance" requires of his audience a certain latitude, a freedom from specificity of fact and act and motive? Or to confess that the practitioner of this putative genre knows himself to be, every moment, skirting the edge of an absurdity? Or is one now and then required to say exactly what the hell he is talking about? Or else—theory aside—merely agree to

> trust, there may have been no crime in Miriam, but only one of those fatalities which are among the most insoluble riddles propounded to mortal comprehension; the fatal decree, by which every crime is made to be the agony of many innocent persons, as well as of the single guilty one. (93)

You mean, like Hilda? Oh no, wait, that hasn't happened yet. What then?

One can easily imagine a notebook entry that proposes an artist and her model shadowed by some dark secret: maybe he's a monk; maybe she's a Jew. But in the

---

45. As his editor has observed, Hawthorne had initially intended to write up a romance out of his English experience—possibly even a novel, as he was, in these latter years, expressing an interest in "another class of works," like those of Anthony Trollope; then, in Rome, he discovered The Faun of Praxiteles (and the portrait of Beatrice Cenci by Guido Reni); so that, while dealing with the dire illness of his daughter Una, he "scribbled fitfully [...] with many idle pauses, & no good result" (xxiv–xxv) on a work he knew was more or less certain to raise both formal and thematic questions; see Claude M. Simpson, "Introduction," to *The Marble Faun* (Columbus: Ohio State University Press, 1968). And, for the sense that Hawthorne experienced "some kind of writing blockage briefly," see Edwin Haviland Miller, *Salem Is My Dwelling Place* (Iowa City: University of Iowa Press, 1991), p. 439.

published version you have to work it up. Even in a Romance. Otherwise your readers—and not just Beef and Ale Brits—will be sore puzzled. Maybe she saw the Monk push one of his fellow monks off a cliff, to hush up their same-sex affair; he's afraid she'll go to the police. Or, maybe she paid him to kill the father who abused her sexually, somewhere back there in Cenciville. Or maybe they have been secret lovers: artist and model, I've heard of that. But to suggest, and then (almost) to deny, that she herself is in any way guilty will require an explanation that is likely to become abstruse. Mystifying, even. And not in the end very convincing. From the author who gave us the untrustworthy but brilliantly executed narration of Miles Coverdale, we have the right to expect something better than embarrassed but incompetent omniscience. Especially from a Narrator without a local habitation and a name.

Or, in a mood less analytical, shall we say that *The Marble Faun* is really about conscience—that formal register of guilt and innocence—which the Count of Monte Beni was said to lack but which others in the novel have in large measure. Indeed one could argue that this was Hawthorne's flood subject, there from the beginning. What has driven the absconded wife and mother in "The Hollow of the Three Hills" into the arms of a fortune teller badly disguised as a latter-day witch? What, more subtly, keeps the two "Wives of the (Un-)Dead" from sharing the knowledge that the husband of each I actually? What exactly does Hawthorne mean when he suggests that it is conscience—or "something in its stead"—that makes Reuben Bourne feel he really ought to lie down and die with his Freudian father. But what is conscience after all? A "faculty," as the old psychology used to say? A necessary exercise of the practical reason? A confused memory of a mother's voice? A sort of psychic indigestion? And how, in any event, do we account for the self-deception that makes it possible for Goodman Brown to venture alone to a witches' coven with every intention of returning at once to the bosom of faith? Why does Parson Hooper imagine he can't reveal his secret sin (or sorrow) to anybody but God? How, at a later date, do mad scientists like Aylmer and Baglioni disguise from themselves the obscure motives they have for experimenting with the lives of trusting women? Can there really be, in the sad case of Arthur Dimmesdale, such a thing as a "subtle but remorseful hypocrite"? Wherein does it differ from the flagrant self-posturing of Judge Pyncheon? And then there's Miles Coverdale: he, himself, was, well, who knows what the hell? Can you really forget a murder and then, less hysterically, find your way back to the scene of the crime? Like Reuben Bourne to Lovell's Rock? Which is to ask the lurking question, well asked if not entirely answered in a Freudian study of Hawthorne, whether psychoanalysis will yet obviate or subsume the old-time science of casuistry.[46]

But if Frederick Crews, whose Hawthorne gives us Freud in advance, then surely K. M. Harris as well, who offers hypocrisy as Hawthorne's métier; and even Austin Warren, who long since sought to diagnose the chronic disease of Puritan conscience. Maybe even Martin Green, whose study of "The Problem of Boston" is not unaware of

---

46. Thus, in reference to Frederick Crews, I once framed the question on the moral foreground of Reuben Bourne's noticeable "Logic of Compulsion" in "Roger Malvin's Burial; see my *Province of Piety* (Cambridge, MA: Harvard University Press, 1984), pp. 109–13.

its long prehistory.[47] The literary history of New England properly begins with the determination of certain Puritans not to get along by going along, not to say well, nobody's perfect—let alone I'm ok, you're ok—but to "make conscience" of their lives in every aspect. This and not the relishing of some psychotic image of hell is their distinguishing mark. That of Hawthorne, the determination to identify and to trace the history of this crowning glory and sad affliction.

5

One further point to be made about *The Marble Faun* concerns its number pattern. Clearly it identifies a thematic plurality of successive places and cultures called Rome: Pagan, Catholic, Modern at the very least. And, nominally, it involves three young American artists all discovering the curiosities of this many-layered venue—and the problem of a childlike sociopathology—at the same time. But the real point is the pairing, the partnering, and what it reveals. Miriam's putative Jewishness—not to mention the possibility of that "one burning drop of African blood" (23)—makes her far less typically American than her paired companions. Somehow she is the worldly equal and opposite that cannot but be attracted to the Adamic Donatello. Hilda and Kenyon are the proper Americans. Hilda, reprised from Phoebe in *The House of the Seven Gables* (and from Rosina in "Egotism"), is, in troubled tribute to the simple amoral purity of Hawthorne's wife, Hawthorne's posited exception to the rule that there is "something which leads mortal man to sin." Man here ought to mean human, but evidently it does not quite. Not only can she not seem herself to sin, she cannot bear its sight. Never could she grasp the point of Hooker's "true sight," and in the end she abruptly resists Kenyon's referring the moral of the Donatello story to the familiar paradox of the *felix culpa*. Not only Calvin is being rejected but St. Paul as well. Hilda is, once again, "Hawthorne's Pelagian heresy." And Kenyon, not fully agreeing, but repenting his dalliance with what his suddenly moralistic companion fears as the high road to Antinomianism, agrees to let her conscience by his guide. As if Eve had talked Adam out of something. Happy wife, happy life, except perhaps in Eden. Where uxoriousness appears to have begun.

Kenyon is also familiar in Hawthorne's gallery of American moral types. A little more alert than the sculptor who, in "Egotism; or, the Bosom Serpent," understands but never thinks to deconstruct the reptilian allegory, who apparently accepts the proposition that puritanical solipsism can be cured by "the idea of another," he seems nevertheless a version of the sort of cool-mode artist who is more than a little out of touch with ordinary sensual life. Marble is cold: he needs to take a mud bath. Further, he is, like Holgrave, more an observer of than a passionate intervener in the plot unfolding before him. In this he also resembles the Coverdale who thinks himself a sort of chorus in a tragedy—and who seems to have forgotten that he himself is the murderer. He also

---

47. See Kenneth Marc Harris, *Hypocrisy and Self-Deception in Hawthorne's Fiction* (Charlottesville: University of Virginia Press, 1988); Austin Warren, *The New England Conscience* (Ann Arbor: University of Michigan Press, 1966); and Martin Green, *The Problem of Boston* (New York: Norton, 1966).

resembles the book's own Narrator, who can intervene and interpret endlessly but never quite get the point. Incompetent Omniscience: almost as interesting as the duplicitous first-person experiment of *Blithedale*. Here, at the end, this guiltless but relatively passive American is full of interpretative high sentence, as an obtuse enough American audience appears to require something such. But you cannot imagine him as a man who would kill for love. They only do that in Europe.

It has become customary to refer to *The Scarlet Letter*, *The House of the Seven Gables*, and *The Blithedale Romance* together, as Hawthorne's three "American Romances," leaving *The Marble Faun* separated by more than half a decade, to stand somewhat alone: after America, Europe; well, Italy at least; after noticeable nationality, an international novel. Yet this fourth romance is as interested in the distinguishing marks of American character as any of the former three. Full of information about galleries full of Italian art, it disclaims any intention to imitate or estimate "the Italian character." Quite rightly: the monk who stalks Miriam wanders in from one or another Gothic novel and the innocent aristocrat with the funky ears, well, they don't call it romance for nothing. But the Americans are emphatically represented as such. Maybe not Miriam: the complicated rumors of whose ethnic origins and her noticeable ability to do as the Romans do make her a fictional nonesuch. But Hilda and Kenyon, those quintessential Innocents Abroad, are nothing short of Hawthorne's attempt to represent the thinning out of an unlovely yet vigorous New England Puritanism into some rare but hothouse provincial purity.

The fragile sensibility which found itself *in extremis* at the thought of when and how impoverished girls lose their virginity in the slums of London here finds itself unable to go with the fertile flow of the Roman Holiday and in the end unwilling to face up to the question of Miriam's sexual history. The London scene is of course a very heavy dose, daunting enough to test the mettle of writers more suited to the morale of naturalism; and no doubt our frightened author deserves some credit for wandering into such an arena at all. But there as here we are forced to realize that Hawthorne's wish to evolve himself into a more worldly sort of writer is largely a fantasy. As a "realist" his offerings would have been every bit as "smiling" as, famously, those of William Howells.

The best we can say—and it is much more than nothing—is that this prime product of latter-day New England knew with a certainty that there were other worlds as well. In the beginning all the world may have been America, but somewhere along the way, Salem, Roxbury, Concord, and Boston had developed an odd half-life all their own. England bespoke the historic reality of class. And Rome? Old, multiform, intriguing, corrupt, inevitable, enticing. Worth an extended visit. Certainly a Romance. For someone else, maybe, a proper novel. But a Puritan has got to know his limitations. Hawthorne died young, to be sure, but he lived quite long enough to learn his own. The author of *The Marble Faun* cannot quite solve the problem of conscience and culture. But, puritanic historian of the Puritans that he is, he knows it when he sees it.

INDEX

"About Warwick" (Hawthorne) 251
"Al Aaraaf" (Poe) 138
"Alice Doane's Appeal" (Hawthorne) 1, 41–42, 43, 55, 83, 163
American Magazine of Useful and Entertaining Knowledge, The 99
"Artist of the Beautiful, The" (Hawthorne) 108, 137–38

Battle Pieces (Melville) 280
Blithedale Romance, The (Hawthorne) 1, 18, 121, 183, 184, 187, 192, 203, 212, 216, 218, 219, 220, 221, 222, 223, 225, 226, 227, 228, 229, 233, 234, 235, 237, 239, 242, 245, 261, 278, 287, 292
Bostonians, The (James) 287
Brand Pluck'd out of the Burning (Mather) 144
Bunyan, J. *Pilgrim's Progress, The* 22, 23

"Celestial Rail-road, The" (Hawthorne) 17, 22, 23, 25, 28, 86, 106, 107, 174, 209
Channing, W.E. 2, 125, 210, 241
Child, L. M. 39
"Christmas Banquet, The" (Hawthorne) 89–90, 93, 102, 239
"Custom-House, The" (Hawthorne) 115

Dante 134
Defense of the New England Charters (Dummer) 51
Descartes, R.
 Philosophical Meditations 90
Divine Comedy (Dante) 134
Dunciad (Pope) 24
Dummer, Jeremiah 51
Dwight, T. 23–24, 149
 Triumph of Infidelity, The 23

"Earth's Holocaust" (Hawthorne) 18, 84, 86, 104, 105, 231
"Egotism; or the Bosom Serpent" (Hawthorne) 77–79, 94, 96, 102, 211

Eliot, T.S.
 Wasteland, The 138
"Elixir of Life, The" (Hawthorne) 265, 277
Emerson, R. W.
 English Traits 3, 261
 Essays 87
 "Experience" 87, 89, 95
 Nature, 2, 90–91
 "Nominalist and Realist" 9
 "Self-Reliance" 105
English Notebooks (Hawthorne) 277
English Traits (Emerson) 3, 261
Essays (Emerson) 87
Essence of the Christian Religion, The (Feuerbach) 126
"Ethan Brand" (Hawthorne) 139, 141, 143, 144, 151, 152
"Evidences of Christianity" (Paley) 125
"Evidences of Revealed Religion, The" (Channing) 125

Faerie Queene (Spenser) 27, 42, 150
Fanshawe (Hawthorne) 39, 1
Faust (Goethe) 26
Fuller, M.
 Woman in the Nineteenth Century 184

"Gentle Boy, The" (Hawthorne) 61, 185, 206, 245
Grandfather's Chair (Hawthorne) 51
"Gray Champion, The" (Hawthorne) 61

"Hall of Fantasy, The" 18, 85, 86, 104, 231, 241
"Haunted Mind, The" (Hawthorne) 14
Hawthorne, N.
 "About Warwick" 246
 "Alice Doane's Appeal" 1, 41–42, 43, 55, 83, 163
 "Artist of the Beautiful, The" 108, 137–38
 Blithedale Romance, The 1, 18, 121, 183, 184, 187, 192, 203, 212, 215, 216, 218, 219,

Hawthorne, N. (*cont.*)
220, 221, 222, 223, 225, 226, 227, 228, 229, 230, 233, 234, 235, 237, 239, 242, 245, 261, 278, 287, 292
"Celestial Rail-road, The" 17, 22, 23, 25, 28, 86, 106, 107, 174, 208
"Christmas Banquet, The" 89–90, 93, 97, 102, 239
"Custom-House, The" 115
"Earth's Holocaust" 18, 84, 86, 104, 105, 231
"Egotism: or, The Bosom Serpent" 77–79, 84, 94, 96, 102, 203, 211
"Ethan Brand" 139, 141, 143, 144, 151, 152
Fanshawe 39, 167
"Fire-Worship" 143
"Gentle Boy, The" 43, 61, 185, 206, 245
Grandfather's Chair 51
"Gray Champion, The" 61
"Hall of Fantasy, The" 18, 85, 86, 104, 231, 241
"Haunted Mind, The" 14
"Hollow of the Three Hills, The" 12
House of the Seven Gables, The 1, 6, 7, 9, 18, 37, 38, 83, 163–64, 174, 205, 207, 242, 245, 277, 292
"Leamington Spa" 246
"Lichfield and Uttoxeter" 246
Life of Franklin Pierce, The 234
"Main-street" 1, 11–12, 116, 153, 156, 158, 162, 169, 211, 245
Marble Faun, The 18, 277, 278, 279, 290, 291, 292
"May-Pole of Merry Mount, The" 11, 28, 29, 30, 32, 34, 36, 61, 101, 171, 199, 285, 286
"Minister's Black Veil, The" 11–12, 28
Mosses from an Old Manse 2, 9, 52, 115, 167, 168
"My Kinsman, Major Molineux" 28, 43, 58, 61–62, 167, 245
Our Old Home 3, 7, 277
"Pilgrimage to Old Boston, A" 246
"Provincial Tales" 100, 167
"Rappaccini's Daughter" 5, 6, 25–26, 112, 123, 134, 167
"Recollections of a Gifted Woman" 251
"Roger Malvin's Burial" 37, 43, 64, 167, 245
Scarlet Letter, The 7, 9, 27, 38, 39, 45, 52, 53–54, 55, 57, 70, 82, 119, 139, 140, 154, 160, 164, 168, 184, 215, 233

"Seven Tales of My Native Land" 12, 41, 99, 167
"Seven Vagabonds, The" 49
"Story-Teller, The" 17, 41–42, 48, 49, 54, 99–101, 154, 163
Tanglewood Tales 3
Twice-Told Tales 81, 99, 101, 167
Wonder-Book for Boys and Girls 3
"Young Goodman Brown" 12, 27–28, 42, 45, 58, 60, 68, 77, 116, 211, 245
Herder, J. G.
Spirit of Hebrew Poetry 128
History of Boston (Snow) 27, 181, 182, 199
Hobomok (Child) 39
"Hollow of the Three Hills, The" (Hawthorne) 12
Hooker, T.
Firebrand 144
Hope Leslie (Sedgwick) 39
House of the Seven Gables, The (Hawthorne)1, 6, 7, 9, 18, 37, 38, 83, 163–64, 174, 205, 207, 242, 245, 277, 292
Hume, D. 96

Italian Notebooks (Hawthorne) 247

James, H. 3
The Bostonians 217
James, W.
"Moral Equivalent of War" 279
Johnson, E.
Wonder-working Providence 189

Lawrence, D.H.. 5, 54, 176, 188, 191
Life of Franklin Pierce, The (Hawthorne) 234
"Little Speech on Liberty" (Winthrop) 190

Magnalia Christi Americana (Mather) 28, 39–40, 80, 189
"Main-street" (Hawthorne) 1, 11–12, 116, 169, 211, 245
Marble Faun, The (Hawthorne) 18, 277, 278, 279, 290, 291, 292
Mather, C.
Brand Pluck'd out of the Burning 144
Magnalia Christi Americana 39–40, 80, 189
Wonders of the Invisible World 171
Maule, M.
Truth Held Forth 210
"May-pole of Merry Mount, The" (Hawthorne) 11, 17, 28, 29, 32, 34, 36, 61, 101, 171, 199, 285, 286

Melville, H. 6
  Battle Pieces 280
  "Benito Cereno"
  "Hawthorne and His Mosses" 137
  "Israel Potter" 248
  Moby-Dick 139, 140–41, 143, 151, 152
  "Paradise of Bachelors" 271
  Redburn 265
Milton, J. 28
"Minister's Black Veil, The" (Hawthorne) 11–12, 61, 81, 101, 171, 245
Miss Ravenel's Conversion from Secession to Loyalty (De Forest) 277
Moby-Dick (Melville) 139, 140–41, 143, 151, 152
"Model of Christian Charity" (Winthrop) 190
"Moral Argument Against Calvinism, The" (Channing) 126
Mosses from an Old Manse (Hawthorne) 2, 9, 52, 115, 167, 168
"My Kinsman, Major Molineux" (Hawthorne) 28, 43, 58, 61–62, 167, 245

Nature (Emerson) 127

Our Old Home (Hawthorne) 3, 7, 277

Philosophical Meditations (Descartes) 90
Pilgrim's Progress, The (Bunyan) 22, 23
Poe, E. 27
  Al Aaraaf 138
Pope, A.
  Dunciad 24
"Protest, The" (Emerson) 241
"Provincial Tales" (Hawthorne) 167

"Rappaccini's Daughter" (Hawthorne) 5, 6, 25–26, 112, 134, 167
"Recollections of a Gifted Woman" (Hawthorne) 251
"Roger Malvin's Burial" (Hawthorne) 64, 167, 245

Scarlet Letter, The (Hawthorne) 1, 6, 9, 11–12, 16, 17, 38, 39, 45, 52, 53–54, 55, 57, 70, 82, 119, 139, 140, 154, 160, 164, 215, 233, 235, 245, 253, 254, 292
Sedgwick, C.
  Hope Leslie 39
"Seven Tales of My Native Land" (Hawthorne) 12, 167
"Seven Vagabonds, The" (Hawthorne) 49
Shelley, P.
  "The Cenci" 113
Short Story of the Rise, Reign, and Ruin of the Antinomians, Familists, and Libertines (1644) (Winthrop) 189
Snow, C.
  History of Boston 27, 181, 182, 199
Specimens of Foreign Standard Literature (Ripley) 123
Spenser, E.
  Faerie Queene 42
Spirit of Hebrew Poetry (Herder) 128
"Story Teller, The" (Hawthorne) 17, 41–42, 48, 49, 54, 99–101, 154, 163

Tanglewood Tales (Hawthorne) 3
Taylor, J.
  Ductor Dubitantum 79
Twice-Told Tales (Hawthorne) 81, 99, 101, 167

Uncle Tom's Cabin (Stowe) 121, 215, 216
"Unitarian Christianity" (Channing) 126

Warner, S.
  Wide, Wide World 44
Wide, Wide World (Warner) 44
Winthrop, J. 1, 7
  Journal 27, 172, 180–81, 182, 189, 199
  "Little Speech on Liberty" 190
  "Model of Christian Charity" 196
Woman in the Nineteenth Century (Fuller) 184
Wonder-Book for Boys and Girls, A (Hawthorne) 3
Wonder-working Providence (Johnson) 189
Wonders of the Invisible World (Mather) 171

"Young Goodman Brown" (Hawthorne) 13, 27–28, 42, 45, 60, 68, 77, 116, 211, 245

www.ingramcontent.com/pod-product-compliance
Lightning Source LLC
Chambersburg PA
CBHW021137230426
43667CB00005B/148